W9-AAT-637

The Myths of Motherhood

The Myths of Motherhood

HOW CULTURE REINVENTS THE GOOD MOTHER

Shari L. Thurer

Houghton Mifflin Company
BOSTON NEW YORK 1994

Library of Congress Cataloging-in-Publication Data
Thurer, Shari.
The myths of motherhood : how culture reinvents the good mother / Shari L. Thurer.
p. cm.
Includes bibliographical references and index.
ISBN 0-395-58415-9
1. Motherhood — History. 2. Motherhood in popular culture — History. I. Title.
HQ59.T48 1994
306.874′3 — dc20 94-2807
CIP

Printed in the United States of America
MP 10 9 8 7 6 5 4 3 2 1

Book design by Melodie Wertelet
Printed on recycled paper

To all my good mothers

and my daughter

"Good wombs have borne bad sons"

— WILLIAM SHAKESPEARE, *The Tempest*

CONTENTS

INTRODUCTION

AS A PSYCHOLOGIST I cannot recall ever treating a mother who did not harbor shameful secrets about how her behavior or feelings damaged her children. Mothers do not take easy pride in their competence. Popular mother culture implies that our children are exquisitely delicate creatures, hugely vulnerable to our idiosyncrasies and deficits, who require relentless psychological attunement and approval. A sentimentalized image of the perfect mother casts a long, guilt-inducing shadow over real mothers' lives. Actual days on Planet Earth include few if any perfect moments, perfect children, perfectly cared for. Watching a three-year-old dress in agonizing slow motion, or a ten-year-old gorge herself on junk food and then despair of her appearance and blame us, provokes powerful emotions in us that do not cohere with our notion of the maternal. We have become highly judgmental about the practice of mothering, and especially about ourselves as mothers. Parental performance anxiety reigns.

Did parents always feel this way? Did those staid nineteenth-century people blankly staring out from the family album experience such self-doubt? What about all those Madonnas in Renaissance paintings? Were children of the seventeenth century more neurotic than children of today because their empathic needs were not met? Were children always so precious? If so, how did my great-grandmother ever bear the loss of three children? Did women want children when delivery may have meant their own death? Did fathers love children when they had to share already meager food supplies? What is good mothering? Am I a good mother? Was Medea? The old woman who lived in a shoe? Donna Reed? Aunt Jemima? Is Murphy Brown? How important is mothering, anyway?

This is not a "how to mother" book. I wish it were. I wish there could be such a guide, a compendium of foolproof techniques for raising a happy child. As a mother, I desperately want to do whatever it takes to do it right. But as a social scientist, I know that the ideal parent does not exist. There are no easy answers, no magical solutions, no absolutes. Good mothering is *not* a formulaic procedure, despite the assurances of all those books on the shelves of your local bookstore.

The current ideology of good mothering is not only spurious, it is oblivious of a mother's desires, limitations, and context, and when things go wrong, she tends to get blamed. This has resulted in a level of confusion and self-consciousness among mothers that their predecessors never knew. There is a glaring need to restore to mother her own presence, to understand that she is a person, not merely an object for her child, to recognize her subjectivity.

The briefest glance at history will dispel any notion that there is but one correct way to mother. Your grandmother may have bottle-fed your father on a rigid schedule and started his toilet training when he was the tender age of three months, practices generally regarded as ridiculous today. Yet he managed to grow up. Youngsters tend to survive their parents' bungled efforts on their behalf. By examining the patchwork of changing expectations for mothers — in psychology, child-rearing manuals, cultural history, the arts, anthropology, and religion — I will show that many of our cherished ideals of parental excellence are about as useless and ephemeral as daily doses of castor oil. Such an analysis has the potential to free mothers from arbitrary, culturally imposed restraints. Mothers may stop worrying about how they stack up against some capricious, external standard. The nervousness parents feel about their adequacy will dissipate when decent people are encouraged to mother in their own decent way. ❍

TODAY, we all want to be the mom in the baby food advertisements. (You know her: the mother who is always loving, selfless, tranquil; the one who finds passionate fulfillment in every detail of child rearing.) It's only natural. The vulnerability of children makes us want fervently to be our best selves, to embody tender nurturance and sweet concern. Besides, how our children turn out has become the final judgment on our lives. Even Queen Elizabeth's image has been tarnished by the marital failures of her children. The rising generation has the power of rendering history's verdict on us.[1] This is a daunting prospect. We want to do a good job. One false move and our precious bundle of joy will turn into an ax-murderer. But as we do more, we seem less sure of ourselves and of what we ought to do for our children. If we enroll our children in day care, we may deprive them of personalized parental attention; if we isolate them in the home, they may not become socialized. We wonder whether we are hurrying our children or, worse, not providing sufficient stimulation. We obsess about creativity, values, lead poisoning, violence on television, responsible diapers, and, of course, about spending "quality" time together. And these are only some of our *overt* concerns.

Beneath them lurk greater fears, for even as we experience a fierce attachment to our children there is the suspicion that we are not cut out for this. We are too impatient; we are haunted by the cultural ideal: the mommy whose love for children is unconditional. In spite of our having grown up with our own mothers — or, some might argue, because of it — we cling to the romantic version of mother, a chilling reminder of our own inadequacy.

But to suggest that mothers are made miserable by mothering is egregiously inaccurate. Bearing and caretaking a child tapped feelings in me that I did not know existed . . . manic highs, extravagant joy, monumental wonder, syrupy tenderness. In a cold and ruthless world, the relation between mother and child may be the most genuine, natural, spontaneous, and exquisite love there is. A baby answers the existential questions. The mere smell and texture of the baby's clothes and skin will evoke a Proustian reverie in most persons who have mothered. When a woman nurtures an infant, she creates someone who loves her passionately and exclusively, who needs her more than any adult does or will. And a mother is socially rewarded for her work by the shared pleasures and confirmation of other mothers, often by the gratitude and pride of grandparents, and by the intense appreciative love of her mate. When a child flourishes, most mothers enjoy a sense of well-being.[2]

But not every child flourishes all the time. Even the luckiest may become ill, lonely, mean, selfish, sloppy, lazy. And the mother may succumb to occupational maladies — possessiveness, parochialism, fearfulness, lack of interest, self-righteousness, and a rage for order that frightens even her. Sometimes she takes out her frustrations on the child, who is often by no means the cause. A mother can infuriate her offspring and disappoint herself.[3]

If the truth be known, many of us are, at times, less than fascinated by the endless chores of socializing a little human being, of living at a pace established by the child, of the relentlessness of it all. Maternal altruism is difficult to sustain. While our children fill us with cosmic joy, while we would defend them with the fierceness of a lioness protecting her cubs, they also provoke in us at times such anger and frustration that we hardly recognize the fury as our own. If motherhood is the dreamy relationship it is often billed as, then those flashes of hostility must be unnatural, traitorous, destructive of all that is normal, good, and decent. The resulting self-doubt is not much talked about. Mothers may joke about it, but they do not talk about it seriously. It is a cultural conspiracy of silence.

Even the daughters of the *Feminine Mystique* generation — those 1950s' housewives who finally admitted that life behind the Electrolux was itself a vacuum — shy away from acknowledging their ambivalence. While women today are freer than their mothers to complain about domestic chores, on the maternity front they are as silent as ever; it is the last stronghold of Friedan's "problem that has no name." Our society simply refuses to know about a mother's experience — how being yoked to a little one all day transforms her. To confess to being in conflict about mothering is tantamount to being a bad person; it violates a taboo; and, worse, it feels like a betrayal of one's child. In an age that regards mothers' negative feelings, even subconscious ones, as potentially toxic to their children, it has become mandatory to enjoy mothering.[4]

So we work at enjoying it. We try hard to improve our attitude, to bury unacceptable feelings, or at least to disguise them, even to ourselves — all of which is pointless. This turbulent inner war is not only unwinnable; it will, ironically, make casualties of those we are fighting to save. Children know very well when they have irritated us; they see right through our bluff. Covering up conflicts does not resolve them; indeed, it allows them to fester and grow larger. Besides, it sends out bad signals to our children: that anger is shameful (why else hide it?); that they should deny their own hostilities (that's what mommy does); that to think of violence, even subconsciously, is to commit it; that negative feelings cancel out positive ones, as if emotions were like arithmetic.

Truth in mothering is a far better policy. After all, criticism of the role of mother is not the same thing as disapproval of children or lack of love for a particular child. ❍

MOTHERHOOD — the way we perform mothering — is culturally derived. Each society has its own mythology, complete with rituals, beliefs, expectations, norms, and symbols. Our received models of motherhood are not necessarily better or worse than many others. The way to mother is not writ in the stars, the primordial soup, the collective unconscious, nor in our genes. Our predecessors followed a pattern very different from our own, and our descendants may hew to one that is no less different.[5] Our particular idea of what constitutes a good mother is only that, an idea, not an eternal verity. The good mother is reinvented as each age or society defines her anew, in its own terms, according to its own mythology.

As with most myths, the current Western version is so pervasive that, like air, it is unnoticeable. Yet it influences our domestic arrangements, what we think is best for our children, how we want them to be raised, and whom we hold accountable. Because we are inevitably caught up in our own cultural vortex, we fail to question our most basic suppositions. Today we assume, for example, that little children should be free to explore. Forget that for two thousand years infants were swaddled and managed to grow up without dire consequences. We now assume that a good mother should dutifully drag around her child's "security blanket." Never mind that granny regards it as unhygienic and would have summarily thrown it out. Her children managed to survive the loss, just as ours survive the germs.

But the current standards for good mothering are so formidable, self-denying, elusive, changeable, and contradictory that they are unattainable. Our contemporary myth heaps upon the mother so many duties and expectations that to take it seriously would be hazardous to her mental health.

Today, mother love has achieved the status of a moral imperative. Our current myth holds that the well-being of our children depends almost entirely on the quality of their upbringing (read *mother,* since it is she who usually has primary responsibility for raising children). An intense, prolonged loving bond between mother and child is essential. Though many believe that the mother need not be the biological mother or even female, it is considered fundamental that children have the continuous and exclusive presence of at least one devoted adult, and that anything separating children from their loving caretaker is psychologically damaging.

Mother love is powerful stuff. Even the least sentimental among us regards parental affection as a child's birthright, average and expectable, a signifier of harmony. A mother's kisses and hugs provide the building blocks to a future of mental health, but — and this is important — only when they are adequately bestowed on a child during its infancy and early years. Later, mother must gradually relinquish her intense attachment. As her child grows up, she must accept obsolescence with grace. The myth tells us that timing is everything. If the dispensation of mother love is stingy, excessive, or ill-timed, harm to the child is irreversible. There are no second chances.[6] The precise dose of a mother's love, punctually delivered, is the central factor in the well-being of the next generation, that is, the future.

With this in mind, common sense has given way to an obsession with the mother-child relationship. Yet even a cursory examination reveals this preoccupation to be a linear way of thinking. At worst, it makes a scapegoat of mom; even at best, it leads to an overemphasis on what she does, at the expense of a broader understanding of child development. It obscures the importance of family dynamics, of the social environment, life events, and the character and inner psychodynamics of the child.

The all-importance of mother love has been fueled by a giant collective wish for perfect mothering. It is bolstered by a religion that gave us the Virgin Mary, nursery tales that supplied us with fairy godmothers, and a psychology that failed to question many cultural assumptions. It is supported by a history that forgot the benign effect of centuries of wet-nursing, an anthropology that romanticized the child-rearing practices of "primitive" cultures like the Trobriand Islanders and Samoans, and by post-Freudian psychoanalytic thought implying that a mother's moods could cause mental illness in her children. Added to this are modern literary classics like D. H. Lawrence's *Sons and Lovers* and Philip Roth's *Portnoy's Complaint,* plus decades of popular movies like *Now, Voyager; Psycho;* and *Mommie Dearest,* all of which are alarming tales about maternally induced psychic paralysis.

It is no wonder that mother is terrified by her own power. Yet, even as mother is all-powerful, she ceases to exist. She exists bodily, of course, but her needs as a person become null and void. On delivering a child, a woman becomes a factotum, a life-support system. Her personal desires either evaporate or metamorphose so that they are identical with those of her infant. Once she attains motherhood, a woman must hand in her point of view. Midcentury psychoanalytic thinking assumed that motherhood is essentially the child's drama, with mom in a supporting role. The popular French version of psychoanalysis of Jacques Lacan and even feminist revisionist psychoanalysis colluded in her obliteration, as have our "dead white male" literary canon, religion, and, to a certain extent, feminism, until very recently. No one spoke with a mother's voice. Apparently, it never occurred to anyone that Portnoy's mother might have a complaint of her own.

Even baby experts acquired the cultural amnesia for the personhood of mothers, thereby biting the hands that feed them, for mothers are their target audience. During the first half of the twentieth century, child-rearing manuals — which, in actuality, are mother-rearing tracts — dramatically increased demands on the mother. In the beginning of the century, advice books offered a vast sympathy for mother and were filled with practical shortcuts. But by midcentury, most notably with Dr. Benjamin Spock's *Baby and Child Care* — the all-time best-selling book in American history after the Bible — the sympathy was switched to the child. Mother's role was greatly complicated: she had to serve as a constant comforting presence, to consider the child's every need, to create a stimulating environment exactly suited to each developmental stage, and to tolerate any regression and deflect all conflict.[7]

Now, for example, the mother not only had to offer her child vitamin-rich food, but had to "enjoy him [sic]," "don't be afraid of him," and to remember that "feeding is learning."[8] Spock's book imposed a psychic workday on top of the physical workday, presuming a two-parent family, where the mother has nothing to do but care for one child. The role is not only more time-consuming than before; it is highly ambiguous. Exactly how does mom proceed to "enjoy" the baby who is spitting out food, mashing it into every crevice in reach, and throwing it in her face? While child-care specialists intend to reassure mothers, in fact they often foster a nagging sense of bewilderment, wrongdoing, and guilt. In effect, they have invented a motherhood that excluded the experience of the mother.[9]

The prevailing mythology does concede that some mothers have to work outside the home, but it classifies such an endeavor as a necessary evil. The really good mother is a full-time mother. One senses a stubborn feeling in the land that stay-at-home mothers will redeem family values and restore morality to our citizenry. There was an almost audible sigh of relief when the wholesome, family-centered Barbara Bush replaced the too-thin, too-fashion-conscious Nancy Reagan as First Lady. Mrs. Bush projected motherliness; Mrs. Reagan projected narcissism. Her brittle image suggested that she had never been maternally preoccupied, a fact corroborated by her daughter. The jury is still out with regard to Hillary Rodham Clinton, the first First Lady who has made no pretense about her professional ambitions.

The public does not warm to mothers who are otherwise engaged, especially when they don't have to be. We grudgingly accept it when a woman "has" to work, meaning that her family's survival depends on her income. It is when a woman chooses to pursue a career that a shadow is cast over her motherliness. After all, what kind of mother could leave a shiny new baby unless her bottom line depended on it? Maternal devotion, it seems, is contingent on economics. The 1992 film *The Hand That Rocks the Cradle* was a parable of what happens to a bourgeois mother who hires a nanny: she must be punished. Nobody believes in the efficacy of Mary Poppins anymore.

It was the hiring of an illegal alien as a nanny ("Nannygate") that cost Zoë Baird the post of attorney general, for which she had been nominated by President Clinton. Yet it is hardly a secret that there is virtually no pool of legally acceptable candidates for domestic work. The extent to which child care is degraded as gainful employment in this country betrays the real value of mothers' work, despite the idealization of the stay-at-home mom.[10] The Baird ordeal begs a lot of questions on the wide front of the gender wars, but it can't have escaped anyone's notice that this woman, this highly paid successful career woman, lost her opportunity to become a member of the cabinet on a maternal technicality, a technicality that had never been invoked to derail the candidacy of a man. The fiasco showed how raw, divisive, and unprocessed are people's ideas about mothers and work.

The truth is that working mothers are doing what mothers have always done. Throughout most of human history, mothers have devoted more time to other duties than to child care and have delegated aspects of child rearing to others, except for a brief period after the Second World War.[11] Fleeting as it was, this period was ossified in a number of TV sitcoms (a new rage in the 1950s), like "The Adventures of Ozzie & Harriet," and "Leave It to Beaver," so that even now we think of those midcentury family arrangements as good and right, and the way things were since time immemorial. But the 1950s was a decade unique in American history, and the breadwinner-housewife form of family was short-lived.[12] As for the decade itself, it was never the familial paradise it was cracked up to be, even in white, middle-class suburbia, where outward domestic cheer often masked a good deal of quiet desperation, especially among women.

This is not to say that full-time, stay-at-home mothers were uniformly miserable; most mothers at the time preferred domestic to outside work. But keep in mind that their options were largely pink-collar. At least 1950s' culture accorded its full-time mothers unconditional positive regard. Today such mothers experience a jumble of mixed messages. The stay-at-home mothers I know dread the question "And what do *you* do?" They know full well that adults who keep close company with children all day long, though applauded in some circles, raise eyebrows in others. Child rearing, inherently a splendid experience for many, is not a source of money, status, or power in society or even in the family. If it were, more men would probably choose to rear children.[13]

Consider the plight of Snow White's stepmother. She has a story, too, but we have not had a chance to hear it. Until just twenty years ago, no one spoke with a maternal voice. No one wrote about the experience of mothering. We have a literary tradition in which a mother existed only in relation to her children — she was trivialized or idealized or disparaged — and was never allotted a point of view. Mothers didn't star in their own dramas.

"Snow White" is a daughter's story. From beginning to end, the girl orients the perspective of the narrative. It is she who must flee from the murderous intentions of a jealous mother figure. The daughter is an angel; the mother, a witch. But if we were to look at the situation from the vantage of the stepmother, could we blame her for her desperation? In a kingdom where a woman's reflection in a mirror determines her access to power, why would the stepmother warm to a woman younger and more beautiful than she? Female bonding is extraordinarily difficult in patriarchy.[14] What were the stepmother's options? Indeed, what will Snow White's be, once she marries the prince, has babies of her own, and proceeds to age? She will face the same dilemma that terrified her stepmother. This tale, like most Western fiction and poetry, offers mother no viable option. She can die like her good biological mother or defend her position like her bad stepmother. Self-annihilation or odiousness: those are her alternatives.

Consider, too, the plight of Hamlet's mother. Hamlet cannot forgive his widowed mother for marrying too hastily and too happily (in Hamlet's view) his father's brother after his father's murder. But is his mother's conduct inexcusable?[15] Why should she be denied a new lease on life simply because her "lust" is shameful to her son? A mother's sexuality is usually threatening to her nuclear family: that is the human condition. But how long should a son's discomfort determine the moral culpability of a mother's behavior? Sex and motherhood have not mixed well since the demise of the goddess religions, when men began to split women into madonnas or whores in every sphere. Presumably a good mother extinguishes her libido with conception or else expels it along with her placenta in childbirth. The extent of the anxiety aroused by the convergence of sexuality and maternity may be seen in the outraged reaction to a stunning photograph of the very pregnant and very naked actress Demi Moore on the cover of *Vanity Fair* in August 1991. The idea of subjecting a maternal figure to an erotic gaze was just too transgressive for many people, and the editors were forced to conceal Moore's protruding abdomen by a white paper wrapper in some cities.

The adulterous mother Mrs. Robinson, played by Anne Bancroft in the film *The Graduate,* remains a character we love to hate. She has impressive forebears. Passionate mothers take center stage in *The Scarlet Letter, Anna Karenina, Madame Bovary,* and *The Awakening,* novels that are among the greatest of the nineteenth century. Though initially sympathetic toward their heroines, the authors were all severely punitive to them in the end. The implication is that had these mothers been less sensual, more self-denying and conventionally maternal, they would have escaped their fate. But the conclusion (maybe even the goal) was punishment or, worse, self-punishment: Hester Prynne could not give up the scarlet embroidered A on her breast as penance for her adultery; the others committed suicide. The situation of amorous mothers may not be much better today. In her recent novel *The Good Mother,* Sue Miller pits a mother's maternity against her sexuality; she ends up losing both.

Psychological theories, especially those which have trickled down to a general audience, also have not been kind to mothers. If a mother is too involved with her children, whatever that means, she is considered overprotective, stifling, or intrusive. If she is not sufficiently involved with her children, whatever that means, she is rejecting, cold, and narcissistic. Some psychotherapists are so sure that bad mothering is the cause of all later idiosyncrasies that they tend to discover it in every patient they treat. For almost every "victim" of paternal incest, a mother is accused of collusion; for every person with an eating disorder, there is, presumably, an emotionally hungry mother behind the scenes emotionally starving her child. One therapist wrote recently that in the dozen years she worked in an outpatient psychiatric service at a major Harvard teaching hospital, she could not remember ever having heard a clinician suggest that a patient had a really good mother.[16]

Taking cues from the experts, the media reflexively look at

mothers when assigning blame. A recent *New York Times* story on cannibalistic mass murderer Jeffrey Dahmer is a case in point. The article prominently featured a head shot of Dahmer,[17] next to which was an equally large head shot of his mother. I suppose that the juxtaposition gratified the public's presumed interest in the manner of creature that produced such a monster. But why would the public be curious about Dahmer's mother if it did not already, on some level, somehow, insinuate her into his crimes?

All of this is not to deny, of course, that mothering does have an enormous impact on child development, or that many mothers do fail their children. Nor, by defending mothers, do I mean to condemn fathers. (Indeed, fathers are getting their share of censure these days for sexual abuse, violence, alcoholism, for being "dead-beat" or just plain absent.) In my psychotherapy practice, I have come across parents of unconscionable vileness, grotesque mothers, hideous fathers. It is just that the indictment of parents (usually mothers) in the psychological literature has been so automatic, so nasty, so massive, so undifferentiated, and so oblivious of the limits of a mother's power that it precludes a sensible assessment of any clinical situation.[18] A sympathetic evaluation of the social context of the mother is virtually ignored in nearly all accounts of parenting. Yet poverty, sexism, racism, or war can undo any mother's best efforts. Mothering is largely socially created and, sometimes, politically remediable. And the power of a child's own psychodynamics should not be underestimated.

But in the current mother mythology, children are seen as eminently perfectible. There are no bad children, only bad parents. What is at issue here is the old nature-nurture controversy about the determinants of child behavior, now heavily weighted in favor of nurture. Just why this view has taken hold probably has to do with its inherent optimism and impartiality. It resonates in these multicultural times; it is hopeful, egalitarian, pragmatic, and it seems to offer endless possibilities for transforming a child, if only mom were to do the right thing. Never mind genes, class, adversity. Biological differences (a factor that makes people nervous) do not matter. No one believes in the "bad seed" anymore. All children are redeemable. If there is parental will, there is a way.

This wishful idea, that there is a way, keeps parents permanently on the hook. Parenting is a precarious business. Do it wrong, suggest the advice columns and child-care manuals, and your child will be warped. But, as we shall see, child-care experts disagree on the "right" way. To be sure, now that the extended family is no longer around, parents probably can't do without baby-care manuals of some sort, if only to tell them about teething and whooping cough. But what Drs. Spock and Brazelton and others convey is merely kindly, humane folklore, not incontrovertible fact. Their advice is based not so much on scientific comparisons of child rearing as on their experience with babies, on child-development theories still in flux, on studies of discrete child behaviors that do not lend themselves to broad child-rearing generalizations, along with a big dollop of their personal philosophies. What they offer is informed opinion, not child-raising absolutes. To quote the wise old Native American in the film *Little Big Man,* "Sometimes the magic works . . . sometimes it doesn't."

It goes without saying today that every child is precious. We put so much emphasis on the individual child that it is widely held we should produce a child only if we have a reasonable prospect of giving it the prolonged and intensive loving care we believe it needs.[19] Our society has become unabashedly pronatal. People are going gaga over parenthood, especially in older, educated, baby boomer circles, where the consumers and tastemakers wield an influence far exceeding their numbers. A rash of movies in the 1980s portrayed procreation as redemptive, even for men — *Baby Boom, Three Men and a Baby, Mr. Mom, Look Who's Talking, She's Having a Baby,* and *For Keeps.*

Never has a baby been so delicious. Capitalizing on this sentiment, hospital administrators boost business by romanticizing their maternity services with gourmet postpartum dinners and private Jacuzzis. Advertisers from the Gap to IBM to Tyson Chicken and Calvin Klein fragrances have turned to photographs of babies to sell their products. Giving birth turns out to improve the popularity ratings of female television newscasters. Children have become fashion accessories in women's magazines. Politicians and British royalty need only demonstrate affection for their offspring to add warmth and likability to their image. Motherhood is utterly sentimentalized.

What we have today is a myth of motherhood that defies common sense. Never before have the stakes of motherhood been so high — the very mental health of the children. Yet never before has the task been so difficult, so labor intensive, subtle, and unclear. At the very moment when women have been socialized into wanting more than a diaper in one hand and a dust rag in the other, they are obliged to subordinate their personal objectives by an ideology that insists that unless they do, they will damage their children for life. Media images of happy, fulfilled mothers, and the onslaught of advice from experts, have only added to mothers' feelings of inadequacy, guilt, and anxiety. Mothers today cling to an ideal that can never be reached but somehow cannot be discarded. ❍

I RECALL treating a young mother whose care of her gravely ill child was nothing short of heroic. She told me of nearly two years of terror during which she stayed up night after night to monitor her child's breathing, performed nursing procedures of frightening complexity and delicacy, and fought medical bureaucracies to obtain the best care for her child. She was labeled a "nuisance" by hospital staff and "overly intrusive" by a therapist, though, in fact, she insisted on a hospitalization for her child which turned out to save the girl's life.

Months after her child was well, the mother developed severe agoraphobia, which was why she was seeing me. This bravest of young women was now afraid to leave her home. Her panic turned out to be self-punishment for ambivalent feelings, now breaking through, about her little girl and the traumatic course of events. While her child was acutely ill, my patient had functioned on automatic pilot; but now that her youngster was out of danger, she found herself dreaming of murdering her. It was all so irrational: her little girl was the most precious thing in the world to her. In her mind, a good mother would never wish to harm her child, whose sickness had not been the child's fault. What this mother came to recognize was that her resentment toward her child was understandable in light of the hell she had been through when caring for her and that despite her suppressed rage, she had functioned wonderfully. Coming to accept her own ambivalence helped her shed the crippling agoraphobia. Unfortunately many women never gain that insight, and live forever in the shadow of an impossible maternal ideal.

My aim in writing this book is to make mothers' internal lives acceptable to them, to undo some of the *angst* among mothers (and mothering persons) at large. I do not mean to quell the guilty conscience of the mean-spirited mother, or the frivolous or neglectful or self-centered mother (who, in my view, needs treatment and some sort of social intervention), but to calm the jangled nerves of your garden-variety mother, the one who is neither villain nor saint. I want to soothe the mind of a mother who mostly loves her children, who worships them at times and is repelled at others, who appreciates their beauty and intricacies, but is still tempted to lead her life outside and beyond them (to paraphrase Tillie Olsen). I want to free this mother from an uncritical dependency on an ideology of good mothering that is ephemeral, of doubtful value, unsympathetic to caretakers, arbitrary, and, literally, man-made.

Our current ideal of the mother is, like all ideals, culture-bound, historically specific, and hopelessly tied to fashion. And, of course, fashions change. As we shall see, the diverse roles that women play in raising their children are not linked to timeless truths, but to more mundane things, like subsistence strategies, population pressures, biology, technology, weather patterns, and speculations about women's nature.

Children may not have been precious when they competed with their parents for limited food and resources or were evidence of their mothers' "immoral" behavior. Remember that well into the nineteenth century many children arrived unbidden (there was little access to reliable birth control). Many inadvertently caused their mothers' death in delivery; often they themselves died before their fifth year. Infanticide seems to have been a part of Western European life until the late nineteenth century, when women finally gained some measure of control over their reproductive capacity.[20] Usually the killing of infants is related to desperate poverty and illegitimacy — themselves related — but sometimes the cause is not at all clear. In both Classical Athens and Renaissance Italy, for example, parents may have abandoned babies, mostly girls, for motives far more frivolous than economic desperation. Misogyny, perhaps?[21]

Even when child-rearing practices spring from parents' best intentions, they may seem questionable to another generation.

What was considered ideal at the end of the last century — devices to prevent masturbation, cold baths, the participation of children in elaborate mourning rituals — may be considered insensitive or even abusive in this one. How history will choose to interpret modern mothers' mandate to bond instantly, flash flashcards, shake the ubiquitous clear rattle, exude round-the-clock empathy, breast-feed again (after decades of bottle-feeding), is anyone's guess.

One of the great curiosities of maternal history that this book explores is wet-nursing. Michelangelo, Juliet, Scarlett O'Hara, and Winston Churchill all had wet nurses. This was not an obscure enterprise; it involved most infants born in certain European cities at various times.[22] Such a practice, if benign (and we have no evidence one way or the other), seems to contradict some of the most cherished beliefs about mother love and attachment held by today's psychologists, child experts, and, indeed, almost everyone.

Just as the practice of mothering has veered widely with the mores of different epochs, so has the status of mothers. From the beginning of time, woman was an awesome being; she seemed to swell and spew forth a child by her own law. Perhaps in those early days, twenty-five hundred years before the birth of Christ and other male gods, the idea of woman as mother endowed all women with respect. But as men realized their contribution to procreation and seized control, organizing much of what we know as mainstream history, the mother has been dehumanized, that is, either wildly idealized (with mothers becoming prisoners of their own symbolic inflation) or degraded (with mothers viewed as brood mares). In men's imaginations, the mother was the selfless nurturer or the wicked stepmother. Since the onset of male domination, mothers' sexuality has been split off from her maternity, and her bodily processes — menstruation, childbirth, lactation — have been deemed indecent. It was only during 1993, for instance, that the state of Florida guaranteed women the right to breast-feed in public.

This book traces the evolution of maternal personae from prehistory to present day. In the last half century alone we have witnessed vast diversity in parenting ideals; good mothering has abruptly shifted from training and control to permissiveness and empathy. And on the psychoanalytic front, an upheaval of such dimension has occurred that psychoanalysts, who previously had ignored mothers, now find themselves scrupulously scrutinizing mothers' behaviors during the first few weeks of an infant's life. The watchwords vary — attachment, mirroring, attunement, empathy, bonding, unconditional positive regard — but the required maternal *modus operandi* remains the same — altruistic love. "The ideal mother," wrote the psychoanalyst Alice Balint, "has no interests of her own."[23]

In retrospect, I realize I began practicing psychotherapy and had a baby at precisely the time when psychological theories were least charitable to mothers. I worked outside the home when experts had not yet given mothers approval for doing so. The women's movement urged me to maximize my potential, but the dominant culture called me selfish for doing so. I tried to be a good mother and a good worker just when the prevailing wisdom insisted that those were mutually exclusive enterprises. I was confused. And it seems to me, more than a decade later, that mothers are even more conflicted and guilt-ridden.

In a time when society values the fulfillment of women as persons, we have an ethos of maternity that denies them that very thing. Just when some of us have been teased into believing that we have vocational options; just when we assumed we could share the burden of child raising; just when we have been driven by economic necessity to work outside the home and to jury-rig a child-care plan, we have a mythology that insists, with rising shrillness, on perfection in child care. No caretaking arrangement can be that perfect. Nor, for that matter, can any full-time mom. Clearly the myth of motherhood deserves a hard reckoning, and that is what I have aimed for.

The Myths of Motherhood

ONE

Mothering— The Old-Fashioned Way

What Becomes a Legend Most?

God used to be a mother who worked outside the home. For thousands of years — from the Old Stone Age[1] to the closing of the last goddess temples, about A.D. 500 — She did it all. The Great Mother, as She has come to be called, gave birth, underwent transformation, death, rebirth, and everything in between, and She caused mortals to do the same. This maternal goddess was the oldest of all the gods, the original deity, and She was all-powerful. She made the rules. Mother has come a long way, baby . . . down! Even if the Great Mother's human counterparts had been but pale shadows of their formidable goddess, they would still give today's "civilized" mothers pause.

The best archeological evidence available indicates that the role of the earliest mothers was wider than at any other time in history, their nature more fully expressed, their contributions to their society more valued, their creativity more celebrated, and their influence on civilization more influential than a modern, particularly a Western, observer might imagine. Far from being the twentieth-century caricature of cavewoman, led around by a club-wielding male holding her ponytail, a mother in the very earliest society often had a better chance of freedom, dignity, and self-actualization compared with her mate than a mother has today. I do not mean to suggest that there has been no progress in thirty-five thousand years, but to emphasize that women in the past were not bound by the repressive expectations for good parenting that have come down to us through the millennia.

Old Stone Age mothers weren't burdened by the modern fetishes of chastity, modesty, maternal altruism, or, in today's terms, "quality" time. And cavebaby may not have been worse off for it. To be sure, prehistoric women nursed their children, but there is no evidence suggesting that they were in their children's thrall. The requirement of exclusive devotion to one's child came much later. Perhaps this lack of personalized maternal attention was so provoking to early man that, when he finally attained the upper hand, he slowly but insistently displaced the Great Mother by multiple male sky gods — later, one male god — and created a patriarchal social order.[2] Over time, a sexually equitable society was effectively replaced by one in which men dominated women socially, politically, economically, and spiritually. It should be noted, however, that even when God was a woman, women did not rule men, but that females and all things feminine enjoyed a higher status than they have ever since.[3] With the masculine God takeover, the Great Mother — and mortal cavemothers, for that matter — were banished to the intellectual ghetto of women's studies, where they remain all but forgotten except by the most intrepid historians, archeologists, theologians, and Jungian analysts.

But why resurrect the Great Mother or her flesh-and-blood counterparts? What do these plump, preliterate museum relics have to say to the harried mother of today, who is most assuredly unassisted by the supernatural? If we begin by looking at the distilled experience of the ancients of our tribe, we may discover what is natural about motherhood and what is culturally induced. We may figure out what is original and what is acquired, what is primitive and what is derived. If we can formulate a bottom-line basis of mothering behavior, by which we may describe future incarnations, perhaps we can determine what is essential and good — for babies, mothers, and societies. These prehistoric mothers jog us out of our twentieth-century models and our impudent assumptions that up-to-date is always better. By analyzing the evolution of mothers, we discover that our present attitudes, far from being eternal verities, are historically specific, and not necessarily superior to old-fashioned ways. The institution of motherhood can be seen as a device used to condition women to a particular social role, which may or may not be in the best interests of their children or themselves, and from which parents may decondition themselves if they choose. So cavemother, and her descendants throughout history, give us perspective and options.

Besides, prehistoric mothers may be a source of some of our "gut" associations to motherhood. Our ideas of the maternal are not invented anew in each era but are historically linked. For example, the symbols of the cave as female womb, mother as pregnant earth, the magical fertile female as the mother of all animals, seem to have persisted some ten thousand years, from the Late Stone Age, when they originated, to the Renaissance, when they may be seen in depictions of the Nativity, with its central image of the Sacred Child in a cavelike shelter surrounded by magically tamed animals;[4] and, six hundred years later, in contemporary America at Christmastime, when Nativity scenes sprout annually on suburban lawns. Our present attitudes toward motherhood are part of the prehistoric mother's legacy. To understand her and her lineage is to begin understanding ourselves as parents.

Moreover, cavemothers and their heiresses make great source material for feminist speculation. In them we have liberated maternal figures — women as mothers who were active and admired participants in their culture. It is reasonable to assume that if female parents were once powerful, they may be so again. If mothers were not always subordinated, reduced to endless caretaking, we have proof that they are not subordinate by nature. And these very ancient people's conception of the deity as a maternal figure provides us with a welcome infusion of nonsexist mythology. Here at last is an antidote to male chauvinist religious ideology, validation for female material and spiritual power. The Great Mother did not undergo job discrimination because of her pregnancy; She did the discriminating. The Great Mother did not mask her protruding belly; She flaunted it (unlike many of us who would not dare to wear a two-piece bathing suit on a public beach when pregnant). Motherhood was divine.

The Old Stone Age, then — the period during which *femina erecta* and *homo erectus,* having become *sapiens,* banded together in small nomadic clusters to hunt and gather, developed tools, and sought shelter in caves — may have been a high point for the status of mothers.

Cavemother: Old Stone Age Mom

Women, because of biological constraints (or opportunities!), have always been the breeder-feeders of children. The key is milk. Milk goes far toward explaining the earliest division of labor, wherein the male hunted and the female gathered. Foraging for food was much more amenable to simultaneous nursing, which obviously was the mother's domain. Sustained nursing gradually evolved into child care. While contemporary feminists may chafe at the rigidity of Paleolithic (Old Stone Age) role assignments, they would do well to understand that mothers performed two of the most life-sustaining tasks of the Old Stone Age: the caretaking of the young, which assured the survival of the species; and the gathering of edible plants, eggs, insects, and what-not, which provided 80 percent of the nourishment. The number of calories obtained through the hunt was fewer and far less dependable.[5]

Archeologists have only recently begun to appreciate the imprint of prehistoric women on culture. Paleolithic mothering, for example, was not a task for weaklings. Hominid babies were heavy, and they got heavier as brains, and therefore skulls, became larger — this as the evolving bodies of mothers presented less hair for their infants to cling to. The mother, not the baby, had to do the clinging. She could not depend on absent males or on a pool of older, postmenopausal women for assistance, for most early women did not live beyond their twenties. The buck stopped at mom. So even by the Paleolithic, mothering was definitely an intentional enterprise; it did not just happen. Then, too, human young take far longer to grow and become self-supporting than did their primate forebears. Mothering had to be sustained. It was not a one-shot deal, as in "now you mother; now you don't." Children need protracted, sensitive care, and cannot be simply swatted off the nipple and pointed in the direction of the nearest banana. Moreover, the human has to be initiated into a far more complex system of social and intellectual activity than does any other animal. Mothering was arduous, earnest, time-consuming, intellectually challenging, and prolonged; this was not a passive process, like laying an egg.[6]

Given the magnitude of the endeavor, why did women bother? No Paleolithic police or child protective service or media campaign dictated that mothers care for their offspring; indeed, there were no institutions — no property, no inheritance, no jurisprudence, no clear idea about paternity. Children in this period were not keepers of the flame, chips off the old block, perpetuators of the gene pool, exemplars of masculine or feminine prowess, the fulfillment of one's duty to state or god. One's offspring may have had little symbolic meaning. Indeed, according to an ecological view of history, Paleolithic children may have been a handicap. Each baby was another mouth to feed.[7] Then, too, mothers could not comfortably rear more children than they could carry as they gathered food. So, given all these drawbacks and unclear incentives, why did Old Stone Age mothers engage in this difficult enterprise?

The short answer is that we do not now know. Even more interesting may be the range of information and speculation the question has engendered among scholars in a mélange of disciplines. I suggest that Old Stone Age mothers mothered because they wanted to. To state the obvious, mother care had to do with mother love — bonding, attachment, empathy, call it what you will. I suspect that newborn babies may have quickened the prehistoric pulse just as they do ours. Even today, despite our sophisticated medical technology and scientific knowledge, childbirth remains awesome. Each maternity reminds even the most jaded among us of the great saga of life, and invites us to revere the marvelous scheme of things in which we are placed. Imagine how miraculous, how magical, how glorious the reproduction of a tiny human being must have been to the unschooled prehistoric mind! My guess is that a baby's smile has always pulled at one's heartstrings.

This does not mean that mother love, or father love, is automatic, like uterine contractions, a cosmic yearning demanding fulfillment, or, strictly speaking, an "instinct." While the term "maternal instinct" has come to have many meanings, scientists are quite precise in their definition: an instinct is an innate and invariant behavior pattern, common in "lower" animals but rare in humans, whose sophisticated nervous systems enable them to adapt to the environment, so that whatever pure urges they may have started with are rapidly overlaid, perhaps overturned, by the effects of learning. Nor does mother love exist apart from mother hate. Children drive us crazy and always have. Indeed, murderous impulses (to be distinguished from actions) toward one's children are universal. Rather, I suggest that mother love is a stubborn, hardy emotion in both men and women that can and will occur — at least in some attenuated form — in all but the most extreme situations, that is, life-threatening, personal, or social conditions, mental impairment, sociopathy, ignorance, or in a society warped by misogyny. In other words, attachment to one's children is usual in ordinary, decent circumstances. Any human being in his or her right mind, when presented with a helpless infant, will tend to provide for its care rather than kill it, eat it, or ignore it. Mother love, though it is vulnerable to environmental manipulation, seems to be a fact.

I suspect that child neglect, battering, incest — those instances where parental attachment goes awry — may have to do with societal misogyny. If we set aside disasters, like war and plague, and individual psychopathology, then we find a higher incidence of child abuse where there is egregious sexual inequality. Women respected in their own right are free to love their babies. The corollaries are also true. Women who are not forced to compete with their children for social status are better able to bond in a healthy manner. Women who can choose whether to bear children are able to mother well. Fathers who help with mothering enhance mothers; the more help, the better.

Astonishingly, the Paleolithic, despite its being, by definition, the most primitive human era, seems to have presented the necessary and sufficient conditions for parental attachment. The first proof is in our existence: babies could not have survived without mother care, and their demise would have meant the demise of humankind. In other words, society could not have persisted unless the majority of women devoted most of their adult lives to childbearing and breast-feeding. Perhaps we can say: We provide care (or our forebears did), therefore we are. The Paleolithic Age allowed mothers to do what comes naturally, to care for their babies.

If, as many feminists mightily wish, a matriarchy ever existed in the distant past, it must have been during the Old Stone Age, though it is more likely that the social organization was based not on female superiority, but on equality between the sexes.[8] The key factor seems to be, as I mentioned before, that women in foraging societies provided more food than men, and as a result of searching for it, they gained equal knowledge of the territory and contact with other people. Mothers, as the most consistent food gatherers, are also thought to have developed the material and social techniques to make their task more efficient: storage containers,[9] the carrying sling, sticks for digging, and, perhaps, regular patterns of food sharing . . . the proto-dinner party. Were women always the primary hostesses? If not, they were still seen to be as important members of the community as men, and their tasks, though different, were rated as highly as the male skill of hunting. It was much later that man came to bully woman.[10]

Paleoanthropology now tells us that life may have been quite pleasant in the Old Stone Age. There was an ample food supply, and, with little competition for resources, there may have been less stress, petty rivalry, greed, and exploitativeness. By analogy with modern foragers — with Richard Lee and Irven DeVore's bushmen or Colin Turnbull's forest people — Old Stone Age societies may have had population control (abortion and contraception), which meant that the children born were wanted. And if the analogy holds, these people may have had some leisure time, a rich ceremonial life, and relative peace.[11]

Plant gathering is thought to have been a friendly, boisterous activity, carried out together by all the able-bodied women of a band. Young children could play about, receiving attention whenever necessary.[12] There was no need for rigid discipline, as there would be later, when youngsters had to earn their keep. Growing up without harsh punishment, perhaps expecting kindness from others as a matter of course, children may have developed into nonviolent adults, free to love their own offspring.

Although there was some ritual human and child sacrifice and cannibalism in times of drought and great hardship, it is thought they were by no means as dominant as they were to become in more "civilized" periods. Moreover, skeletal remains show that these prehistoric people sometimes kept alive even severely disabled infants, a group frequently sacrificed in many societies, even, at times, our own. So we are dealing with a complex, humane, child-respecting culture. Perhaps this was a heyday for mothering.[13] ❍

WHEN OUR FOREBEARS attempted to answer such universal questions as where we come from when we are born, they confirmed the obvious — life emerges from a mother. Indeed, what first inspired worship was Great Mother. They developed a religious theme connecting woman with the mystery of life. Of course the word *religion* is problematic in a prehistoric context; way of life would be more apt. Religion for Paleolithic people was not a dimension of experience separate and apart from the ordinary. All life was sacred, and the Great Mother created all life.[14]

The very earliest known religious icons were naked female figurines, often in advanced stages of pregnancy. Over sixty of these remarkably uniform little statues have been found in Europe, at sites as far apart as western France and Siberia. In caves, on mountaintops, at home altars, and in the earliest shrines, the fecund goddess appeared, carved from soft stone or mammoth ivory or baked in clay. The wide dispersal of the figurines attests to the ubiquity of the awe attributed to woman's capacity to create life.[15] The same idea seems to have happened all over, a powerful hint that as soon as hominids began to wonder, a woman's reproductive power inspired near-universal wonderment.

Though no two figurines are exactly alike, the Great Mother is almost always stout, erect in posture, self-contained, sometimes faceless, and only inches in height, a miniature fireplug of a woman. She may have been held in one's hand, or, because she sometimes lacks feet and her lower half comes to a point, she may have been "planted" in the ground. Her most obvious features are her enlarged breasts and buttocks, unfortunately seen as "tits and ass" by a previous generation of archeologists, who categorized the statues as "Venus" figures, after the goddess concerned with sexual love. By far the most famous is the Venus of Willendorf, a four-and-an-eighth-inch limestone figurine from Austria, around 30,000 to 25,000 B.C., whose likeness is much copied.

But these Venuses are no chorus girls. They are not erotic in the modern sense — they are too independent to be projections of male sexual desire. These figures are probably more sensibly understood as symbols of fecundity. By and large they portray pregnancy — not birth, nurturing, or sensuality. Interestingly, it was not until the Middle Neolithic (New Stone Age)[16] that figures of the Great Mother holding a child appear.[17] This suggests that among the first "thinking" humans, it was specifically woman's capacity to reproduce that inspired worship.

In the Paleolithic mind, the Great Mother came to be associated with the earth, on which these people fully depended for sustenance. It was only much later that divinity was connected to the heavens. The Goddess was immanent, not transcendent; She was located within each individual and all things in nature, not above them. As Old Stone Age men and women observed the natural processes in a woman's body — menstruation, pregnancy, birth, lactation — the earth was understood by analogy to be the great womb from which all life emerged. The dead were buried in the fetal position, with their arms crossed over their chests, their bodies marked with red ocher, the pigmented earth, symbolic perhaps of life-giving uterine fluid or menstrual blood. Thus, humans were returned to the earth's womb at death, perhaps to be born again, like plants in the great seasonal round. Recent interpretations of cave paintings and engravings suggest that figures once thought to represent arrows, barbs, and weapons of the masculine hunt are actually plants, trees, and reeds, products of feminine foraging. The mysterious carved notches found on many cave panoramas are now understood to be a recording of the menstrual cycle and the lunar months of pregnancy. Also, depictions of triangles and flowers are currently thought to represent the vulva. For example, the French archeologist André Leroi-Gourhan solved a riddle of the early cave paintings that had defeated anthropologists for decades when he decoded the recurrent and puzzling "double egg" figure as symbolizing the vagina. Similarly, in a remarkable sculpted frieze of animal and human figures at Angles-sur-l'Angline, the female forms are represented by pure abstract triangles of women's bodies with the sexual triangle prominently emphasized. Perhaps phallic symbols became "phallic," that is, signifiers of power, only after men gained ascendancy. Vagina symbols may have been the phallic symbols of the Paleolithic. This should give pause to those men with an *Iron John* mentality who turn to caveman myths for a masculinity infusion.[18]

While we cannot assume that there is a fixed relation between the status of women and the worship of a goddess in all cultures — in contemporary India, for example, the widespread oppression of women exists alongside the worship of a female divinity, the Hindu Devi — in many civilizations where the Goddess held sway, women did too, to a certain extent.[19] The open veneration of woman's natural rhythms and monthly flow contrasts sharply with the secret shame and "curse" they later became. It is important to note that in this very early conception of a maternal goddess, She had a dual nature: She gave life and She took it away. The early civilizations understood very well the strong association of the divine woman with the mysteries of death. They were not wedded, as we are, to an all-loving, all-forgiving stereotype of mother. The Great Mother was not expected to be all-good. Instead, She expressed her complete psychic reality. Worship of her was sensual and erotic, embracing all that was alive. Sex was associated with life-giving powers, renewal, rebirth, and transformation. But She also had a dark side — irrational, chaotic, and destructive — all of which was acknowledged when the Goddess reigned supreme. She was whole in ways that future female divinities and their human counterparts would be denied.

The Divine Womb: New Stone Age Mom

As time passed, the earth's temperature warmed and the glaciers receded, ushering in nothing less than a new world order in which life centered on the farm, not the cave. But the Goddess still reigned; indeed, Her incarnations multiplied. There is little evidence that male-dominated politics, economics, religion, or family had come to the fore. On the contrary, much evidence suggests life was fairly equal between the sexes. Women were buried in sanctuaries, celebrated in art, and are thought to have hunted alongside men; they were not subordinate in social status. Motherhood remained mother-defined. Patriarchy was but a gleam in the masculine eye, still thousands of years off. This was the Neolithic — the New Stone Age[20] — a prehistoric period that has stirred the imaginations of generations of writers from the ancient

Greeks to the late Victorians to New Age pagans. The Neolithic gets good press today and has spawned a veritable industry in books, religions, guides, tapes, and paraphernalia that extol the goddesses and depict this period as egalitarian, peaceful, warm, playful, and nature-loving.[21] To some feminists, the ecology-minded, various and sundry utopians, and even numerous sober scholars, the goddesses are not only sources for artistic and spiritual inspiration, but role models as well. Their depictions of this so-called Lost Golden Age tend toward the rhapsodic.[22] They argue that the coincidence of Goddess worship and social harmony is hardly accidental, that a motherly outlook would naturally be associated with peace and balance, nature and sensuality.

These ideas, however, are only speculative, as are even the received academic views of the Neolithic period. Much of our "unshakable" evidence is archeological — assorted physical remains — not written records. And debris is not very informative. Or else the evidence is anthropological, derived by analogy with contemporary cultures having similar characteristics. Again, conclusions are hypothetical. So mainstream scholarship may be no less skewed than the hyperbolic outpourings of zealots. But while little is actually known about the Neolithic, the period begs for thoughtful, interpretive work. It offers a unique opportunity to contemplate a time when the central religious image was a life-giving woman, not, as it is today, a brutally murdered man; when, for that matter, the primary maternal image was lusty and willful, not, as with the Virgin Mary, virtuous and self-sacrificing. The implications are "pregnant" with meaning. Were these maternal goddesses symbolic expressions of how New Stone Age mothers experienced reality? Or did the goddesses' image shape reality? Perhaps these maternal divinities were products of wishful thinking, and bore no relation to actual mothers. The possibilities are intriguing.

The persistent portrayal in popular culture of the Neolithic as a feminine Elysium is in itself interesting. Historical interpretation reveals much about the historian. Perhaps we all yearn for a time when we might have had perfect mothers, or when we were free to be perfect mothers — the nagging wish for a history of which we may be proud, to contrast with, or to correct, a dreary present. The longing for a past relationship to a warm, tender, protective female body, stronger than our own, is understandable, given that most of us, in earliest infancy, lived under the power of a mother. Prodded by slumbering memories (or wishes) of infant bliss at the breast, we re-create our personal past in dreams, myths, and so-called history. But we create an improved version, an idealized mother, one who would never be so rude as to wean us, to exile us from paradise! In some of the heated writing about the Neolithic, we easily see how the powerful wish for a good mother has shaped perceptions. But even if we were to turn down the temperature, we would find enough evidence to suggest that New Stone Age cultures esteemed mothers and, in turn, children.

WHAT WE KNOW ABOUT THE NEOLITHIC

With radically changing geological conditions, the abundance of game lessened. Tales of a woolly mammoth that could feed sixty persons would probably have sounded as unlikely to the Neolithic ear as the chance of buying inexpensive beachfront property does to ours. Successful hunts became rare, forcing our migratory ancestors to abandon their way of life and to develop new ways to supplement their diet. Gradually, in different regions at different times, the gatherers and hunters became horticulturalists[23] and, later, agriculturalists[24] and breeders of animals, settling down in clans, villages, and towns. It is significant that people no longer roamed, but stayed put to cultivate their gardens and to tend animals. A fixed home is stabilizing. Human energy and imagination were freed to develop new technologies (pottery, basketry, the weaving of textiles, leather and jewelry crafting) and art (painting, clay modeling, stone carving). With a regular and sometimes even surplus food supply came stirrings of materialism, greed, an unequal distribution of wealth — the beginnings of complicated social dynamics and of what we call (with some irony) Western civilization.[25]

The center of culture shifted from the caves in Western and Southern Europe to the then moist and fertile valleys of the Near East, where the first systematic cultivation of grain occurred. By 7000 B.C., agriculture was well established in Jordan, Iran, and Turkey. We now know that Mesopotamia was not the only "cradle of civilization," and that town life appeared thousands of years earlier than was thought just thirty years ago.

The role of the male in reproduction, which was probably not fully understood in a foraging society, may have become somewhat clearer once animals were kept in captivity. How could a Paleolithic man guess that sex and babies were connected, separated as they are by so many months and intervening variables? Some feminists[26] regard this knowledge as the beginning of the end, leading to the devaluation of women, the demise of equality, and the rise of the phallus (pun intended!). But the story is not so simple. Even if Neolithic man completely understood his biological contribution to pregnancy — and chances are he did not — he would have had no way of staking claim to any particular child or designating an heir for his possessions. Monogamy was a future invention (of about six thousand years!). In this early period, fatherhood was probably a frail bond if it was recognized at all. Besides, the Neolithic was relatively egalitarian, as we shall see.[27]

The discovery of agriculture served to reinforce the power of the Great Mother, whose connection to the earth had already been established during the Paleolithic period. It must be remembered that a farming economy, perhaps even more directly than foraging, binds people to the biological rhythms of plants and animals on which their existence depends, and it would be a small step for them to discern a likeness between these rhythms and the cyclical changes in the female, and to attribute them to her supernatural powers.[28] Does not the female's body share with the moon its periodicity, and with the earth its power of generation? In the Neolithic cultures of Palestine, Turkey, and Southeast Europe, religious imagery was overwhelmingly dominated by women.

At Catal Hüyük,[29] for example, a Neolithic excavation site in Turkey that has proven to be an archeological watershed, the whole town seems to have been dedicated to goddess religion and to religious artisanry. At least forty shrines have been found, one for every four or five home dwellings, all to a female divinity, none to a god. Depictions of the pregnant goddess on shrine walls bear a startling resemblance to the Paleolithic "Venuses." This same goddess is also shown in other wall paintings as a slim maiden who is running or dancing or whirling, her hair streaming behind her, perhaps foreshadowing the later lascivious goddesses of Minoan Crete.[30] Perhaps she is a missing link between the two eras. Yet other depictions show her as a menacing old crone, sometimes accompanied by a vulture. There are numerous paintings of swooping vultures, with five-foot wing spans, eating headless humans. Apparently like her predecessor, the Great Mother, this goddess was a deity of death as well as life. In her more terrifying aspects, the Neolithic goddess is shown as a kind of stalactite with a human head, emphasizing what scholars call her chthonic, or earthy, qualities, connecting her to caves and the underworld. Here, in 6000 B.C., was concrete evidence of the dual nature of the mother goddess, symbolically both the terror and hope of the human race during the Neolithic and later eras. Like her ancestor, but unlike her well-known descendants, the Greek and Roman goddesses, she is a model of (mother) nature in its fullness — creative and destructive, tender and fierce, good and bad. She is not impossibly benign or forever young. Indeed, she inspires awe even as a postmenopausal woman.

At Catal Hüyük and in nearby Hacilar, we find two tantalizing figures of a Mother Goddess holding a baby, one of the oldest "madonna cum bambinis" to date. The mother-child configuration, now virtually imprinted on our brain, obviously became a central religious and secular image that has survived the millennia. The Catal Hüyük version, carved in gray-green schist, shows the goddess as two female bodies, back to back, one nursing an infant and the other embracing a lover (a figure smaller than she, implying youth and subordinate status). The Hacilar clay statuette shows a nursing male child with his genitals near the mother's vulva. Both show the beginnings, within the goddess religions, of a companion worship of a young male who may be both son and lover,[31] which was to become a common theme. Do these statues depict Neolithic mother love? Do they suggest incest? Surely the proximity between sexual organs of mother and child would be behavior unbecoming a late-twentieth-century Western parent. But given finite biological avenues for expressing human bonding, and the absence of social constraints, perhaps Stone Age maternal attachment was overtly sexualized, at least for deities.

Over time the Neolithic Mother Goddess is thought to have evolved into the great personified goddesses — Ishtar of Babylon and Assyria, Astarte of Canaan, Isis of Egypt, Cybele of Phrygia, and Gaia of pre-Hellenic Greece — a motley crew, powerful, whimsical, and, in turn, nurturing and cruel, the infamous subjects of Old Testament scorn. Even later, her personality was splintered. The famous goddesses of the patriarchal cultures of Greece and Rome may best be understood as diminutions of the Neolithic goddess. In contrast to the more ancient goddess, the Greek and Roman goddesses are one-dimensional and are defined by their relation to men. Not one is a full-blooded, multifaceted mother. Motherhood was severed from all other attributes of womanhood.

What did a Neolithic mom, in the shadow of her feisty three-dimensional goddess, feel about her babies? We do know that the folk of the New Stone Age, in their cozy farm communities, bred like rabbits! There was a population explosion of sorts around 10,000 B.C. These people are thought to have had rudimentary means of contraception, so presumably they wanted their children. Why? Ethnologists show us time and again — and as recently as the 1960s among the !Kung bush people — that as nomadic people go sedentary, they tend to suspend their use of birth control. A child becomes an asset, not a handicap. In agricultural communities a youngster is another pair of hands to work the land. Laborers are much valued, and New Stone Age people worked like dogs. Ironically, nomads have a much easier life than farmers. If our ancestors only knew what they gave up when they put down roots![32]

In agricultural societies, children start to work at the age of three, chasing birds from food plots. Older children watch the animals and keep them out of planted areas.[33] The Neolithic, then, may have marked the true end of childhood innocence. Youngsters had serious responsibilities. It makes sense to speculate that punitive child-rearing practices must have developed concurrently. Children are human, after all, and are not likely to work hard without a little prodding.

As women settled into individual huts in villages, keeping their children with them, there was a greater restriction in living space. Eventually, these dwellings housed men, though men still had to hunt to supplement the agriculture and modest domestic herd, so they probably were not around very much. With a more confined lifestyle, motherhood must have undergone some elemental changes compared with the time when mothers and children lived in a series of caves. Since a child moves in the mother's orbit up to the first ten years of life, constriction in space for one is also a constriction for the other. We all know that familiarity breeds contempt. Here we have a situation ripe for mother-child conflict, adding credibility to the theory that punitive child care developed around this time. But familiarity may also breed empathy. Mothers may have had a better chance to observe their babies grow and develop. The Neolithic may have been the beginning of nuclear family intimacy — assuming that women limited themselves to one mate. Many scholars[34] believe this period to be matrilocal and matrilineal, meaning that "married" couples lived in the "wife's" family domain, and descent was reckoned through the mother. The dad would move into her hut and produce her children, which implies a very different family dynamic from the one we now know.

Just as we found scattered evidence of child sacrifice in the Paleolithic, so we find traces of the same practice in the Neolithic. A group of baby skulls found under a basinlike structure in the earliest layer of Jericho probably indicates human sacrifice. But the fact that such findings are infrequent — in stark contrast to the grisly mass murder of children some millennia later — suggests that the practice was not widespread.[35]

This evidence, then, for maternal attachment during the Neolithic is impressive: women had babies in abundance; they kept them nearby; they trained them in adaptive skills; and they did not frequently engage in child sacrifice. But the strongest proof, to my mind, derives from the descriptions of excavations at Catal Hüyük. There, the dead were buried under sleeping platforms inside the houses. The larger platform, always on the east wall, belonged to the mistress of the house. The small corner platform, belonging to the man, was often moved about. Children were buried with their mother. Sometimes they were buried under their own platform, but never with the men.[36] The important point is that burial of children was never careless, disrespectful, or isolated from the family; it was with family, especially the mother. Proximity in life; proximity in death — what more powerful evidence could there be of a strong, indeed, an eternal bond between Neolithic mother and child?

Because these societies were based on agriculture, on the domestication of animals, on weaving and pottery making — all activities associated in some degree with woman's invention and control — the prevailing view is that women played a major part in these cultures, as further evidenced by the dominance of female religious images. In the Neolithic, women were respected, and they seemed to respect their children. The condition and position of women proves to be an index of the condition and position of children. Let me add that the Neolithic Catal Hüyük community lasted for fifteen hundred years — seven times as long as the existence of the United States — seemingly free of massacre or war. Perhaps the contemporary disciples of the Mother Goddess are not so misguided after all.[37]

WHAT WE FANTASIZE ABOUT THE NEOLITHIC

The Neolithic period is a veritable Rorschach test, an inkblot on which generations of people have projected their wishes, fears, values, and dynamics. Each age interprets it anew, reinventing it according to unconscious blueprints drawn by their own early needs and wishes for a perfect past, for a good mother, as it were. Each version of the New Stone Age brings into relief a lot of the tics and assumptions of everyday life of the interpreter. The Greek philosopher Plato saw prehistory as a Golden Age, free and easy, with no such thing as private property and families; the sentimental Victorian Swiss jurist Bachofen understood the Stone Age as nurturing and altruistic; feminist contemporary goddess worshipers view it as unabashedly prowoman. As a prehistoric period without written records to dispute anyone's claim, the Neolithic is ideal for continuous interpretation.

It is also a hotbed of primordial maternal associations, a "mother" lode of newly minted symbols, many of them so powerful and tenacious that they have survived the millennia. It is the *source* — a mythologist's dream. Because maternity was the preoccupation of the age, many of the Neolithic symbols are maternal; agrarian people, as noted before, are understandably interested in the natural cycle of gestation, birth, and regeneration. Of course we do not know this for sure. An inventory of Neolithic symbols does not conveniently come with an interpreter's guide, so, like the age as a whole, the signs and artifacts have been subjected to massive distortions and transformations over time. Recall the meanings given by the Bushman to the Coke bottle that fell from the heavens in the film *The Gods Must Be Crazy*. All the interpretations he made of the bottle were logical in his context but preposterous in ours. Analogously, the meaning we attribute to a particular Stone Age symbol may have little to do with its original meaning. We must tread carefully, but let us look at a few.

Remember that the magical force and wonder of mother in the Neolithic was no less a marvel than nature itself, and the association of mother and nature, though inherited from the Old Stone Age, was the pre-eminent symbol of the New Stone Age. The equating of mother with nature was mutually enhancing, implying prodigious power for each. It was everywhere — in shrines and houses, on wall paintings, in the decorative motifs on vases, on sculptures of the round, clay figurines, and bas-reliefs — a rich array of Mother Goddess representations intertwined with images from nature. The Mother Goddess is shown amidst pillars or trees, accompanied by goats, snakes, birds. At Catal Hüyük she consorts with such powerful animals as leopards, vultures, and bulls. In some of her presentations she is part human and part animal. Sometimes she gives birth to a bull.[38] (Indeed, the most common depictions show her squatting in the posture of birthing.) In Old Europe,[39] the maternal goddess is variously portrayed as an egg, a bird, and a fish. She is often associated with life-sustaining water, indicated by the presence on many objects of what scholars call meanders, patterns of wavy lines. As the "Vegetable Goddess," she is fertility itself.

Even today the association between mother and nature taps feelings so basic, so universal, that it seizes the observer in an unforgettable vise of common understanding. Today, nature is mother herself: Mother Nature! "Mother is the root," wrote the early feminist Simone de Beauvoir, "which, sunk in the depths of the cosmos, can draw up its juices; she is the fountain whence springs forth the living water, water that is also a nourishing milk." Freud made the connection in his *Civilization and Its Discontents*. Our cultural language and imagery are replete with comparisons of a woman's body parts to flora and fauna — a peaches-and-cream complexion, doe eyes, swanlike neck, teeth like pearls, hymen as cherry, breasts like melons. We almost never hear of a man's skin as dewy or his lips like wine. Images of males are rarely organic, except when effeminacy is implied, as in "he's a fruit." Note that the masculine association with nature is derogatory. Real men have wills of iron, nerves of steel, ramrod spines, and razor-sharp wits. "Super" men are faster than speeding bullets, more powerful than the locomotive, able to leap tall buildings in a single bound. These metaphors are mechanical, urban, warlike.

But while the association of mother and nature remains strong, its significance has changed. It has been downgraded, probably reflecting the ambiguous status of motherhood these days. Nature is something that every culture now defines as being of a lower order of existence than itself.[40] Granted that nature and that which is "natural" are sentimentalized as innocent and pure and lovely in certain circles (witness the proliferation of the words "natural" or "organic" and the use of the color green in advertising), still, nature is more generally regarded as raw, uncivilized, uncontrollable, tilting toward the barbaric, something to be improved upon. Men, on the other hand, are associated with products of culture (technology, rationality). What was once a glorious association — motherhood and nature — is now mutually devaluing.

Dorothy Dinnerstein, a feminist author, has taken this one step further. She argues that in our failing to distinguish between nature and mother, we assign to each properties that belong to the other. We cannot believe how accidental, unconscious, unconcerned — unmotherly — nature really is; and we cannot believe how vulnerable, conscious, autonomously wishful — human — mother really is. We overpersonify nature (which is wholly impersonal and nonsentient) and underpersonify mother (who is fully sentient and not a force of nature).[41] If we could only outgrow the feeling that our female parent is omnipotent and responsible for every blessing and curse of existence, we might figure out what can be expected from mom, and what is owed to her, a human person.

While "mother as nature" has sunk in prestige over the millennia, other Neolithic symbols have been virtually turned upside down. The horns of the bull, though always representing the male, were once the benign accompaniment of the New Stone Age goddess and a manifestation of her power. At Catal Hüyük, bull horns form rows of altars under her images. Today, horns are symbols of Satan or evil. But this metamorphosis pales in comparison to the humiliating fate of the snake. One need not be a Freudian to guess its phallic significance. In the Old Testament, it was the serpent who tempted Eve, and ever since then the snake has come down to us as a pejorative symbol — of male sexuality, immoral sex, malevolence, and treachery. But in the Neolithic, the snake symbolized eternal life, since each time it shed its skin it seemed reborn. Ironically, it appears to have been primarily revered as a female and was generally linked to wisdom and prophetic counsel. Snake prestige reached its heyday in Bronze Age Crete, where gorgeous statues of serpent-entwined priestesses abounded, and where "snake tubes," cylindrical clay objects used to feed or contain the sacred serpents, were kept at the best addresses on the island, the sanctuaries of the Cretan goddesses. What a comedown this poor reptile has endured.[42]

Probably the most telling indicator of mother's declining reputation is her association with the now lowly pot. Today we do not often refer to the mother as a cooking utensil, yet we do hear women called "old bags," "weaker vessels," or "air heads," terms that conjure up empty containers. In a more benign "take" on this, the psychoanalyst Erik Erikson has associated women with "inner space," thereby attempting to explain the feminine tendency (or requirement, in my view) to mind "interiors," such as one's home.[43] Perhaps Erikson may not have realized that he was merely recapitulating the time-honored ideas of the Greek historian Xenophon, who wrote, "It seems to me that God adapted woman's nature to indoor and man's to outdoor work,"[44] or later ideas, following industrialization, about women's and men's "separate spheres." But "interiority" as a mode of existence lacks the status of "exteriority" — getting out there, going on a mythic quest, conquering the world, the exclusive province of heroes, not heroines.[45] Worse, the interior aspect of the mother seems to evoke dread for some men. During sexual intercourse, the vagina, as a receptacle, takes in the penis. In these males' horrific fantasy, woman, by taking into herself the body of man, "consumes" him. Hence the worldwide popularity of *vagina dentata* (toothed vagina) legends and metaphors — the castrating mother, the devouring witch, the monster into whose belly the hero must go (as Jonah went into the whale).[46]

The association of the mother with the pot no doubt developed because of the container's likeness to the shape of her womb or vagina or breast. The connection was probably enhanced because pottery making has been a primary occupation of women since the Neolithic, and is thought to have been developed by them during that period. Erich Neumann, in his pictorial *The Great Mother,* traces the "mother as vessel" imagery in artifacts of ancient cultures. But a pot during the New Stone Age was not just a bit of enclosed empty space. It was the very implement in which prehistoric woman transported her young, cooked her food, stored perishables; it was the premier primordial labor-saving device! Before the development of the pot, people were obliged to follow their food supply; they could not settle down and store provisions. Neumann views the pot as "transformative" — it transforms, or cooks, food — as is the womb, which transforms bodily fluid into life. Symbolizing the mother as a container was a supreme sign of respect in prehistoric times. Wombs — mothers — are far less magical today (more like incubators). And so, of course, are pots.[47] ❍

AS WE HAVE SEEN, the meanings assigned to Neolithic symbols of maternity have varied according to the moods of the times. But at the turn of the century there was a flurry of thought among intellectuals about the importance of motherhood. Largely armchair philosophers who spanned the disciplines of anthropology, political theory, religious history, and psychology, they shared the fanciful conviction of the mother's absolute virtue and her dominance in the Neolithic. Their theories grew out of the Romantic movement, with its renewed appreciation of nature and emphasis on imagination and the emotions — a period when anthropologists did not venture out into the field, when psychology was not yet an objective science, and political theory did not depend on verifiable facts. This was the era when European social philosophers looked for universal themes of human experience and grand evolutionary theories to explain our mist-shrouded history and development. It was the age of exaltation of the so-called primitive, the noble savage.[48] Reflecting the prejudices of their day, these scholars wove together inflated, sentimental ideas about motherhood and prehistory, some of which need disentangling even today.

Foremost among this group was the scholar Bachofen, who

came up with the notion of a maternal noble savage, in *Das Mutterrecht* (*Mother Right*). Bachofen suggested that all societies had to pass through a matriarchal stage (when women subdued men's animal lusts) before becoming patriarchal and monogamous. His data were mostly his idiosyncratic interpretations of myth, language, customs, and the works of ancient writers, all tainted by his mushy views of women's nurturance and altruism and by his Victorian prudery. Though universally discredited now, he influenced a generation of anthropologists who fastidiously assembled evidence for a prehistoric matriarchy and social evolution theory. Among them were James Frazer, whose now classic *The Golden Bough* ran to twelve volumes; Robert Briffault, whose three-volume work *The Mothers* exceeded Bachofen's in his assessment of mother love as the be-all and end-all for civilization's salvation, and who staunchly maintained that Amazons once abounded; and Helen Diner, who reinterpreted Bachofen in her *Mothers and Amazons* (which, interestingly, was endorsed by Joseph Campbell, the renowned popularizer of anthropology, in its first American edition). Her book was reissued in the 1970s, during the height of the women's movement, nourishing women's wish for a glorious past. Working in this less than scholarly tradition, Robert Graves traced the origin of the European great goddess and her connection with world mythologies in *The White Goddess*. He is now regarded skeptically by some feminists, who are miffed by his description of the goddess as a "bitch," and by academics for his insistence that the world alphabets were invented by women. And finally there was the renegade scholar Elizabeth Gould Davis, who dabbled in "creative" history in *The First Sex*, published in 1971. She argued not only for the existence of Neolithic matriarchy, but for the superiority of women in all realms — biological, moral, artistic. "The first males were mutants," she wrote without a hint of self-consciousness, "freaks produced by some damage to the genes."[49] Her impartiality may be questioned, but she should get credit for assimilating a vast amount of material pertaining to the patterns of female influence on civilization, even if she presented it impressionistically. Her bibliography alone is a worthwhile contribution to our understanding of ancient mothering.[50]

All these writers envisioned a Neolithic civilization centered on mother, both as head of the family and deity. Unfortunately, they interpreted the relative absence of female *subordination* and *inferiority* as implying women's *dominance* and *superiority* — this without any basis in fact. There has never been a true matriarchy — equality, perhaps, as we have seen in prehistory — never female dominance over men, the inversion of patriarchy. And these scholars' view, that women are superior to men, are more virtuous, and are more altruistic because of their so-called maternal instinct, distorts the biological sex differences. Simply, it is unscientific. Their argument that women, as mothers, are better equipped than men to improve society is pure idealization. They overvalue mothers' nurturance and undervalue mothers' humanity. These ideas were a malady of the Victorian Age and, to some extent, ours. While ostensibly "pro" mom, they actually undermine her by failing to see who she really is. They set impossible standards for her and engender needless guilt. Perhaps these writers are best appreciated not as chroniclers of absolute truths or proto-feminists, but as mythic storytellers who prime our imagination, who challenge men and women to conceive of modes of existence other than their own.

Bachofen had some strange bedfellows — Friedrich Engels and succeeding generations of Marxists, for example. In Engels's *The Origin of the Family, Private Property, and the State,* prehistoric matriarchies were the original sites of communism — and this was a compliment! Recall that Engels wrote a hundred years before the fall of the Berlin Wall. His argument went something like this: mothers first controlled communal property, but when agriculture was introduced (in the Neolithic), man used and therefore owned the farming tools, especially the ploughs and domesticated animals. Men thus became the first sex to have *private property.* Of course, by that time man had figured out his biological contribution to reproduction. And in order to pass on his property to his children, he had to make sure they were indeed his, so he introduced monogamy to control the descent system. As a result, women were subordinated economically and restricted sexually. If we follow Engels's logic, we would expect the abolition of private property to liberate women, but, of course, it has not. We have only to observe the appalling condition of women in China today to understand that it is not capitalism alone that is the oppressor of women. Furthermore, Engels was wrong about the New Stone Age as a period of prehistoric matriarchy. He was, however, insightful about the connection between economic dominance by men and the control of women's sexuality. To be sure, economic factors have been a major influence on maternity, maternal affection, maternal status. More than one child was begot to produce an heir; more than one child was killed to reduce poverty.

Using methods as evocative and speculative as those of Bachofen and his followers, a number of Jungian psychoanalysts, particularly Erich Neumann, looked to the art and mythology of the Neolithic and other ancient civilizations for inferences about human behavior. Like Bachofen, they worked outside the realm of strict historical truth. Their goals, like his, were less literal; they sought psychological truths. In the image of the Great Mother, for example, Neumann saw an archetypal figure, an eternal symbol, a signifier of psychic issues we all associate with mothers. In Neumann's reading of ancient artifacts, these Mother Goddesses are both "good" and "terrible" and both "elementary" (possessive) and "transformative" (facilitative of change). We have already spoken of Neumann's linking of mother with the transformative pot. Whether, in fact, Neolithic people experienced their mothers this way is questionable. Yet his interpretations have psychological resonance with respect to the way we sometimes feel about our mothers, and in the way parents feel about children — that they are all good or all bad. Similarly, Neumann's interpretation of the Great Mother as "elementary and/or transformative" bears on the all-too-human parents' dilemma of whether to hold on to or let go of their children; and children's corresponding conflicts about being cared for versus becoming independent. From Neumann's perspective, then, these Neolithic goddess figurines tell *our* story. ❍

IN CONJURING UP Neolithic motherhood, I wonder whether we are not, in a sense, speculating about the nature of Mother Eve before she partook of the apple. What was she like while she was still innocent and free and surrounded by nature? How would she have felt about babies before God's punishment of pain in childbirth? Was the grass greener? Was her milk sweeter? We may never know. The Neolithic was nonliterate. By the time recorded history began, we were long banished from the garden. The idyll, if there ever was one, had faded.

TWO

History Begins, Herstory Ends

The Decline and Fall of the Great Mother

It did not happen overnight. The Neolithic idyll — the supposed age of peace and sexual equality — faded slowly, over twenty-five hundred years, from approximately 3100 to 600 B.C.[1] In the beginning we might have overheard a Near Eastern mother sing a Sumerian lullaby to her baby as she rocked her or him to sleep, but by the end, as humankind ironically emerged from the darkness of prehistory, we might have observed terrified young children — mostly under two but some as old as twelve years — being placed in the mechanical arms of a carnivorous deity as sacrifice. Thousands of urns containing the cremated remains of babies and youngsters have been found, for example, in Carthage.[2] What happened in between was the establishment of patriarchy, the universal domination of women by men that has continued in one form or another ever since. This is not to say that patriarchy alone accounted for the dramatic change in maternal attitude or that mothers' feelings reversed themselves worldwide. But historical events and social forces did bump up against one another, resulting in a kaleidoscope of shifting patterns of power relations among men and women, and changing forever family dynamics and affective bonds.

The onset of patriarchy, even in the ancient Near East, occurred at a different pace and at different times in several distinct societies. Further, the change was not across the board. Women seemed to have greatly different positions in different aspects of their lives. So, for example, early in the transitional period, Babylonian women may have had high status in society, yet, in accordance with the Code of Hammurabi (a collection of laws), they incurred the death penalty for adultery though their husbands might go scot free for the same crime.[3] But with the coming of one God (Buddha, Yahweh, Christ, or Allah), women's standing in all realms was leveled to a position subordinate to that of males. Political, social, philosophical, religious, and economic thought became the exclusive domain of men. (Note that every parvenu God is male.)

By 600 B.C., patriarchy was established over much of Europe, Asia, and Africa. In its most basic manifestation, female virgins and mothers were commodities (much as Engels speculated), the former valued for their breeding potential (children were still needed as labor), the latter for their nurturing. Should a hapless woman not fall in either category — if, for instance, she had been raped by someone other than her designated mate, or if she was barren — her life could be jeopardized. She might be stoned, drowned, or discarded. Property was transmitted from father to son, and all benefits of women's and children's labor accrued to the father. So the accurate identity of the father became highly important, lest goods be inherited by the wrong person. Men were economically constrained to curtail sexual access to their mates, which helps to explain the fetishes that arose about virginity, chastity, and sexual exclusivity. The laws that developed in ancient times to regulate women's sexuality may be understood on one level as protective measures for what were essentially economic transactions between fathers and husbands.

Evidently, once the idea of patriarchy entered our consciousness, it altered the way we saw the world, so it perpetuated itself. The subordination of women became reality, and we could imagine no other. Every age automatically reinvented it, with its own battery of justifications. The historian Rosalind Miles points out that masculine supremacy has been so resilient over time as to withstand all revolutions, all democratic experiments. "All demands for equality have so far stopped short of sexual equality."[4]

As recently as the 1960s and 1970s, in the student protest movement, it was the women who typed, the men who grabbed headlines; in the proliferating communes, supposedly models of egalitarian living, it was the women who cooked, the men who bossed. The males were the lead performers; the females, as always, the supporting cast. Patriarchy felt natural, God-given.

Moreover, the patriarchal takeover preceded the development of writing. Every written word, then, has been refracted through the prism of a male-dominated consciousness. Virtually all the messages we get or ever got through reading — subliminal, liminal — have been mediated by a patriarchal sensibility. All history is biased. It was written from the point of view of the victors of the gender conflict. And because patriarchy is so pervasive, because it permeates language and the written word, it is hard to grasp. Perhaps that is why women took twenty-five hundred years to notice.

Finally, and this cannot be dodged, women have colluded in their own subordination. To a certain extent, once patriarchy was in place, women had no choice. Handed over as children by one man (the father) to another (the husband), they were legally, financially, and physically subject to the power of men for thousands of years.[5] But interestingly, men did not often have to use overt physical pressure to keep women down; it was assumed for centuries — from Aristotle to Freud — that women were naturally subordinate, that anatomy was destiny.

Today, superseding biology as an explanation for women's inferior position is social conditioning, the barrage of psychosocial messages — in ritual, tradition, language, customs, etiquette, and education — that serve to shape women to men's demands. Certain feminist psychoanalysts and theorists[6] look to the infants' early environment — the gender arrangement around the baby cradle — to account for the lopsided power relations between men and women. The crucial variables are the baggage of patriarchy: the socially isolated mother-and-child unit and the absent (relatively speaking) father. Because of being mothered by someone of the same gender as themselves (with whom they identify), it is speculated that girls emerge from childhood with a capacity for nurturance, empathy, and selflessness. In contrast, boys, in order to be perceived as males, must disidentify with their mothers and disavow "femininity." In the end, males tend to be more autonomous and personally ambitious, and sometimes they defensively denigrate women. Here we have an explanation for women's odd complicity with their own subjugation. Obviously, this is partial and simplistic, but it is persuasive. All theories seem to be "works in progress" at this time.

At the beginning of recorded history, we behold the finale of the long pageant of prehistory, when a baby was its mother's child exclusively, when women alone were thought to have the wondrous power to reproduce. Arguably, Copernicus's insight that the earth is not the center of the universe, and all other occasions of radical transformation in consciousness, are dwarfed by comparison with what happened when men discovered that mothers are not the center of the universe. Yet even today, the revolutionary patriarchal takeover is overlooked by school curricula, despite abundant new scholarship. To do otherwise, I suppose, would be to interpret history from a female perspective, which is still regarded as a peculiar angle from which to view things. Also, the transformation was not marked by a single, cataclysmic event, so it is tricky to conceptualize.

The essential change, the one basic to all others, was in the nature of mentality. What was gained was a new kind of cognition — logic — the connection between cause and effect (as in the link between men and babies), an emphasis on rational thinking, a gradual drawing away from the natural world, a retreat from magic in favor of science. No small advance! What we lost, however, was the supremacy of the maternal metaphor, a gentler way of conceptualizing, ordering, and valuing reality. When God was a mother, perhaps all things maternal enjoyed higher prestige — things reproductive, nurturing, preservative. All artistic expression was characterized by dancing goddesses, vegetation, and birthing women, never by war imagery. All natural phenomena were candidates for elevation to sacred status because nature was regenerative and therefore wondrous. And motherhood itself, the source of generative power, was the be-all and end-all.

During the twenty-five-hundred-year transitional period, in which patriarchal attitudes gained ascendancy, woman was still valued for her ability to reproduce. Her fertility potential, as noted, determined her worth as a commodity. But now woman was valued *only* for her maternity. Her scope and dignity were reduced; she had become an instrument for reproduction. And now this power was not solely hers. Woman had become a mere stop on the assembly line of baby production, a means to an end. Patriarchal man impregnates "his" wife and expects her to deliver "his" child; her elemental power is perceived as a service she renders, a function she performs.[7] She has no value beyond childbearing and child rearing.

Not surprisingly, there was a shift in magic, ritual, and imagery from the womb to the phallus. The number of female figurines diminished with respect to male figurines. The penis replaced the womb as the primary symbol of generation, of power. The penis as an icon entered our dreams and from then on has affected the very way we experience the world. Freud knew this, and so did Jacques Lacan, the influential French psychoanalyst, though they may not have suspected that there was a symbol of a very different organ at an earlier point in history. Paradoxically, women were the first worshipers of the phallus, but not on its own account. Rather, they regarded the penis as an adjunct to the goddess. It was in service of woman's sexuality and, may I suggest, erotic pleasure. In Egyptian mythology, it was Isis herself, the primary deity, who ordered a wooden lingam of Osiris to be set up in her temple at Thebes. Subsequently, the women of Egypt carried images of the male god Osiris in their sacred processions, each one equipped with a movable penis of disproportionate magnitude. Later, in Greece, the women carried on in much the same way. Phallus statues sprang up everywhere. By the third century B.C., the ancient city of Delos boasted an avenue of mammoth penises, supported by bulging testicles, shooting skyward. Even later, it was rumored, Roman women sat upon the erect penis of the statue of Priapus in order to become fruitful.[8]

Once man was promoted from bit player to leading man in the primal drama, the penis took center stage. It became the central preoccupation — indeed, the obsession — of men, who celebrated it as a symbol of manhood and individual paternity. From this epoch onward, male superiority became vested in and expressed through this one organ as an ever-present reminder of male power. Man, even today, glories in his member. Phallic symbols abound: church steeples, the Washington Monument, the sword, rifle, baton, billy club, rocket to the moon, and our supreme gesture of scorn — "the finger" — all partake of the power of the penis. The phallus, displacing the womb as the center of all creative power, became the symbol of masculine domination over women, children, Mother Earth, and other men.

Of course, all this attribution of power to one's organs is arbitrary; the penis is no more sovereign than the vagina or, for that matter, the liver. And for all the penis's symbolic value and supposed significance as a cause of envy in females, it has never been a popular subject for their pen or paintbrush. The coveted object hardly appears in the graphic arts or in literature unless the artist is male (with the recent exception of Sylvia Plath's *The Bell Jar,* where the male organ is compared to a "turkey neck and turkey gizzards"). Yet man has long sung the charms of woman's bosom, curved neck, smooth waist, inviting cleft, and so on.[9] It makes one wonder who envies whom for what body part.

It is fascinating to observe that the power shift from female to male was reflected in virtually all the ancient mythologies, as every Mother Goddess, one after the other, was deposed. This occurred after the actual subordination of mortal women, and the pattern was roughly the same. At first, an earth-centered Mother Goddess was pre-eminent. She created the world and had children as she pleased (by parthenogenesis, as it were — no male needed). Next, one of her male children was promoted to lover-consort, and she eventually shared her power with him. His identity conflated with that of a creator–sky god. In the ensuing power struggle between him and the goddess, he won, and he ruled, initially, with a whole galaxy of gods. She was demoted. Later, he became supreme and ruled like a despot from heaven, and the transfer of the power of creation from goddess to god was complete.[10]

Variations on the theme of the dethronement of the Mother Goddess appeared in different mythologies at different times, but the result was always the same: the masculinization of the gods. For example, in Sumeria, Dumuzi replaced Inanna; in Babylon, it was male Marduk who defeated Ti'amat (the Great Mother); the Hittite deity Arinna, Queen of Heaven and Earth, actually changed sex, becoming a man. But the replacement of the Mother Goddess by male gods did not occur without a hitch, quite literally. It appears that in the historical development of these mythologies there was a period in which the goddess, much like a black widow spider, copulated with her male consort, after which he died. Later, in some renditions, he returned. Historians and anthropologists call this the "sacred marriage" ritual, and it may be seen in numerous versions of the "goddess dethronement" story; it is usually connected with the promotion of agricultural fertility. In all these myths, an immortal mother (always an older female goddess) takes a beautiful but expendable youth as her lover (sometimes he is her son); for example, the goddess Ishtar copulates with Tammuz; Venus with Adonis; Cybele with Artis; and Isis with Osiris. Afterward the lover dies, though occasionally he is reborn. The rebirth symbolizes the cyclical nature of the harvest. If the flower is to bloom, the seed must fall. After the youth dies, there is "plenty" in the land.[11] The "dying and reborn sun god" theme is probably a precursor of the Christ story.

A number of aspects of the sacred marriage ritual are pertinent to the image of mothers, notably the dominance of the Mother Goddess, who selects the ruler privileged to cohabit with her. She actively and explicitly enjoys him sexually. The issue of this union is specifically *not* a baby; it is luxuriant vegetation and fertility throughout the land. The bountiful harvest generates jubilation among the populace. The message is that sex — even nonmonogamous, incestuous, nonprocreative sex performed by a mother — is good! Also notable is that the male god — at least for this period, before he becomes ascendant — is a sacrificial lamb, a disposable drone, a female sex object. Quite a switch from the sexual politics of today!

Much like the medieval passion play, the mythical sacred marriage rite was re-enacted publicly in rapturous celebrations all over the Near East for two thousand years, with worshipers taking the parts of the goddess and her young, virile, doomed consort. These events involved real sexual activity on temple grounds, where priestesses imitated their goddess by copulating with designated male strangers, all in the service of a bountiful harvest. Though rites of worship, these cultic sexual acts were labeled by later prudish biblical patriarchs as "temple prostitution," an unfortunate misnomer that has contaminated the good name of goddess worship ever since. Sadly, by the time of the Phoenicians, in the first millennium, the sacred marriage rite had devolved into the sexual exploitation of women and included actual ritual human sacrifice, symbolizing, I suppose, the mythic death of the consort. But it would be a mistake to blame the Mother Goddess for the later excesses of her worshipers . . . a little like holding the Venus de Milo accountable for her numerous schlocky knock-offs. For most of paganism's long life, its practice was joyful and benign, even by contemporary standards.[12]

What should a twentieth-century mother make of the Mother Goddesses? Do they speak to us? They are a complicated lot, these female deities. By the transitional period of history, when patriarchy took root, they became individualized personalities with dramatic, bloodcurdling life histories that would make soap operas look tame. I am referring here to such goddesses as Ishtar, Isis, Kali, and so on. Their exploits are chronicled in elaborate myths set down in the Sumerian *Gilgamesh,* the Indian *Mahabharata,* and the Egyptian *Book of the Dead,* for example. Present-day artists as diverse as the director Peter Brook, the painter Judy Chicago, and the sculptor Louise Bourgeois have turned to them for inspiration. The theological scholars Carol Christ and Christine Downing and the Jungian Esther Harding find in them universal truths of feminine being and urge other women to search for the "inevitable" goddess within themselves.

I remain somewhat guarded about their value as role models. On a positive note, an affirmative view of the goddesses is useful as an antidote to the entrenched historical tendency to demonize pagan goddesses, most notably in the Old Testament, whose authors were hell-bent on eradicating any flattering reference to goddess worship (which continued to be a threat to male-god monotheism) and on disclaiming any evolutionary debt for their own existence to any prior theology. If nothing else, it balances the scale. And to the extent that these deities provide a wider definition of mothers' behavior (sexy and willful) than later goddesses, like the eternally compassionate Buddhist Kwan Yi or the Blessed Virgin Mary, they have value. Extreme conceptions of the divine mother as perfect are hard acts for mortals to follow, and they obscure an inevitable and essential component of mothers — imperfection. But the trouble with romanticizing these particular maternal goddesses is that they have so many grim aspects. There is Anath (of Syria-Palestine), who dances with the heads of her victims tied to her girdle; Beltis of Babylon, with the heads of slain prisoners bound to her neck; the Hindu Kali, dancing with the skulls of her victims tied to her neck and waist. Perhaps all this bloody decapitation was the goddesses' desperate revenge on the usurping male gods. A Freudian might regard it as "displacement upward," that is, the taking out of anger not on the penis, symbol of manhood, but on the head. But sadism, however justified, is hardly model behavior.

Whether or not these divinities are worthy of our deification is probably a moot point. About three or four thousand years ago they were deposed, or at least sufficiently undermined as to become innocuous. Relegated to the status of wives or mothers of new powerful male warrior gods, they ceased to matter all that much. The goddesses suffered a diminution in status from which they never recovered, much like mortal women. They were replaced by their babies!

Historians heatedly debate the causes of the patriarchal takeover. We are familiar with some of their ideas already: man's knowledge of his biological role in procreation; the switch from the hoe to the male-run plough and ox (resulting in a masculine dominance of food production); private property (Engels's idea). Add to this the theories of structural anthropologist Claude Lévi-Strauss, who attributed the subordination of women to the universal incest taboo; this forced men of different clans to exchange women in order to mate, thereby making women into objects of barter, like meat. Then, too, there were historical events that may account for the downfall of women, namely, the invasions of iron-wielding warrior tribes from north of the Black Sea. The Kurgans, as they are called, brought with them their male-dominated hierarchy and aggressive male deities and caused wide-scale destruction and dislocation. A competing hypothesis has patriarchy the result of the transition from village culture to city culture. As people began to congregate in cities, there was a clearer separation between private and public realms. Women, relegated to the private realm as an outgrowth of their caretaking, were excluded from the creation of a political community. They were isolated. Men, on the other hand, remained in the public domain and assumed more power. Whatever the cause for the shift in power, it was reflected in religion by the dominance of male deities, who were not infrequently pictured as slaying female monsters, symbolic, perhaps, of the Mother Goddess religion or of woman herself.[13]

But we should not be so surprised that mother and, in turn, those dreadful goddesses were dethroned. It was probably inevitable. They were much too threatening; they must have struck cosmic terror into the hearts of men. Ironically, their fabulous power — the power to create life — contained the seeds of their downfall. There had always been a dark side to their prodigiousness: she that giveth can taketh away! The goddesses were capricious, uncontrollable, destructive, and wanton. Just as they were associated with fertility, so were they associated with death and decay. They were terrible, and, worse, they were terribly necessary. What a conflict for man!

Besides, men are vulnerable. Their genitals are more precariously situated than the female's, more exposed to injury. Women can feign or hide sexual arousal; a man's penis is prey to unbidden erection, stubborn refusal to arise, and unpredictable deflation . . . mortifying situations. In sexual intercourse, a woman can experience multiple orgasms; a man has a more limited capacity. A man's impotence will, among other things, prevent him from inseminating. Even if a woman is not sexually aroused, she is still capable of intercourse, conception, and motherhood. A man's sexuality is no match for a woman's. No wonder men have an eternal fear of women.[14]

This fear is probably not unlike that which we all experience as helpless infants when we are at the mercy of the good will of mom for physical and emotional support — that "ferocious, voracious dependence" on mother, as Dorothy Dinnerstein[15] calls it in her classic feminist book, *The Mermaid and the Minotaur.* And she is a "dirty goddess," untrustworthy, impossible to please. If man lets her, mother can readily shatter his adult sense of masculinity any time.[16] Naturally, he hates her for her power. The psychoanalyst Melanie Klein wrote about the infant's understandably sadistic, aggressive response to this dependency. In this precarious predicament, the child cannot overtly act on these feelings — one must not bite the hand (or, in this case, the nipple) that feeds him or her. That might incur retaliation. No, the child must attempt to behave or pretend to behave. But what if mother can read its mind, sense its murderous feelings toward her? The child is always fearful of mother's possible reprisals. According to Klein, the boy compensates for his feelings of "hate, anxiety, envy, and inferiority . . . by reinforcing his pride in possession of the penis."[17] This is what appears to have happened at a global level with the onset of patriarchy.

Before his complete takeover, man resorted to numerous measures to exert some control over woman, some of which persist. In prehistory, man attempted to appease the fickle goddess through sacrifice, prayer, ceremonial gifts, rites, magic, and incantations. He tried to mollify mortal woman in much the same way, though his attempts evolved into ritualistic taboos, mostly associated with her reproductive functions. Remember that man was caught in a tangled web of associations between the Mother Goddess, a woman's menstrual cycle, the cycle of the moon to which it mysteriously corresponds, and the seasonal round of harvest and decay. So in order to direct woman's biological powers, he had to confine her to a special place or develop special rules limiting her expression. Hence, we have the beginnings of female suppression — the worldwide system of menstrual taboo, for instance, by which menstruating women were excluded from society so that they could not infect men, pollute food, or, as Aristotle believed, tarnish mirrors with their breath; the rites of birth (such as the eating of the placenta[18]); the wide range of rules in all societies which regulate the pregnant woman, such as the taboo against sexual intercourse among the Mbuti of the Congo and the Jamaican belief that a pregnant woman must not view a corpse, lest her blood turn cold and her fetus die.

Over time, the suppression was manifest as a myriad of strict cultural expectations, all designed to separate woman from nature. The battery of social and legal controls covered every part of her anatomy, from top to toe. (Having a woman's body is evidently considered an ignominy.) It is embarrassing and obscene to man to be aware of woman as flesh, perhaps because it reminds him that his mother was a carnal being and that she refused to be possessed by him. Luxurious hair could excite lust; accordingly, the Jewish Talmud from A.D. 600 onward allowed a man to divorce a wife who appeared in public with her hair uncovered; Saint Paul went so far as to instruct Christians that a woman who came bareheaded to church had better have her head shaved. The women of ancient Greece shaved their pubic areas to be more appealing to men. Even in America today, depilation is a *sine qua non* of femininity: shaved underarms, tweezed eyebrows, hairless legs. Man prefers woman denatured. He is frightened of the raw form.[19]

But it was not only fear and embarrassment that made man wish to dominate woman; it was outright jealousy. The locus of much male envy is the female bosom, continually hymned, extolled, bedecked with all the qualities of loving — kindness, fullness, and softness — wishfully attributed to mothers. Perhaps because they were once rudely weaned, men are, quite simply, avid for breasts, looking at and longing to touch as many as they can. Why should women and not men have the power to nurture, to provide or withhold milk? Man wanted this power, so he socially commandeered the woman's breasts. Though they are on her body, man laid claim to all access, reserving his wife's bosom for his use (and eyes) only. Breast-feeding was devalued, and women were forbidden to nurse in public; for centuries, they were urged to employ wet nurses or, later, to bottle-feed. In this way, man made himself the greater resource for humanity.

Similarly, man is awed by woman's capacity for motherhood. The idea that men secretly wish to give birth is not new. In 1926, Karen Horney, an early psychoanalyst, wrote of her startling discovery of the intensity of that jealousy. Boys, she suggested, defended against this envy (of birth, breasts, suckling) by promoting the sour grapes idea that motherhood is really a burden, and that what woman basically wants is not a child but a penis. In Horney's view, then, penis envy is really a defense against womb envy. So much for one of Freud's pet theories! In the 1950s, Ashley Montagu added, in *The Natural Superiority of Women,* that through womb envy, man has devalued woman's pregnancy and her birth and nursing abilities, and turned them into handicaps.[20]

But man has gone way beyond devaluing woman's mysteries and capacities by trying to appropriate them for himself. Resentful of woman's monopoly of maternity, man strove to imitate it. Although this idea of man stealing the ability to give birth may seem far-fetched, consider what is going on now in the baby-making industry: *in vitro* fertilization, wombs for rent, fetal surgery, technologically oriented births. All of these are opportunities for man to meddle in childbirth. These techniques are double-edged; they may produce "better" babies, but they separate the birth process from the mother.

Man's appropriation of woman's reproductive abilities is even more apparent in some anthropological studies, such as the oft-mentioned custom of carving up the pudendum, a ritual that dates back to the remotest antiquity. That the slitting of the penis is an overt attempt to emulate woman is attested to by the fact that in Australia the name for the *slit penis* derives from the word *vulva,* and those who have undergone the procedure are known as "possessors of the vulva." The male initiation cult of New Guinea is another conspicuous example of "womb envy." It involves the symbolic death of a boy who, until that point, has been in the maternal domain, and his subsequent rebirth as a man, a birth effected by *men*. Particularly fascinating are rituals of "male menstruation." Here, selected older men and the initiates are made to bleed either from the genitals or from nose or tongue, and this bleeding is referred to as the male period. The couvade, wherein men imitate their parturient wives, is found globally in preliterate and peasant societies. Sometimes the simulation includes a period of the father's lying-in while the postpartum mother goes about her usual prepartum business![21]

As we move closer culturally to modern Western society, appropriations are no longer quite this blatant. Within our own culture we find the persistent literary use of the procreative powers of females as a metaphor for men's creativity. When poets and scientists create a product, they call it a "brainchild." The feminist poet Judy Grahn argues that man's many blood rituals — circumcision, the slash in Christ's side and His blood-dripping crown of thorns, the blood bandage on the traditional hero — all are versions of male bleeding-for-life magic, imitations of menstruation and bids for power. The recent image of a naked father cradling a beautiful naked baby against his sleek, muscular chest (seen in magazine advertisements for baby powder, camera equipment, and faceless corporations) also suggests the male's unconscious desire to nurse his offspring. La Leche envy, perhaps?[22]

The ultimate usurpation of women's life-giving ability is probably the ubiquitous revision of the creation myths, edited so that man is no longer born of woman; he is born of man. For example, in Egyptian lore, Re created humankind of his tears; Zeus gave birth to Athene from his head; and, of course, Adam produced Eve . . . from his rib, no less! Any way you slice it, motherhood was written right out of the myths.

The Cradle in the Cradle: Sumerian Mom

Come sleep, come sleep,
Come to my son,
hurry sleep to my son
Put sleep to his restless eyes . . .

So sang the wife of Shulgri, ruler of Ur in Sumeria, at the end of the third millennium B.C. This lyric must be among the earliest recorded references to mother-child interactions. Indeed, it is among the earliest recorded interactions of anything at all! For history is said to begin at Sumer, an ancient empire that preceded Babylonia and Assyria on the alluvial plains of lower Mesopotamia, now Iraq, the area that has been called the cradle of civilization. We now know that civilization was not born there, nor was history, but the Sumerians are often given credit because they wrote it all down. They invented cuneiform writing, a kind of wedge-shaped script, that was a great advance over Egyptian hieroglyphics. The ancient Sumerian culture is one of four we will examine in the development of patriarchy.[23]

Shulgri's wife went on with her lullaby:

In my song of joy, I will give him a wife,
I will give him a wife. I will give him a son!
The nursemaid, joyous of heart, will sing to him;
The nursemaid, joyous of heart, will suckle him.

In this brief fragment, thousands of years old, we hear, unmistakably, mother love, a "song of joy." We discern that the bestowal of a baby is a gift. And it is specifically a male baby that is wished for, which suggests the influence of the patriarchal value on boys more than girls. Another Sumerian lullaby pleads with the ghost of a deceased wet nurse not to let harm come to her former charge.[24] Again, we sense parental attachment. How poignant that among the possibilities of things to be first recorded by women and men we find gentle lullabies. Of course, most of the earliest outpourings of the Sumerians were not lullabies, but lists, records of transactions, economic registers. Only later did Sumerian writing become more philosophical and reflective, containing hymns, sagas, laws, and narratives with poetic content.

The Sumerians were an ingenious stock, with dazzling technological ability and rich culture. They built an elaborate drainage and irrigation system — dikes, ditches, canals — which enabled them to maximize the use of their farmlands. Floods must have been very much on their mind. According to Sumerian tradition, the priest-king Ziusudra was warned by the god Enki of an impending deluge, and he built a big boat (prefiguring Noah). In fact, various Sumerian legends eerily presage a number of Old Testament stories. The Sumerians, for example, have their counterpart to Moses. Sargon as an infant was supposedly placed in an ark of bulrushes, but was rescued and became king. And one of their creation stories warms the hearts of feminists. It has a cast of characters similar to the Judeo-Christian version — a garden, forbidden fruit, and a tree of life — but women and men were created simultaneously. Moreover, woman was not blamed for the fall. Yet for all the political correctness of this creation myth, the Sumerians were a society increasingly dominated by patriarchal ideas, which were ultimately reflected in their religion. The earliest Sumerians worshipped Ti'amat, the Great Mother, but their descendants ended up revering the male god Marduk, who murdered her.[25]

The food surplus from the Sumerian farms was large enough to support bustling city-states of twenty-five thousand or more, including artisans of all sorts, clergy, educators, merchants, traders, and a military (yes, there was warfare). The cities had winding streets and bazaars, were surrounded by walls, and were dominated by ziggurats — immense, many-storied ornamented temples — dedicated to hundreds of gods. (Ishtar was of Sumerian origin.) It was in Sumer that the wheel and astrology were invented, probably also the plough and the chariot. It was also in the city of Ur that Sarah (Sarai) married Abraham (Abram) of Old Testament fame.

Another Sumerian clay tablet reads:

> Our earth is degenerate in these latter days. Bribery and corruption are common. Children no longer obey their parents . . . The end of the world is evidently approaching.[26]

Sound familiar? These could be the words of Jesse Helms or Pat Robertson expostulating on the decline of American culture, but they are the lament of a Mesopotamian scribe nearly four thousand years ago. There is something timeless about his complaints and in his assumption that children used to behave better. Perhaps nostalgia is eternal. Perhaps parent-child conflict is also eternal. Indeed, Freud thought that conflict is built into the human condition.

"Where did you go?" asked still another scribe of his shiftless son. "I did not go anywhere," replied the son. "If you did not go anywhere, why do you idle about?" What exquisite irony it is for us to decode a cuneiform tablet and discover what could be an episode on "The Simpsons"! We can almost hear the father's voice rising. "Go to school!" he continued. "Stand before your teacher, recite your assignment, open your schoolbag, write on your tablet . . . After you have finished your assignment and reported to your mother, come to me and do not wander about in the street!"[27] Surely we can empathize with this ancient father's frustration. There follows, in the essay, a bitter rebuke of his wayward son, who, his father claims, has made him sick to death with his impossible behavior. He, the father, is deeply disappointed at his son's laziness; after all, he never made him work behind the plough and ox, nor carry reeds, as other fathers expected of their sons. Yet other sons appreciate their relatives and support their parents by working, while his own son is a "good for nothing." To help the son become a man, the scribe offers him advice in the form of proverbs. Though the father's anger is almost palpable over the millennia, it is notable that he does not use corporal punishment on his son. He does not commit child abuse, withdraw his affection, or ignore him. Rather, he employs rational exhortation, admonishment, and guilt — modern, Western, middle-class methods of discipline. What we hear in this essay is not only the Sumerian respect for education, for mental work over physical labor, for honoring one's elders; we also plainly sense strong parental concern — by both mother and father. This is not indifference or disregard.

In short, Sumerians seem to have bonded with their children. Their culture obviously facilitated the bonding. At this point in history, most cultures were well on the way to patriarchy, but they were not oppressively patriarchal. They were cultures in transition. In Sumer, women, unlike their forebears, were elbowed aside from farming and were relegated to unskilled and various miscellaneous tasks. More and more, they were confined to their homes. Society was becoming stratified, with a domestic slave class (mostly war captives, criminals, and the wives of debtors) available to men for sexual use. Unlike living arrangements in the Neolithic, households were now male-headed, and descent was reckoned through the father. An adulterous wife would be placed in a river (her fate to be determined by the river god), but an adulterous husband might merely be divorced. Yet there was a legal code (a forerunner of the Babylonian Code of Hammurabi) in which women were guaranteed certain rights: their names appeared on land deeds, for example; they were protected as widows; they were donors and recipients of food offerings.[28] And while there were few female scribes (an honored position), there were many priestesses (also an honored position).

Prostitutes were still sacred, not profane. Deceased female consorts were buried with almost as much splendor, and with almost as many human sacrificial subjects, as their husband-rulers. Daughters would sometimes serve as stand-ins for their ruler-fathers. In other words, women's status was eroding in the Sumerian culture; it had not bottomed out. Even at the culture's demise, Sumerians were not misogynistic. Mothers were accorded enough respect so that they did not need their children to bolster their status. There is no evidence in Sumeria of the exposure of unwanted babies, a practice inflicted on female infants in other cultures. This was a society in which a woman rarely had more than four children, frequently more girls than boys, arguing against the use of selective infanticide, and suggesting, instead, the practice of birth control (probably prolonged nursing and *coitus interruptus*). Wanted babies are easier to love — or more readily loved; the dynamics are cleaner, less sullied by ambivalence. Sumerian mothers and babies seem to have been valued members of society.

Honored Tombs, Honored Wombs: Ancient Egyptian Mom

Just as New Yorkers regard residents of Los Angeles as an inferior cultural species, so did ancient Greeks turn up their noses at ancient Egyptians, whom they dismissed as an effete, wishy-washy group, dominated by their womenfolk. Herodotus wrote mockingly of Egyptian men, in the fifth century B.C., that "women go in the marketplace, transact affairs, and occupy themselves with business, while their husbands stay home and weave." The Greeks were surprised that the Egyptians did not practice infanticide, which says as much about themselves as parents as about the Egyptians.

The Greeks also found it curious that the Egyptians did not swaddle their children. According to the historian C. John Sommerville,[29] writing in the 1980s, there are as many justifications for the practice of swaddling as there are societies that do it. Some societies claim that it gives children a straighter spine; some say it keeps them warm. It has been thought to be a means of keeping children from tearing at themselves, frightening themselves at the sight of their own limbs, or masturbating. But it would be naïve not to think that swaddling might be more for the parents' convenience than for the children's benefit. The Greeks, like most peoples of their day, took the binding of infants for granted.

From our distance, it appears that the Egyptians were a wealthy, stable, sophisticated, family-oriented society, lighthearted and fond of life, despite their preoccupation with death and mummification. They supported a basic equality between the sexes, and responded with warmth and tenderness to both daughters and sons. But like the Sumerians, Egyptian women suffered a two-thousand-year diminution of status and opportunity, though Egyptian women held their own for longer and to a far greater degree. This is probably because their energetic, resourceful goddesses were more firmly entrenched in the ancient villages of Egypt than were the goddesses in the more urbanized Near East; also, a dominant military, often a bastion of male chauvinism, never developed in Egypt to the extent that it did elsewhere.[30]

Ancient Egyptian women were devoted to their offspring. In a papyrus letter from about 2000 B.C., one child wrote: "Dear Mother, I'm all right. Stop worrying about me." Another scribe was not above inducing guilt in Egyptian children to get them to look after their elders: "Repay thy mother for all her care for thee . . . Give her as much bread as she needs, and carry her as she has carried you, for you were a heavy burden to her. When in due time you were born she still carried you on her neck and for three years she suckled you, nor did she shrink from your dirt."[31] Add to this the abundant images of Egyptian Mother Goddesses (mostly Isis) holding a nursing infant, and we have a portrait of what was undoubtedly a baby-loving culture. By the way, the child in these depictions is held in the mother's left arm, sucking at the left breast, nearer to the mother's heart, an artistic convention that persisted late into the Christian era. A concern for children can also be seen in Egyptian medical texts, which describe pediatric regimens — like the use of opiates to get youngsters through rough periods — with which one would presumably not bother if one were not invested in children. Then, too, children were grievously mourned when they died, by fathers as well as mothers. We know this from grave inscriptions.[32]

The milk of the wet nurse in ancient Egypt was thought to bind the baby to the nurse. Kings were depicted suckling the breast of a goddess, thereby attaining divinity.[33] It is no wonder that wet nurses were chosen with great care by the wealthy (contracts exist that reveal this) and were accorded great status. Indeed, wet nurses were always among the honored guests at the funeral feasts of royalty. This was certainly a measure of their elevated status, as funerals were occasions of high seriousness. Much of an Egyptian adult's life was spent in the preparation of his or her own tomb; witness the Pyramids.

Egyptian artists routinely portrayed children engaged in family activities — party scenes, the hunt, fishing, funerals — often accompanied by their parents. Clearly, youngsters had an accepted role in the family.[34] Egyptians had a propensity for large families, though they had a number of methods of birth control, and could have limited their number of offspring if they chose. Then, too, even ordinary families buried their children's toys with them, a touching gesture whose emotional resonance survives the millennia.

That ancient Egyptians loved their children is not surprising; they also loved their wives and mothers. A common depiction of the Egyptian family shows father and mother holding each other by the hand or about the waist. In written expressions a husband's name is often coupled with his wife's, along with an affectionate sentiment, as in "his beloved wife, his darling." And though a man was free to be polygamous, it was rare that he made use of this privilege. Also, special respect was due one's mother, according to the Egyptian *Books of Wisdom*.[35]

Women were not only esteemed as wives; they were powerful in their own right. There were times, during the Middle Kingdom, for example, when descent was specifically reckoned through the maternal line. As a result, Egyptian girls, as heirs of the family property, had to supply their brothers with dowries so that they could attract wives! Palace women who were members of "harems" — which were not, at this time, male-owned repositories of voluptuous, sexually available maidens, but female intellectual and cultural courts — held considerable clout in political affairs, both for the women themselves and for the government as a whole. And love poems discovered in Egyptian tombs strongly hint that Egyptian women wooed the men, not the other way around.[36]

As patriarchy became entrenched, women slowly lost their prestigious position. In earlier times the goddess Hathor was served by sixty-one priestesses and eighteen priests, but by the middle of the second millennium B.C., women were no longer even part of the clergy, but served only as temple musicians.[37] Also, at this time, the word *pharaoh* took on a different meaning. In an earlier usage it meant "great house"; later it was used to signify the royal men of that household. Over time, males continued to be respected for their age and wisdom, particularly if they were obese, but women were expected to be slender. Yet even as patriarchy was making inroads, the female sex could, for a time, find partial compensation in the great female pharaohs, still wielding power over great numbers of men. Nefertiti and Cleopatra are perhaps the most famous (though the latter has had a bad press: she was less pretty and far more intelligent than billed, and she had a genius for politics). Probably the most powerful female pharaoh was the earlier Hatshepsut, who seized the throne after the death of her husband (and half brother), Thutmose III. She declared herself a male god, and she sported a false beard and phallus. Here, we can easily see the influence of patriarchal attitudes.

Things got worse for women. Family life broke down. During the first century B.C., when the misogynistic customs of Greece and Rome were superimposed on Egyptian life, the abandonment of infants, especially girls — an act that Egyptians had once considered an atrocity — became common. Babies were often placed on rubbish heaps. People who wanted an inexpensive slave could visit such places and choose an abandoned baby. This practice is inferred in the naming of such infants Coprus and Corpise (that is, picked off a dunghill).[38] Incidentally, the status of wet nurses plummeted: they were now slaves.

The Abyss: Phoenician Mom

The Romans, no innocents themselves, were shocked by the practices of the Phoenicians, who "did things so abominable that they cannot be described," continuing a long tradition of Phoenician bashing that persists today. Anyone familiar with the Bible may recall the Old Testament prophets' railing against the so-called excesses of the Canaanites (the early Phoenician residents of Palestine). And while most of the critical material about this society was written by their enemies, it is a hard society to admire, especially in its North African version. It is an incontrovertible fact that the Phoenicians participated in a long-term holocaust that rivals the Nazis' and Cambodians' for sheer horror — the formal, ritualized execution of babies that occurred on a massive scale in Carthage during the first millennium B.C. One estimate suggests that as many as twenty thousand burial urns, each containing the remains of one or more slaughtered babies, were interred between 400 and 200 B.C. alone![39]

Who were these people and why did their parenting go awry? Legend has it that Carthage (in Tunisia, in North Africa) was founded by the bewitching Phoenician princess Dido, who sailed from Tyre, on the coast of Palestine, a little before 800 B.C. She was immortalized by the Roman poet Virgil in the *Aeneid*. Whether Dido existed is doubtful, but the Phoenicians did settle in that part of Africa around this time. The Palestinian Canaanites are probably best known as those pagan people whom the ancient Hebrews conquered after escaping from Egypt, crossing the Red Sea, and wandering for forty years in the desert. Canaan is also the birthplace of the infamous Jezebel, who married Ahab, a king of Israel, and who defiantly worshiped the goddess Astarte (another name for Ishtar), influencing her husband to do the same. She and her husband were murdered in a civil war fomented by the Hebrew God's devotees. The Bible describes her gruesome murder in morbid detail, and it is surely intended as a cautionary tale to all idol worshipers. Incidentally, Jezebel's reputation has recently been revamped by feminists,[40] who now regard her as a courageous defender of her faith.

In the millennia before 1200 B.C., dramatic developments in the history of civilization took place in the area of Canaan: the construction of Jericho, which may have been one of the world's earliest cities, rivaling Neolithic Catal Hüyük; the invention of the alphabet; the building of one of the world's oldest "superhighways," the Way of the Sea, connecting Egypt and Mesopotamia;[41] and the invention of the chariot. The Canaanites themselves were originally Semitic nomads and herders, like the early Hebrews, but they eventually became wealthy and urbanized, and created the great coastal cities of Byblos, Beirut, Sidon, and beautiful Tyre. In the course of seafaring, this savvy people amalgamated the advanced cultures of Mesopotamia and Egypt, colonizing not only North Africa, but Cyprus and areas throughout the western and central Mediterranean in the process. At their height, they were the master merchants of the Mediterranean, superbly organized into a wealth-gathering and -distributing machine. But in amassing their fortunes, they may have lost their conscience; at least this was the view of the Phoenicians' contemporaries, who, of course, may have been motivated by envy.

In Roman accounts, Phoenicians are portrayed as disreputable, artless, and money grubbing. From the Greek perspective, Phoenicians could never be trusted. They were known to kidnap children at the drop of a hat, sail off to sea, and sell them into slavery at the next port of call. If given half a chance they would make off with unprotected women, and they had little regard for human life and dignity. Even today, accounts of Phoenicians tend to be disparaging: one recent Italian scholar went so far as to say, "Having invented a marvelous instrument [the alphabet], the Phoenicians proceeded to do little or nothing with it." Indeed, the Phoenicians perfected and transmitted a form of writing that has influenced dozens of cultures, but most of their surviving writing is of interest neither in its decorative form nor in its content; it is certainly not poetry or literature, but mostly pleas to the gods or records of transactions, and is not useful even for historical reconstruction.[42]

Naturally, history is a protean thing, changing its nature as well as its shape when viewed from different angles. A single set of facts, arranged and rearranged, can point to contradictory conclusions. It is therefore possible to understand the Phoenician practice of murdering their children as a religious ritual — to avert disaster, palliate the gods, preserve the health of others, or achieve union with a divinity. But under what circumstances would a society develop such an atrocious rite, and persist in its observance for hundreds of years?

Let me describe the ritual. It occurred at open-air shrines, known as *tophets,* of which a number have been found. The most infamous is located in Carthage, in an area that has now become an upscale resort. Apparently, thousands and thousands of infants were slaughtered there, presumably to appease the goddess Tanit and the god Baal. No one knows the "rate" of execution, but it was probably in the hundreds, maybe more, every year. The charred ashes of the victims were swept up into ceramic urns and buried in pits capped with funerary markers (*stelai*).

Various ancient accounts of these rites are surprisingly uniform. The child's throat was slit and the freshly killed child placed in the outstretched arms of a bronze statue of Baal; the child then rolled down into a fiery pit beneath the statue. All this took place to the accompaniment of flutes, drums, and perhaps tambourines. Most of the offerings were children between one and three years of age, though a third of the children slaughtered were between two and three. It is conjectured that in the early days of the sacrifice, the murdered babies were children of royalty (thus linking their death to the sacred marriage rite, wherein, you may recall, the consort-son of the goddess dies), but over the centuries the practice became democratized to include babies regardless of class. Though animals were sometimes substituted for children, the use of animals seems to have decreased rather than increased in this ancient period. It was precisely when Carthage attained the height of urbanity (in the fourth and third centuries B.C.) that child sacrifice flourished as never before.[43] The rite of child sacrifice seems to have been followed with considerable frequency right down to the Roman conquest.

At this time, no sacrifice shrines have been found in Israel, though scholars[44] do connect the Canaanite practices associated with Moloch in Palestine (as mentioned in the Old Testament) with the child sacrifice that was practiced later in Carthage. Infants' skeletons found at Tirzah and Schechem, and infants buried in jars in the subsoil of Gezer, may testify to these customs.[45] But this is all very controversial. The early Hebrews, influenced by their neighbors, perhaps engaged in such activities, as well — Abraham, for example, was certainly willing to sacrifice Isaac, until a ram was substituted at the last minute — though child sacrifice came to be strongly denounced by the patriarchs. The proof of Canaanite and early Hebrew child sacrifice is more biblical and inferential than archeological, but it is persuasive. Interestingly, overall influence of Canaanite practices on the early Hebrews has spawned a mini-library, especially with regard to suspected Hebrew goddess worship.[46] Many feminists regard the association of early Hebrews with the goddesses as a positive thing, but by the first millennium B.C. pagan religion had become so degenerate, so strongly associated with human sacrifice, that I wonder why so many revisionist historians are eager to find a connection. The awesome Neolithic Mother Goddess seems to have given way by then to her greedier aspects. In all fairness, I suppose we should not blame the goddesses for their desperate, bloodthirsty characteristics. They were, after all, in their death throes.

So why did these North African parents do it? What impelled Phoenicians to develop a religious practice in which their own babies were slaughtered? Unfortunately, Phoenician artifacts are far less easy to interpret than are those of contemporaneous cultures. They left no first-person accounts; and we must be cautious about psychologizing at this distance. Nevertheless, the systematic Phoenician degradation of women may provide a clue: the cultic sexual practices, which by this time had degenerated into crude caricatures of earlier ones based on cyclical fertility celebrations, had become rituals that were particularly dehumanizing to women. The description by Herodotus, the Greek historian of the fifth century B.C., is illustrative. He discussed religious prostitution in Babylon and compared it with that in Cyprus, a Phoenician stronghold.

> Every woman born in the country must once in her life go and sit down in the precinct of Venus, and there consort with a stranger . . . The woman goes with the first man who throws her money, and rejects no one . . . Such of the women . . . who are ugly have stayed a long time before they can fulfill the law. Some have waited three or four years in the precinct.[47]

Clearly the sexual politics of Phoenicia appear to have been especially exploitative of women at this time. This was not mere patriarchy; it was misogyny. It makes sense to speculate that a society with an affinity for one atrocity, woman hating, might have an affinity for another, child sacrifice. Moreover, if Phoenician women were as objectified and subordinated as it seems, then understandably they may have been so damaged as human beings as to adhere to a belief system that would sanction the murder of their own youngsters. This may be an example of just how virulently perverse people can become when they are in the grip of misogyny.

A Mother Love Story: Ancient Hebrew Mom

We can only imagine the desperation that Jochebed, an ancient Hebrew mother, felt as she placed her three-month-old son in a wicker basket caulked with bitumen and pitch, and concealed it among the reeds beside the Nile. Seti I, the pharaoh of Egypt, had decreed the death of all newborn Hebrew males, and Jochebed was a woman *in extremis*. How could she save her baby? She concocted a wild plan: she would leave the infant in a strategic place on the river where princesses of the royal house were known to bathe. Perhaps one would feel pity for the foundling and take him in. Her gamble paid off! Not only did a daughter of the pharaoh adopt the boy, but the woman she employed to nurse him was, though she did not know it, the mother of the child, Jochebed herself. This Bible story may be the first tale of multicultural mother love. A Hebrew mother abandoned her child in order to save him, and an Egyptian woman raised another woman's child for the same altruistic reason. The boy grew up to be the man we know as Moses.

The ancient Hebrews,[48] like the early Egyptians and the first Sumerians, clearly loved their babies. Hebrew women, unlike the Egyptians and Sumerians, did not suffer a dramatic loss in social position during the twenty-five hundred years when patriarchy took over. They were born into patriarchy, and were subordinate at the outset. The Hebrew God is Himself a patriarch. Some scholars[49] do note a decline in women's standing as the Hebrews changed from a tent-dwelling culture, where descent was matrilineal (a vestige remains today, because children's Jewishness is determined by their mother's bloodline), to a centralized monarchy in Canaan and then to life in exile, when Jewish males recited the prayer: "Blessed art thou, O Lord our God, for not making me a woman." However, any real change in women's social position is a matter of only a few degrees: ancient Hebrew women were certainly not the equal of men, but they were not abused. Their situation was never equitable, but it did not worsen much. Unlike the Phoenicians, the Hebrews do not appear to have been misogynists. But in the scholarly disagreement over the relatively minor issue of a "decline," we begin to see the enormous complexity of analyzing the social history of the ancient Hebrews; it is a hotbed of interpretative controversy.

In reconstructing the parent-child relationship of the Egyptians, Sumerians, and Phoenicians, we do not have to worry about offending the followers of Isis, Astarte, or Tanit, for they are long gone (except, perhaps, for a few recent converts). But an enormous number of people still connect with the ancient Hebrews and their texts. And everybody has an opinion! There is an avalanche of biblical interpretation extant, much of it conflicting, and all presumably deriving from the same source. The most disparate people seem to find justification for their own point of view in the traditions and laws of the ancient Hebrews — right-to-lifers, feminists, evangelists, pagans, not to mention the Jews, Christians, and Mohammedans, all of whom bear a common heritage but have a different perspective on that heritage. Add to this the imprecise nature of the sacred texts themselves. In the Hebrew Bible[50] (which contains the history, law, and social commentaries of which we have been speaking), we are dealing with several layers of expression: the actual content, which is internally inconsistent and was recorded eight hundred to sixteen hundred years *after* the events described; the ancient consciousness that produced the doctrine (assuming it wasn't divinely inspired); and the consciousness of the numerous — male — Judaic scholars of late antiquity who devoted many volumes to "clarifying" the sacred texts. These volumes are known collectively as the Talmud.

For the sake of comparison, let us confine our observations of the Hebrews to the second millennium, the very ancient, pre-Talmudic period of Jewish history. Sarah and Abraham, having left Sumeria, made a covenant with God and settled in Canaan. Their group became what is called now by anthropologists borderland nomads — they had simple community centers, and they herded their flocks in prescribed family areas. A number of early Hebrews migrated to Egypt because of a food shortage. Eventually, over a sketchily described period of four hundred years, they were enslaved. Moses led these Hebrews out of Egypt and made another covenant with God, which committed the Jews to the Ten Commandments. The Egyptian Jews joined the descendants of Sarah and Abraham and settled in the city-states and areas around Canaan. Many Jews became farmers, and they developed an allegiance to a centralized government rather than to a clan.

But what did they feel about their children? One point does not appear to be controversial. They loved them fiercely, and they were not shy about recording their feelings for posterity. No static yet. Given the precariousness of life in the desert and fields of Canaan, coupled with the need for labor, it is no wonder that Jews regarded their offspring as blessings, veritable gifts from God.[51] Over time, as the Temple was repeatedly destroyed, the Hebrews were forced to disperse, and they understandably turned to their children to prevent their vanishing from history altogether. If a mother refused to nurse her weakened child, the mother was considered worse than a monster. Children, especially male children, were "the crown of man," a "reward, like arrows in the hand of a hero; happy the man who has his quiver full of them." And though there undoubtedly were periods when the early Hebrews practiced some of their nature-worshiping neighbors' religious rituals (when in Canaan, do as the Canaanites do), including child sacrifice, the vehemence with which those behaviors are later denounced suggests that evolving Hebrew values lay in the repudiation of such rites, not in their observance. Child sacrifice is repeatedly referred to in the Bible as an "abomination," bespeaking the preciousness of children to the Hebrews. Moreover, there are many stories of Hebrew mothers grievously mourning dead children. The story of the mother who tells Solomon she would rather give up her baby than have it divided between herself and another claimant became a classic parable of virtue that signals — indeed, broadcasts — maternal love.[52]

Children were important as individuals and not just as family legacies. The Hebrew God often favored younger brothers for their personal qualities, not, as was conventional in this ancient period, the eldest son, who was the designated heir. Thus, God preferred the ingenious Abel and Joseph over their jealous brothers; or the wily Jacob, whose persistence was rewarded; or David, whose winning personality made him such a successful leader. Moses, too, was a younger sibling. Education was important for children in the biblical era: some things never change! It was the mother who gave her children moral guidance. As children grew up, they were entrusted to the father. Later in Jewish history, schools took over the burden of education from their families. Unlike educators today, teachers were persons of great status, reflecting not only the Hebrews' reverence for knowledge, but their recognition of the importance of the rising generation.[53]

The main way that Hebrew women proved their worth was in bearing children. Pity the woman who was barren. Rachel, in the Old Testament, cried, "Give me children, or else I die." If she did not soon become a mother, a Hebrew wife wondered whether she had sinned before the Lord. Sterility was a disgrace from which Sarah, Rachel, and Leah all tried to clear themselves by adopting the child their maids bore to their husbands. This solution was not without its problems. Sometimes, if the maid proved fruitful, she gained greater favor and real status by giving the husband what he most desired. This probably goes far toward explaining Sarah's deplorable behavior to Hagar and her son Ishmael (Abraham's child), whom she banished to the desert. They were probably rivals for Abraham's affection. The childless widow was a stock figure of sorrow and poverty, because she had no one close to care for her. Barrenness was legitimate grounds for divorce.[54]

The importance of the mother-child relationship was always acknowledged in Jewish tradition; the Fifth Commandment, after all, enjoins children to honor father *and* mother. This respect is probably most exquisitely illustrated by an old Jewish proverb, according to which, since the Almighty could not be everywhere, He created mothers, and, so to speak, delegated part of His power to them.[55] Mother love was so potent a theme in biblical literature, according to the religious historian Denise Carmody, that it eventually became a metaphor of God's love for Israel. "Can a woman forget her sucking child?" Isaiah asks. "As one whom a mother comforteth, so will I comfort you," says God.[56]

Now for some static. It has been argued by a number of Jewish apologists that a woman's value exceeded that of her womb.[57] A few scholars cite the Talmudic edict: "When it is a choice between the mother's life or the baby's life at the time of labor, the mother's life comes first." But the Talmud was compiled a thousand years after the period we have been observing. I suspect that ancient Hebrew women in the earlier period were appreciated as compliant "helpmates," but not as women. When they obediently looked after the flocks, worked in the fields, cooked the food, cared for the young, and did the spinning, then they were esteemed. In other words, they were valued contingently. This was not unconditional love. Most of the last chapter of Proverbs sings the praise of the good housewife, not the good woman.[58]

After all, a Hebrew wife called her husband *ba'al* (master), addressing him as a slave addresses his master. Her position was definitely inferior to that of women in the great countries around her. In Egypt, the wife was often head of the family; in Babylon, she could acquire property and take legal action. But the Tenth Commandment ranks a Hebrew wife among her husband's possessions, along with his servants, his ox, and his ass! Moreover, there are grisly passages in the Bible, such as Genesis 19, where virginal daughters are virtually pimped by their own fathers so that Sodomites will not get their hands on male guests, reminding us that when push came to shove, women were expendable. Wives and daughters did not inherit, except in the absence of male heirs. And while a husband could repudiate a wife, she could not ask for divorce, and remained legally a minor through life.[59]

Strangely enough, far more women than men were willingly converted to Judaism. Perhaps this has to do with the many items of protective legislation in the Bible — a man, for instance, could sell his slaves but not his wife; if a man did divorce his wife, she was allowed to keep part of her dowry (a predecessor of alimony). Again, there is a diversity of interpretations. Some scholars[60] regard these laws as restrictive and patronizing; others[61] feel that they were primarily philanthropic, designed to help women. One law that has provoked endless speculation is that of the levirate, wherein a childless widow could continue as part of her husband's family (her brother-in-law was obliged to marry her). Cynical scholars regard this law as a way of preserving family property; those who are sentimentally inclined regard it as a way of preserving the widow. The sexual politics among these people were very complicated.

Despite the woman's ambiguous status, there are numerous images of female strength in the Bible — the "builders of Israel" like Rachel and Leah; national saviors in the mold of Judith and Esther. Deborah is a case in point. A fiery religious mystic, who prophesied and sang, she organized a coalition army (which no man was able to do) and destroyed the rival force of a major Canaanite king. And, as if that was not enough testimony to female power, the defeated Canaanite foolishly took refuge in the tent of Jael, another ferocious woman, who proceeded to drive a stake through his head after he fell asleep. Deborah memorialized this event in a famous victory hymn.[62]

Sarah, the original matriarch, is the first person in history recorded as laughing — this at the birth of her son Isaac, whom she delivered in her old age.[63] Indeed, many Old Testament women convey an emotional resonance, an affective dimension that has survived four millennia: the shy but kindhearted and loving Rebecca; the sorrowing and mutually devoted Naomi and her daughter-in-law Ruth.

Yet, for all their strength and emotionality, these women were subject to strict sexual codes. A Jewish bride had to be a virgin, lest she be stoned for betraying her father. In the early days, polygamy was allowed, but never its opposite, polyandry. Menstruating women were barred from the tabernacle. There is a pervasive sense in the Bible that women were temptresses (remember Eve!) whose sexuality had to be controlled. Of course the Mosaic laws were very strict in all matters of sexuality for men as well. In contrast, Sumerian law permitted fornication, adultery, bestiality, and incest in certain circumstances (those goddesses were loose women!). The Hittites would allow some forms of bestiality (though not incest). The Egyptians regarded consanguinity as unimportant, and many siblings married. But the Hebrews banned all forms of "irregular" sex — sodomy, bestiality — and they had an elaborate list of forbidden degrees of blood relationship that would preclude persons from marrying each other, including affinity as well as consanguinity. Also, "harlotry" and "sexual lewdness" were severely castigated. The vigor with which morality (some might say prudery) was promoted probably had to do with the patriarchs' attempts to destroy all vestiges of cultic sexuality and goddess religion, which continually threatened monotheism.[64]

Ironically, the very puritanism of the early Hebrews' lifestyle and emphasis on sexual restraint — which seems so repressive, inhibiting, and unfair to women from our perspective — may have served to protect them from extreme sexual exploitation. Though the Bible is hardly a feminist document, it did promote strong, stable family dynamics. Sexuality within marriage was celebrated. In the sanctity of family life, the Jewish mother, despite her second-class status, probably found greater fulfillment than the forthcoming, more sophisticated women of Greece and Rome. The vital part played by the mother-child relationship was always acknowledged. So, though Eve's daughters were bound and fettered in many ways, the Hebrew tradition held woman-as-mother in sentimental, if subordinate, regard, a position that enabled her to lovingly nurture her children.[65]

THREE

The Sublime and the Ridiculous: Classical Mom

The Secret History

Today the good mother provides good care, presumably, for all her children. In fifth-century Athens, the good mother cared for only those children chosen to be reared. The choice was her husband's, and, as a rule, he preferred the healthy male baby whose paternity was uncontestedly his. In the birthplace of democracy, it seems, parental affection was hardly democratic. While all Athenian newborns were prospective candidates for elimination, the rate of female infanticide, in particular, may have ranged from 10 to upward of 20 percent. By the time of the Roman conquest, around 200 B.C., sisters were a rarity. Only one family in a hundred raised more than one daughter.[1]

Unwanted children were "exposed," that is, abandoned, a practice that persisted quietly in Western culture in one form or another well into the Middle Ages, when the process became institutionalized in the form of foundling homes. In the Athenian version, children were wrapped up, supplied with a birth token (usually a piece of jewelry), put in a crockery pot, and entrusted to either the midwife or to a household slave, who would carry the pot outside the residential area and place it on a roadside or near a temple or in some other public place, thereby abandoning it to the mercies of the elements. By leaving the infant in a conspicuous spot, parents perhaps indulged in the dubious hope that someone else would rear their child. Interestingly, dung heaps and cesspools were popular sites, suggesting the Greek equation of these babies with other forms of human waste. The right of the father to expose an excess baby was unquestioned, but he had to carry it out by the fifth (or tenth) day after birth, prior to a naming ceremony. No less a character than Oedipus was abandoned. He was left on a mountainside by his parents to obviate the prediction that he would murder his father and marry his mother — all to no avail, as any Freudian knows — and humankind presumably symbolically repeats his story *ad infinitum*. But child abandonment was not only a subject of classical tragedy; it was much used in Attic comedy as well, for the exposed-infant scheme proved to be a rich source of comic material, with its possibility of mistaken identity and unintentional incest if the child survived. The very presence of references to exposure in Classical drama implies that it was not all that unusual. One can only assume that the audience must have understood.[2]

Historians have no good explanation for the prevalence of this phenomenon, and until just twenty years ago remained largely silent on the subject of exposure, though they have known the murky truth for centuries.[3] There were no tragic plagues in Athens[4] to provide a facile excuse, no widespread famine, nor any known situation sufficiently desperate to justify the abandonment of unwanted infants. The death of some children did not ensure the survival of others. There were enough material goods to go around. Life was not so wretched in this period. When the topic of child abandonment finally began to be examined in earnest, in the 1970s, it was initially seen as a product of parental defect. Parents in early history were viewed as indifferent, self-centered, and unempathic. The psychohistorian Lloyd deMause, in 1974, was the leading proponent of the grisly view of premodern parents. According to him, children existed to love and admire their parents, not vice versa. Babies were vehicles for their parents' projections, "toilets," as it were, used to collect their parents' unacceptable feelings.[5] In viewing their children as "bad," early mothers and fathers were then able to view themselves as "good," and therefore justify their rigid child-rearing methods, abuse, even murder. Today, deMause's thinly veiled moral indignation is unfashionable, and most historians have retreated from the outright blaming of parents for exposure.

Rather, they paradoxically tend to blame the victim[6] — the child — though this is by no means their intent. The most common explanation for the past neglect of children is the high infant mortality rate.[7] In other words, children's tendency to die "caused" their parents' indifference. According to this thinking, affection for one's children in preindustrial societies was not the prudent thing to feel. Mother love was not expected. Instead, parental detachment was normative. This lack of emotional involvement could be construed as a defense, an unconscious means of softening the likely blow of a child's death. Psychologically, it may be understood as the parents' "rejection" of the infants (through indifference, abandonment) before the infants "rejected" them (by dying).

But even this idea was never comfortably absorbed by mainstream scholars. Perhaps the thought that mothers did not love all of their children is just too painful to contemplate. Despite the fact that the practice was rife with misogyny, even feminist historians[8] skirt the issue, maybe unintentionally. Maternal indifference is not a view that is especially flattering to women. Let me emphasize that the feminists are not alone; indeed, the majority of contemporary scholars, in the time-honored tradition of their forebears, evade or underplay the issue of child abandonment. Illustrative of this "head in the sand" approach is one recent author[9] who attempted to compute away the statistical evidence for Athenian infanticide. His data are hotly disputed.[10]

Very recently there have been some valiant attempts to put a good face on the matter.[11] The apologists argue that exposure was in the baby's best interest. They point out that Greek abandonment was not the equivalent of murder; at least some of the exposed babies were rescued, if not by childless couples, then by people who used the children as slaves or prostitutes.[12] But surely such a rescue was not much of a kindness and did little to exonerate the parents from deliberate, willful neglect.

Then there are the arguments of "social usefulness" to explain exposure (eerily reminiscent of Fascist theories of eugenics two millennia later); these bypass the moral and psychological implications of the act altogether. According to this view, child abandonment was practiced because it was practical. It reduced the number of heirs and prevented undue fragmentation of Athenian property. (Primogeniture — inheritance by the eldest son — had not yet been invented.) The exposure of girls, in particular, diminished the number of marriageable women, and saved their fathers the expense of a dowry. Evidently, a "responsible" Greek father did not raise daughters unless he foresaw a proper marriage for them at maturity. Better dead than unwed, I suppose. In other words, exposure was a form of family planning. To an ancient Greek, abandonment may have been merely the emotional equivalent of late abortion — with the advantage of preserving mother's health. In this view, the failure to nurture certain newborns was not a personal failure, just a social dynamic. These historians make no judgments. They do not deny the occurrence of exposure, but they cast no blame, as if the deed had been performed by robots. If pressed to be evaluative, they are conveniently free to argue that the Greeks *could* love their *wanted* babies.[13]

But while this view is politically correct, admirable for its scholarly restraint in not imposing today's values on a past culture, it is morally bankrupt. What "social usefulness" theories achieve in common sense, they lose in sensitivity. They fail to appreciate that Greek parents were routinely neglecting — if not murdering — babies who would otherwise have thrived. They neatly bypass the implications of this act. They provide an external rationale for the behavior, not an internal one.

It is the internal rationale that is necessary for an understanding of the permutations of mother love. And though these internal dynamics may be unappealing to a modern sensibility, they beg for consideration. While not as flamboyantly perverse as Phoenician child sacrifice, which occurred in noisy public rituals, the Greek practice of exposure may have been all the more insidious because it was banal. At least the Phoenicians spaced their sacrificial spasms over intervals, and seemingly needed to work themselves up into a frenzy to perform their religious rite. The ancient Athenians, on the other hand, seemed to regard child abandonment as ordinary. How did Athenians come to decide that certain children were expendable, an idea, incidentally, that was abhorrent to neighboring Egyptians and Jews? Why did they develop such an egregiously inconsistent pattern of parental loving? The Phoenicians were sacrificing "wanted" children; the Greeks, "unwanted" ones. How did the Greeks come to "unwant" their offspring? What made them attach to some babies and detach from others? What would move a Greek mother, still engorged with milk, to let her baby be taken away?

Since there was no realistic, pressing need for child elimination, as could be argued for later societies, there must have been a powerful cultural force operative on the Greek psyche, a force strong enough to distort character, to warp parental affection. Could this have been sexism? Was Greek misogyny so pernicious that it undermined the most basic human emotions?

Sexual Politics in Ancient Greece

There is a supreme irony in criticizing Greek culture in this way, for Classical Athens has long been considered a Golden Age of unmatched artistic, intellectual, and philosophical expression. To our founding fathers (and mothers), ancient Athens was the model of the democratic state. We deify the Greeks, if not their gods. We idealize them, sentimentalize them. Boston, the city I live in, boasts that it is the Athens of America. The exquisite sculptures of Phidias, the philosophy of Socrates, Plato, and Aristotle, the dramatic masterpieces of Aeschylus, Sophocles, and Euripides are part of the underpinnings of Western civilization. Yet these same high-minded Greeks who so valued the "examined life" (as Socrates put it) failed to notice that they enslaved about a third of their population, that their society was ridden with class conflicts, that their relentless combativeness was often unprovoked and left destruction in its wake. They were committed to a barbaric view of violence — one that Nietzsche called "a tiger's lust to annihilate." And though females loomed large as powerful goddesses and tragic heroines, women were radically marginalized in everyday life. Athenian men sequestered their wives and daughters, derogated the female role in reproduction, erected monuments to penises, had sex with the sons of their peers, sponsored public whorehouses, created a mythology of rape, and engaged in saber rattling. The model Greek man was macho in the extreme.[14]

A female who did survive infancy in ancient Athens was not a creature to be envied. She was considered secondary to men;

restricted to her home; politically disenfranchised (though she could be a citizen, she was a lifelong minor); undereducated; and was given food of poorer quality — as noted by the historian Xenophon. She was disregarded and without identity other than as baby maker, prostitute, or slave. Her subordinate social position was enforced by a series of venerable legal measures, beginning at the time of Solon and continuing into the Classical period, that kept women out of sight. Conjugal bliss was not a priority, and the Athenian woman may have been sexually ungratified, at least by sexual intercourse. Indeed, the ideal "pinup" penis was short and thin, with an elongated foreskin, behaving in a modest fashion, not exactly a woman's dream; and the use of dildos was commonly portrayed in vase painting.[15]

To be called "womanish" in Classical Athens was to receive a serious insult. The female was the object of male scorn. "The two days in a woman's life a man can best enjoy are when he marries her and when he carries her dead to the grave," wrote the poet Hipponax.[16] Central to Athenian thought was the belief that women are not just physically but intellectually and morally weaker than men, designed to be dominated and kept indoors. Aristotle considered women unreliable, deceptive, and overly passionate. These ideas have been amazingly tenacious, and there is today a popular psychiatric diagnosis called "hysterical personality" (technically known as histrionic personality), which lists the same characteristics and is arguably overapplied to women. The word *hysteria* is from the Greek for womb. In the Greek myth of the first woman, Pandora, as recast by Hesiod, we see the prototype of the Athenian "hysterical" woman. She is a scheming temptress with the capacity to arouse man's desire and the shameless disposition of a bitch. When Pandora opens her infamous box (a vagina symbol?), she releases the evil that now affects humankind. The Pandora myth achieves what Saint Paul's version of the myth of Eve achieved in the story of the Fall, placing the blame on woman and her nature for Original Sin. All hell breaks loose when a man succumbs to a woman's attractions. Here we see the continuing legacy of patriarchy symbolized in the imagined dangers of women's sexuality.

While the male citizen might engage in art, politics, and war — highly public and valued activities in the early Greek status hierarchy — his wife was relegated to domesticity. She occupied and dominated the private realm of the *oikos* (household). She did, in fact, belong to it, and throughout her life was in the charge of the male relative who was legally entitled to her. Before marriage she belonged to the *oikos* of her father and after it to that of her husband. Marriage was arranged by the father, who provided a dowry, intended to be passed on to her children. The woman had no say in any of this. No wonder Euripides' Medea said, "We women are the most wretched of creatures" when speaking of these arrangements. Marriage was no love match.[17]

The respectable woman spent most of her life indoors, managing the household and making fabric, that is, spinning, weaving, and decorating material. The gymnasium, which non-Greeks saw as the hallmark of Greek culture, was an exclusive men's club. A woman could not go out walking or riding; she could not entertain or visit whom she chose, unless she was chaperoned. Of course only a small percentage of all women were actual citizens. Let us not forget that there were multitudes of poor women, slaves, prostitutes, and foreigners. But though the physical movements of these less respectable women were less restricted, their devalued social standing was probably an even greater form of entrapment.[18]

The strict segregation of females probably had something to do with the Athenian fetish for biological legitimacy. All-important citizenship in the Athenian *polis* required that both parents be citizens. Therefore, premarital and marital chastity of women was rigidly enforced, lest a child who was not the offspring of a bona fide citizen be insinuated into the citizen body! The common practice of men in their thirties marrying girls in their teens reinforced male dominance in conjugal matters.

The Athenian husband was not expected to be sexually monogamous. Quite the contrary. The dictum of a fourth-century sage describes the situation for men: "We have mistresses for our enjoyment, concubines [*hetairai,* the Greek geishas] to service our person, and wives for the bearing of legitimate offspring." It was common, too, for middle- and upper-middle-class men to enjoy the company of other males sexually. Such relationships were considered not only acceptable but often far more rewarding than relationships with women. Even as sexual objects, women in ancient Athens were second class.[19]

Where's Momma? Maternal Images

The pervasive misogyny served to subvert ancient Greek motherhood. Though there never has been a monogamous society in which the role of the woman was more restricted to one specific function — that of bearing children, particularly male children, and not too many — there probably never has been a society in which the role of mother had such lowly status. The mother was so diminished as to be practically erased in religion and art. Or she was depicted as evil, incompetent, and almost always a negative influence. In Greek mythology there are countless stories of *male* motherhood, in which offspring are actually born from parts of the male anatomy. Long gone is the powerful Mother Goddess. Her descendants, the goddesses of Greek mythology with whom we are more apt to be familiar, are dominated by the father Zeus and are cut off from their own mother.[20] Athene emerged full-grown from her father's head. Aphrodite was born out of the semen that surrounded her father's genitals. Demeter, Hera, and Hestia were swallowed by their father immediately after birth. Of the major Olympian goddesses, only Artemis had a mother, and a fairly insufficient one at that. Artemis became the prototypical parentified child, caring for her own mother instead of the other way around.

Having received inadequate mothering, the goddesses, in turn, failed to mother. Even Artemis, who was invoked by women in labor — goddess of the hunt, overseer of childbirth — was herself childless. So was Athene, though she was the protectress of the young children on whom the *polis* depended. And so was Hestia, who was ironically the goddess of the hearth and family. All three were virgins. The beautiful Aphrodite, though hardly a virgin, was not a mother figure. Her priority was sexual passion, not the result of that passion. And Hera's role was pre-eminently that of wife (of philandering Zeus), not mother. Her children were incidental. In fact, she tortured her stepson Dionysus. Only Demeter, goddess of corn, seems at first glance to represent maternal devotion. She literally raised hell (in this case Hades) to repossess her abducted daughter, Persephone. Hades had snatched the lovely Persephone away to the underworld, promising that, as his queen, she would be a great power and mistress of her own domain. But Demeter was inconsolable, and in her grief, she ravaged the earth. Eventually Demeter was able to accomplish the return of her daughter Persephone for two thirds of the year (and so restored vegetation to the earth for that period). But whose needs was Demeter fulfilling? Hades' proposition to Persephone was not bad compensation for leaving mom. Persephone's point of view is never considered. A close reading of the myth suggests Demeter's overinvestment[21] — a mother's inability to let go of her child. Even among the lesser characters in Greek mythology, there is nary a "good" mother: Procne killed her son in a jealous rage and served him up to his father in a stew. The Maenads ate children raw.

In their reinterpretation of mythology, the playwrights hardly upgraded these maternal images. Medea, protagonist of Euripides' tragedy, claimed she would prefer armed combat to giving birth, and later, in an orgy of revenge on her unfaithful husband, she killed her own children. Clytemnestra, in Aeschylus's telling, cast her son Orestes out in infancy. So much for Greek mother love!

Of course, these goddesses were hardly bound by the Athenians' rules of domesticity, which required earthbound women to relentlessly weave and/or bear sons. They were not sequestered in women's quarters. Nor were they paragons of virtue, role models, in the way that later deities, such as the Madonna, became. Rather, they animated the collective Greek imagination, and as products of the unconscious, they symbolized the conflicts, behaviors, and wishes of the populace. Reality unavoidably informs the artistic or the spiritual in some way, shape, or form. So the omission of nurturing mothers from Greek mythology and Greek tragedy implies something about Greek life. Mothering's significance is in its absence. The exclusion suggests that parenting, the actual task of nurturing, was not on the Greek mind. Evidently the process of child rearing was not highly valued and did not bring the mother much in the way of prestige or honor.

Indeed, the maternal contribution to conception did not matter much either; at least it did not matter as much as paternity. Interestingly, the question of maternity — its importance relative to paternity — was one that preoccupied the Greeks. Despite the fact that a baby is so obviously born of woman, the philosopher Aristotle, representing a majority view, was determined to upgrade the importance of the father. According to Aristotle, it is the male seed that in reproduction "cooks" the female residue, converting it into a new being: the seed, in other words, has an active role, but the female blood has a passive role. In essence, the male converts female matter with his sperm, according to his treatise *Generation of Animals*. Aristotle then uses women's so-called passivity in reproduction to justify her social inferiority. His misogyny parading as science is legendary; it reached its nadir in the ludicrous observation that women have fewer teeth than men. It is rumored that the philosopher Bertrand Russell once commented that Aristotle would never have made this mistake had he let his wife open her mouth once in a while.[22]

The reproduction debate raged in ancient Greece but was made most vivid in the Orestes myth, which had more incarnations than the "male buddy" plot does today, relatively speaking. It was the subject of seven Greek tragedies out of the thirty-two extant, and was treated by all three of the great dramatists — Aeschylus, Sophocles, and Euripides — suggesting that matricide, or at least mother bashing, was a Greek obsession. In it, Clytemnestra murdered her husband, Agamemnon, who had killed one of their daughters. To avenge his father, their son, Orestes, then murdered his mother and her lover. When brought to trial, Orestes was acquitted of his mother's murder, since it was thought by the male-dominated society of Athens more important to avenge one's father than to respect one's mother.

Men won the reproduction debate, too. This was spelled out in the famous trial scene. Though the Orestes trial represented an advance in jurisprudence, because justice was obtained through an impersonal legal instrument of the state instead of through clan vengeance, it can also be read as the ultimate put-down of maternity. In Aeschylus's version, mother-murder was dismissed by the god Apollo as less significant than father-murder. He had this to say about the role of woman in parenthood:

> The mother of the child that is called hers is not really its parent. She just nurses the seed that is planted within her by the child's true parent, the male . . . and if you want proof of what I say, here it is:

> here is Athene, child of Zeus, who was born with no help from a mother's womb; she is living proof that the male can father a child with no help from a female.[23]

So Orestes was freed on the grounds that, in killing his mother, he had not shed kindred blood! One's mother is no kin. The "one who mounts" is the true parent. The mother-child bond is denied in the context of this profoundly patriarchal point of view.

One wonders about the frame of mind of Athenian women as they read philosophy or observed plays — if they read philosophy or went to the theater. Indeed, their education was far inferior to men's, and it is thought that respectable women may not have attended theatrical performances at all in Classical Athens. (Men wrote, staged, and acted in the plays, including the numerous female parts and choruses.[24]) While it would be a mistake to read feminist frustration back into the women of ancient Athens, surely complicated feelings must have unfolded as women mothered.

We already suspect that mothers colluded in the exposure of their infants. What could the Greek mother have felt? What were her assumptions about her role and the nature of children? Did she bond with her offspring? Given the fragmentary nature of our evidence for reconstructing Greek lives, it is unlikely that an absolute determination can be made. But a pattern is emerging, one that suggests attitudes and behaviors similar to ours — affection, attention, nurturing, the valuing of the child — but also extremes of detachment and overinvolvement for selected children that would be considered monstrous in our age. Let us look at the facts of life of the Athenian mother, as best we can, to sort out her mental state and child-rearing methods. How did the Greek mother mother?

She Loved Them, She Loved Them Not: Maternal Reality

The ancient Greeks preceded exposé journalism, confessional memoirs, and even naturalistic fiction by twenty-five hundred years. As a result, we can determine the nature of parental affection only from such secondary sources as moral and medical tracts, art, literature, legislation, religious imagery, burial patterns, demographics, all of them subject to interpretation. If only, for example, Perictione (Plato's mom) had left a diary so that we could confirm or deny the provocative inferences about mothers in Plato's *Republic,* wherein haughty, narcissistic, glory-seeking men (he called them "timocratic") are said to hail from frustrated mothers who press their sons for accomplishments beyond their fathers'.[25] From that we might discern whether Greek mothers were indeed frustrated, if in fact they used their sons to further their own ambitions; we could surmise whether their sons complied, or if their flaws were connected to their mothers' inadequacy. Unfortunately, the data we have are much more oblique.

There is evidence suggesting mothers and fathers in Classical Athens were devoted to their offspring.[26] They appear to have grieved deeply when children died. (This was true for wanted children; others were treated very differently, as we shall see.) Numerous *stelai* (grave markers) from that period convey much pathos. One epitaph, for example, informs us that the deceased child, nicknamed Little Chatterbox, was a consolation in life and will be missed by all. Another depicts a delightfully pudgy infant (presumably the deceased) straining upward to reach a bird. Still another shows a young grandmother holding her dead grandchild, one of the earliest successful renderings of a baby. The familiarity of these images tugs at our heartstrings. But do they represent a true emotional attachment to the child or a formalistic codified Greek response?[27]

The fourth century B.C. witnessed an increased artistic attention to the depiction of children. Until this time artists portrayed children as miniature adults, with heads disproportionately small, who functioned merely as appendages in any composition. But now Greek vase painting regularly pictured young children, usually plump little boys, at play with wagons, pets, and toys. There is other artistic evidence — terra cotta statues, clay models — of delightful representations of children and their activities: from toddlers being carried on adults' shoulders to boys playing with knucklebones to a young girl getting a cooking lesson from her mother. These images have a kind of Norman Rockwell resonance, but, again, do they represent a composite picture of Greek childhood? Or are they the ancient equivalent of Hallmark cards?[28]

It is important to note that the pictorial representation of mother and child, one of the great and enduring iconographic images in Christian art from the tenth century, never occupied a position of comparable significance in classical history. There are depictions of women nursing male babies, called *kourotrophoi,* but these are typically composed of an inert, wooden-looking child, cradled awkwardly in the arms of an expressionless mother. Only occasionally is the theme treated with a degree of emotional involvement. For example, a vase from 440 B.C. shows a rare scene of a mother (a legitimate wife!) breast-feeding while her husband looks on. The mother cups the head of her child in a gesture of gentleness and absorption. But whether this depiction, together with the profusion of representations of children in general, suggests an increase in sentiment for children or merely reflects increased technical mastery in the pictorial arts is debatable. It is fair to say that the tender depiction of mother and child was not a prominent ancient Greek motif.[29]

Philosophers like Plato and Aristotle devoted considerable attention to children and to making sure their education equipped them for life as good citizens. They present what are essentially theories of physiological and psychological development (corresponding quite remarkably to contemporary models of child development), along with "how to" advice for proper child care. One of Plato's dicta is much like that of experts today, who decry the impact of television: more care should be taken in the stories told to children. He goes on to explain that tales of bogies like Medusa and the Cyclops, which were meant to scare children into behaving, might actually damage them. Of course Plato's and Aristotle's writings may not reflect public opinion. They were surely unrepresentative men, perhaps eccentric, and quite possibly childless. Their interest in children, moreover, was prompted not by a humanitarian concern for child welfare, but for the perpetuation of the state. Their goal was preservation of the *polis.* Nor, it may be noted, were their comments directed primarily to parents.[30]

Instances of mother love and father love may be found in literary and mythological sources (although the aforementioned images of monstrous parents, infanticide, incest, parricide, and the eating of children's flesh predominate). Euripides, who knew how to pull out all the emotional stops, has Hercules exit with this line: "The best mortals, and those who are not, love children; they may differ in means, the haves and the have-nots, but all love children." That in his ensuing madness he then kills his own children is the height of pathos.[31] Equally poignant is the myth of the overly proud mother of twelve, Niobe, who is so full of sorrow when her children are slain that Zeus turns her into a weeping statue (an image that presages the Mater Dolorosa — the tearful Virgin cradling the dead Christ — which dominates art from the twelfth through the fourteenth centuries).

More incontrovertible evidence was found elsewhere. Excavations unearthed a veritable cornucopia of childhood paraphernalia: bassinets, cradles, feeding bottles, potty chairs, and many kinds of toys. The range of toys, which would impress F.A.O. Schwarz, included dolls (some with articulated limbs and real hair), miniature pots, tools, and furniture, pull-toys, balls, tops, marbles, and hoops. Surely Athenian parents would not have bothered to create such objects, so specifically directed to children's special needs, if youngsters were of no account. This material evidence is paralleled by inadvertent references to parental attachment, particularly in law-court speeches, where appeals to mother love were almost a cliché. Defendants routinely swore oaths on their children's heads and brought them into the court to win the jury's sympathy. Such emotional bids were obviously based on the assumption of parental affection for their offspring, without which such appeals would have been meaningless. Finally, medical writers like Hippocrates observed that children had their own particular problems — tonsillitis, teething, and so forth — which often required a different kind of medical care. The interest in pediatric medicine strongly suggests that at least certain children were deemed worthy of keeping healthy.[32]

There is another take on all this, however. These data may signify not a positive feeling toward children, but merely a realization of their practical value. An old and venerable law required Athenians to provide food and shelter for their parents.[33] This, in a society that did not have pension plans, and in which the maintenance of burial plots was highly important, must have been a strong incentive to care for one's offspring. Children were one's insurance policy in old age.

The more accurate interpretation of the evidence may be that ancient Athenians, though fond of certain offspring, basically lacked interest in the separate nature of the child.[34] They lacked a detailed apprehension of the child as another human existence. Though often perceived as charming and cute, children were described chiefly by negatives, as being deficient in intellect, morality, strength, self-control, courage, in short, as being nonadult. Aristotle said, severely, that no rational adult would wish to be a child. Taken as a whole, Greek society was anything but child oriented. Much like slaves and women, youngsters had virtually no legal rights, in stark contrast to American culture today, when, in some cases, children may "divorce" their parents. Some Greeks said straight out that they had little inclination for children. "Most men treat their private business in a careless manner," says Plato's Laches; "that concerning children and other things too."[35]

Apart from the philosophers, who address childhood from a purely theoretical standpoint, and a few medical treatises, other literature is provocatively silent. In Greek tragedy, the appearance of children is generally confined to moments of crisis, when their lives are endangered. They are used as a plot device. The child's point of view is not addressed in Greek writings; the subjective experience of the youngster is beside the point. The child as person is of little interest.

What stands out in bold relief from the evidence is the predicament of the Greek mother and how her situation conspired to make her detach from her offspring. We can only imagine the mental state of a girl, age fourteen or so, as she is about to deliver her first baby. Childbirth was a dangerous undertaking, and many women died.[36] A pregnant girl had only to look about her to observe the funerary monuments bearing melancholy witness to the many casualties among young mothers. The fact that Greek society would glorify her death in childbed as female martyrdom, especially if she produced a live male, may have provided little reassurance as she underwent the risk of delivery. Women who survived the painful and exhausting labor of giving birth, some as many as ten or twelve times, probably shortened their life expectancy, which was thirty-five, while men could expect to live longer than women by as much as ten years or more.[37] The newborn was also at great risk.[38] Ten pregnancies might yield four grown children. In a society in which early deaths and burials were routine, the nature of a mother's emotional response to her baby would have to be questioned. It is painful business to love and lose, perhaps making one vulnerable to never loving at all, as has been noted. This perhaps helps to explain mothers' presumed collusion in the practice of exposure.

Pregnancy and all matters gynecological were considered women's business. Male physicians did not ordinarily deal with such matters. This may have been a blessing, because in later centuries physicians and their unsterilized instruments spread puerperal fever, which ravaged the population of mothers. Greek women gave birth from a seated position on a stool, attended by a midwife, away from male eyes. The thrust of the ancient medical literature on the subject was the production of a viable male baby, not prolonging the life of the mother.[39] The implicit devaluation was not a message likely to be lost on women.

Women were defined by their fertility. Celibacy was not an option. (No nunneries yet.) Infertility was grounds for divorce. But while women were under pressure to produce male heirs, they were simultaneously under pressure not to produce too many. Theirs was a delicate balancing act. They had to balance the need for enough children to continue the line, support them in old age, and tend their grave, while allowing for high infant mortality, war, and illness with the risk of diluting the family property and endangering their status in the *oikos*. The importance of this point cannot be overemphasized. It was the rule throughout the Greek world that inheritance must be divided equally among the sons, so the head of household was under a strong compulsion to limit his family and avoid dissipating his estate and impoverishing his heirs. The desirability of having only a single male heir was advocated by a variety of philosophers, including Plato.[40]

It is a curious thing that excess population was even a possibility in Athens, given the acceptability of homosexuality and various sexual practices, like sex with slaves and fancy *hetairai,* which would not exactly increase the incidence of pregnancy in their legitimate wives. And given the aforementioned high mortality of babies, the death of young men in war, and a fifth-century Athenian state policy promoting childbirth,[41] one would expect each infant born of a citizen to be wanted. Besides, contraceptive practices were known — though they varied in effectiveness (as they did until the 1960s) from moderately reliable pessaries and spermicides to mere superstition — suggesting that mothers had at least some choice in whether to bear a child. Also, an early form of abortion was practiced, though, ironically, it was eschewed in favor of exposure! While the Greeks expressed reservations about terminating a pregnancy, they paid not the least regard to the rights of the newborn child, which underlines the difference between the ancient Greek mentality and our own.

These fertility concerns present a very confused picture. From our perspective, Athens did not seem in danger of a population explosion, making any motive for exposure all the more morally incomprehensible. The socioeconomic dynamics further complicate matters. What was deemed good for any one family (the wealth of the *oikos*) was not necessarily good for Athens as a whole or for the individual in particular (in this case, the exposed newborn). So while Athens may have wanted more citizens, a particular household might not. The situation strikes me as schizophrenic, not unlike our national policy of subsidizing food wastage in the Midwest while a family in a ghetto may go hungry.

Having borne an heir, a woman consolidated her identity. It was in the delivery of sons, not the raising of them, that she achieved status. No wonder the thrust of maternal concern was childbearing, not child rearing. That was where her bread was buttered. Any attachment to the child, any joy she might have from her children, was incidental to the system. Children belonged to their father. Such social contingencies were a setup for lack of maternal interest.

The manner in which Athenian mothers dealt with their offspring bears this out. Mothers were in charge of infants and children, except boys after the age of six, and their methods, on the whole, convey a certain remoteness. Though avoided by the Egyptians, swaddling was practiced on Greek babies, as noted. The motives for binding up a baby must be understood in context. It is a practice that continued in parts of Europe well into the nineteenth century, and was thought to keep a child warm and safe and to straighten its arms and legs. Today the idea of swaddling a child may seem ludicrous, yet it was not inherently harmful. But given the Athenians' lack of interest in children, their use of swaddling would only seem to emphasize their aloofness. By its nature, swaddling is an impediment to expressiveness, communication, and interaction between mother and child. While it conveniently frees mom to go about her business, it has just the opposite effect on her baby, frustrating its movement, curiosity, and, perhaps, its will. In a loving atmosphere, these factors may not be deleterious, but when a child is of little account, they may be highly operative.

It was customary, as well, for Athenian citizens to employ wet nurses, who remained with the family until the child reached adulthood. Taken purely at face value, the presence of a wet nurse in the *oikos* might suggest a distancing between the mother and her child, and in the Athenian context that interpretation may be valid. But as with swaddling, we cannot automatically assume that the employment of a wet nurse represented a lack of regard for a baby. The Egyptians and Sumerians, you may recall, used wet nurses and seemed to love their children. ◑

IT SEEMS extraordinary that so little remains today of this once flourishing aspect of child care. Wet-nursing seems to have vanished from the collective European memory, perhaps because we are so ambivalent about it. Yet it flourished in Europe from antiquity and reached its heyday in the eighteenth century, significantly dying out only *after* bottle-feeding became a safe alternative in the nineteenth century.[42] For hundreds of years the practice was confined to the wealthy classes, but in the Early Modern period, the middle and working classes began to ape their superiors, and they too sought wet nurses for their children. The question is why.

Certain advantages are evident. In an age when alternatives to human milk were unknown, wet-nursing was a necessity for those infants whose mothers had died or were physically unable to nurse. The use of a foster nurse freed the mother to follow her daily pursuits, unhampered by the round-the-clock obligation to respond to her child's needs. Such freedom may not have been frivolous but essential to the family's economic survival or smooth functioning. But not all the reasons were so worthy; undoubtedly the hiring of a wet nurse was a status symbol, and it may have served to preserve the appearance of the biological mother's breasts (at least, that was the thinking at the time). Then, too, because breast-feeding reduced the possibility of conception, the use of a wet nurse by a wealthy woman served to restore her fertility, while simultaneously reducing that of the nurse's, thereby redistributing the birth rate so that it favored those who could most afford to support children. (Whether this outcome was considered desirable or not by any one woman is speculative.) And since the indulgence in sexual intercourse by a lactating woman was thought to curdle her milk, employment of a wet nurse enabled the employer to resume sexual relations with her husband. (The wet nurse, of course, was supposed to abstain.) Finally, the use of wet nurses by bourgeois women created a viable, respectable, decently paid occupation for other women (especially unwed mothers) who otherwise might have had to resort to prostitution.[43]

Yet there is an obvious downside to reliance on wet-nursing. It deprives the biological mother and baby of that overwhelming, single-minded clutch of mutual attachment so many modern mothers rhapsodize about as they gaze into their newborns' eyes while they nurse or bottle-feed. (Of course, in some instances, like ancient Athens, that "deprivation" may have been the whole point of the enterprise; that is, mothers purposely sought to distance themselves from their offspring.) Another disadvantage — an egregious one — is that in many centuries there appears to have been a higher death rate for babies who were wet-nursed than for babies who were nursed by their mothers. Then, too, there was the delicate issue of the disposition of the nurse's baby. The lactating mother's occupation may have resulted in the abandonment, and perhaps death, of her own baby,[44] since the breast-feeding of more than one infant at a time was forbidden, as it was mistakenly thought to dilute a woman's milk.

Despite these drawbacks, in all recorded history there has been a subset of women, a stubborn percentage of mothers, usually privileged, who have resisted the idea of nursing their own babies. Psychoanalysts have speculated that resistance to breast-feeding may have to do with women's unconscious feelings deriving from their own infancies, their damaged characters, or shame over the erotic stimulation involved. All this may be true, but we must be careful not to equate the use of a surrogate nurse with the rejection of the child. Nursing is not the *sine qua non* of a good parent (just ask any loving father!). And the presence over history of a group of mothers who choose not to breast-feed suggests that resistance to maternal nursing is neither unnatural nor pathological. Evidently nursing, like music, has enough charm to soothe the average breast, but not all breasts. Some women love it; some hate it; most find it moderately pleasurable at times.

The fact that, for centuries, it was the father who brokered the wet-nursing transaction with the husband of the lactating woman hints at a more salient explanation: patriarchal control. We have already discussed men's envy of women's ability to lactate. When a man's wife nurses his child, he may also feel envy of his baby. He may feel excluded and replaced by his child in her affections. In a defensive attempt to restore the previous balance in the marital relationship, he may devalue her nursing (and mothers' nursing in general) and encourage her to disavow such an unseemly endeavor. In the end, a mother's reluctance to breast-feed may have much to do with patriarchal preference, and hence social conditioning, since the man usually has the power to enforce his prerogative. ☽

IT APPEARS THAT ancient Greek women were not overburdened with child care. In addition to wet nurses, *paidagogi* (male slaves) were employed to accompany young boys as soon as they were old enough to leave the women's quarters. Clearly, the wives of the citizens of Athens did not suffer from overexposure to their children. The chances for mother-child intimacy seem rather obscure.

Children may have had a bad time of it in Athens. Practices in the school were notoriously harsh. Despite Plato's advice to the contrary, nurses terrified children with stories of bogies who preyed on little children in order to keep them in line. Boy brothels flourished, and child prostitutes could be rented. The Greek penchant for the smooth, unbearded skin of male youths is hardly a secret; it is immortalized in the poetry of Philip of Thessalonica, Strato, and others. Here is a bit from Meleager: "I was thirsty. / It was hot. / I kissed the boy / with girl-soft skin. / My thirst was quenched." Quite apart from these revealing verses, we know about the Greek obsession with pederasty from many other sources — art, legal statutes, history. Even Plato, certainly one of the most respected philosophers of any era, recommended that boys be kept in common and shared by different men. Lest anyone conclude that this behavior constituted not child abuse but creative sexual expression, let him study the many painted vases depicting such scenes. Invariably, the penis of the seducer is erect while that of the young boy remains flaccid. If not victims of seduction themselves, children of citizens may well have seen their father have sexual relations with a child slave.[45]

An inference about latent maternal hostility, advanced by Philip Slater in *The Glory of Hera* (1968), goes far toward making sense of the abundance of powerful female figures in Classical Greek tragedy (those menacing, sexually ravenous mothers who go about killing their children or eating them or getting them to avenge their wrongs). Slater asserted that Greek men, and hence Greek playwrights, were misogynistic because of their mothers' frustration with their own restricted lives. Mothers projected their sexual and social frustrations onto their young boys, whose future they envied. Wives dared not voice their unhappiness to their husbands, who, according to Slater, were mostly absent on military campaigns anyway. Instead, repressed and isolated, these mothers used their sons to vent their complicated feelings. They alternately bombarded their boys with stifling possessiveness, as they sought to make them into substitute marital partners, or with venomous hatred, as they jealously tried to live vicariously through them. Young boys, who were unavoidably in their mothers' orbit until they went to school, sensed and internalized their mothers' hostility and turned to fearing and hating women. Misogyny bred misogyny.

Slater decoded all those images of women in Greek tragedy whose power seems so unaccountable in light of woman's actual powerlessness in society. The images are part of a projective system, patterned to man's psychic fears, that inverts reality. In myth, man is the innocent victim and mom (who in real life is the object of his guilt-tainted thoughts) is the villain — not the other way around. Greek literature caricatures every aspect of motherhood that terrifies males: prodigious mothers, suffocating mothers, emasculating mothers, and so on. Such exaggerated portrayals, perhaps, served to exorcise man's underlying dread of the real thing — his conflicted tie to his mother.

Mothers' self-centered involvement with their sons could also explain the self-absorption that has been said to characterize the Greek personality — exhibitionism, competitiveness, thin-skinned combativeness, and "lust to annihilate." These behaviors are signs of insecurity, attempts to shore up poor self-esteem by grandstanding. A child who was never loved for himself may have sought attention in this way.

Unlike Slater, I suspect that Greek women were less repressed than they were self-centered and needy (because of their own upbringing). Their frustration, in my view, was due not so much to their husbands' absence (which has been disputed), but to their husbands' disdain. It was the rampant misogyny that rendered these women unable to love empathically. Psychoanalysts call this unloving condition "the narcissistic personality." The Greek mother's narcissistic attachment to her children would include her daughters as well as her sons. Her children were not people but objects employed to regulate her self-esteem. When insufficiently useful (because of their redundancy or failure to gratify mother's needs), sons and daughters were discarded, either emotionally, by the mother's withdrawal of interest and love, or physically, by exposure.

Narcissistic parenting replicates itself in a vicious circle. In the Classical Athenian version, as a boy grew up, understandably hateful of women, he avoided marriage until the sake of the *oikos* absolutely demanded it. He then married a girl half his age. She, like his sisters, was undereducated and not much of a partner for him. He felt justified in neglecting her in favor of the male society of public life. Never valued or loved herself, she was unable to value and love her offspring, except in the narcissistic way I described above. The father, himself narcissistic, could not empathize with the child either. So here we have the explanation for the radical inconsistency that employed both exposure and nurturing in ancient Greek parenting. Of course this schema is oversimplified. But the dynamics of narcissism may help us unravel the mystery of exposure — how parents could treat some of their children as expendable objects. At the bottom of this is, of course, misogyny, the degeneration of a patriarchal social order.

Interestingly, it may well be that the tensions and conflicts that produced narcissistic personalities also fueled the creation of Greek art, literature, and philosophy. It does not discredit this art to think it owed something to sublimation. Instead, we are reminded that beauty has its price.[46] The tragic view of life which Greeks recognized so clearly, and their exhaustive competition for recognition, show a craving for the love their parents could not give. The vulnerability made them people with whom we may easily identify.

As a footnote to this period, it is interesting to observe that the Spartans, the long-time rivals of the Athenians, whom Athenians regarded as dull-witted boors, engaged in infanticide. In fact, infanticide was a Spartan social policy, mandated by law, though the decision to murder was determined less by gender than by the physical perfection of the child. Spartan society functioned as a kind of communal war-preparation machine. The conjugal goal was the production of future warriors. A mother's loyalty was unambivalently co-opted by the fatherland, not her child. Recall the story of the "brave Spartan mother" who sent her son to battle with the admonition "With your shield or on it," meaning the young man was to return victorious or dead. Amidst this overflow of testosterone, the position of women in Sparta was actually better than in other Greek cities.[47] As breeders, women were highly valued. Obviously there is more than one type of social arrangement that can produce parental detachment. Dysfunction is not always in the form of misogyny. In the case of Classical antiquity, however, all roads led to Rome.

Some four hundred years after Athens, the Roman mother's use of her own sons toward the attainment of power was elevated to high art. How else can we explain Seneca's letter to his daunting mother, Helvia, in which he transparently tried to exonerate himself in her eyes by explaining away his fall from grace as chief minister to the Emperor Nero? Seneca's experience of scheming mothers was considerable, since he had no doubt witnessed the machinations of the Emperor Claudius's fourth wife, Agrippina, who had engineered the succession of her son, Nero, to the imperial throne (whence she acted as co-ruler). No less notorious was Livia, the wife of the Emperor Augustus and the mother, by an earlier husband, of his successor, Tiberius; she supposedly resorted to murder to ensure Tiberius's place as emperor.

Rome adopted the culture of Greece as its own and managed to retain many of the glories of Greece (though bastardized) — the literature, art, and religion — but also its vices — slavery, male supremacy (*patria potestas*), infant exposure.[48] But compared to her Athenian predecessor, the Roman matron could be considered emancipated. She was hardly sequestered and undereducated. As women gained power, the birthrate plunged, suggesting that when women are given the choice, many would as soon not assume the burdens of motherhood. (The declining birthrate has been cited as one of the causes of the fall of the Roman Empire.) It is likely that as women's social gains increased, so did their internal conflicts over child rearing. Roman men tantalized them with a taste of freedom, but kept its trophies just beyond their grasp.[49]

Among the most recent scholars[50] who have studied the Roman parent-and-child relationship, there is general agreement that during the Roman Republic there was little emphasis on satisfying the child's emotional needs. But this may have changed during the transition from Republic to Empire, when fathers and mothers took a keener interest in their offspring and mourned their decease with such intensity that a new literary genre, the *consolatio,* was invented. There is also evidence for romance within marriage during the Empire. All this is energetically debated.

We do know that the abandonment of newborns persisted — as did the prostitution of children, their use in circuses, and the castration of young boys to produce eunuchs. The famed book by Petronius, *The Satyricon,* contains a veritable trove of examples of Roman sexual abuse of children, both boys and girls. Petronius depicted a scene in which the youth Giton deflowered Pannychis, a girl approximately seven years old. A group of elder women observed the proceedings, encouraging and applauding the violation. Even though *The Satyricon* would be classified as a work of fiction, it appears to reflect real behaviors in Rome, especially among the upper classes. For example, the Emperor Tiberius, successor to Augustus, certainly ranks in history as a notorious abuser of children. He trained a cadre of little boys to swim between his legs in the pool, and to lick and nibble his genitals. He called them his "minnows." Tiberius's successor, the infamous Gaius Caligula, savagely executed children in public spectacles.[51]

Rome did have a "favorite woman" in the second century B.C. whose virtues as a mother were extolled by the populace. She was Cornelia, a paragon. As a widow she turned down lucrative marriage offers to be faithful to the memory of her husband, by whom she had borne twelve children — all for the glory of Rome. Her fecundity was much praised, as was her devotion to her children's education. Under her tutelage, two of her sons, the Gracchi — Tiberius and Gaius — led a reform movement of the plebeians against the patricians. Both sons died in the ensuing unrest, but Cornelia was stoical. She owes her fame to her reply when asked why she did not wear jewels. "These," she said, pointing to her children, "are my jewels." What a maternal prototype! And on the statue erected in her honor, she was remembered with the inscription "Cornelia, Mother of the Gracchi."[52]

It would appear that the Romans, unlike the Greeks, did start to develop a maternal ideal. This undoubtedly elevated child rearing to an activity of worth. It put maternity on the map. But, as we shall see, idealized images of mothers may further serve to undermine women. If every hope of fulfillment is bound to the one duty of childbearing, which is not universally fulfilling and frequently impossible to perform in the prescribed manner, motherhood is in danger of becoming an instrument of women's annulment as persons. Which brings us to the Middle Ages.

FOUR

Sacred and Profane Callings: Medieval Mom

Madonna Fever, the Original Version

The Middle Ages, that period of European history stretching from the fall of the Roman Empire, around the year 500, to the time of Columbus, witnessed the rise of a maternal image so irresistible, so brilliantly tuned in to human needs, and of such enduring appeal that she has been impossible to relinquish. I am referring, of course, to Mary, mother of Jesus, the Madonna, the Blessed Virgin, whose selfless devotion to her Son has provided boundless wish-fulfillment to the Western world for a millennium and a half. In some circles she is automatically appealed to in times of stress, her very name achieving the status of an exclamation — Mary! Mother of God! — which reveals something about our feelings toward the Virgin, whom one may respectably implore long after it is acceptable to cry out for one's own mama. The enormous impact of the Madonna cannot be overestimated. Even today, when mainstream religion is supposed to be in decline, how many religious figures can still attract the twelve million pilgrims a year who go to the Shrine of Our Lady of Guadalupe, or the four and a half million a year who go to the shrine at Lourdes?[1]

Mary is one of few female characters to have attained the position of archetype. Attachment to Mary (mariolatry) and the reverse, contempt for Mary (which, in itself, may be read as a form of attachment, but of a negative variety) run very deep. Her exaltation has been the cause of wars, schisms, masochism, impotence, as well as songs, liturgies, fabulous works of art. The veneration of Mary arguably remains the single greatest obstacle to the eventual reunification of the Christian churches. Over the years her cult has acquired stories, visions, shrines, miracles, and sightings. She is also the stuff of big business as sites of miracles turn into lucrative roadside tourist traps. Should one doubt the power of Mary's image, one need only note the popularity of Madonna (Ciccone), the media megastar, who makes cunning use of that image, if ironically, to promote her own persona — very successfully thus far.

A myth of such dimensions cannot but exercise a sway over our unconscious lives. Whether we revere her or not, whether we are churched or not, we are in her thrall. Though many of us have never given her a second thought and would regard sightings of her as utterly preposterous, her brand of motherhood is embedded in our psyche. The Virgin's way of nurturing has become *the* maternal ideal, the pinnacle of feminine ambition. Her bond with her Son, her inalienable, irreducible, indestructible love for her Baby, now defines the parameters of mother love. Moreover, it has been elevated to an implicit entitlement, a kind of basic right for all children, a shared expectation, without which one is permitted to feel shortchanged. Mary set the standard, though, interestingly, this standard has been acknowledged more widely in the centuries later than her period of origin or greatest veneration.

The Virgin Mary's popularity is not surprising. Who would not want such a mother? Indeed, she is so abundantly gratifying as a concept, so responsive to suppressed human longings, that it is a wonder she was not invented before. She is everything the Great Goddess, the Neolithic goddesses, and the Greek goddesses were not: merciful, trustworthy, overflowing with goodness. Imagine how soothing the contemplation of her must have been to hapless medieval women and men in the throes of Black Death, spiritual agony, endless crusades, or capricious feudal fiats. The Madonna and Child is a picture of comfort and peace, visual Prozac. Her maternal tenderness tugs at our collective heartstrings.

And it was specifically this — the Madonna's maternity, her exquisite bond with her Son, her inexhaustible caring — which accounts for her enormous grassroots appeal. Her mothering is one of the few aspects of her story that has remained constant over time. Indeed, for two thousand years, Mary's biography has been so transformed and embellished that the social activist Mary of today would barely recognize herself in the majestic and remote Virgin of the early Middle Ages, or the ordinary historical Mary of the first century, who was, after all, a socially marginal Jewish mother from the backwater town of Nazareth. Yet she was always a perfect mother, a pluperfect mother. The Blessed Virgin was so pure, so self-abnegating, so nurturing, and so ecstatic in the performance of her tasks that she made humility and submissiveness look good. And note the result of her ministrations . . . Divine!

Mary is the archetypal devoted mother, dream mom. In psychoanalytic terms (the Melanie Klein rendition of psychoanalysis), she could be considered the consummate breast, ever full and flowing, which we all wish we once had, or thought we had but were rudely forced to give up. To the psychoanalyst D. W. Winnicott, she could be regarded as a "good enough mother," to say the least, and psychoanalyst Heinz Kohut might have considered her the ultimate "selfobject" (a compliment, as we shall see). Garden variety Freudians would undoubtedly focus on the convenient appeal of her virginity. But we are getting ahead of ourselves. We shall examine psychoanalytic explanations later. The point is that Mary presses all the right psychic buttons; that is, all the right psychic buttons for the child. But what about the mother's psyche? There is an underside to Mary's selflessness if we consider that Mary has no self. She has no needs of her own. The only female biological function permitted her is the act of nursing.[2] She is modest to the point of prudery, servile, pious, entirely self-erasing, a primeval co-dependent. Whose dream is she, anyway?

The Madonna's image poses knotty problems. Was it a social advance for women, or a regression? Did the revered image of the Madonna raise the social standing of flesh-and-blood medieval women over their predecessors? Or was it an emotional straitjacket of impossible expectations, the source of all our later maternal guilt? Was the Blessed Virgin a trendsetter or a follower? Did her fervid adoration of her Son influence mothers to feel the same way about their offspring? Or did her tenderness merely mimic medieval reality? Was she a kind of opiate for the collective inner child of the masses? Is her way of mothering good for mortal children?

The answers to these questions would provide considerable mileage in our quest for the truth about motherhood, about what is natural and what is acquired, about what is necessary and what is sufficient. Unfortunately, there is no perfect key to unlock the secrets of a medieval mother's heart. Hard data of the medieval period are maddeningly sparse and inconclusive. Diaries, letters, and genre painting all came later, and when they appeared at all in the Middle Ages, were restricted to the nobility, flattered the author, and typically made few references to children. The information necessary to arrive at the truth always proves to be incomplete; every point of view, no matter how persuasively argued, collapses for lack of some crucial piece of evidence. To date, all views are partial and reductive, and fail to do justice to the full complexity of motherhood.

But the mere scarcity of data has not stopped historians from historicizing — at length! So as we grapple with questions about medieval mother love we are irresistibly drawn into the vortex of a controversy that has been storming wildly for thirty years. It is a debate that has polarized historians since its inception and continues to inform most recent scholarship on the family from the Middle Ages on.

Does She Love Me?

Broadly speaking, the argument concerns whether or not preindustrial European mothers loved their children, but it really concerns many other issues as well: the very existence in history of the nuclear family, for example, or of conjugal love and privacy; and larger issues, such as whether nonpublic phenomena like sexuality, death, boredom (the French call them *mentalités*) even have a history, or whether they are timeless and intractable, as people tend to assume.

These factors have been habitually overlooked, but in reality are essential for the development of mother love. Surely a mother cannot bond with her baby if, for example, she is never in its proximity. And she may not have been. Certain revisionist historians contend that the nuclear family of father, mother, and children living under a single roof is a modern invention. Before the sixteenth century, families tended to be large, often embracing several generations, and not housed in familiar modern ways. More important, such a family group was primarily an economic entity — all members working the same fields — rather than the psychological unit of modern times. For contracting a marriage, love and sexual attraction counted for far less than did material interest, and marriages were often arranged by parents. This arrangement was no haven in a heartless world, and affective ties between parents and children did not have much weight.

The thinkers who take this darker view[3] of maternal affection have been far more flamboyant than traditional historians. Given to grand theorizing, they aim to demonstrate the cultural variabilities of sentiment, the most notable being that family life is progressive (that is, getting better and better over time). As a group, they are determinedly unconventional, dogged defilers of sacred cows. Their data are drawn from a mosaic of resources — art, architecture, literature, toys, dress — and tend to be impressionistic and untidy; and though they are often persuasive and inspired as evidence, they are somewhat muddled by a certain looseness of time-perspective, and the historians' tendency to lump together disparate fragments from many epochs.[4]

The granddaddy of these thinkers is the man to whom all social historians pay tribute (if only to refute him), the Frenchman Philippe Ariès, who, in the early sixties, published *Centuries of Childhood,* in which he reported his remarkable discovery that children used to be invisible, meaning that children were mostly overlooked in the Middle Ages, and, in fact, were not much cared about until the eighteenth century. He did not mention Madonna worship at all and surely did not see it as influencing medieval mothering, which was hardly tender, in his view. In early historical periods, according to Ariès, there were no clearly defined categories of adults and children, as there are now, with the former striving to comprehend the special needs, vulnerabilities, and sensibilities of the latter. The idea of childhood as a separate phase in the human cycle simply did not exist. But, then, the concept of adulthood as a phase hardly existed either. Social divisions were determined less by age than by social status. In one bold stroke, Ariès abolished our collective fantasy of the universality and necessity of the loving nuclear family — the shared idea of the domestic hearth (today the TV) around which are eternally gathered mom, dad, and the kids, all dedicated to maximizing the happiness of the children. Of course Engels and Marx, as we have seen, freed us from the legacy of a biological tendency toward a nuclear family long before, but not in so gripping a manner. To a generation of readers bred on Dr. Spock, infused with a philosophy of peace, love, and flower power, such cynical ideas as Ariès's *l'absence de sentiment* were shocking, but shocking was appealing in the 1960s. Young academics applauded his iconoclasm. Besides, Ariès's implication that parents were self-serving struck a responsive chord among those readers who did not trust anyone over the age of thirty.

Mother love atrophied in the medieval period, speculated Ariès, because of unfavorable conditions. Owing to the high infant mortality of the times, estimated at one or two in three, the investment of love in a child may have been so unrewarding that, by some ruse of nature, as when overcrowded mice in captivity will not breed, it was suppressed.[5] Given the high likelihood of death for their newborn children, parents developed psychic defenses against attachment. Perhaps also the frequent childbearing put less value on the product. A child was born and died, and another took its place.[6] It was better not to waste affection. Babies in the Middle Ages were swaddled, left unattended for long periods of time, sent out to wet nurses, and, later, were flogged and apprenticed — all of which Ariès's school cites as evidence of parental indifference.

Children who survived until the age of seven were treated as adults. They dressed as adults, worked as adults, and even went to war, all verified in remains of their garments, games, and assorted matter. For example, everyone, young and old, wore tunics and bowled hoops. Within each social class and gender there was a democracy of lifestyle: children were not differentiated. But Ariès's most brilliant proof of the evolution of childhood, his most original contribution, was his understanding of the power of portrait psychology to convey history (for which art historians still pay him tribute, unlike their "pure" historian counterparts).

Ariès pointed out that before the twelfth century — when children were presumably not much thought of — there were no portraits of individual children. Indeed, there were few representations of children at all in art, not even on children's tombs; that is, until the sixteenth century (Ariès does not deal with antiquity). Even then children appeared not on their own, but on their parents' gravestones. It did not occur to anyone to keep a picture of a dead child.[7] Medieval illustrations do show people in every other human activity — having sex and dying, sleeping and eating, in bed and in the bath, praying, hunting, dancing, ploughing, in games and in combat, trading and traveling — but so rarely as youths or with children that the absence is notable. Youngsters, when depicted at all, were shown as smaller-scale adults.[8] Ariès "discovered" childhood in medieval representations of Jesus nursing at His mother's breast, saw it develop in the games of the *putti,* those babies, representing cherubs, which ornament Renaissance art, and traced its full bloom through seventeenth-century family portraits, where nearly naked, real children were finally allowed to inhabit the canvas. Not coincidentally, the callousness toward children presumably softened somewhat in that century as privileged French parents sought to educate their sons so as to improve their value on the marriage market. In Ariès's view, it was in the seventeenth century that children finally emerged from their anonymity, and they did so even more in the eighteenth century, when parental concern for children grew intense and each child was precious, charming, and irreplaceable (first in the upper classes and later in the laboring classes). Maternal tenderness was now *de rigueur.* The modern concept of parenthood was born.

The history of childhood unfolded in tandem with the development of the nuclear family. Prior to the seventeenth century, according to Ariès, the idea of family as mom, dad, and their biological children did not penetrate far into consciousness. Collective life dominated society. A medieval man may have felt as much loyalty to his servants, his bastards,[9] or business associates as to his wife and legitimate family. The nuclear family was not factored out as a unit from the mass of one's neighbors and kin, even in living situations where space was at a premium and privacy was nonexistent. According to Ariès's reading of the Middle Ages, life among all but the elite meant a great press of bodies. It was not important that the conjugal family be together at their very own dinner table. This was *not* the classic family of Western nostalgia — the large household of parents, grandparents, and kids living happily together.[10] The household was large but not necessarily "happy." The continued presence of outsiders in the household, the argument goes, worked against the development of sentiment as we know it. Family solidarity, marital intimacy, parental love, the sense that family members have more in common with one another than with anyone on the outside, that home is a place, in the words of the poet Robert Frost, "where they have to take you in," all came later. Despite all this, Ariès was actually somewhat nostalgic for the early period, though he is not often billed that way. He thought modern schooling and social control were intrusive, depriving children of the freedom and spontaneity they may have enjoyed in medieval communities. He saw family life as growing restrictive and repressive over time. Not so Ariès's followers.

These later "theory-driven" historians have little nostalgia for the past.[11] While they take their major cues from Ariès, they do not sentimentalize the good old days, preferring to deconstruct the romanticized images of history recapitulated by Disney or the BBC or Quaker Oats. Unlike the so-called New Right, whose members denounce the decline of the family (citing high divorce rates, the prevalence of premarital and extramarital sex, abortion, and homosexuality), and who blame its deficiencies for every conceivable social ill, these scholars insist that family life was actually worse in earlier times.

According to Lloyd deMause, Edward Shorter, and Lawrence Stone, family life was never entirely harmonious; certainly it was never the delightful environment we envision as ideal for raising children. Mothers in premodern Europe may not have cared for their babies, may have allowed them to stew in their own excrement for hours on end, to be rocked to insensibility in their cradles, to be farmed out to neglectful wet nurses who might feed them "pap" — a protein- and vitamin-deficient mixture of flour, water, and sugar that deprived children of the natural immunities they might have received from human milk. One historian, Edward Shorter, goes so far as to say that medieval mothers' indifference to their children led to the babies' high death rate — not the other way around. Why did mothers behave this way? Shorter speculates that material circumstances may have been the cause. But the relentlessly gloomy deMause, in *The History of Childhood,* suggests that medieval parents' monstrous behavior toward their offspring was the sorry result of their own horrific childhood. Themselves victims of narcissistic parents, they became, inevitably, as awful as those who bore them. While in antiquity, according to deMause, parents freely killed unwanted babies, by the Middle Ages they resorted to less direct means of ridding themselves of offspring. Having converted to Christianity, parents were morally obliged now *not* to murder their children. Instead, they abandoned their children to wet nurses, to the monastery or nunnery, to foster families, to the homes of other nobles as servants or hostages, or subjected them to severe emotional deprivation at home. Child life could be an abusive nightmare.[12]

Few other historians are this extravagantly morbid about family relations in the Middle Ages. But they would concur that if, like Mark Twain's Connecticut Yankee, we went adrift in time and washed up centuries earlier, we would encounter social arrangements so different from our own as to constitute a foreign civilization. Were we to wander into a town dweller's house in England in the fourteenth century, for example, we would be struck by the crush of people residing in one undifferentiated space. In addition to the immediate family, which was often large, it contained employees, servants, apprentices, friends, and protégés. Households of up to twenty-five were not uncommon. In the absence of restaurants, bars, and hotels, the home served as the place for entertaining and transacting business as well as residence. The medieval home was sparsely furnished; the few furnishings were multipurpose and movable. A few tables on trestles, benches, and chests doubling as beds were pushed around the perimeter of the room to accommodate the hubbub of people who cooked, ate, played, worked, and slept in a single chamber. People did not so much live in a house as camp in it. Even sleeping was a communal business. Not only were there usually many beds in a room; there were usually many people in each bed. This explains the size of medieval beds; ten feet square was normal. We can only assume that the tiny one-room hovels of the poor (who made up the vast majority of the population) were even less private. How did people achieve intimacy under such conditions? It appears they did not.[13]

This was life in a fishbowl. The medieval family was embedded in the community. Authority was vested in the village, not the conjugal unit; therefore life took place in the entire community, not at the household level.[14] Boundaries — one's sense of personal or family space — were obviously very different then, probably much more porous. There were no separate spheres of work and home. Family members were fellow laborers. Production of food took place in the same rooms where children grew up, where babies were born, and where couples came together. Before industrialization, the word *housework* would probably have been nonsensical, since almost all people, regardless of gender, worked in or on the grounds of a house — if not their own, then someone else's. According to the *Oxford English Dictionary,* the word *housework* finally made it into recognized use in 1841.

The universe outside one's front door did not consist of strangers or near strangers, as it does today. Rather, most people lived among those they had known since childhood, whom they would expect to have dealings with for the rest of their lives. Collaboration was of the essence. Laundry was done in great communal tubs; crops were planted and harvested by villagers working together.

While such a familiar community may sound cozy and appealing to the many lonely, alienated men and women of the twentieth century, it actually entrapped people in a sticky, tangled social web. Ariès's followers suggest that there was no such thing as social anonymity. Medieval common folk were subjected to the tyranny of public scrutiny. Outsiders could enter the household freely and were entitled, even encouraged, to observe, meddle, and report. The flood of church denunciations for domestic transgressions instigated by "well-meaning" neighbors, for example, as well as noisy rituals in which wayward community members were paraded and shamed, attest to the ubiquity and acceptability of prying eyes. Even a wedding couple was accompanied to the bridal bed by neighbors who exposed the sheets the next day! There was nowhere for medieval folk to run, nowhere to hide. Given the family's vulnerability to outside influence, and the sheer number and variety of household members, it is no wonder that medieval family dynamics were vastly different from what they are now. The main ties were not "nuclear" (between husband and wife; and parents and children and designated pet), but were bound to the wider group (the village, community, distant kin, ancestors, future generations). One need not be a family therapist to imagine the variety of possible alliances and misalliances among such a confusing configuration of people. At the very least, affection must have been widely diffused.[15]

And there may not have been much of it.[16] Marriages were remote affairs, according to Ariès's disciples. Indeed, a "love match" is almost an invention of the late eighteenth century. Marriages were entirely a matter of property, units for production and reproduction, rather than for emotional satisfaction. Love was irrelevant and was discouraged lest it get in the way of dynastic arrangements. Sex was regarded as a sinful necessity, a duty, its enjoyment considered a temptation to mortal sin. Husbands were not to behave like romantic lovers. Wives could not refuse their husbands sex. Happiness was something to be anticipated in the next world, not this one.

While medieval marriages may not have been "happy," neither were they long (lasting only about twelve to seventeen years); they were frequently dissolved by the death of the husband or wife. Then another spouse was taken and often another family was introduced and yet another produced. Lawrence Stone has remarked, "Indeed, it looks very much as if modern divorce is little more than a functional substitute for death."[17]

Into this impersonal, precarious hybrid family came a long succession of children, or serial progeny. Almost half died, but many were replaced. Could a mother love her children in other than a mechanical manner, appearing as they did as if on an assembly line? Indeed, there was her own death to consider. Childbirth was often lethal for mother and child. Life was cheap. Besides, the absolute number of children who survived, when the average age of human populations was considerably younger than today, meant that the amount of time, energy, and resources that the relatively few adults had to devote to the large number of children was enormous, though each child received only a minuscule bit. And there were few grandparents to help, since adults tended to die young, not long after their own childbearing years. Given these conditions, it is not surprising that the response to children was tepid. If they survived, they did not stay long with their parents. They were handed over to wet nurses and later to other households as servants or apprentices. As infants they might be left alone for hours on end while caretakers worked, which meant that accidents were common. When they died, they were not much grieved. Parents seldom attended their child's funeral, for example, and, at death, even the children of the rich were treated as paupers, their bodies "sewn into shrouds made of cheap sacking and thrown into big, common graves."[18]

As bleak as this sounds, the story concludes happily — that is, if you accept the version of Ariès's followers, who see emotional relations between parents and children as undergoing a long trek toward the sentimental. But even among that group there is no consensus as to *why* this trend developed. DeMause, for one, feels that, as in psychoanalysis, successive generations of parents "regressed" to the psychic age of their children and so, over the centuries, came to understand and sympathize with their children better and to treat them more kindly and thoughtfully. Others attribute the progress in parent-child relationships to the rise of capitalism or the emergence of a general spirit of benevolence. Whatever the cause for progress, most agree that the eighteenth century (or thereabouts) was the beginning of a veritable tenderness revolution.

The nuclear family became more closed-off, bounded, defined. Domesticity, that mesh of privacy and intimacy encircling the family as a whole, flourished while members' ties with the outside world of aunts, uncles, peers, and associates weakened. The family unit became more of a shelter against the outside: "us" versus "them." Middle-class domestic architecture has long since reflected this tradition. There were now more rooms devoted to specialized uses, additional floors and hallways and corridors; in short, private space. Privacy facilitates intimacy, bonding, family identity, not to mention new possibilities for erotic expression without public display of the "primal scene" (undoubtedly much to the relief of the later Freudian community). The historian Randolph Trumbach found evidence of permissive, even "Spockian," child-rearing practices in the eighteenth century, and Allan MacFarlane, who has traced modern English family patterns back to 1300, found a general shift toward a more passionate and erotic form of marital love, which he called "instituted irrationality."[19] In this newly invented conjugal state, private emotions, not public functions, came to predominate. Marital partners were now companions, according to Lawrence Stone. Henceforth, the ideal marriage would require the locking-together of souls. Wedded bliss

... ently achieved in reality. ... earlier, but in the eight- ... he model to emulate. In ... l objects of the coddling ... ight assume babies have

... ed to Ariès and his fol- ... academics rely heavily ... gisters and tax lists from ... rts, wills and legal stat- ... al documents, and bio- ... re far more conservative ... the nuclear family has always been the norm and that the indifferent mother exists only in the cynical imagination of Ariès and his coterie. Far from being a modern creation, the family of father, mother, and children, united by bonds of affection, as well as by common interest, is probably a natural phenomenon, or, at the very least, an inescapable convention. It has sometimes been abused and disfigured by economic scarcity and by enemies, but it has invariably reasserted itself.

Their response to Ariès — swift, sharp, and vehement — suggests that the absence of so basic an emotion as mother love was an offense too painful to endure. Peter Laslett and this school — John Hajnal, David Herlihy, Barbara Hanawalt, Linda Pollock, and others — feel that Ariès's disciples interpreted paintings altogether too literally. Depicting children as miniature adults may have been merely a convention or a flaw in technique. Besides, there are certainly examples of realistic representations of babies in the Middle Ages.[21] More than a quarter of the illustrations in the Utrecht Psalter, an illuminated manuscript of the ninth century, for example, depict children as children.[22]

Further, they argue that the Ariès school mistakenly gives medieval parental behavior an overly negative "spin." Swaddling may have been a safety precaution, not a form of repressive confinement. Wet-nursing outside the home may have been a harmless convention, not rejection of the child. And a good flogging now and then may have been considered necessary and beneficial. Besides, medieval adults in servile positions were often beaten too. These were violent times. Also, Ariès's followers ignored or distorted evidence of positive treatment of children. In the eleventh century, for example, Saint Anselm was celebrated for his sensitivity and compassion toward the young. He declared that he always tried to behave to others with the same gentleness and understanding that his mother had shown him when he was a child.[23] Should the reader doubt the veracity of a long-dead saint whose goal was more likely moral propagandizing rather than self-revelation, the school points to further evidence found in the fourteenth-century statements of French peasants from the village of Montaillou. These sad and sometimes desperate stories were inadvertently recorded by Jacques Fournier, the Bishop of Pamiers, who was busy gathering data for the Inquisition. In Fournier's record, the grief of mothers forced to abandon or bury their babies is achingly evident. There is a description of a weeping and wailing mother tearing her hair out and beating her breast and head; a mother fleeing to the forest after the death of her infant; a bereft mother refusing to hand over the corpse of her little son for burial; a father paralyzed with grief.[24] If that is not parental love, what is?

Finally, there is a continuing debate about actual household size. Peter Laslett's followers claim there has been a nuclear family in Europe since time immemorial — not a huge, amorphous household, but a simple family of five or six living in its own house. So, presumably, there was opportunity for privacy, for sentiment expressed by family members, and for mother love. However, these historians, with very few exceptions,[25] survey households from the sixteenth century on, at least fifty years *after* the Middle Ages, usually much later, to generalize backward about earlier times. And they tend to take snapshots of families; that is, they look at families at one point in time instead of observing them over their life cycle. The resulting picture of family size is distorted. Ultimately each group of historians — both the "theory-driven" (Ariès's disciples) and the "data-driven" (Laslett and his) — has manipulated evidence to some extent to further its own ideas — or hopes — about mother love.

Even Ariès acknowledged in 1980, shortly before his death, that had he looked more carefully at medieval sources, he might have modified his conclusions about the lack of parental sentiment in that period.[26] Yet any claims by data-driven historians for the presence of exclusive, private, affectionate nuclear families during the medieval period would be presumptuous, given the flaws in their methodology. The history is still being excavated, and the jury is out regarding mother love in the Middle Ages.

Medieval Mixed Messages

If medieval mothers were like Mary, we would have to ask — which Mary? The Virgin underwent numerous personality changes, as we shall see. And to complicate matters further, the Virgin Mary is only the most famous of a cast of maternal characters populating the medieval imagination, all of them possibilities for imitation. There is the wicked temptress Eve, the Virgin's moral opposite. Or Héloïse, the world-famous lover of Abélard, who forsook not only him but their son to join a nunnery. Or Patient Griselda, the apotheosis of male chauvinist wish-fulfillment, whose pathetic story of servitude to her husband (which included child sacrifice) was set down by no less than three of the "greats" of the period — Chaucer, Boccaccio, and Petrarch. Or Grendel's hellish mother, the only active female in *Beowulf,* the earliest extant epic in English, a horrible monster to all except her son, to whom she was devoted. Each maternal figure conveys vastly different priorities regarding her offspring. Indeed, the dispositions of the characters are so contradictory that they practically cancel each other out.

But medieval men and women displayed an inordinate capacity for tolerating all sorts of contradictions. Knights talked of honor but turned brigand. Clerics and nuns preached asceticism but practiced debauchery. Filthy, starving peasants in squalid hovels lived alongside prosperous peasants who ate pork, fowl, and game, slept in featherbeds, and enjoyed frequent baths in village bathhouses. After a morning of solemn devotion in a cathedral, a medieval scholar might attend a gaudy public execution in which punishments of obscene cruelty were carried out according to the most pedantic etiquette. A cathedral itself could be a combination of medieval sanctum sanctorum and bestiary. So motley was medieval life that it was said to have "the mixed smell of blood and roses." The Madonna is hardly the whole story.[27]

Perhaps a more accurate emblem for medieval motherhood than any of the aforementioned figures is one that, oddly, does not impersonate a female at all, but better conveys the complexities, ambiguities, hypocrisies, and ideological clashes of parenting in that period — the foundling hospital. Established in the eighth century in Italy, these institutions spread there and northward from the fourteenth to the sixteenth centuries. If you count oblation (the offering of children for service to a monastery) and believe the recent scholarship of the Yale historian John Boswell, then the abandonment of children was routine right through the Middle Ages and beyond. The problem of foundlings grew to such an extent that by 1450 most large cities of Europe were forced to establish hospices, lest people encounter unwanted children in the streets. (One cannot help being reminded of the use of mental institutions today.) No doubt foundling hospitals reflected a humane, even desperate, effort to keep abandoned babies alive — the Christian solution to the ancient problem of exposure — but they also suggest that there was no dearth of abandoned babies. Surely there would have been no need of a solution had there been no problem. The existence of the institutions reflects profoundly contradictory attitudes toward parenting in the Middle Ages: the impulse to abandon and the impulse to rescue. To complicate the issue, it turned out that over time the conditions within these hospitals degenerated to so deplorable a degree that a majority of the children died shortly after admission. What was intended as an instrument of mercy turned out to be an instrument of death. The contradictions are epitomized in a most curious architectural feature of foundling hospitals, the "tour," a box in which an unwanted baby could be placed outside the hospital; when turned 180 degrees, it deposited the child inside, allowing whoever had abandoned the infant to depart unseen. Such a contrivance suggests that the act of abandonment was considered shameful (why else the anonymity?), yet it provided a mechanism for carrying out the deed. How are we to understand this?[28]

Of course, no age is tidy and seamless, and though none has a more checkered fabric than the Middle Ages, a few patterns have been discerned by modern scholars. The period was a rather benign one for sexual politics. Both the medieval lady in the tower and her counterpart, the poor wench, may have been more "liberated" than their sequestered ancestors in the Greek *oikos* or their descendants in the Renaissance palace. Men did not usually relegate their wives to positions of household drudges and seek pleasure from prostitutes to the extent they had earlier, nor did they cast women into the role of ornamental object or witch as they did later. This was not because medieval man was politically correct. Equality of function — if not status — was thrust upon women by circumstance, not liberal ideology. Noblemen were often away fighting crusades, so women ran the manor. The advent of Christianity afforded women an alternative to their often lethal biological destiny of motherhood; in the convent, females had access to education and positions of considerable responsibility.

Of course, the majority of people in the Middle Ages lived in neither the manor nor the convent but on farms. There, in the field, mothers toiled alongside their husbands and children. Toiling is a great equalizer. The situation would change later on, but at this time the feelings toward mothers warmed a few degrees. While the early medieval period did not give mother a precise persona, it at least restored to her a presence she had been denied in antiquity, where, you may recall, she was portrayed as a devouring monster — if she was portrayed at all. As feelings toward mothers softened, so did feelings toward children. Babies were hardly coddled, but they were not wantonly murdered. Infanticide and abandonment occurred, as noted, but were performed more out of desperation, and with remorse, than with indifference. (This all changed by the late Middle Ages.) Once again, the esteem for children seems to have been related to esteem for mothers. But the esteem for both is not without crosscurrents.

Devil or Angel: Images of the Child

Christianity raised the status of babies. Jesus Christ, after all, arrived on earth as an infant, which no doubt lent prestige to that age group. But Christianity also lowered the status of babies, transforming the heretofore inconsequential reputation of children into something inherently tainted. During this thousand-year period, children were perceived as holy innocents or as depraved containers of Original Sin. But despite the mixed messages, Christianity at least paid attention to children. For the first time in history the moral status of children was important.[29]

With the Christ Child as the model, how could children be anything but innocent? And, at first, that was the prevailing view. Scripture said that one must become as a child to enter the Kingdom of Heaven. To be childlike was to be Christlike. Such metaphors are implicitly flattering to children, sublimely complimentary (literally!). Of course, the childlike behavior to which the Bible refers would presumably not include temper tantrums and diaper rash, but, rather, innocence, the capacity to be amazed by wondrous things, a freedom that gravitated toward truths presumably hidden from cynical adults. Also, it was thought then that children did not yet know "evil" (that is, sexual desire or the threat of death) and so were blessedly naïve. The use of "child" as a metaphor of high praise is abundantly sprinkled throughout the Bible: the way of the child is the Way; Christ with His sacrifice purchased paradise for His followers, who were called Children of God; and so forth. That the Slaughter of the Innocents is one of the most repeated motifs in medieval art also betrays an unmistakable horror of violence visited on the young, contradicting Ariès's idea of maternal indifference during this period. This Slaughter refers to a hideous incident in Bethlehem, when all the children were killed by King Herod in his desperate attempt to destroy the Infant Christ. The depictions of this event, like the one on the frieze that threads across Chartres Cathedral, invariably portray parents in anguish over the death of their offspring. A final example of New Testament affection for children: once, apparently on the Day of Atonement (Yom Kippur), the Disciples, probably with the best of intentions, sought to protect Jesus from their clamor. His response was, "Suffer little children, and forbid them not to come unto me: for of such is the kingdom of heaven." In other words, don't bar youngsters from my midst; they are my most divine followers.[30]

Until this point in history, children were only potentially human. Childhood and children's needs raised few questions to the men and women of antiquity. They evoked only the slimmest stream of associations. The child may have contained the possibility of perfection, according to Plato, but until the possibility bore actual fruit, the child remained subrational and therefore less than interesting. This attitude was undoubtedly convenient when it came to disposing of unwanted infants. In striking contrast, Christianity, like Judaism before it, respected the child. Christianity unequivocally condemned infanticide and the exposure of infants (not wholly effectively, as we have seen).

But even though Christ gave privilege to the child, as He did women, outcasts, and other unfortunates (a radical gesture at that time), His interpreters supported a much harsher appraisal of youth. Saint Augustine, for example, argued that children were conceived and born with Original Sin. In other words, babies enter the world bearing the stain of Adam's initial rebellion against God, along with irrepressible carnal lust and an inevitable propensity for evil. Here we see a tendency to regard sin as a kind of material pollution that is inheritable. The argument to Augustine was propounded by Pelagius, who felt that children start life with a clean record and are responsible only for such sins as they themselves commit. When the lines of battle were drawn between Augustine and Pelagius, the early church favored Augustine. This meant that all infants were inherently depraved and therefore had to undergo baptism to wash away their inborn evil. In actuality, the practice of baptism had been carried out for four hundred years but had been more of an initiation rite into a new faith. Now, according to the revamped dogmas, an unbaptized child, upon death, was consigned to the flames of Hell. Such was the unpleasant but inevitable conclusion of the stated premises of Augustine.

To a modern mentality, this doctrine may be viewed as an extreme example of "blaming the victim" — compounding the misfortune of an early death with eternal damnation. Even the early church was uncomfortable with its thinly disguised hostility toward children. Theologians immediately began searching for arguments to show that though unbaptized children might go to Hell, they would not suffer, and what the thinkers came up with was the sentimental concept of Limbo, a kind of void where there was no torture.[31] In the end, the church wobbled, but it did make the child a centerpiece of Christian doctrine. So where children had been previously neglected in Western civilization, they were suddenly of great moment.

Seen in a modern light, Augustine's observations on the nature of children are highly evocative of Freud's theory of infantile sexuality. After all, Augustine was getting at something deep and original in his soul-searching autobiography: that children are motivated by processes as "perverse" as those which motivate adults and that adult traits can be traced back to one's earliest years. He certainly did not mean that children are worse than adults. No earlier writer had taken children so seriously.[32] Augustine's doctrine also laid the foundation for the child as a literary and artistic image. Henceforth, the child figure was associated with sin or innocence. In the Middle Ages, it was innocence, a heavy burden, as it turns out.

The chief role of the child in medieval literature was to suffer. Children in every literary form — ballads, romance, folklore, verse narrative, even biographies of saints — faced mutilation, drowning, smothering, and especially abandonment, perhaps in a forest on the orders of some prophecy-fearing king or mad husband testing his wife's endurance.[33] In the stock romance (the precursor of the fairy tale), the typical task of the youthful hero, who has been invariably spirited away from his high-born but true biological parents, is to return and claim his heritage. In the course of so doing, he undergoes severe hardships but displays his noble lineage by distinguishing himself in feats of great physical prowess or savvy or both. He passes years of adversity, fights dragons and other mythological beasts in enchanted forests, and eventually returns to his place of origin to marry a princess (just like dear old dad). Such was the fate of Sir Degare, Octavian, and many others, including Sir Percival, one of the Knights of the Round Table of Arthurian legend.

The abandoned child hero of the romance does not perish, of course, for that would be the end of the romance, the purpose of which was to be marvelous. Having taken the listener or reader on a trip into an extraordinary world, at its end the tale returns the hero (and, by extension, the listener-reader) safely back home. The hero (always male, by the way) conquers adversity and finds his identity. No wonder romance was hugely popular. It was pure escape. The medieval romance revealed little about actual childhood beyond the universal quest for identity. The hero, though young, was not really childlike.

While the romance usually preserved the life of the child hero, other medieval genres were far less fastidious. One popular fourteenth-century English alliterative poem tells of "Mary, a mild wife," who cooks and devours her own son during the Roman siege of Jerusalem. This particular story must be deeply embedded in the European consciousness, for it has appeared again and again over the centuries with little variation.[34] Similarly, children undergo barbaric ordeals in the many stories about miracles performed by the Virgin which had become highly popular in the eleventh century. Admittedly, each child was ultimately rescued, but in the meantime he may have had his tongue cut out, swallowed glass, or drowned, for the sole purpose of being spared by the Virgin's merciful intervention.[35] Here and elsewhere, the child is a figure of pathos, used to demonstrate someone else's wondrousness (in this case, the Virgin's) or evil. Heroes need victims in order to define themselves.

In six of Chaucer's *The Canterbury Tales,* the only ones in which children are given any substantial treatment, they suffer extreme violence. They are never developed as characters, but are always innocent pawns caught up in the misfortunes of their parents.[36] Patient Griselda in "The Clerk's Tale," for example, readily surrenders each of her children to be killed, merely because her husband asks it of her. This turns out to be only a test of her devotion to him, but at the end, she willingly reunites herself with the odious author of her trials! The apparent function of the children's potential suffering in the story would be to demonstrate the slavish loyalty of their mother to their father at their expense. Whether Chaucer meant Griselda's "patience" to be a virtue is hotly debated in feminist and literary circles. But the fact remains that the children were readily sacrificed.

The frequent use of child figures as victims of violence seems to presuppose a sympathy toward children. Medieval children served to elicit pity and compassion because they were able to arouse pity and compassion. Children were tortured in fiction precisely because medieval people cared about them in reality. But the very frequency with which children were tortured in stories, the excruciating detail in which the suffering is sometimes described, and the fact that there is no alternative literature featuring careful parenting all suggest some aspect of social reality, either as mirror or smoke screen. It is doubtful that child abuse and abandonment were merely literary devices invented purely for storytelling. Surely the maltreatment of children was not fabricated out of whole cloth.

The presence of the abuse of children in imaginary literature is so ordinary, so ubiquitous, so unchallenged that it must reflect if not literal truth, some psychic truth; that is, children's power to evoke warm, sentimental, and sympathetic feelings in people of the Middle Ages. Yet it also suggests an unconscious hostile wish. The quantity of aggressive content in medieval literature betrays its author in the same oblique way that the quantity of pornography perused by a censor betrays his or her prurient interest. Like the theology of the period, medieval literature is fickle about kids; medieval men and women probably loved *and* hated their children.

Mother Superior, Mother Inferior: Maternal Images

This fickleness was magnified to almost mythic proportions in medieval attitudes toward mothers: one moment they are idealized in images of the Holy Mother; the next moment they are denied access to sainthood precisely because they gave birth. Sainthood was reserved for the celibate until the thirteenth century.[37] Much of the confusion stems from Christian attitudes toward sex.

In the early Middle Ages, Christians prohibited intercourse on Sundays, Wednesdays, Fridays, Ember days, during Lent and Advent, and before Communion. Sex was also forbidden when a woman was menstruating, pregnant, and recently postpartum, as she was "unclean" (we can see Jewish influence here). On the occasional free Tuesday, married couples had to observe the regulations governing the appropriate position: "missionary" was in; "after the dogs' fashion" out.[38] Since the process for begetting children was so ignominious, it is no wonder that parenthood was damned with faint praise by the early church fathers.

Jesus preferred celibacy for Himself. He declared that there would be no marriage in heaven. The Apostles were even more emphatic in their deprecation of marriage. "But if they cannot contain," said Saint Paul, "let them marry: for it is better to marry than to burn." Marriage is merely the lesser of two evils, a preferable alternative to burning (presumably with unsatisfied lust, or in the fires of Hell for fornication). In other words, marriage was to be tolerated only because it provided some sort of regulation of sexuality, but it was a concession. Married people ought to blush at the state in which they live, according to Paul. The message was clear: matrimony is morally inferior to celibacy.

Ironically, then, marriage in the early Middle Ages was viewed as having a subversive quality because it was tainted by sexuality. It was the only sanctioned arrangement in which sexual intercourse could occur, but its occurrence, ironically, polluted any virtue in the arrangement. These prudish ideas long predated the Christians. Certain groups of late Greek philosophers like the Stoics and Neo-Platonists preached self-denial and austerity as an antidote to Roman excess, the violent games and conspicuous consumption, for example. To these Greeks, the passions were suspect. Sexuality was pitted against reason, with reason being accorded the higher status. So the Christians did not invent sexual repression; they merely amplified these attacks on the pagan lifestyle (as had the Jews, by the way). The vigor of their protest against sensual pursuits was probably fueled by their wish to differentiate themselves from these idol-worshiping libertines, and to define a "superior" morality. But they overshot their mark (assuring psychotherapists of the future a healthy practice). In attempting to end debauchery, the early Christians ultimately objected to almost every manifestation of sexuality, from abortion, divorce, adultery, masturbation, titillating thoughts, to *coitus interruptus*. In the early medieval period, this resulted in outright revulsion toward the body, especially the female body.

Closely infused with this condemnation of sexuality was a fear of women's seductive influence, which was construed as a possible peril to men's souls. Paul recast the story of the Fall, placing major guilt on Eve (merging her with the Greek Pandora) and exonerating Adam. Eve's act of disobedience became evidence of women's inherent weakness and evil and the principal justification for her eternal subordination to her "natural" superior, the more spiritual, rational, and cleaner male. Paul established a precedent for misogyny in the church that has persisted. His zealous reinterpretation has led some feminists to say that Eve did not fall; she was pushed.[39]

In the thirteenth century, Saint Thomas Aquinas, as was the fashion among intellectuals, revived some of the "scientific" views of Aristotle, namely, that fathers should be loved more than mothers, since they supplied the *active* element in conception. Unfortunately, Thomas Aquinas's thinking was later used to pave the way for one of the most frightening battles in the war of the sexes: the sixteenth-century witch hunts.[40] But in all fairness to the church, it also provided a goodly dose of idealization, down-to-earth respect, and opportunity for women. The story of Christianity and gender grows more inseparable and convoluted.

By the time of the early church fathers, the Christian aversion to sex and the subjection of women had hardened into universally accepted dogma. All women were temptresses like Eve. Their bodies were nothing more than vessels of filth. Salvation required the extinguishing of sexual passion. Naturally, all this ran counter to human nature. And eventually the church was forced to make concessions to the flesh. Marriage began to be absorbed into official Christian ritual, but it was sanctified only for the purpose of procreation. Sexual intercourse undertaken for pleasure — even with one's spouse — was declared a venial sin. Saint Jerome specifically warned men against loving their wives too ardently. Interestingly, the original reason that Christianity condemned birth control was not out of sympathy for the fetal life (about which it did not yet have a clear concept), but that the use of contraception would imply that the couple had engaged in sex merely to enjoy it (God forbid!), rather than to reproduce. Motherhood was, in effect, the payment extracted for carnal indulgence.[41]

All this did not bode well for the status of family life. In elevating asceticism over marriage, the early Christian hierarchy not so subtly rejected domesticity. The claims of kin were seen to compete with the claims of God. The entangling world of secular ambitions and family squabbles was just too distracting. The medieval church placed no absolute value on close and emotional family attachments. After all, Jesus' relations with His own mother are obscure. In the Synoptic Gospels, she does not even attend His death and resurrection, though other female disciples loyally do so. The early Christians, both men and women, specifically had to surrender family ties to follow Christ, not strengthen them.[42]

Not surprisingly, the baby was thrown out with the bath water of sexuality. Jerome saw nothing in the least attractive about motherhood; to him, pregnancy was "the tumefaction of the uterus," and pregnant women were a "revolting sight," and he could not imagine why anyone would want progeny, "a brat . . . to crawl upon his breast and soil his neck with nastiness." The intent of the early ban on birth control most assuredly was not to produce more children! While the First Commandment to Adam and Eve was "Be fruitful and multiply," the early Christians, who were convinced that the end of the world was at hand (at midnight, December 31, 999, to be exact), were indifferent to the issue of producing heirs. Both Tertullian and Ambrose believed that the end of the human species was not too great a cost for extirpating human sexuality. This, by the way, was in marked contrast to the first-century Jews, who, as we have seen, regarded children as a blessing, and barrenness a divine curse. There was no interest among them in virginity or celibacy as a permanent status. To the Christians, however, spiritual descendants were more important than biological descendants. They regarded the world as already filled up with people. Augustine, like other church fathers, was not desirous of large families for Christians. He hoped that if they had to marry, they would have no more than one or two children, and then mutually agree to live a life of continence.[43]

In sum, biological motherhood was second-best. It was deemed better to renounce physical maternity.[44] But the plot thickens.

Much as early Christians devalued actual motherhood, they appropriated the imagery of motherhood and applied it to a spiritual relationship. Motherhood became the model for the monastery. Among the nuns, the abbess was called "Mother." This was also true for female saints, who, in turn, called their followers "children." I suppose these designations implied tenderness and a special awe (which says something about the medieval concept of motherhood). In the writings of the church fathers, the Christian church is also seen as a mother who bears children (that is, new worshipers). The waters of baptism are seen as a womb of rebirth, fertilized by the power of Jesus. Carrying this analogy further, a number of medieval writers from the twelfth to fourteenth centuries, especially Cistercian monks, used explicit and elaborate maternal imagery to describe Christ Himself. So motherhood was not all bad. But what was valued in the early medieval period was spiritual motherhood, not the real thing. Biological mom was "Mother Inferior," compared with her celibate counterpart.[45]

Yet, let us keep in mind that, unlike other male monotheisms, Christianity claims for itself a central sacred female who is a mother — Hail Mary, Mother of God! There is no more maternal figure. Surely a woman with her immaculate credentials could rehabilitate the Greco-Roman goddesses, who would just as soon murder their children as nurture them. Ever since the Virgin's womb was touched by eternity two thousand years ago, she has become one of the most potent imaginary constructs of Western civilization. Every age, including our own, has cried out for her. The demand for her milky sweet portraits was an obsession of the late Middle Ages. Since then, among all the women who have ever lived, the mother of Jesus Christ is the most celebrated, the most venerated, the most portrayed, and the most honored in the naming of girl babies and churches. Even today, she causes unease in Vatican circles because her recent worldwide populist revival presents competition for worship over her Son.[46] Indeed, claimed sightings of her far exceed sightings of Him. How can a woman with such cosmic appeal fail to enhance the prestige of motherhood?

Unfortunately, those cloistered celibate males doing most of the writing in the twelfth and thirteenth centuries emphasized the *contrast* between heavenly Mary and the biological version of mom. The Virgin was presented as an alternative to one's actual mother.[47] Those men did not exhort mothers to emulate Mary in relation to their own children. That would have been a trivial concern, compared with saving women's souls. Instead, they exhorted females to be celibate. For most of the Middle Ages, Mary's virginity was celebrated over her child-rearing capacity. As we have seen, medieval woman was accorded more points for "spiritual" motherhood (remaining a virgin, joining a convent, and nurturing Christians) than physical motherhood.[48] It was almost as if the fact that terrestrial mothers and the Virgin Mary had the same reproductive equipment was inconsequential. A human mother's defloration precluded her comparison with the Virgin. To be like the Madonna, one must have an intact hymen, not a baby.

Though the Virgin Mary's biography may not reveal much about real mothering in the Middle Ages, her story does illuminate something about the nature of people's fantasies of mother. She was a protean symbol who changed shape to meet the requirements of her devotees. In a sense, except for her questionable early stay on earth as a human being, Mary did not have much of an existence to call her own. She depended for her existential reality on the early Christian spin doctors. If we examine the change in her shape over time, we can learn much about those Christian spinners, about what they wished for in a mother then. And about what people wish for in a mother now, for the Christian imagination, which included a near monopoly of Western cultural expression in the Middle Ages, forms the basis of our own. Besides, I suspect that yearnings for mother have not changed very much.

Mary is mentioned in only about a dozen brief passages in the New Testament, sometimes not by name, and not always flatteringly. This was an inauspicious beginning, to say the least, but it provided a lot of room for invention. Here we have practically a blank screen, a perfect canvas for our projections. As veneration of Mary grew, the original references to her were found to be woefully inadequate, and the lack gave rise to a collection of glorious stories — the Apocrypha — which conveniently filled in the blanks, especially around her birth and death. In them, the humble, obedient maid of Nazareth who silently pondered her Son's mission became a heavenly queen with the power to influence and even control human destiny in this world and the next. Gradually, she began to take over some of the characteristics of her Son.[49] Interest in Mary has always originated among the simple, devout people, the rank and file, the vulgar masses, so to speak, and has been resisted by the church hierarchy. But bit by bit, the church grudgingly absorbed into itself and metabolized many of the legends about her, all the while emphatically denying her status as a co-equal of Jesus. The Protestants, of course, never exalted her at all.

Mary was not much thought about until the latter part of the fifth century. Perhaps the persistence of pagan goddess worship during that period satisfied any grassroots hunger for female divine imagery. Mary certainly fits neatly into the protective and sustaining aspect of the role of ancient Near Eastern fertility goddesses. Her devotees may also have borrowed trappings from Classical goddesses in which to clothe her. In Ephesus, for example, fervor for Artemis-Diana smoothly gave way to equally deep devotion to Mary.[50] In the sixth century, the church set up the Feast of the Assumption of the Virgin on August 15, the very same time as the old festival celebrating Artemis. It is interesting to note that the demise of the goddess temples coincided with the rise of the cult of the Virgin.

Coincidence or not, for about four hundred years the church fathers never considered her a significant image in her own right. In Christian art of that period, Mary was invariably placed in a position lower than Jesus, even lower than the Magi, who were encircled by haloes, while she wore none. (She finally got one in the sixth century.) The fathers did make a point, however, of casting her in the role of "the Second Eve," to be distinguished from the first, fallen Eve. This splitting of mother into good and bad feels very familiar (recall Neumann's analyses of the Neolithic goddesses) and continues to resonate today: the lovely stay-at-home mom in the 1987 film *Fatal Attraction* versus the "pregnant" homicidal career woman. Mary and Eve, in sum: "pure" and "impure." The common woman was uncompromisingly associated with the latter — or with her counterparts Mary Magdalene and Mary the Harlot, all fallen women.

And then there was the brouhaha over the Virgin's hymen. The Gospels clearly state that Mary was a virgin and that Jesus was conceived miraculously without a human father. But what about after He was born? Did delivery rupture her hymen? About this, as about most things pertaining to Mary, the Gospels are silent. Did Mary *never* have sex with Joseph? Are the brothers of Jesus mentioned in the Bible merely stepbrothers, sons of Joseph by a previous marriage? The problem is that if Mary ever engaged in intercourse, then she would be no better than Eve, a "cauldron containing the hell of lustfulness," to paraphrase Augustine. How could such a vessel of filth produce the Lord, even if it became defiled technically after the birth? The solution to this embarrassment was found after protracted doctrinal councils.[51] The Blessed Virgin Mary, it was decreed, was a perpetual virgin. This decision came just in time. Devotion to Mary was growing, and it was important that she be a suitable object of reverence.

What brilliant public relations! Unwittingly, the early dignitaries of the church had created an image ingeniously tuned in to unconscious human longings. Here is a mother figure whom a son could strongly desire without fear of retaliation from dad. The Virgin is so dissociated from sex, her nature so pure, her hymen so impenetrable that she is virtually unseducible. She presents no threat of impropriety. She appeals to daughters, too. In identifying with her, women may derive vicarious fulfillment of their desire for sexual association and impregnation by a powerful father.[52] Yet they too remain untainted, free of guilt. These unconscious Oedipal longings for the parent of the opposite sex are presumably operative in us all to some extent after babyhood. It is what makes the world go around, according to Freud. But perhaps the so-called Oedipal gratification is really secondary to Mary's more basic appeal as perfect nurturer. She stands for maternity itself. Her unsurpassed position as a needs-satisfying object may in itself explain her widespread appeal, and it provides even more enticing grist for the mills of the current revisionist psychoanalysts than do her Oedipal associations.

But should anyone really doubt that there is an erotic component to her appeal, they need only examine portraits of Mary from the late Middle Ages. While not exactly pornographic, they do convey a certain seductiveness. She is ravishingly beautiful, young, delicate, and, since the fourteenth century, often partly unclad. Though her *déshabille* is not obviously licentious, she reveals her breast to nurse the Child, creating a tension in the viewer between erotic attraction and religious meaning. Christians up to this time made a point of clothing figures in art. The Child, by the way, is also partly nude now, His masculinity prominently displayed (even if the genitals are sometimes lightly veiled) in various positions of intimacy with His lovely young mother. Mary had begun to resemble an idealized version of the sexually appealing lady of the courts. She is now officially the Bride of Christ, as well as His Mother, an incestuous combination of roles from my perspective, but one that did not particularly bother church dignitaries. Divine privilege, I suppose. Churchmen rhapsodized over what it must have been like to become impregnated by the

Holy Ghost. To Saint Bernard, the Virgin conjured up imagery that a post-Freudian reader might rate X. She was "the bush, the arc, the star . . . the nuptial chamber, the door, the garden . . . etc.," all voluptuous, passionate allusions that would seem more appropriate to a sexual object than a sexual neuter.[53]

One does not have to be a psychologist to realize that this bursting through of sexual imagery in the writing of fanatically prudish ascetics was almost inevitable. It may not be totally possible to repress erotic instincts without those feelings appearing in one form or another. Freud called this the "return of the repressed." The beautiful Virgin of Heaven was a perfect vehicle for the safe direction of those feelings. At the same time, such devotion could allow, and perhaps even reinforce, an aversion to real women, who were thought defiled by sex and procreation.[54] And, in fact, this splitting of affect for women was characteristic of the era.

More and more the language used by the clergy in their worship of Mary merged with the language of the lover to such an extent that the art historian Kenneth Clark commented that one hardly knows if a medieval love lyric is addressed to the poet's mistress or to the Virgin Mary. The greatest of all writings about ideal love, Dante's *Vita Nuova,* is actually a quasi-religious work, and in the end it is Beatrice who introduces Dante to Paradise (which is a role switch with the Virgin).[55]

What was happening during this period was a fusion of the cult of the Virgin Mary with the worship of the beloved, *amour courtois,* courtly love, as it is popularly known, that highly conventionalized code of conduct that was expected of medieval nobles. Courtly love required a knight to lust in his heart for a highborn lady, to whom he was utterly subject. No sacrifice was too great for her. A whole lifetime might be properly spent in paying court to an exacting, unapproachable lady, who was, according to the rules, married to someone else. (A basic tenet of the code is the incompatibility of love and marriage.) This (supposedly) unconsummated love ennobled the knight and presumably inspired him to poetry. And it is this very poetry, sung in the feudal courts, that blended with sermons in praise of Mary.

How very strange that two conventions arising from such dissimilar impulses — one sacred and one profane — would merge.

Yet both the worship of Mary and courtly love involved the sublimation of erotic desire. Both put women on pedestals yet denied their sexuality. In neither was there a trace of love and respect for motherhood for its own sake. Neither woman seemed particularly encumbered by offspring. Feminists might object that both Mary and the lady of the court were focal points of men's aspirations,[56] prisoners of men's dreams, male inventions. Yet some of us, alas, may regret the passing of a time when the supreme object of love was an older woman.

For all this glorification of woman, there was the separate and equally powerful tradition of denigrating her. Women were gloriously extolled by the troubadours, the trouvères, and the minnesingers at the same time that they were contemptuously sneered at in popular antimarriage tracts and comically debased in bawdy fabliaux.[57] In fact, those fabliaux are the source of the familiar stock-comedy situation of shrew wife–henpecked husband, which has been regularly repeated in works as variable as Shakespeare, Dickens, "Rumpole of the Bailey," and *Popeye*. Sometimes women are exalted and deprecated in the very same work. *Le Roman de la Rose,* the thirteenth-century bible of love and a veritable best seller for two hundred years, begins in the conventional female-worshiping courtly manner, but concludes with mocking abuse of women and marriage, and praises carefree lechery at such vituperative and monotonous length that it is unreadable by today's standards. The voluminous second part, by Jean de Meung, was completed fifty years after the first, written by Guillaume de Lorris. Jean's work was not an isolated incident of savage misogyny but part of an established tradition with which the church felt highly comfortable. This fluctuating response to women — idolizing them and insulting them — while apparently contradictory, is in fact two sides of the same coin. It is a way of distancing oneself from females, and represents a failure to recognize women as all too human. The opposite of love is not hate but indifference. Medieval men loved and hated women, but were, most assuredly, not indifferent.

Let us return to the early Middle Ages. In A.D. 431, at the Council of Ephesus, Mary was declared to be not only mother of the human Jesus, but Mother of God. This new script for Mary combined with her prior image readjustment (the pronouncements of her perpetual virginity and her revised role as the "new and improved" Eve) boosted her popularity among the masses. Or perhaps it was the reverse: her popularity provoked a change in church doctrine. In any case, her celebrity took off. Gradually, over the next seven hundred years, she became the be-all and end-all. Great festivals came into being honoring the newly minted events of her life, including the Annunciation, the Visitation, Candlemas, the Assumption, and eventually the Immaculate Conception. (She, too, was deemed to have been conceived without sexual intercourse, thus freeing her from the taint of Original Sin, like her Son.) Men built soaring Gothic cathedrals to her, monuments of dazzling, unequaled magnificence, like Notre Dame of Paris, of Chartres, of Rheims, of Amiens, of Lyon, and of Senlis in France alone! They wrote hymns to her of unsurpassed beauty ("Ave Maria," the "Salve Regina," "Regina Coeli"), moving, exquisite hymns that are beloved even today. She progressively emerged as a miracle maker. From the eleventh century on, the collection of Mary stories grew by leaps and bounds. In her various appearances, she wept, lactated, spoke, led armies to victory, cured ailments. The church simply could not put a brake on this popular groundswell of Mary worship. She became so popular, in fact, that in the thirteenth century one author bluntly declared, "God changed sex."[58]

Nothing illustrates better the changing outlook toward Mary — and, by extension, mother — than the gradual humanizing metamorphosis of the Virgin-and-Child image in art. Keep in mind that to the largely illiterate people of the Middle Ages, religious paintings were almost the equivalent of television today. Accessible to everybody, seen on a daily basis, they conditioned attitudes. Their importance cannot be overestimated. One of the earliest cult figures of the Virgin and Child (a duo that became an utter fixation of artists) is a painted wooden statue in the Cathedral of Saint Denis that dates from 1130. It is prototypical: both figures are majestic, remote, and face forward solemnly. The Child sits on His mother's knee as if on a throne, holding up His right hand as a sign of benediction. The figures do not relate to each other. By the thirteenth century, Mary has acquired the accouterments of a Byzantine empress — luxurious robes, jewelry, a throne. Angels worship her. Still closer to the people than either Mary or the Child, however, are the saints.[59]

Humanization proceeds slowly. The Child's expression becomes more mobile. He chuckles, plays with a ball or apple, twists around to engage the viewer's eye (perhaps inviting us to participate?), and caresses His mom. It is an odd fact that for centuries artists were more likely to show the infant caressing His mom than the reverse. In general, Christ is now a large, well-fed baby boy, who in dozens of snuggly ways and postures reveals His close emotional bond with His mom. Gone are His symbols of wisdom and authority.[60]

Mary, too, begins to lose her aloofness and majesty. She has become like a human mother with a baby. Increasingly, the spotlight focuses on her. She appears alone in such scenes as the Annunciation and the Visitation. In fourteenth- and fifteenth-century Renaissance Italy, she is shown as a humble peasant woman, sometimes barefoot and seated on the floor or ground. Painted in a naturalistic style, these Madonnas of Humility could hardly be a more striking contrast with the depictions they replaced. The visual message of the new Madonnas suggests the Virgin's sweetness, sympathy, and emotional richness. There is a marked painterly emphasis on the Virgin's exposed breast, representing, perhaps, the furthest extension of her homey simplicity, earthly eroticism, and unpretentious accessibility.[61]

Mary has been transmuted by the late Middle Ages into the bearer of a vast weight of Renaissance emotional overload. She is recalled, from older images, as exalted, powerful, and queenly, a mother who could protect her children from harm. She is a paragon of virginity able to protect her children from their own impulses. She is young and beautiful, so as to gratify latent erotic wishes. She is modest and accessible, capable of responding to her children without intimidating them. Above all, she is lactating, supplying her children with endless quantities of mother's milk. In the Renaissance, as before, breast-feeding by one's mother was extolled in literary and didactic works (though the advice was rarely heeded: mothers of means continued to resort to wet nurses). The Virgin's milk, that white, gleaming, moist equivalent of astral light, became magical. In the numerous miracle stories of the

Virgin, which had become so popular in the eleventh century, her milk cured blindness, cancer, and other maladies.[62]

And in the late eleventh century in the West, the Virgin was permitted another bodily effluvium of psychological resonance: tears.[63] She weeps for the dead Christ. This is the oft-repeated, sorrowful image of the Pietà. Recall that in the Gospel accounts, Mary is not around for her Son's crucifixion (except in the Gospel of Saint John). But a powerful legend grew up in which she suffered as a witness to His execution and participated in His agony. Her pain was understood to be no less than His. The intensity of her anguish, and the tendency of devotees to identify with her, were most dramatically expressed in the "Stabat Mater," a thirteenth-century Latin masterpiece, set to music variously by Palestrina, Haydn, and Rossini. The cult of the Mater Dolorosa flowered in the fourteenth century.

What unmet need was filled by this weeping mother — who so powerfully evokes the Egyptian Goddess Isis and the dead Osiris? Why should mother suffer? Perhaps her agony gratified an unconscious wish for a mother who feels as we do, for a mother who hears our sorrow, who, above all, understands our pain. And tears are water, after all. Water washes. Perhaps she satisfies the hunger in us not only for empathy, but for cleansing, for purification.[64]

What we have, then, by the late fourteenth century, is a Mary fine-tuned to the needs and desires of the Southern European Renaissance: the wishes for protection, stimulation, compassion, and nurturance. Some of these longings persist today, and so do some medieval qualities of the Virgin. Did the Virgin Mary rehabilitate the image of mother? If she did, it was a rehabilitation accomplished through her defeat, to paraphrase Simone de Beauvoir.[65] Mary always played second fiddle to her Son. She endorsed self-sacrifice and renunciation as the highest accolades. A "liberated" mother, a free woman, even a complete goddess, she was not.

If images are a measure, then things got worse for mothers in the Renaissance. Mary's portraits eventually became mawkish. Raphael used his glamorous mistress for his model of the Virgin in *Madonna della Sedia*. He clothed her in a modish, richly embroidered shawl, and supplied her with a "come hither" glance as she embraces the Child. Perhaps patrons wanted stylish women to adorn their walls and churches. But this manner of representing the Virgin tests the boundaries between the respectable and the fashionable. Raphael's work is a masterpiece. Unfortunately, many who followed did not share his consummate genius. Their Virgins are feeble, mannered, self-conscious, merely conventionally pretty. And the Renaissance habit of populating the heavens with *putti,* while testifying to a consciousness of the fragility and evanescence of childhood, is downright sugary.[66] In other words, the images became stereotypes, cheap shots, easy appeals to superficial sentimentality, having less and less relevance to genuine emotion. They do not suggest that people esteemed real mothers or real children. And there was another twist in the imagery.

Someone else was added to the eternal grouping of Mother and Child: Dad. Until this time, Joseph had been a peripheral figure, often a figure of fun, fast asleep by a rock during the miracle of the Nativity, for example. When he appears in medieval writing, which is rare, he is called "old man," and he is painted that way.[67] But in the late fourteenth century he was modernized, de-aged, empowered, and embellished with a story. Artists now depicted not only Mary and Jesus, but the Holy Family, including a newly scripted Anne (Christ's grandmother), and, above all, the reconstructed Joseph at its head. The Holy Family became a model for the "best" Christian family. The loving, loyal relationships among its members dignified those sorts of bonds. A new feeling about family was emerging, a renewed paternalistic dynamic, which came to fruition in the Reformation and Early Modern period. And with it came a whole new set of issues for mother.

Facts of Life: Maternal Reality

THE EARLIEST MODEL: A.D. 500–1000

Everyone had a "blood price" in early medieval Europe. The Visigoths, those so-called barbarians who sacked Rome in the fifth century, set a fee, to be paid for by the perpetrator, for the injury or murder of any individual. The amount of the fee varied according to the age of the damaged party. This makes the determination of the value of a mother conveniently easy. A woman of childbearing age was worth 250 soldi, which is more than seven times what she was worth as a girl, and an impressive five-sixths the worth of a man. Not too sexist, relatively speaking. Indeed, if you believe the old Roman historian Tacitus, Germanic women were highly prized by their spouses, who paid a goodly sum (called a bridewealth) to marry them, in contrast to the practice of Roman and Renaissance Christian men, who, instead of paying out money, received it in the form of a dowry. According to Tacitus, Germanic mothers were paragons of domestic virtue. They were faithful and fertile. They eschewed contraception, and instead produced many robust children with "marvelous girth of limb." They nursed their sturdy offspring themselves and forbade infanticide. Unfortunately, or fortunately, depending on your perspective, this rosy picture of Germanic family life is not quite accurate. Tacitus had an ax to grind, shaming his fellow Romans by exaggerating the strict morality of German society. The fact is, Germanic men of means kept several wives and concubines, did engage in the killing of newborns (though not systematically), and certainly did not invest heavily, either psychologically or materially, in their care. Since children presented such low maintenance costs, why not produce multitudes? These Germanic people were also preliterate, engaged in ferocious reciprocal revenge feuds among clans, were contemptuous of traditional culture, and abducted and raped women with impunity.[68]

That period, between the fall of Rome and year 1000, is the most obscure in all Western history. Few voices survive, certainly none of mothers or children. Literacy was rare, records few. A subsistence (or less than a subsistence) economy prevailed. The great urban centers of culture and learning declined, and in their place grew small pockets of population around fortified castles or churches. Slaves on farms had been replaced by families of indentured serfs, who constituted the great majority of people. One would guess that in this environment children were welcome, if only as cheap sources of labor.

It appears that mothers shared equitably, not unduly, in the harshness of the times. Over time, Germanic law allowed mothers to act as guardians of their children, to own property, and to inherit: mothers now had some economic leverage.[69] Interestingly, during this period men and women were roughly the same age at first marriage, which is often a positive indication of equality in family dynamics.

By the millennium, the church had achieved its goal of converting the "heathen" people of the West to Christianity and possessed considerable clout regarding lifestyle. Reluctantly, the church had resigned itself to the reality of people's propensity to mate, and it incorporated marriage into Christian ritual. At least marriage produced more virgins, one church dignitary rationalized. Christian customs were devised, such as the solemn blessing of the bride and groom. Some were accompanied by rites taken over from pagan customs; at Rome a veil was placed on the heads of the married couple.

In expanding its control over marriage, the church unintentionally may have become a champion of women's interests. As a corollary of its hostility to sensuality, it forbade the keeping of concubines, treated adultery and rape severely, and denounced polygamy. In this instance, the church's aggressive prudery probably worked in favor of females and protected them from the caprices of their husbands. It also distributed women more equitably across all social classes, preventing elite men from hoarding, giving non-elite men a better chance of obtaining a spouse, and thereby reducing the need for abduction and rape (which tells you something about the nature of the times).[70]

The church also limited child marriage and marriage among relatives (endogamy), which, though a self-serving move by the church to undermine the power of pagan families who used these internal marriages to strengthen group ties, had a happy result for women. It enabled them to circulate, encouraging their public activity.[71] The church also put obstacles in the way of divorce, heretofore easily obtained, which worked to women's advantage, as it assured a stable environment for the raising of children. Mothers could not be readily abandoned by their spouses.

But for all the benefits the church gave to women, it took away others — namely, the ones that granted women control over their own bodies. Contraception and abortion, known in antiquity though not widely used, were absolutely forbidden. In commandeering the rules of marriage, the church policed the bearing of children. Emerging as a progressively conservative, hierarchical, and male-dominated institution, the church gained more control over motherhood.

How women felt about this situation remains a mystery. Most of our knowledge of the early Middle Ages comes from the pens of monks. This situation is not as dire as it sounds for historians, because, though celibate, the monks, oddly enough, were positioned to know something about attitudes toward children. The practice of oblation (wherein children were donated to monasteries) developed during this period, peaking in the eleventh and twelfth centuries. Monks were in charge of caretaking and educating little boys; nuns prepared girls for spiritual vocation. Records indicate that they did so, for the most part, sensitively, softening the harsh pedagogic practices of antiquity by allowing play time and rest periods, and eschewing corporal punishment.[72]

But the practice of oblation implies that children were sent away from families. The historian John Boswell sees oblation as just another form of abandonment, which, he claims, was routine. If traffic lights imply traffic, then the abundance of injunctions against the abandonment of children by the early church implies that abandonment was widespread among Christians, as it had been among pagan Romans. The difference is that churches replaced the dungheap as the preferred location for leaving infants. The church acted as a kind of clearinghouse for distributing the youngsters. It was unsystematic, but the majority of abandoned children survived — in the early Middle Ages, anyway. The first foundling homes were started under the auspices of the church. If parents supplied a "dowry" for their left child, then he or she would become an oblate in the monastery. If not, these children probably became servants, either in the church or in wealthy households. Apparently, some became prostitutes. This may be deduced from the stunning fact that early theologians — like Clement of Alexandria and Justin Martyr — argued that a man should not go to brothels lest he unknowingly commit incest with a child he had abandoned. Peculiar logic from our perspective, although rife with implications! Was abandonment so common that a father was likely to encounter his own child in a brothel?[73]

Boswell also astutely points out that Christianity may have ironically augmented the rate of abandonment. Through its churches and monasteries, Christianity provided a readymade, honorable receptacle for the relinquished infant and remitted child. Oblation in particular ensured not only economic melioration for the family, but social prestige and divine grace. Even church-doorstep abandonment (wherein no money was left for the child's keep) forestalled the death of the youngster, at least in the earlier centuries; so Boswell argues that abandonment did not imply a lack of parental sentiment. Parents believed they were acting not only in the best interests of their own material survival, but in the best interests of the child. Good fortune or, at the least, a normal life span might ensue where the sole alternative was death.[74] I am less convinced that parents' motives were benign.

Historians have unearthed another stunning cache of information from the swelling documentation now available for decades as early as the middle of the eighth century; it includes actual surveys of households. The most famous of these surveys describes the ninth-century families of Saint Germain (now part of Paris). The most pertinent piece of information reveals that there were 3601 females to 4857 men, or only 100 women for every 135 men in the district. The ratio challenges credibility. Assuming that an equal number of girls and boys were born, what happened to the missing females? Surely they did not all die at birth. Demographers often smell a rat with data like these — for they suggest the killing of female babies. There may be other explanations, such as that surveyors simply failed to report women; but the entries themselves show that, if anything, census takers were interested in inflating the number of residents so as to boost the monastery's rights. Underreporting of either gender would have defeated the purpose of the survey.[75]

The sheer number of times that infanticide is mentioned in the penitentials (much used quasi-handbooks of Christian sins, with associated disciplinary codes) also suggests that the killing of babies occurred. The offense of "overlaying" is especially prominent in the penitentials. Evidently, it was common for newborns to be smothered or crushed to death in the beds of their parents or wet nurse, where they usually slept. Obviously, the church suspected, probably with reason, that some cases of overlaying were disguised acts of murder.[76] That, or a lot of people must have gone to bed in a drunken stupor.

We may never know. Most historians regard infanticide and

neglect of children by Christians in the early Middle Ages to be acts of desperation, strongly associated with poverty. Such behavior was not socially condoned, as we can infer from the many injunctions against it. The mother was undoubtedly not the wondrous, all-giving Virgin Mary in this period. But, then, the Virgin Mary was not the wondrous, all-giving Virgin Mary in the early Middle Ages either.

THE HIGH MEDIEVAL MODEL: ROUGHLY 1000–1400

Much to the astonishment and relief of the teeming masses, Judgment Day did not begin on midnight, December 31, 999. The world not only did not end; it entered a period of such extraordinary ferment and accomplishment that one historian has called the eleventh century "radioactive."[77] There was an extravagant outpouring of energy during the High Middle Ages, a grandiosity of gesture that included the suicidal crusades to recapture the Holy Land; pedantic rules of chivalry and courtly love, all taken with high seriousness, though they served no apparent purpose other than their own perpetuation; colossal Gothic cathedrals with luminous stained glass windows of transcendent beauty; the proliferation of education and formation of universities; the gestation of great cities — so much intensity that it is easy to forget that most people lived routine lives. The new burst of achievement was made possible by economic prosperity, due in no small measure to relative political stability, the use of the deep plough, and crop rotation, which, combined with a long spell of good weather, quadrupled food production. There was an increase in population. For the first time since antiquity, people had energy to spare.

And with it came — what else — paperwork! Proliferating in these centuries are the chronicles, tax rolls, "courtesy" books, the lives of saints, legal and manorial records, and medical writing from which we construct history, though, of course, none of these documents speaks with a mother's voice. Any "facts" we glean are necessarily inferential, pieced together from offhand records denoting, for example, the feeding habits of saints' mothers or burial rates of newborns. As it turns out, even these "hard" data are maddeningly inconsistent, as inconsistent about mothers as the "soft" data of medieval theology, imaginative literature, and paintings.

Contradictions abound. For example, church and philosophical writings downgrade the mother's part in conception and reproduction; on the other hand, midwives know very well that women contribute something important; animal milk is uniformly condemned for feeding children, yet the existence of nursing horns suggests that it was used; courtesy books, those guides on manners which became popular in the twelfth century, variously advised men to treat women reverentially, as in *The Art of Courtly Love,* Books I and II (not III!) and to beat them to a pulp for mere disobedience, as in the popular book written by the Chevalier Geoffrey de la Tour Landry. His manual was so successful, by the way, that it was translated into English and German and went on being read as a sort of textbook right up to the sixteenth century; in fact, an edition was published with illustrations by Dürer.[78]

And how did women respond to these conflicting cues? Latter-day feminists should take heed. These medieval ladies seemed to exercise whatever rights they had with vigor, and they did not take the abuse lying down. One gets the impression that the battle of the sexes was a hot topic (and this was before widespread use of the printing press in the sixteenth century). Jean de Meung, the consummate male chauvinist author of the second part of *Le Roman de la Rose,* got his comeuppance from the pen of Christine de Pisan, a French poet and a darling of today's feminist scholars because she is the only known woman to have earned her living by writing in the Middle Ages. Christine launched a counterattack against Jean's misogynist work so effective that it provoked a debate about the nature of femininity that went on for centuries and even came to have a name: "The Woman Question." This debate was at times combative, ironic, indignant, passionate — and playful.[79] Even the greatest writer of the age, Geoffrey Chaucer, joined in the gender wars. He contrived an alter ego for his pre-eminently meek Patient Griselda in the bawdy Wife of Bath (precursor of Roseanne Barr?). That feisty woman outlived four husbands and walloped the fifth into submission.

No, contrary to the myth, medieval women did *not* wear chastity belts, the use of which was merely a literary conceit. The romantic image of the *châtelaine* of a castle standing guard at the barbican, preparing to pour hot oil on the heads of the manor's attackers, however, turns out to have been accurate. The lady of a manor more often than not had to manage alone when her husband was occupied elsewhere, as he generally was, for the sun never set on warfare. It was not at all unusual for a child to use the matronymic (mother's last name) instead of the patronymic, signaling that his or her mother, not father, owned or managed an estate. Property rights for women naturally corresponded to, and were interwoven with, occupational and legal rights as the great trading cities of the Middle Ages began to flourish. In German cities this equality was explicitly stated. Women could now inherit, sue, and, thanks to the church, had the right to withhold consent from a marriage proposal (though papa's grip on the purse-strings probably rendered her true power in choosing a mate virtually nil).[80]

In the ecclesiastical sphere, abbesses, no less than abbots, were likely to become mighty magnates. The convent gave women at least one option beyond their biological destiny in this age, and though the choice involved renunciations that some people of today would regard as unacceptable, many nuns converted this disability into a source of strength, using their retreat as a way of gaining an education and performing good works. Of course, life for the vast bulk of the medieval population, the peasants, was so elemental, so constrained by the rules of feudalism and exhausting labor, that to argue that one gender had it worse than the other would be trivial at best. Serf husband and serf wife were partners in a life of harrowing drudgery.[81]

Despite certain gains, most medieval women were basically under the thumb of, first, their fathers, and, later, their husbands. They were largely debarred from public life, in church and state, both of which were patriarchal organizations. The surest route to power was widowhood, which was an artifact of the legal system. This must have been an age of merry widows. But, murder aside, widowhood was never a guaranteed life phase, and most women never gained ascendancy.

Regardless of their status, there are many reasons that women may have wanted babies in the prosperous High Middle Ages. Children were a source of labor for the poor and middle classes. By the time youngsters were five or six they were assigned real chores.[82] For the rich, they were important as heirs. Lineage was a high priority: the elite needed descendants to be recipients of their legacies. Primogeniture, wherein the eldest son inherited, had been instituted, thus removing the persistent worry among nobles of dilution of their holdings. Successive sons could always embark on a career in the church or seek their fortune in war. Girls merely had to be given a dowry, a practice that had been restored in this period, and did not usually present an undue strain.

But the most powerful reason for wanting children had to do with "supply and demand." There was a short supply; fertility was low. This may seem odd for an era in which all forms of birth control were forbidden, but the number of offspring was determined by the length of a marriage. In the Middle Ages, people married late (especially in England) and died young. "No land, no marriage" was the order of the day. A son had to wait for his father's death or retirement to gain sufficient economic independence for the establishment of a new household. And so he postponed marriage and probably dreamed of patricide. (The psychodynamics of this setup would be manna from heaven to Freudians.) A large percentage of people never married (all those younger sons and dowry-deprived daughters and persons with spiritual inclinations) and so were not a rich source of babies. And given the high infant mortality rate — estimated at 30 to 50 percent — and the reality that only half the population reached the age of twenty, the dearth of babies is understandable.[83]

So how did all these factors conspire to affect mothers? In spite of all the hype about Mary — all those tender depictions of Mother and Child — Mary's influence on medieval child rearing was mild, and she ultimately did little to elevate motherhood's prestige. For one thing, the Virgin was the Mother of God, not God the Mother. Her power was always derived. For another, *mortal* mom was not identified with Mary. As a nonvirgin, she dwelt not in paradise, but in the shadow of the fallen Eve. Happily, this spared her from the impossible task of having to deliver perfect mothering. Careful child rearing simply was not a priority. It would never have occurred to medieval mom to gratify her child in as unconditional a way as Mary, nor would material circumstances even remotely have permitted such indulgence. Regarding the Virgin's maternity — the medieval mother wished to be the recipient of its beneficence, not the deliverer. But let us recall that, though Eve was a sexual being, she was not an abusive mother. Neither, for the most part, were mothers in the High Middle Ages. Because these women were married to men near their own age and were reasonably respected as people in their own right, one would not expect them to abuse their children.

Medieval biographies and autobiographies suggest how ordinary routine affection was between parents and children. Here are a few glimpses. The writer of the twelfth-century *Ancren Riwle* describes a peasant mother playing hide-and-seek with her child, who, when he cries for her, "leapeth forth lightly with outspread arms and embraceth and kisseth him and wipeth his eyes." Another writer pictures a child playing peek-a-boo, covering its eyes and thinking no one sees it. And there is Adelard of Bath's charming vignette of a tiny child, not yet able to speak, standing by the fire, listening to music, and becoming so excited that he begins to bounce and giggle to the music.[84]

Children in the High Middle Ages had toys: dolls, doll carriages harnessed to mice, puppets, hoops, stilts. They had hobbyhorses, which must have been ideal for imitating knights. Cradle rocking did exist, and, not coincidentally, the manger was added to Nativity scenes at this time. Probably nothing could better demonstrate affection for youngsters than the rise of holidays infused with delights for children, holidays whose primary goal seemed to be the indulgence of youngsters, with parental pleasure merely a byproduct. Christmas, formerly ignored, was reinvigorated as a part of a specific recognition of Christ's childhood. People started to give presents to children on Saint Nicholas's Day, December 6, in honor of the saint who brought murdered children back to life. Additionally, a boy bishop was elected on that day to rule until Holy Innocents' Day, December 28, yet another commemoration of the slaughter of the children in Bethlehem. This little "bishop" was allowed to parade through the streets and even to preach a sermon, usually written for him, but always affecting childish sentiments. Adults thought these festivities charming.[85]

The Children's Crusade during this period bears on medieval attitudes toward children and is worthy of consideration. According to scattered comments in chronicles, around 1212 thousands of children undertook to free the Holy Land. They marched from areas of France and Germany and made their way to the Mediterranean. There, they were purportedly robbed, raped, and kidnaped by unscrupulous traders and were sold into slavery in North Africa. The historian C. John Sommerville suggests that the zeal with which Pope Innocent III appropriated the misguided, naïve passion of these youngsters (thereby enhancing the glory of Christianity) represented an exploitation of children's "good press." With the church's self-serving approval, the incident was highly sensationalized: in actual fact, only a portion of the crusaders were children, and they were more like the wanderers following the Pied Piper of Hamelin than an organized battalion of liberators.[86] The pathos of the event evidently captured the medieval imagination and was continually embellished. The point here is that the plight of the youngsters obviously played on medieval sympathies, suggesting that these people had a soft spot for children, one evident enough for the church to capitalize on it.

The High Middle Ages were, on the whole, more lenient and permissive toward the young child than the centuries that followed. In the eleventh century, an abbot described to Saint Anselm his difficulty in controlling obstreperous boys in his charge, complaining that he beat them day and night but still they would not behave. Anselm replied:

> Feeling no love, or pity, good will or tenderness in your attitude towards them, they have no faith . . . [and] so regard everyone with suspicion and jealousy . . . Are they not human? Are they not flesh and blood like you?[87]

Anselm was not the last medieval man to suggest that discipline could be accomplished by love rather than by force. Bartholomew of England took this line. So did Philippe of Navarre, a secular writer of that century. One German writer ruled out physical punishment altogether. Of course beatings still happened, but it is interesting to note that they were not condoned by the education establishment.

It was routine at the time for mothers to make grants to monasteries in order to obtain prayers on behalf of sick children. They also made pilgrimages and implored saints for favors in that regard. In a haunting incident from fourteenth-century inquisitorial records, a fanatically religious father instructed his hapless wife to impose on their daughter the "ultimate fast" (*endura*) of the Catharist sect, to which they belonged, denying the child milk and giving her only water and vegetables until she died, at which point she would immediately enter heaven. But when the father left the room, the distraught mother proceeded to nurse the daughter. Upon his return, the father rebuked her harshly and, according to the wife's testimony to authorities, withdrew his love from both herself and the child.[88] This was hardly an indifferent mother.

If grief at the death of a child is a measure of attachment, here is a painful example from the journal of Giovanni Morelli, an especially articulate fourteenth-century Florentine, describing the death of his son at the age of ten. The child had been ill for two weeks and the father never left his bedside; the loss of the boy threw Morelli into an agony of despair and self-reproach. His greatest joy ironically brought him his greatest sadness, he noted in his diary. "You loved him but never made him happy. You never kissed him when he wanted you . . . now you have lost him and will never see him in this world."[89] This occurred during the Black Death (bubonic plague), when presumably the death of a child might almost have been routine. Clearly, for Morelli it was not.

But child rearing was not all cradles and Christmas. For a medieval woman, the bearing of a child was a fearful prospect, literally the punishment of God on Eve for her duplicity. Some 20 percent of all married women who died in Florence in the early 1400s died in childbirth. Methods of delivery were no better than in ancient times; the pain was unrelieved. Most complications meant death for both the mother and child. Childbirth was still a matter for women and midwives (not physicians, who did not know much about delivery anyway). Though savvy, midwives had few aids beyond potions, poultices, appeals to saints, and magic stones. Women, by the way, delivered in a sitting or crouching position. In her autobiography, Margery Kempe, a fourteenth-century mystic, reports visions of Jesus instructing her to abstinence in marriage. Even if her visions were not divinely inspired, they would be understandable in light of her frequent and difficult pregnancies, which resulted in fourteen live children. Her amorous husband finally conceded to Margery's "religious" requirements and stopped touching her, which supports my suspicions about the true source of her spiritual inclinations (avoiding sex). Not that I blame her. Mothers who survived the ordeal of childbirth often lived to face the death of the baby they had borne at such risk.[90]

Birth control techniques were known in the Middle Ages. Chaucer's "Parson's Tale" provides an impressively full catalogue: potions, pessaries, suppositories, *coitus interruptus,* abortion, and the use of orifices of the woman other than the vagina. Prostitutes had few children. Nevertheless, most medieval women became mothers. It is safe to assume that motherhood defined a woman's life and occupied most of her years. From her mid-twenties on, life was a cycle of childbirth and nursing and childbirth. The intervals between pregnancies were governed by the length of the period of lactation, which prevented further conception with some effectiveness. When a child was weaned, very often a new conception would take place.[91]

Because peasant women tended to nurse their own babies, they had the opportunity (luxury?) to space their children. Not so, well-to-do women. They did not nurse, so they tended to conceive at shorter intervals, and produced ten, seventeen, even nineteen children. Also, they tended to be married very young, since they served as pawns in the cementing of alliances or in building up land holdings.[92] They had a relatively long marital career in which to conceive.

We can only imagine the psychological effect of all this: the hazards of delivery, the pain, the high mortality of newborns, the inevitability of pregnancy, church denunciations of sexuality. At least one of the saints of this period — Francesca Romana de'Panziani — is said to have vomited every time she was forced to have intercourse with her husband.[93]

Despite the abundance of tender vignettes, many of the child-rearing practices betray a certain degree of coldness toward children. For most newborns of the wealthier classes, life began when they were farmed out to a wet nurse. Usually the nurse was a poor peasant who lived far away from the parental home. On a positive note, much forethought was given to the choice of a wet nurse, a task assigned to the biological father and a role jealously guarded by him (which may be, as noted before, an example of male nursing envy). The baby's father bargained not with the wet nurse for her services, but with the nurse's husband, and the two men ultimately agreed on a fair price. Children were thought to exhibit characteristics reflecting the physical appearance and personality of their milk source. (Hence, Michelangelo attributed his interest in sculpting to the fact that his wet nurse was both the daughter and the wife of stonecutters!) Obviously animal milk was out of the question (lest one's child resemble a cow), which was probably a good thing anyway, since purifying and preserving foods were unknown in the Middle Ages. Anyway, the father sought a nurse who bore some likeness to the child's mother and was of good character. The nurse's breasts came in for scrutiny; if too large, they would flatten the child's nose. As in antiquity, it was also desirable to get a nurse who was not sexually active. Pregnancy was thought to corrupt a mother's milk and harm the baby; this had something to do with the idea that milk and menstrual blood were the same substance and would be oversupplied to the fetus at the expense of the nursing infant.[94]

Away in the country, infants were seldom visited by their parents. Sometimes the children were handed from nurse to nurse — if a nurse became sick or pregnant, for example. There was a suspiciously high death rate among wet-nursed babies. Even if death did not ensue, the child often suffered neglect. The situation was ripe for this: the wet nurse's motives were mercenary. She had to displace her own child at her breast with a stranger. (The disposition of her own child is unknown.) This was an accepted part of the contract, for people did not understand until the nineteenth century that feeding more than one child at a time did not affect the quality of the mother's milk. And breast-feeding, because of the belief system of the time, interfered with the conjugal rights of her husband. Not a happy set-up. The child would return to its birth family at any time between the ages of two and seven. Thus, many children were raised by a nurse well beyond weaning. When the child returned to his or her family, it was to a group of strangers.[95]

The nature of the job of wet nurse required either a certain defensive callousness or outright desperation, for frequently the woman was expected to put her survival ahead of her child's, as the following episode shows. "I have found one in the Piazza della Pieve whose milk is two months old," wrote an Italian merchant's wife to her husband, "and she has vowed that if her baby, which is on the point of death, dies tonight, she will come as soon as it is buried." This makes the problem brutally clear. Those who could afford to pay for a wet nurse's service did so at the expense of the nurse's baby. The startling injustice of this system, where the life of a well-born infant was favored over that of a low-born, is apparent. In effect, the children of the rich were fed from the breasts of the poor.[96]

The reluctance by women of means to nurse their own babies flew in the face of an overwhelming body of advice from physicians, humanists, and priests, drawing on authorities as old and honored as Aristotle and Plutarch.[97] Much as these men harped on women's obligations, lavished praise on maternal nursing, nagged, and cajoled, mothers continued to demand the luxury of sending their newborns away. They were, of course, no worse than the wealthy women of antiquity, who also failed to heed the admonitions of Aristotle and Plutarch, though Greek wet nurses often became part of the *oikos*. Even the proliferation of paintings of the lactating Madonna did not seem to persuade earthbound mothers to imitate her. Though wet-nursing does not always bespeak parental indifference, here it points in that direction. Certainly it suggests that medieval women did not want to enjoy their children as infants.

Another custom of medieval parenting, also derived from antiquity, that seems highly questionable from our vantage point is swaddling. All children were swaddled through the first year of life, which meant that they were wound tightly in woolen fabric so that they ended up looking like miniature mummies. A child could not move its appendages and remained in a rigid position. Obviously all that wrapping was not terribly efficient for diaper changing or bathing. Again, questions may be raised about the mother's motives. Did swaddling represent a fundamental level of concern for molding a child's body into a desired shape? Was it an attempt to re-create the womb's security? (We do things like that today with our Leboyer baths and toys with heartbeats.) Was it for the child's protection? For the mother's convenience? Did the child's swaddling interfere with communication and bonding? Did it render impossible a child's search for autonomy?

Like everything else, maternal affection escapes a generalization. After wet-nursing exile, children until the age of seven were left in the charge of their mothers, who schooled them in manners, religion, and, to some extent, letters. Undoubtedly, youngsters were coddled, bounced, and sung to. But lest we become too enchanted by the cozy picture of a medieval mom softly singing a lullaby to her child, it is well to note that an analysis of the text of those lullabies reveals hints of resentment, sometimes even hatred and blood-curdling threats. But then the best-known lullaby in English today, "Rock-a-Bye, Baby," also suggests child neglect: a baby falling out of a tree. The ambivalence of parents toward their children runs deep.[98]

The common folk belief in the changeling — that is, in the kidnaping by the Devil of one's real, wonderful child and its substitution with one of inferior quality — also provides a clue as to how medieval parents felt about their children (or at least about the decoy in the cradle). The idea of the changeling often led to extraordinary and brutal practices by parents toward their baby aimed at reversing the exchange. It is amusing to note that the changeling fantasy is a perfect foil to the "family romance" fantasy, which is very common among children. Here a youngster believes that, due to an unfortunate mix-up in the hospital nursery, it was not given to the true parents, who are exalted persons, but instead assigned to the wretches with whom it now resides. Surely those pitiful creatures could not be its real parents! Both fantasies repair the disillusionment with one's real child or parents by denying a blood relationship. These reciprocal revenge fantasies which so neatly and benignly distance one's relations from oneself also cleverly obscure one's anger toward them from oneself. And they are enormously self-aggrandizing. Imagine being the child of royalty or the parent of a child so desirable that the Devil cannot resist stealing it![99]

Let me add another bit of medieval unconscious hostility toward children. Multiple births were regarded with suspicion because it was thought that a woman could not conceive twice, consecutively, and that, accordingly, twins were not born of the same father.[100] And what was an occasional solution to this frightful circumstance? One child, the "legitimate" one, was permitted to live; the other was abandoned.

Evidently having one's child under the parental roof was not a medieval priority. When the child was seven and education began in earnest outside the home, the son of a noble destined for knighthood was likely to be placed in the household of a seigneur (probably his father's lord), where his training was largely in horsemanship and the martial arts, with a smattering of letters. The child of a merchant or an artisan was likely to be apprenticed in the household of a "master." Children destined for the church were deposited in a monastery as oblates, if they had not already been so donated. Peasant children, of course, did not leave home, but took on a more serious round of tasks. (The fact that poor children lived with their parents and were nursed by their own mothers suggests that attachment to one's children in the Middle Ages varied in inverse ratio to wealth and social standing.) Girls of the nobility, too, were sent away from home: some went to nunneries; and some, who were betrothed early — a practice limited to the nobility — were sent to the future husband's home for rearing. Poor girls entered service at around the age of twelve. Surely these practices represent a systematic shifting of upbringing away from parents. But perhaps parents were not so much ridding themselves of offspring as ensuring their children a place in society, supplying them with a means of survival. Social norms underlay the system, not parental indifference. Yet what kind of society would develop such social norms?[101]

Rumors about atrocities carried out against children seem to be associated with this age in particular. It has been said that "the rivers and latrines of medieval Europe resound with the cries of children who have been plunged into them." Well, not quite. It *is* true that overlaying and exposure were railed against in the eleventh- and twelfth-century penitentials, but actual evidence for their occurrence has proven impossible to obtain. Extremely few cases of child murder by a parent were tried, and in most instances the killer, usually the mother, was regarded as out of her mind, suggesting that medieval folk believed, as we do, that no sane person would commit such a hideous act. With regard to the murder of newborns, court judgments show remarkable mildness toward the perpetrator (a fact that changed radically during the early modern period). While this may appear to reflect an indifference about the sad fate of murdered infants, it is more likely a compassionate response to the mother, who was typically unmarried and poor.[102]

If the outright killing of children was rare, the accidental death of youngsters was not. For the unsupervised toddler (the most frequent victim), the medieval home was fraught with peril: hot kettles to be scalded by; wells to be drowned in; horses to be crushed under; and, most of all, the glowing hearth, an abundant source of burns and fires. Indeed, cottage fires account for a third of infant deaths, and unattended swaddled babies were unable to maneuver out of the way of flying cinders. The continuing problem of overlaying was noted in a fourteenth-century English confessional manual; the priest was instructed to examine the consciences of husbands: "Hast thou also have i'layn / And so bytwen you thy chyld i'slayn?"[103]

From our perspective, medieval parents were careless. Obviously "child-proofing" their home was not a part of their mental furniture. Does this apparent negligence imply indifference? We may never know. It is interesting that accidents among children were seasonal, occurring most often during periods of planting and harvesting, when parents were required to be away from home.[104] Perhaps the accidents were unfortunate byproducts of necessity, not the result of parental indifference.

During the eleventh and twelfth centuries, the abandonment of children decreased. This was a period of economic expansion, after all, and children were desired. Oblation also increased, largely as a result of primogeniture, since parents had to do something respectable with those of their children who would not inherit their property. However, by the thirteenth century there was overpopulation, which was corrected in the next century by the Black Death and Hundred Years War. (The Black Death of 1347–1348 reduced the European population by a half to two-thirds.) But in the meantime parents resumed abandonment, especially since they had an official and orderly system for doing so within the newly emerging foundling homes. Established in Florence, Rome, southern France, Genoa, Pisa, Siena, Venice, Marseille, Chartres, Ulin, Freiburg, and Nuremburg, they grew as the plague spread and, in a paradoxical way, eventually presented a parallel menace, as we shall see.[105]

The "report card" for the High Middle Ages is decidedly mixed. Mothers were idolized in art, and in reality were treated well or misogynistically. Women were feisty but ultimately ruled by their spouses. Children were often portrayed as innocents, and there is much evidence of affectionate feelings for them: holidays, toys, and a softening of pedagogy. But wet-nursing, the frequency of accidents, and general lack of proximity to their parents suggest a certain indifference. It appears that mothers were respected enough in their own right to be able to nurture their children, but not in a manner that would be applauded today. Yet if their methods of child rearing appear cold and rejecting by our standards, they may have been especially suited to the precarious life during these brutal centuries. Unfortunately, the High Middle Ages' C turns to F during the next period.

THE LATE MODEL: ROUGHLY 1350–1500

The Renaissance. The word alone conjures up such shimmering images — dazzling art, splendid scientific achievements, the rediscovery of "the freedom and dignity of man" — that historians are barely able to contain their enthusiasm when they describe the period. But it turns out that mothers may not have had one — a renaissance, that is — and neither did kids. However surprising it may seem, the Renaissance worsened the maternal condition and saw no end to the flood of unwanted children, who by now were dying in droves in those presumably humanitarian foundling hospitals.[106]

What happened? The gender roles hardened. "Women" became a category, and, as with any label, it served to stereotype and objectify real women. In fact, all forms of life, civil and religious, were being codified at this time, all in service of a bureaucratized and centralized government and church, both of which were predominantly masculine organizations. Bureaucracies, by definition, thrive on oversimplification and codification.

Charm became part of a woman's job description. Precise standards of beauty were established for every part of a woman's body. These were immortalized in works of art and canonized in various written works and became fixed in the Western European imagination: thick, light hair; pale complexion; plucked eyebrows; large eyes; straight nose; prominent breasts; long legs; small feet. In attempting to achieve the ideal, women resorted to makeup and artifice, for which they were mocked. "They grease themselves with monkey fat, they puff out their hair with sulphur and resin," scoffed Sebastian Brant, the author of *Ship of Fools*.[107] It was a no-win situation. Joan of Arc, the Maid of Orleans, who claimed that heavenly voices had sent her to lead the French troops against the English, was turned into the enemy by her own countrymen and burned at the stake. One of the complaints against her was that she failed to conform to gender expectations: she wore men's clothes! This was the age when women were molded into aesthetic objects — decorous, chaste, dependent. They were not supposed to lead armies, never mind wear pants.[108]

With the development of capitalism, production was organized on a larger scale, and the workplace and home were separated. More and more, women stayed inside, men worked outside. The woman's sphere of influence narrowed. The age, which so idealized the Greek Classical period, ironically assumed some of the worst characteristics of Athens as its own; namely, the disappearance of women from the public domain. There was a simultaneous decline in the power of churchwomen; fewer roles for women in guilds; less opportunity for women in agricultural administration.

Though the humanists of the period advocated equality of education for both daughters and sons, their texts and programs of study for the two genders belie their rhetoric. With varying degrees of cruelty and patronization, they indicate that the purpose of education for women was to make them perfect wives. Latin and Greek (the foundation for learning in the 1400s) were described as dangerous because they might distract a woman's mind and render her unfit for motherhood. Humanism rediscovered "man" but forgot woman.[109]

The disappearance of the tower and the loggia in Florentine domestic architecture in the late fourteenth and fifteenth centuries was emblematic of the new order. Without the loggia, women had no window upon urban life. There was a turning toward the inside, a growing emphasis on an elegant interior space. Complementary to this was a demand for personalized portraits and pictures idealizing family. Hence all those domesticated Madonnas.

Family dynamics were changing. With a notion of gender in reserve to call upon, Europeans redefined women's work. Woman became exclusively the psychological helpmate of her husband and mother to her child. Moreover, as a result of early capitalism, her work was no longer considered real or valuable, because it did not directly contribute to capitalist production. These factors served to reinforce the despotic authority of husband and father.[110]

The church joined in, energetically promoting devotion to Joseph. The veneration he attracted seemed to be a thinly disguised cult of paternal care.[111] This is all clearly apparent in paintings, where, you may recall, Joseph had been added to the Holy Family. Mary had to share her authority, marking the beginning of the demise of her exclusive parental power.

There was now a glut of marriageable women, and this resulted in the runaway inflation of dowries. Owing to their overabundance, little value was attached to daughters as products, and families had to accumulate a fortune to get rid of them. We can imagine the disappointment parents must have felt on learning of the birth of a female child. Families who could afford dowries chose one daughter to make a brilliant match and endowed her at the expense of her sister.[112] Obviously, there were fewer marriages; the ranks of unmarried women swelled. Many families contracted their daughters into domestic service, so many that the term *maid,* meaning unmarried girl, became synonymous with *servant.* Many single women joined nunneries or informal religious groups like the Beguines, though the presence of so many members without a true vocation for the spiritual life must have made the environment in a convent arid and hypocritical. Inevitably there were some dark and desperate moments, sexual scandals and what-not, all vigorously publicized by later Protestant propagandists.

With the marital odds weighted in their favor, men began to choose nubile young women as partners. (This was true in Southern Europe only.) The age of marriage for girls dropped, and that for males remained high. It became more unlikely that a married couple could become true companions. Once again, the situation is reminiscent of that in Classical Athens. It is interesting to observe that both eras were periods of great artistic achievement and a high incidence of homosexuality. Whether these factors are related is anyone's guess.[113]

The sentimentalized interest in the Holy Family, the virtual obsession with sweet portraits of a nursing Madonna, would seem to reflect a greater respect for mothers and mother love. Yet this interest occurred against a background of an established system of commercial wet-nursing and a swelling flood of child abandonment (now, as in antiquity, lethal). The disposing of one's child was so routine that the women saints of the period typically extended maternal service to all those in need *except* their own children, whom they abandoned.[114] The gulf between the ideals of mother love and social reality in the Renaissance serves as a sobering reminder that beauty may be only skin deep.

The exquisiteness of the irony becomes apparent when we examine the relationship between the life and works of two painters whose tender but ambiguous depictions of the Mother and Child dominate our cultural unconscious: Michelangelo (1475–1564) and Leonardo da Vinci (1452–1519). It was these two artists who inspired Freud's two most extensive pieces of art criticism, though with regard to the former, he gave motherhood short shrift. In his Michelangelo essay (1914), Freud spent only a paragraph on the artist's life and confined himself to a male-centered view of the mothering role and his preference for identifying with father figures. But other psychoanalysts have connected Michelangelo's exhaustive treatment of the Madonna and Child in his drawings, sculpting, and painting to his own inadequate experience of being mothered and a wish to master the traumatic situation. Michelangelo, like his four brothers, was sent off to a wet nurse immediately after birth and did not see his mother, except for occasional visits, for two years. He returned then to a virtual stranger, only to have her die when he was six. That is why, some scholars speculate, in his portrayals, the Madonna always looks *away* from her Son.[115]

A conception of the mother as one who gives, then takes away, seduces, then shames, lies at the heart of Freud's Leonardo essay (1919). Leonardo also had what may be construed as a maternally deprived, or at best confused, childhood. He was the "love child" of Ser Piero and Caterina, a peasant woman. Later Ser Piero married another young woman, who, it turned out, was unable to conceive. So Ser Piero brought the very young Leonardo to be raised by the pair as their own. With regard to the Mona Lisa's smile, Freud argued that Leonardo found the model for it in Caterina's countenance, which held "the promise of unbounded tenderness and at the same time sinister menace," presumably the menace of abandonment. The inscrutable smile simultaneously conveys reserve and seductiveness, kindness and cruelty, charm and deceit. Leonardo portrayed a number of his maternal women in this haunting, teasing way. In "Saint Anne with the Madonna and Child," Freud suggested, Leonardo composed the picture so as to merge into a single form his two mothers — his true mother, Caterina, from whom he was separated before he reached five, and his father's young wife, who became his stepmother when he entered the paternal household. Leonardo painted both the grandmother (Saint Anne) and the mother (the Madonna) as equally young and beautiful: both are "endowed with the blissful smile of the joy of motherhood."[116] Here, Leonardo romanticizes the mother. Both kinds of depictions — the idealizing and the mysterious — suggest ambivalent feelings toward mother, a failure to recognize her as human. Leonardo and Michelangelo had lost their early mothers (as did many children in the Renaissance as a result of the practice of wet-nursing) and it makes sense that they were wary of a mother's enticements. Having been burned, they experienced mother love as precarious, and they painted it that way. Artists of the period were obsessed with the subject: depictions of the nursing Madonna saturated the cities of Europe. Perhaps they were attempts at repairing the painful feelings resulting from her loss. Like the glorious movie palaces built during the Depression in America, they indulged our fantasies. Renaissance art seems not to have been the product of secure mothering — rather, the reverse.

In the fifteenth century, the abandonment of children mushroomed. In Florence alone, a third hospital was founded exclusively for foundlings to alleviate the burden on the other two. Within a half century, it was accepting nine hundred children a year. All the major cities now had such hospices. The rich deposited their bastard children. But to infer that illegitimacy was the sole cause of abandonment would be an oversimplification. Prosperous families sometimes took bastards in and raised them. Poor families deposited both legitimate and illegitimate children. Wet nurses handed in their own children. Most of the charges were, not surprisingly, girls. A terrible mortality rate reigned within these foundling homes. The majority of children died within a few years of admission; in some places the mortality rate exceeded 90 percent, probably because of unsanitary conditions and the spread of infection.[117]

The extent of abandonment in the fifteenth century is a puzzle. Because of the staggering loss in population during the preceding century, there were sufficient resources for survivors and their immediate descendants. Food prices were low and wages high. The question arises as to whether the very existence of new foundling homes increased the demand by providing a ready and easy opportunity for giving away a child. If so, what does this imply about mother love? Indeed, with mothers increasingly confined to their home, ornamented, ever-more youthful, objectified, perhaps they did not have an environment in which to mature. Immature themselves, they were unable to care maturely for their offspring.

It appears, then, that the Southern European Renaissance had a nasty underside. In the century of the flowering of art and architecture and humanist learning, there was widespread inhumane treatment of children. Exalted in painting, mothers and their offspring were trivialized in reality. ❍

THE MIDDLE AGES were a multifaceted period. One finds mother love in it; one finds child abandonment. There was an epidemic of Madonna fever, but it was a surface affliction. Parents wished to receive Mary's nurturing but did not feel compelled to dispense it. Clearly, the first few months of life were not what they became in the modern family — a time of close bonding with an attentive mother. It is probably safe to say that, contrary to Ariès's assertions, medieval folk most certainly did have a concept of childhood, but children of the Middle Ages did not undergo an intense emotional encounter with their parents.

It is striking that, once again, the degree of respect accorded mothers seems to reflect the degree of attachment mothers accorded their children, and that the absence of mother love coincides with the absence of love *for* mother. As before, a mutually causal relation is suggested: as the status of woman rises, so does the status of children and child care. The more a society values women, the greater importance it will assign to that which is associated with women. To state a commonsensical idea — it seems that we nurture well when we feel nurtured. The greater the degree to which women are esteemed by their society and nurtured by peers, the greater will be their capacity to do many things well, including loving their children.[118] In periods of relative advance — at the end of the Dark Ages and during the High Middle Ages, when women gained legitimate economic and legal rights and responsibilities — there are not many good data about infanticide or wanton abandonment. Later, in the Renaissance, as bureaucratic government and commercial capitalism eroded women's roles, parents dispatched their unwanted children to foundling homes in droves. Abandonment continued in the next centuries but became less frivolous.

FIVE

Father Knows Best: Early Modern Mom

The Obedient Mom: 1500–1700

As the Renaissance crept northward, as Shakespeare wrote and Rembrandt painted, witches burned. Thousands of women — maybe 60,000; maybe as many as 200,000 — were pricked, racked, and strappadoed[1] on trumped-up charges until they confessed to being witches, at which point they were burned at the stake. The witch craze cannot be attributed to ignorance and superstition. It took place not in the Dark Ages, as commonly thought, but in the early modern period, the age of rationalism and the scientific revolution. Yet, even as Galileo formulated the law of inertia, Descartes philosophized, Montaigne moralized, and Kepler discovered the elliptical orbit of planets, countless women were tortured (including Kepler's mother!). Americans are ordinarily appalled by their own witch trials, which occurred in Salem and other New England towns a century after those in Europe, but they pale in comparison. In all, a mere thirty-six persons were executed in the United States, a paltry postscript to the collective insanity that ensued in Europe between 1500 and 1700.[2]

The witch craze in Europe was practically an equal opportunity destroyer of women. Men were executed, too, but 85 percent of those burned were women. Almost all grown women were vulnerable. Almost all could be accused of witchcraft; all women, that is, with one exception — the reproductively correct; namely, mothers. But while reproduction was a necessary condition, it was not sufficient for exempting a woman from trial by ordeal. Not all mothers were safe; only "good" mothers were granted immunity from the society's misogyny. Fewer women were saved from the stake than one might expect. Though many mothers, if not most, were quite competent, they were not necessarily deemed "good."

"Good mother" came to have a precise meaning. You know her well, for she has lingered all these years, with minor variations, in the background of our domestic values, and flourishes still in her pure form in the hearts and minds of the New Right. She is most assuredly not Murphy Brown or Mia Farrow or Hillary Rodham Clinton. She is, rather, properly married, faithful, subservient, modest, a woman who puts aside her own desires to rear and inspire her children. She is part of our mental furniture: the doormat. Her value is so fundamental to our thinking and cultural heritage that it generally remains an unspoken assumption, an "eternal truth." But she is not eternal. She had a beginning, and it was in the early modern period. For those of us who take issue with some aspects of her job description, we have this era to blame.

Prior to the sixteenth century, mothers were not held to much of a standard in relation to their children. The celestial mothers and celibates of the Middle Ages never actually changed diapers or swaddling, as it were. They resided in Heaven or in convents and were too busy preserving their chastity and renouncing worldliness. For a long time, actual motherhood barred a woman from sainthood.

This all changed with the demise of feudalism and the advent of the Reformation. The plain burgher woman, that paragon of homeliness, who arrived with the advent of early capitalism and the Protestants, became the role model for all females, the woman of status.

Motherhood had come a long way since the Middle Ages, when virginity was the more prestigious calling. Now maternity was part of the price of admission to Heaven. There was no other way to be a good Christian woman than to give birth (within wedlock, of course). Former priests rushed out to court wives. Family values were invented, praised, and propagandized. Motherhood was "in." Ironically, it was not Catholics who perfected the image of "good mother," but the Protestants (aided by the humanists), despite the fact that the strongest advocates of conservative family values today are to be found among the deeply Catholic peasantry of Portugal, Spain, southern France, and Italy, and among the Orthodox Christians of the former Balkans and Greece.

And what of mother love? The good mother, basking in her renewed respectability, was well able to love her children. Indeed, the age pioneered self-conscious parenting. But the offspring of women who were victims of misogyny did not fare well. The modern reader should not be surprised. Shakespeare left us a provocative clue, though it is mostly overlooked. When the three witches in *Macbeth* were concocting their magic brew, among the many revolting things they tossed into the cauldron was a finger from a strangled baby who had been thrown in a ditch. Sadly, this ingredient may not have been too hard to come by in Old England.[3] ❍

THE INVENTION of the good mother occurred amidst sweeping economic and political changes. As the Reformation spread across Europe, the Western world discarded feudalism and replaced it with centralized absolute monarchies, nation-states, bureaucracies, and early capitalism — the modern age. Cities grew, swelled by dispossessed peasants, and so did inflation. Society became polarized between the newly wealthy and the newly poor, some of whom became roving paupers. Eventually, the growth of manufacturing (especially cloth making) produced an expanding bourgeoisie. The members of this new middle class, with their Bible-based literacy, wage labor, and social mobility, were freed from the constraints of obligatory loyalty to their noble or clan. Instead, they could be loyal to their king and focus on themselves and their immediate family. Capitalism legitimated people's self-interest. These forces coalesced to create a revolutionary new domestic ideal — the nuclear family.

This is immediately apparent in the architecture. At the beginning of the period, the ordinary home still looked as if the occupants expected a flash flood to sweep away their belongings at any moment. Conspicuous by their absence were comfortable furniture, ornamentation, or any bric-à-brac that would convey the personalities of the house's occupants, furniture arranged for intimate conversation, games for entertainment, or, indeed, any objects that would encourage domesticity, coziness, warmth. The family meal, if one may speak of such a thing, was probably a hurried and primitive affair involving crude implements. Sleeping, eating, and work spaces were not sharply separated. Privacy was not yet a priority. Even the fanciest houses in France, though luxuriously appointed, had no corridors. Each room directly adjoined its neighbors. Architects prided themselves on aligning all the doors so that there was an unobstructed view from one end of the house to the other. All traffic, servants as well as guests, had to pass through a room to get to the next. Even the grandest houses provided about as much opportunity for seclusion as a series of railroad cars. These were not ideal sites for the development of private, intimate relationships between family members.[4]

But by the end of the period, the transition from public household to private home seems to have been accomplished. The number of chimneys per house increased, resulting in numerous warm hearths around which family members could gather. More and more, mats had been replaced by beds, comfortable places to retreat to. Gradually, even the poorest families partitioned rooms and installed glass windows, so houses became more private, with warmer, lighter spaces. The separation of workshop and domestic residence gained momentum; family members were becoming each other's exclusive company. Even sleeping arrangements, which had been based on gender, were now based on family relationship. Parents and their children retreated to a private space to sleep, separated from apprentices, servants, and other nonrelations. Bastards were no longer routinely welcome to reside within. Wealthier households began to hang family portraits on the walls. One's house was becoming a nice place to be. House was becoming a home.

Whether architecture begot home, or home begot family, the sixteenth century saw the rise of the nuclear family as a state of mind that called for the development of close, affectionate relationships between husbands and wives and parents and children.[5] Many historians[6] would hardly regard this as a new turn of events, but almost no one disputes that the nuclear family existed. With growing privacy, the family residence afforded more space in which to develop intimate relationships. Mom could now easily retire from the public gaze and bond with her children.

The nuclear family was given a moral boost by the Reformation — especially the Puritan wing — which dignified marriage and took it out of the realm of the lesser evil. Three years after nailing his theses to the door of the Wittenberg church, Martin Luther, father of the Reformation, pronounced marriage a "holy thing." He himself married a former nun and lived with her until his death, twenty years later. Henceforth, marriage was considered not only superior to burning (to paraphrase Saint Paul), but better than celibacy. Far from being a defense against fornication, it was viewed as a cooperative relationship based on mutual respect, a unity that God actually intended. Divorce came to be seen as a genuine possibility in cases where mutual respect dissolved. This served to enhance marriage, to turn it from a form of ritual entrapment to a potentially friendly bond. Parents even began to consult their grown children before arranging a match for them. While Protestants did not overtly endorse tumultuous sexual passion in marriage, neither did they preclude a positive emotional experience. The Catholic humanists, like Thomas More and Desiderius Erasmus, shared these ideals. And they prevailed. This was nothing short of revolutionary. The concept of happy marriage was born.

Within this newly revised family, motherhood turned 180 degrees. The Protestant cry against the cloister brought a renewed emphasis on childbearing, which dovetailed nicely with population pressures. Fertility was low due to late marriage and early death — Juliet's marriage to Romeo at fourteen was the exception, not the rule — factors that conspired to make children highly desirable. Women, even Catholics, were honored for having babies. Luther, having lived with his wife through six pregnancies, knew something of the pain and danger, and urged upon husbands a new solicitude.

But while he appreciated women's mothering, he offered them no other options: procreation, for women, was the sole purpose of their existence. To Luther, this was self-evident. In one of his Table Talk essays he noted that one only had to look at a woman's body to see what she was naturally intended for. "Were not her narrow shoulders, broad hips, and behind created for sitting at home, bearing and bringing up children?" This was in contrast to men's physiques — broad shoulders, narrow hips. Men were created for more intellectual endeavors.[7] God, according to Luther, had a marvelous sense of symmetry.

The family that Luther and Protestants were extolling was not an equal partnership, but a male-ownership model — patriarchy. Of course, patriarchy had existed for three thousand years by then, sometimes liberally seasoned with more than a pinch of misogyny, but it was more *de facto* than *de jure*. Now, the "rule of the father" was codified and extrapolated to every form of governance — in the home, village, church, and nation. "Honor thy father," the Fifth Commandment, was interpreted as ordering obedience not only to one's dad, but to one's priest or minister and king. Drawing from the Old Testament, political theorists like Sir Robert Filmer, in the seventeenth century, stressed that both monarchs and fathers exercised power as part of a continuous chain of command descending from the first father, Adam, and, before him, from God Himself. Patriarchy was reinforced at every level of social organization. Apparently no one noticed that in the original text of the Fifth Commandment, people were exhorted to honor their mothers as well.

Of course kings championed this ideology; it conveniently justified rule by "divine right." As the divinely appointed father of the nation, the king was naturally entitled to the affection, service, and economic resources of his subjects, just as fathers in families were owed obedience by wives and children. This was a closed self-justifying system, like a Möbius strip, to which women had no access. Patriarchy was inescapable because it was ubiquitous.

It is amusing to note that even in this early age kings understood the power of propaganda. Perhaps the wish to orchestrate audience response is in the royal gene pool. In the sixteenth century, the public relations "concept" was to promote the image of the monarch as father, and portraits were painted with this in mind. The results were very different from the domestic parlor scenes that became fashionable in the nineteenth century, nor were they like the calculated peep shows we have emanating from Buckingham Palace these days (which hint at the extent of distortion involved in royal representation). The early modern versions are closer in spirit to dynastic flow charts. The king dominates the canvas. The rest of his family are lined up like the cast of an opera taking a curtain call, offering themselves as a visual family tree, validating their lineage. If these paintings have a voice, it is that of the king-father, whose will extends to the will of the group. In portraits of the Stuart kings of England, mothers are so insignificant as to be actually absent.[8]

The saying "a man's home is his castle" was coined around this time, as the father was considered king within his own family. If there was a comfortable chair, it was assigned to the male head of household, a practice that seems to have continued to this day, the family cat notwithstanding. Father was freer than ever from such external controls as clan or parish priest. He was a despot — malevolent or benign according to temperament and inclination, lording his power over wife and children. The well-ordered family was considered the foundation of a well-ordered state and world. Because the father's authority was derived from the king and ultimately God, any concession of power to the wife not only would have undermined the delicate structure of this hierarchical pyramid, but would have been blasphemous as well.[9]

The Luther household was prototypical. The stocky peasant nun Katharina von Bora, who married ex-monk Luther, personified the ideal. She was reportedly a strong-minded *materfamilias* with many children, who fed the poor at her table, ran the family farm, and managed household and family affairs with little or no help from her husband — yet she deferred to him in all things. She had no views on public matters, but apparently had wide enough hips and bottom to carry out Martin's idea of her true purpose on earth.[10]

This social order was not all bad for women, for it did provide them with an important role and various safeguards. It valorized motherhood, which, after all, was the vocation open to the largest number of women, as opposed to, let's say, jester or mandolin player. Moreover, motherhood was recognized as vital work, deserving of sympathy and protection. Honorably married women enjoyed a new prestige. The Protestant ideal of marriage as a friendly arrangement may have improved the lot of both genders, if it did not set up false expectations. No doubt the Reformation contributed to an evolving moral climate that would eventually sanction planned parenthood. Finally, the Protestant emphasis on the Word of God, on the universal reading of the Bible in the vernacular, at least assured a modicum of literacy for a great many women. Once women learned to read and had established this privilege for their daughters, their situation would never again be quite the same.[11]

But for every step forward, the Reformation pushed women two steps back. More than in the centuries immediately preceding it, women were tied to their households.[12] At least Catholics had offered the woman an escape route via the convent, where she could obtain a classical education if she was so inclined. Now, her sphere of influence was limited to a single domain — the home — where she was under the thumb of her husband.

Whether this arrangement was oppressive is a matter of conjecture. It would be a mistake to read modern feminist frustration back into early modern family dynamics. In real life many compromises may have been sought by husbands and wives. The formal debate on the "woman question" continued in this era, with essays praising women as convincingly as essays damning them.[13] But the debate was an academic exercise carried on by a rarefied, intellectual elite that probably did not have much effect on the good woman tending the hearth. The bulk of the literature demeaned her. It would have been difficult to ignore the cumulative weight of sermons from the pulpit, prayer books, educational treatises, and household manuals, as well as governmental policies and social norms, all of which portrayed women as second rate. The composite message was emphatic and repetitious: woman existed to serve man. The good woman was a good mother, honorably wed and fertile, and, above all, *pious, obedient, chaste,* and *silent.* Those particular qualities, repeated *ad infinitum,* have become part of our cultural heritage.

Piety meant that the good mother raised her children to be good Christians. Though this has been secularized today in all but the most conservative circles, so that good mothers now raise their children to be good citizens, not necessarily churchgoers, the principle is much the same. The role of obedience to one's husband is no longer legally enforceable in Western countries, but it remains a fact of life for many women for economic reasons. Chastity, meaning sexual fidelity, is still operative, though the vehemence of this restriction seems to be diminishing. Witness the sexually forthright manner of film star–mother Susan Sarandon or countless others these days. Ingrid Bergman, a legendary star, was condemned for just such behavior in 1949. Prohibitions are weakening faster for men than for women, however, and a double standard still prevails.

Vestiges of the rule of silence may be easily seen today in any elementary school classroom, where girls are still typically quieter than boys. Girls' reticence may be short-lived, however. Thanks to feminists like Carol Gilligan and Gloria Steinem, women are developing a point of view and gaining access to media to express that point of view. In the sixteenth and seventeenth centuries the restriction on a woman's voice was of an entirely different magnitude. A woman who talked too much was criminalized as a scold, an exclusively female crime, for which she was subjected to a punishment like cucking (being strapped in a chair to be jeered at and pelted) or ducking (being plunged into water), as well as to sanctioned beatings by her husband. Any extreme violator was accused of witchcraft. Apparently, what went into and out of women's orifices was of major concern to early modern man. Speaking was equated with wantonness. From that perspective, the fact that today women's talk is often considered just female chatter, rather than substantive commentary, is actually a major advance.[14]

Add to these indignities the new definition of work that was emerging, a definition that served to further subjugate women. Work became that which one did for pay: wages were necessary if work was to be adjudged legitimate. So while women, however ill-suited, were obliged to perform domestic duty, they were simultaneously devalued for carrying it out, since unpaid labor was not real work. And because domestic work did not count, it was not considered an undue burden when carried out in addition to salaried work. Here we see the beginning of the "second shift" mentality, which the sociologist Arlie Hochschild has so powerfully documented in today's world: women who work outside the home are expected to do the work inside, too. Also, early modern women were excluded from guilds and confined to low-status occupations like domestic and spinner (from which the pejorative term spinster derives). The lot of an early modern mother was not an especially enviable one.[15]

With no option but to marry and reproduce, a full 40 percent of women — those who could not or would not marry, the infertile or postfertile, and the widowed — were doomed to a life on the fringes of society. By the year 1500 there was a surplus of women in every age group, especially the older cohorts, a situation that went from bad to worse as the Reformation continued to close convents. Some unmarried women joined roving bands of paupers. Some became prostitutes.[16]

Medieval society had tended to shut its eyes to prostitution; it was tacitly allowed. Most cities had brothels and some even passed legislation protecting the women and their customers. That all changed in the sixteenth century. With the Reformation, there was a steadily intensifying official uncharitableness toward unchaste women and their children. The prostitute was demonized and became an object of disrepute, a profligate, a disgrace. The sudden and rapid spread of syphilis in Europe further damaged her image (as if her customers had nothing to do with it. Here is another instance of projection of blame). As prostitution became criminalized, even this most desperate form of employment was denied to a woman. She was damned if she did and dead if she didn't.[17]

The stigma attached to the prostitute was inherited by her offspring. Until the sixteenth century, men often took care of their bastards, were proud of them, and in some cases brought them home to their wives to be reared. After all, the old foundling hospital in Florence is called the Hospital of the Innocents, suggesting, quite literally, that in the Middle Ages illegitimacy was not an automatic blot on one's character. But because the early modern period tightened the definition of permissible sex, the paternity of these children was no longer acknowledged. Bastards were "fatherless" and therefore threats to the patriarchal social order. As such, they were as scorned as their mothers. It was an impossible situation, with tragic consequences, as we shall see.[18]

Scientists were so entranced by this patriarchal design for the family that they actually claimed to have made microscopic observations of spermatozoa containing perfect little embryos. Presumably, a sperm was like a Chinese box, containing all future men in an infinite regression, which goes to show the extent to which science is a product of social influence. The female role in producing babies was reduced to that of a warming oven in which the sperm hatch, an idea that had persisted since Aristotle.[19]

In early modern Europe, grown women were split into two groups: good mothers and everyone else. The former went to Heaven; the latter were consigned to hellfire and damnation, and often they did not have to wait for death to intervene. It is ironic and sad that the elevated status of the good mother served to devalue all other women. On the positive side, many, if not most, women enjoyed maternity and derived pleasure from its enhanced prestige, even if that prestige was patronizingly accorded.

Down and Out: Maternal Images

The art and literature of early modern Europe, if taken at face value, would lead one to believe that early modern Europeans reproduced by cloning. One would hardly know from reading the autobiographies of the theologian Richard Baxter and the philosopher John Locke, for example, that they had been "of woman born."[20] Mothers are practically invisible in the artistic landscape.

Tradition tells us that Shakespeare dramatized the full range of human feeling, that nothing human was alien to him. Are we to suppose he just "forgot" about mothers? Where is the mother of Jessica? Desdemona? Ophelia? What woman carried in her womb Regan, Goneril, and Cordelia? Did all those shadowy, unnamed women die in childbirth? In *A Midsummer Night's Dream,* the maiden Hermia is advised that she owes her existence to her father alone. The subtle message is that the father is the necessary and sufficient parent.[21]

There *are* a few mothers in Shakespeare, veritable needles in a haystack, but they are hardly pious, obedient, silent, and chaste. Lady Macbeth was willing to pluck from her breast "the babe that milks me" and "dash his brains out." Hamlet's mother, Gertrude, wasted no time in marrying her murdered husband's brother, betraying, in Hamlet's view, an unseemly lust. The "problem" with Lady Macbeth's and Gertrude's mothering might not be so important if *Hamlet* and *Macbeth* were not such important plays, probably Shakespeare's most famous, and if there were other early modern literary mothers to balance the negative picture. Children fared a bit better, gaining significance in the last decades of the eighteenth century. Meanwhile, they continued to be used for their sentimental value, mostly as victims of brutality, as in Shakespeare's *Richard III* and *Titus Andronicus*.[22]

Mothers received their worst press in traditional fairy tales, which were being elaborated and collected at this time. In the early versions, Snow White was persecuted by her natural mother, and Hansel and Gretel were rudely abandoned by both of their biological parents. Indulging a cannibalistic impulse, Sleeping Beauty's mother-in-law tried to eat Beauty as well as her grandchildren. In "The Juniper Tree," a woman decapitates her stepson, chops his corpse into small pieces, and cooks him in a stew that her husband devours with gusto. And Cinderella's notorious stepmother turned her into a household drudge, though, interestingly, she was quite nice to her biological daughters. A century later, romantic editors, like the Grimm brothers, rebelled against any desecration of motherhood. In a lame effort to disguise their mother bashing, they transformed all the wicked mothers into wicked stepmothers.[23]

To be sure, the menacing mothers in folklore, like those in classical mythology, serve to work out unconscious conflicts within us. Given the exigencies of life, it is inevitable that children feel ambivalent about their mothers. Fairy tales enable us to transfer unacceptable feelings (like disloyalty) from inside ourselves to outside . . . to fairy tale mom. (You may recall that the Greeks and Romans did this with their myths.) In the stories, as in the myths, mom hates the child, not the other way around. Mom becomes the villain; the child, the victim. Our vague sense of guilt over our "improper" feelings toward our mothers is thereby vicariously cleansed away. Projection is a wonderful detergent for guilt. And because it functions in psychically subterranean fashion, we are able to preserve our comfortable fantasy that we *only* love our mother. Projection also serves simultaneously as a mechanism for attaining sweet revenge against mothers, for, by projecting wickedness onto them in literature, we have tarnished their reputation in a highly public manner. The very popularity of these fairy tales over so many centuries attests to their psychic resonance and to the effectiveness of the unconscious mechanisms involved.

Fairy tales are a thesaurus of so-called archetypal figures, universal truths, unfolding psychodynamics, and moral epiphanies; and their dissection has become something of a vocation among armchair analysts. Feminists love to hate fairy tales for their sexist values, especially Charles Perrault's seventeenth-century versions (later used by Disney), which were embellished with perfume and fashionability so as to be congenial to the French court, where they were talked of.[24] But there are real facts of life at work in these stories too. Stepmothers may very well have been wicked in early modern Europe. In an age of high death rates, few children lived out childhood with both parents alive. Fathers often remarried. Since father's new wife, the child's stepmother, was dependent on her husband for security and status, it is only natural that she would strive on behalf of her own children against her predecessor's offspring — even to the point of murdering them. Sadly, the wicked stepmother may not have been a fairy tale.

Neither, perhaps, was the cruel mother. Mom also remarried after the spouse's death. When a young widow rewed, it was customary (at least in Southern Europe) that she leave *with* her dowry but *without* her children, who remained with her deceased husband's kin. Understandably, this may not have been a happy arrangement for the children. No wonder, then, that the "abandoned" children experienced their mother as "Mommie Dearest." Objectively speaking, these mothers may have been more sinned against than sinning. They were pawns in a social structure that presented them with a choice as bitter as Sophie's: their children or a mate.

In these centuries, the mother image in painting lost ground. Depictions of the nursing Madonna ceased to be an obsession. Suddenly, images of the Madonna's husband proliferated. We see Saint Joseph at the manger, leading the ass in the flight into Egypt, at the carpenter's shop working side by side with his divine Son. The Virgin Mary, once the Queen of Heaven, has become the perfect wife — an obedient, silent spouse, a fit companion to Joseph, her protector, who works to provide for her and her Child. Catholics still produced depictions of Mary in the sixteenth century — the Trinity incarnate inside the Virgin's Womb (as powerful an image of woman as any); the Virgin fainting at the Crucifixion; Coronations; Immaculate Conceptions — but they are fewer in number, more mannered in style, and, if anything, are even more devoid of social reality than earlier versions of Mary. Reform Catholics began to protest the theatricality of the newer portraiture and repeatedly urged artists to stick to the text of the Bible. Protestants tore down Mary's portrait altogether, as part of their campaign against images, whence the term *iconoclasm* derives. It is interesting to note that the demotion of Mary to sidekick coincided with the demotion of woman to *hausfrau*. In retrospect, perhaps even so incomplete a goddess as Mary was better than no goddess at all.[25]

Family portraits became all the rage in the sixteenth century, indicating the rising concept of family. Clearly, the family felt a need to contemplate itself as a unit. These paintings are the visual manifestation of a new self-consciousness of the family bond. Exterior scenes do not disappear — they develop into landscapes — but interior scenes, private domestic scenes, frequently invade the canvas. And they are placed not in church, but in the home. While these portraits are an homage to family, they celebrate only a particular vision of that entity — the patriarchal family. In ordinary family portraits, as in their royal counterparts, dad takes center stage. Around him, stiffly clustered, are family members, both dead and alive. All are in subordinate positions. All are situated so as to highlight the male lineage — by gaze, gesture, or physical resemblance.[26]

Perhaps the most telling index of maternal status is the hype surrounding Queen Elizabeth I of England. To be a woman and a sovereign in early modern Europe was almost an oxymoron. But Elizabeth was a genius at self-presentation. What is especially interesting is that she flaunted her childlessness. Her inviolate status became an integral and positive part of her image, so positive that she named a colony after her unruptured hymen — Virginia. Her childlessness was defiance of her parliament and counselors, all of whom urged her to produce an heir to ensure an orderly succession. But she shrewdly used her virginity to her advantage. By firmly demonstrating that motherhood was not on her agenda, she sloughed off the odium attached to ordinary women. She was able to convince her subjects that she gave them the nurturing that would have gone to a child. With considerable calculation, she fashioned herself into a Protestant Virgin (*sans* Baby), appropriating many of Mary's symbols to foster a kind of personal mythology — the cult of the Virgin Queen — which turned out to be effective in elevating her status. Perhaps only by presenting herself in this way could she hope to overcome the confines of her gender. She intuitively understood that motherhood did not harmonize with real political power. Yet, in the end, she was so transcendent that her imprimatur — Elizabethan — is attached to the culture of the late sixteenth century.[27]

The Reformation dismembered the Virgin. The various facets of her persona were divided up and doled out one at a time to each of the prominent stereotypes of women. In the High Renaissance, you may recall, Mary was maternal *and* alluring *and* powerful. The Reformation split off her maternity from both her allure and her power; motherhood was acceptable only in its nurturing, selfless, and self-sacrificing form. Sensual moms need not apply. The same goes for uppity ones. The good mother was the Virgin minus appeal and magic. Her sensuality was assigned to the "lewd" woman (who was also related to Eve). And her power was assigned to the "witch." The witch became as potent a symbol in this age as Mary was in the last.

Suddenly, out of nowhere, the night sky filled with old crones riding broomsticks, their hair flying, their bodies smeared with toad's excrement, as they traveled to Sabbath celebrations where they copulated with Satan. These "witches" reportedly ate boiled babies, spit on crucifixes, raised hail and thunderstorms . . . and stole penises! For three hundred years, they were perceived everywhere in Europe, and then, for reasons as mysterious as those which brought them, they left, stopping briefly in America before finally disappearing. In fact, there probably were women in early modern Europe who practiced benign pagan rituals, or who were mentally ill and thought of themselves as witches, but I think we may safely assume that they never copulated with Satan, despite testimony to the contrary. Rather, these women, and multitudes of others, were victims of one of the most extensive and ugly assaults against the female gender in all of European history. The collective insanity of the witch craze was not limited to one religion. Both Catholics and Protestants carried out misogynistic inquisitions of excruciating savagery. The feminist theologian Mary Daly has called it gynocide.[28]

At first glance, it may seem that the witch craze had little to do with motherhood, but the personae of witch and mother are closely related. They are inversions of each other. The characteristics of the witch are not random; they are direct perversions of the characteristics of the good mother. The good mother was silent; the witch was verbally aggressive. The good mother was chaste; the witch was promiscuous and perverted. The good mother was always obedient; the witch was wild and insubordinate. And the good mother was pious; the witch flamboyantly sacrilegious.[29] The witch was the anti-mom, the bad mother. She marked off the borders of proper maternal behavior, thus providing the good mother with a clearer definition of herself. And she soaked up all the loathesomeness that could have poisoned the good mother's purer being.

The witch was the anti-mom in another important way: she was barren. (Actually, the typical European woman accused of being a witch may once have had children, but was now menopausal and without a husband.) Not only was she infertile, but she took delight in producing barrenness in others, presumably out of jealousy of their fertility. Her *modus operandi* was witchcraft, which is spelled out in the *Malleus Maleficarum* (or *Witches' Hammer*), a popular handbook for witch hunters written in the fifteenth century under the auspices of the Pope. According to the *Malleus,* witches "bewitched" innocent young girls to turn away from holy, heterosexual matrimony. Witches were also responsible for male impotence, for hindering conception, and for causing infants to stay in the womb, all in addition to the theft of penises. A full quarter of all indictments against witches in England were for bewitching infants.[30]

The witch became a scapegoat for all problems related to childbearing. For every instance of male impotence, a witch could be tortured and burned. Witches, not men, could be blamed for the birth of illegitimate children, for nonconception, even for the death of legitimate (father-owned) children. But perhaps the most ridiculous attribution to the witch was extra breasts, by which she nurtured evil. Witch hunters were encouraged to search for extra teats on the presumed witch by, among other things, pricking birthmarks, warts, freckles, or any skin blemish (they had special instruments for this), and by sucking any "protrusion." Oddly, investigators often claimed to find these teats, which only proves that hate may be as blind as love.[31]

Because witches were prosecuted for producing infertility and abortions, it is not surprising that midwives became a target for witch hunters, since, traditionally, midwives had colluded with women in their birth control endeavors (which, before now, had not been criminal). Besides, midwives were already a degraded group, contaminated by the very nature of their work. Women's reproductive organs were considered evil incarnate, a stigma that attached to the birth process itself, which was, since the onset of patriarchy, thought to be a messy, even revolting affair. Men had been forbidden to attend births, and midwives were censured for doing so. With convenient doublethink, the midwife, privy to the mysteries of female anatomy, pregnancy, methods of facilitating labor, the social rituals of childbirth, and various palliatives, all unknown by the male physician in this period (deprived as he was of empirical experience), was now accused of possessing demonic powers for that very knowledge![32] The midwife's power was her death sentence.

As male physicians began to dominate the obstetrics business in the sixteenth and seventeenth centuries, the mortality rate did *not* decline. Inadvertently, they spread the deadly plague of puerperal (childbed) fever through their unsterile delivery practices. Asepsis and the transmission of disease through bacteria and unwashed hands were unknown until the latter part of the nineteenth century. Midwives carried fewer diseases than doctors because they attended only women in labor, not sick people in general. The story of the male establishment's battle to control and profit from the essential female experience of childbirth, and to "medicalize" that which is normal and healthy, has been well-documented.[33]

The conglomeration of images of mother in early modern Europe — her absence in literature and art; her demonization in the fairy tale and the witch craze — suggests a profound ambivalence in the collective unconscious. Through the grid of psychoanalysis, the witch hunts, the evil stepmothers, the planned childlessness of Elizabeth I may all be read as hostility toward mothers, anger worked out not toward mother herself, but through her "stand-ins" (literary images, queer old ladies). Perhaps this upsurge in mother bashing (reminiscent of the misogynist Classical Greeks) had to do with a feeling that women were exceeding their boundaries, which, at the same time, were becoming more rigid and restrictive. Perhaps the breakdown of social, political, and religious consensus created the massive insecurity for which certain women, especially unruly women, were scapegoated. It is interesting to note that while the good mother was lauded from the pulpit, she was largely invisible in the art and icons of the period. The cultural splitting of women into "good" and "bad" had, as we shall see, a great effect on the institution and experience of motherhood.

One marvelous exception worth noting is found in Dutch painting, where the good mother is far from absent. Some of the most delightfully intimate pictures of parents and children were created by the Dutch painters of the sixteenth century, or by foreign painters, like the Spaniard Murillo, who were selling to a Dutch market. Enduring images abound: lots of babies' bottoms being wiped and moms' good-night kisses; there is one of a mom inspecting a child's head for lice; and another of a mother guiding her child's first steps. These splendid paintings convey the feeling that mother love was the most ordinary thing in the world. Not surprisingly, a common depiction was of a mother nursing her infant. Previously, this subject had been mostly confined to religious compositions, but in one of the most telling inversions of icon and objects in all of European art, the Protestant Dutch abolished images of the Madonna and Child, only to reinstate them surreptitiously in paintings of simple, secular nursing mothers. What is especially significant about this effervescence of depicted mother love is that it occurred in the European country that accorded its womenfolk more freedom than did its counterparts. The Netherlands tolerated prostitution (and, in fact, it still does); it eschewed wet-nursing; and had the lowest rate of child abandonment. The Netherlands of the sixteenth and seventeenth centuries, then, seems to be the exception that proves the rule: respect for women directly correlates with women's respect for their children.[34]

Sparing the Rod: Maternal Reality

As if early modern mothers were not sorely maligned by their treatment in art and literature, they are lumped together by historians with the even more maligned Puritans, about whom almost no one has a good word to say. The Puritans were the early Protestant reformers who insisted that the Church of England (itself a reform church) was not sufficiently "pure." They are best known for their consuming interest in Scripture, infant depravity, predestination, eternal salvation, and odd names, like Tribulation Wholesome and Zeal-of-the-Land Busy, names that even their contemporary, the playwright Ben Jonson, had such fun mocking.[35]

Up to this time, names had not been important. Only a few names were common in English, so few that siblings were sometimes given the same name. Sometimes a newborn was given the name of a recently deceased child. So many people had the same name that they had to be differentiated by name endings, numerals, and nicknames (John II, Johnson, Littlejohn, Jack, and so on). Apparently the Puritans felt that children were less interchangeable and more in need of a personal label with an individually tailored moral message to launch them in life.

The Puritans have a terrible reputation as parents, and early modern mothers suffer by association. Without exception, historians from Alice Morse Earle in the 1890s to Philip Greven in the 1990s have considered Puritans to be little better than child abusers.[36] Until this past decade, scholarship gave the impression that all Puritans were ferocious souls who spent the bulk of their time flogging their kids, beating the will out of them, and beating biblical bromides in. The expression "spare the rod and spoil the child" is usually (and mistakenly) assumed to be Puritan. It is actually from a seventeenth-century poem by Samuel Butler satirizing Puritans. To be called "puritanical" today is to be insulted.

As it turns out, historians' greater error is in their unduly harsh view of Puritan child rearing, and not in their failure to distinguish early modern mothers from the Puritan midst. Though never more than a small percentage of the population, the Puritans cast a big shadow in sixteenth- and seventeenth-century Europe and America. Partly this was because they left a smoking gun — books, diaries, treatises, sermons, autobiographies, and letters. It has been said that they suffered from "extreme loquacity" and an irresistible desire to commit every thought to paper. Their intense interest in child rearing was the beneficiary of these traits, and Puritans came to define and dominate a subject that before had been mostly ignored. They are the true forebears of Dr. Spock. Given the Puritans' dominance in the early modern media, it is no wonder that their preoccupation with morals and child discipline extended to the population at large.[37]

The actual Puritan philosophy of child raising was probably very similar to that of other parents of their day. Where they differed was in their high profile. This was an era of tremendous cultural shifting, and Europeans of all religious orientations may have become reflective about children and receptive to strict ideas about child-rearing techniques in an attempt to exert some control over the future.

Before the Reformation, the Catholic Church enjoyed a monopoly on people's religious affiliation. Suddenly there was competition. Numerous religious sects vied for one's soul. If a particular denomination was to survive, its children's allegiance was vital. The rising generation attained new status as preservers of the faith. Special efforts had to be made to secure their loyalty. Parents had to try harder to win and maintain compliance. This was a situation ripe for stern parental intervention, and, indeed, early modern parents were far more intrusive and strict than the parents we have met up to this point.[38]

In proper households, children were supposed to stand or kneel in their parents' presence, unless bidden to sit down, and to beg their parents' blessing morning and night. Parents were considered God's representatives; their approval was all important. One writer (John Aubrey, no Puritan) remembered the 1630s as a time when

> the child perfectly loathed the sight of his parents, as the slave his Torturer. Gentlemen of 30 or 40 years old, fitt for any employment in the commonwealth, were to stand like great mutes and fools bare headed before their parents, and the Daughters (grown woemen) were to stand at the Cupboards side during the whole time of the proud mothers visitt, unless (as the fashion was) 'twas desired that leave

> (forsooth) should be given to them to kneele upon cushions brought them by the servingman, after they had done sufficient Penance standing.[39]

The Puritans were only the most conspicuous advocates of a hard line with regard to the raising of children.

Of course, these were the habits of bourgeois families. Among the poorer, nonliterate classes, child raising was not much of an issue but was shaped by the round of daily tasks; it was always in part an apprentice relationship. It was not so much something parents did as it was something that happened, or had to happen if the family's work was to be done.[40]

Worry was the hallmark of Puritanism, of which child rearing was but one source. A byproduct of Puritan theology was a haunting sense of guilt. Deprived of all the psychological props of Catholicism, the collective rituals, the opportunities for blowing off steam, Puritans stood alone before their Maker with nothing but their conscience. Their guilt could no longer be assuaged by confessions, indulgences, pilgrimages, or even by miraculous interventions by the Virgin. (Protestants did not believe in her.)[41] Driven by unresolvable anxiety over their salvation, they took to a strict moral account keeping (hence all those diaries) as a means of keeping track of their moral balance sheet. Self-confession, the habit of enumerating one's failings, has taken hold in our own culture to the extent that it supports whole industries: television talk shows, magazines, even psychotherapy. We have the Puritans to thank for this.

And for self-conscious parenting. Four hundred years before Sigmund Freud, the Puritans charged parents with the profound responsibility for the life and prospects of their children: little people could be "set on a true course" or ruined for life by the influence of the home. What happened to a child was its parents' fault. To the Puritans, a well brought-up child was an indication of parental virtue. Conversely, a sinful child signaled parental failure. The quality of the child was a measure of the quality of its parents. Even at the end of their lives, parents could be vindicated or destroyed by the performance of their grown children. Puritans assumed (rather arrogantly) that any event that befell their offspring was somehow related to them. In Colonial Massachusetts, when Cotton Mather's daughter burned herself badly in a fire, her father wrote, "Alas, for my sins the just God throws my child in the fire." This is parent blaming taken to an extreme. But are modern parents so different? To be sure, contemporary moms and dads credit their children with greater self-determination than did Puritans, and are hardly beset with religious matters, but they tend to feel enormous (if not total) responsibility for their children's emotional well-being. To the mother especially, how her child turns out becomes the final judgment on her life.[42]

This gives the rising generation enormous power, and it complicates the parenting process. A mother who could be condemned for any defect in her offspring naturally feels ambivalent toward the child, especially if the child willfully disobeys (as children often do). Invariably, children sense this ambivalence and may wish to retaliate for mom's less than unconditional love. This adds credence to the idea that all those fairy tales featuring predatory mothers were a form of unconscious revenge.

With so much at stake — possible damnation for their children and themselves — it is understandable that parental anxiety about proper methods of child rearing was prominent on the Puritan agenda. Early Protestants, like Catholics, believed that children were intrinsically inclined to wickedness, but, unlike Catholics, felt youngsters needed firm correction if they were not to go to Hell. In the Catholic tradition, children's souls were only briefly in peril, until baptism, which took place a few days after birth. The sacrament of baptism put the whole business to rights and set the infant on the path to Heaven. But the Protestants distrusted the effectiveness of the sacraments. To them, salvation was not so easily acquired. They thought that the child must deliberately choose the way of virtue, and such a choice was possible only after a period of proper indoctrination. Good Protestants were therefore saddled with a new task — the religious processing of children. One might suppose that Puritans would have expected little good to come from their child-rearing efforts, since they also believed in predestination; that is, those children who were bound for Heaven were already selected. Because entry into paradise was rigged beforehand, there was nothing sinners could do to alter their fate. Why, then, bother to discipline a child if its destiny was sealed? This logical inconsistency did not dampen the Puritans' zeal for moral indoctrination. Undaunted, they valiantly persisted in their efforts to mold their children into proper Christians, and they valiantly persisted in writing it all down.

But non-Puritans, as I mentioned, were not exactly permissive parents either. Humanists, Catholics, and others were also stern disciplinarians, though for different reasons. They believed that children were morally neutral (not irremediably depraved) but that a strict upbringing was needed to prevent deterioration. In their view, discipline preserved a fragile innocence rather than corrected inborn vices. If you were a fly on the wall, you might not notice a difference in the way any of these European groups conducted themselves. While John Locke famously argued in 1690 that children are "blank slates" on which parents could inscribe what they wished, he also advocated a hard line, just like the Puritans.[43]

Historians have tended to assume the worst about these parents. Physical punishment and humiliation were thought to be the order of the day. That children were expected to submit, without understanding, was presumed to be standard early modern child-rearing practice. Underlying the harshness was supposed to be a profound indifference to one's offspring.[44]

The predicament of John and Charles Wesley, founders of Methodism, is often cited as a case in point. As youngsters they were throttled, whipped, and chastised, and even required to cry silently so as not to disturb their elders with "odious noise." We know this because their mother, Susannah Wesley, herself the daughter of Puritans, unself-consciously detailed her personal methods of child rearing in a letter to one son. She reports drilling her children in obedience and using "the rod" for punishment from an early age, sometimes before a child was a year old. "When a child is corrected, it must be conquered," she wrote.[45] This was not the mother-child bond we prefer today, but the mother-child Bund.

Harsh discipline was purportedly not limited to the middle and lower classes. Lady Jane Grey, the great-granddaughter of Henry VII and the vehicle of her family's ambitions for the throne of England, was relentlessly beaten by her pious parents in the 1530s and 1540s. She could do nothing right in their eyes and was continually "bobbed" for one supposed infraction or another. By her own account, when in the presence of her father or mother she thought herself "in hell."[46]

Early modern parents were assumed to care so little for their children, some historians argue,[47] that they did not bother to give them individual names. That was why they sometimes named a newborn after a child who had recently died or even one who was still alive. Why not spread a good name around? At least one George or William or Elizabeth might survive.

Presumably, coldness to children was not confined to England. The French philosopher Michel Montaigne commented, "I have lost two or three children in infancy, not without regret, but without great sorrow."[48] And in a letter of August 19, 1671, Madame de Sévigné mentioned a friend's curious sorrow over the death of her little girl: "She is very much upset and says she will never have another as pretty."[49] One is left to wonder whether the girl would have been mourned had she not been pretty.

One of the most oft-quoted documents by historians painting a bleak picture of the bad old days is the extraordinary, obsessively detailed diary kept by Dr. Jean Hérouard, physician to the infant Louis XIII. It is a veritable catalogue of what today can only be considered child abuse. It reads like pornography. Poor Louis was not held by his mother during his first seven months. He nearly starved to death because of his wet nurses' inadequacies (he went through four). Dr. Hérouard reports interfering with Louis's excretory processes from the time the baby was two weeks old by using purges and enemas; he continued this close supervision for the rest of Louis's life. During his first three years, Louis's genitals were frequently caressed, rubbed, and sucked by his nurse. Between four and six, he was taken into bed with a number of ladies-in-waiting and nurses and was encouraged to explore their private parts; he later commented publicly on their size and lubrication. The most charitable interpretation is that the grown-ups performed the activities naïvely for the little king's amusement, not their own. But from our post-Freudian vantage point, we may conjecture that they account for the king's later troubles. Louis was notable for sexual disorientation: he suffered long periods of impotence such that he could father an heir only after twenty years on the throne. As an adult, he was secretive, introverted, and a stutterer.[50]

If these child-care practices were reserved exclusively for the French aristocracy, one wonders why Louis was not granted special treatment regarding beatings. The child was beaten mercilessly. First whipped at the age of two, he was punished continually (usually for obstinacy) after he became king, at the age of nine. On waking in the morning after a transgression, he was beaten on the buttocks by his nurse with a birch or a switch. The whippings increased in frequency when he was three, and on one occasion his father whipped him himself when in a rage about the boy. As he grew older, his nurse could not control him, and he was held down by soldiers when she beat him.[51] How plausible is it to assume that discipline was less severe for those children lower in the social order than for a reigning king?

From evidence like this, historians have inferred an underlying disposition toward children that was at best unfriendly and more likely indicative of outright paranoia. Regarding the Puritans in particular, one of the more common explanations is that, having failed to sway the nation toward their beliefs, they turned their disappointment into compulsive vengeance against the one group within their power — their children. According to this theory, parents were determined to crush the wills of their children because their own wills had been broken,[52] a process that, once initiated, proceeded with a kind of boss-dumps-on-man-so-man-kicks-dog inevitability.

There would be much merit to this analysis except that it now appears that Puritans and their contemporaries may not have been so cruel to their children after all. The accepted view these days is that the sadism of early modern parents toward their children has been greatly exaggerated. Documents like Hérouard's diary and Wesley's letter may not be representative, but were selected by historians, perhaps unconsciously, to support a theory that parents in the past were worse than parents now, a theory that smacks of cultural bias, if not smugness.[53] Actually, the harsh discipline associated with the early modern period belongs to one much later. Hellfire-and-brimstone sermons reached the height of their popularity in the eighteenth century, and suffocating repression came in the nineteenth.

While much of early modern child rearing does seem extreme by our standards, it was not incongruous, and certainly not capricious, given the prevalent views of human nature and society. Far from representing a dark surge of percolating hostility, the severity may have been a manifestation of greater interest in children. So long as no one cared about their offspring very much, they could be allowed to run wild or left in the hands of lazy, easygoing, negligent servants. But in this period it was thought that children had to be thoughtfully disciplined. A careful reading of Puritan child-rearing books reveals that their advice tended to be highly consistent and to follow a predictable pattern. Parents were to set the example for their children; parents were not to spoil their children. Spoiling, called "cockering," was a behavior to which women were thought especially prone, as they were easily led by "passion." The avoidance of wanton indulgence, however, did not preclude affection and playfulness, which parents were urged to display. Discipline was to be carried out with common sense and wisdom, after an assessment of the nature of the infraction and the culpability of the child. It was to be done when the adult was in a *calm* state of mind, after the child had been told why the correction was being made. Spanking was sometimes necessary, but only as a last resort. Care had to be taken not to injure the child. Casual brutality was categorically condemned. Puritans wanted their children to obey freely, without compulsion. Obedience that was extorted was considered null and void before God.[54]

We have no good evidence of whether Puritans took their own advice. But because they were the first group to discuss child rearing at length and always dealt with the question of the "rod" does not mean they invented it or even overindulged in its use.[55] In fact, their advice books advocated a serious, moderate, sensible form of discipline. If anything, they conveyed a genuine sensitivity to children's needs and great care about their welfare. The real difference in discipline between then and now is in the Puritans' religious orientation. Proper rearing was to lead the child to salvation, not necessarily to emotional well-being.

The closer one gets to the Puritans, the more sympathetic they seem as parents. In his diary, the Reverend Ralph Josselin, a seventeenth-century Englishman, wrote that he could not recall ever having been whipped by his Puritan parents, and he never recorded whipping his own children, although he repeatedly threatened to disinherit his dissolute second son, John. Apparently he did not have the heart to carry out his threats, however, for when he died he left the bulk of his estate to John. So much for parental sadism. In fact, brutal punishment of youngsters was a criminal offense in early modern England; it incurred firings, fines, and deep personal remorse. When child abuse occurred, it seems to have been in the treatment of poor young apprentices, which, of course, does not excuse it, but does take it outside the domain of family.[56]

There is much that modern mother might admire about the Puritans. For those who exalt the mother-infant bond, the Puritans were advocates of its importance about four hundred years before contemporary pediatricians. They railed against the use of wet nurses, strongly favoring maternal nursing. And they were the first to define children as a target audience for books. Unfortunately, the books they wrote for children were mostly religious handbooks and tracts used to guide little feet on the path to Heaven. But occasionally there was a masterpiece — John Bunyan's *Pilgrim's Progress* (1678), for one.[57]

Puritans were also the first to promote guided reading for children. Fables, fairy tales, nursery rhymes, all of which came to be the property of young readers (though they had not been written specifically for them), were frowned on by Puritans for romanticizing a life of idleness and violence. Their objections, of course, only served to drive the books underground. Whether one regards Puritan intrusion in children's reading as early censorship or early political correctness is a matter of perspective. But it does convey a certain protectiveness of children's sensibilities and is reminiscent of the many controversies in the air today, about lyrics on rock recordings, sex and violence on television, and even the goriness of early Walt Disney.

What is especially ironic about early modern men is that, though they were male chauvinists, they were most assuredly not absent fathers. When ministers and others in positions of leadership wrote about parenting, they used the pronoun "he," directing their comments to the father. No doubt this was a recognition of the father's final authority in the family, and of the belief that child rearing was too important to be left to women, whose rational powers were thought to be weak, their moral vulnerability great . . . so let's not feel nostalgic for that arrangement. Regardless of the offensiveness of their motives, men shared parenting functions with women to a remarkable degree, especially after their offspring's infancy, and they shared the blame when things went wrong. After the nursing stage, fathers decided what children would learn, eat, and wear. They rocked the babies to sleep, walked them at night, and cuddled them when they traveled. They decided when children were ready to begin work, leave home, and whom they should marry. They were the source of moral and intellectual guidance. This situation reversed itself in the next century, when woman began to be seen as morally superior and children were reared entirely within mom's orbit because daddy was now out of the home, at work. But meanwhile the Puritan father, he that hath become the scapegoat in the popular mind for our civilization's original sin against children, took on child care as his social responsibility.[58]

This is very apparent in early American history. The fathers of the American Founding Fathers were much more fascinating to them than their mothers, if their own writings are reliable testimony. Thomas Jefferson's mother, for example, is shrouded in mystery, primarily because Jefferson was so uncommunicative about her. His silence is the more perplexing because he wrote voluminous and heartfelt words about his two daughters and about his father; yet he is dry and curt on the subject of his mother. The same may be said of Benjamin Franklin and John Adams. Whatever their feelings, those men were not motivated to leave their mothers' stories on the pages of their letters and journals, as they did their fathers'. By all accounts they did not think ill of their mothers; they simply did not think of them much at all.[59]

Much has been made of the staggering death rate of children in this era; it has been cited as the explanation for parents' supposed indifference to their offspring. Presumably, children's deaths were so familiar, so very ordinary, that parents became hardened to their loss and grieved little.[60] We have encountered this explanation before.

Today, the death of a child is an outrage, an offense to the natural order. No pain is thought to be as exquisite. But in the sixteenth and seventeenth centuries, a third of all youngsters died before their fifth birthday. Cotton Mather was outlived by only one of his fifteen children. Queen Anne of England had fifteen pregnancies: all except one of her children were stillborn or died in infancy. The survivor, William, Duke of Gloucester, died at the age of eleven. If these parents grieved their loss as we do, they would have been in perpetual mourning.[61]

Diaries and autobiographies, which have been examined scrupulously in these last two decades, indicate that the loss of a little one was most assuredly not trivial. Mary Lady Verney of England was delirious for two days and nights with sorrow when her baby died suddenly of convulsions; when the news of the death of her daughter Peggy reached her, she felt totally unable to care for two little girls, relatives of her husband, because to do so would have exacerbated her own grief. Even so religious a man as Martin Luther was virtually inconsolable after the death of two of his six children in his lifetime. One of the most poignant of all testimonies of parental grief is Ben Jonson's farewell to his seven-year-old first son, whom he addressed as "child of my right hand, and joy," and described as his "best piece of poetrie." And the notebooks of the astrologer-physician Richard Napier (1559–1634), who functioned as a kind of psychologist for his age, catalogued his treatment of 134 women who were grief-stricken, mostly about the death of their children. These were women of all social classes.[62]

Familiarity with death did not breed indifference. Naturally, many parents were consoled by Christian faith, which counseled resignation to God's will, and by their belief that children were on loan from God, Who could recall them whenever He wished. Some comforted themselves with the thought that the child was in a "better" place.[63] Some refrained from overtly showing their grief because an outright display of misery was regarded as a failing, "unchristian," or, worse, "womanish." But mourn they did. Try as they might, people were consumed by the death of their children. Practice did not make perfect, so to speak.

After all, what would Shakespeare's audience have made of his death scenes if they had been unfamiliar with parental love or parental grief? The anguish of King Lear, mourning for the dead Cordelia, his daughter, in his arms, must have had resonance. The grief of Macduff, when told of the murder of his wife and offspring, must have tugged at the audience's heartstrings. These were not exotic feelings.

Women wanted children. To be "big-bellied" or "great-bellied" was the happy norm. The science of the day indicated that a woman, frustrated in her desire to reproduce, might sicken and turn green. About a third of brides were already pregnant on their nuptial day, suggesting that they needed to prove their fertility before men would marry them. But their wish for babies seems to have transcended their husbands' desire.[64]

Thanks to recent studies of the few samples of women's writings available, we can learn early modern women's ideas and feelings in their own words. And what they say, time and again, is that they love their children. Of course, it was only the "good" mothers (married, obedient, and so on) who were privileged enough to be literate, to afford pen and ink, to have time to commit their thoughts to paper. Undoubtedly these were the women most comfortable with a patriarchal ideology, most at peace with their position. Nevertheless, the repetitiveness of their message, its artless vehemence, its warmth, suggest an authenticity of sentiment. The Englishwoman Dorothy Leigh wrote, in a tract intended as counsel for her sons, that a mother's love for her children was beyond the bounds of reason. Similarly, the gentlewoman Elizabeth Grymeston prefaced a book of prayers for her son in 1610 with this: "There is no love so forcible as the love of an affectionate mother to her naturall child." Here is an excerpt from a poem from the early American mother Anne Bradstreet, written in 1658:

I had eight birds hatcht in one nest
Four cocks there were, hens the rest,
I nurst them up with pain and care,
Nor cost, nor labour did I spare,
Till at the last they felt their wing,
Mounted the trees, and learn'd to sing . . .

If birds could weep, then would my tears
Let others know what are my fears
Lest this my brood some hard should catch
And be surpriz'd for want of watch.[65]

Surely one who so laments the departure of her children was attached to them in the first place.

One of the most remarkable early glimpses of a relationship between mother and child is the correspondence between Madame de Sévigné and her grown daughter, Madame de Grignon. What is obvious from even a cursory examination of the mother's letters is her attempt to *portray* herself as a devoted mother. By all accounts, she was a devoted mother, probably overly so. What is significant is that she felt it important to project this aspect of herself. Letter writing was an art form during this period in France. Letters were read out loud to a circle of intimates, where they were enjoyed not only for content, but for wit and imagination. They were public forums for self-presentation. So, in her correspondence with her daughter, Madame de Sévigné was, in effect, putting on a performance. It is significant that she chose as her role that of "concerned mother." The personification of concerned mother was her bid for status.[66] Obviously, then, that particular persona carried weight, even on the fringes of the frivolous French court. Good mothering, or at least the appearance of good mothering, must have been valued in seventeenth-century France.

To bear no child was unfortunate in early modern Europe, but to bear one outside marriage or to bear too many was disastrous. Apparently, women did have a modicum of "choice," albeit a very small one, in this matter. Frenchwomen were known to suffer from an "epidemic of headaches" to deflect their husbands' amorous overtures. Mary Holden, an Englishwoman, prescribed a diet that would "make a man no better than a eunuch." Women knew about the contraceptive effect of prolonged breast-feeding. They also made use of sponges, *coitus interruptus,* and abstinence, none of which was approved by the church. Condoms made of animal bladders were known but lurked outside the realm of respectability. The English called them "French letters"; the French, in turn, named them *les capotes anglais,* "English hats," each nationality thereby attributing immorality to the other.[67]

None of the contraceptive methods in use was very effective, and women sometimes found themselves carrying a child they would have preferred to be without. Abortion was sometimes resorted to with abortifacients, for which there were numerous recipes. Modern analysis surprisingly reveals that some of these remedies may have been effective.[68] Of course, abortion was roundly condemned by the church and moralists, so the recipes were "billed" as medicines for inducing menstruation. But a rose by any other name . . .

By far the larger concern among "good" women was the conception of children, not contraception — even though childbirth meant certain pain and a reasonable chance of death (estimated conservatively at 7 percent per woman over her lifetime). The level of obstetrics and gynecology was so primitive that Mary Tudor, Queen of England, stayed in confinement for five months waiting to deliver, only to realize, to her humiliation, that she had never been pregnant. The humanist Erasmus wondered why in the world women would ever succumb to men's advances, given the "labor" and the extraordinary pain of the outcome. And to do so a second time, he concluded, could be accounted for only by amnesia.[69]

Understandably, many women approached childbirth with fear. The legacy of Eve in Genesis — "in sorrow thou shalt bring forth children," which people took seriously — must have been less than encouraging. Most women had witnessed, or known of, the death of someone in childbirth. If a problem arose, death was almost certain, and a gruesome, protracted death at that. There was no way of delivering an obstructed child alive. (Forceps had been discovered by then by a male physician, but was kept a family secret until 1733!) This was especially vexing because of the prevalence of rickets in this era, which reduced the size of many women's birth canals so that a baby's head was too large to pass through. Successful caesarean sections were still a procedure of the future. Despite the legend of Caesar's birth, no successful section was performed on a living woman until the eighteenth century, and the operation was not fully safe until the nineteenth century, following the discovery of anesthesia, development of surgical techniques, and the introduction of antiseptic principles. The use of chloroform and ether for pain was 150 years off.[70] Major hazards from hemorrhaging, infection, and eclampsia had to be negotiated. In 1660, puerperal fever killed two thirds of the women in the Hôtel Dieu, the public hospital in Paris. Childbirth was not for sissies!

So it was not uncommon for women to make arrangements for their death as they prepared for their confinement. In 1622, Elizabeth Joceline, expecting her first baby, composed a book saying how she wished her child to be brought up if she died in childbirth. Reading *The Mother's Legacy* is wrenching, for nine days after the birth of her daughter, Joceline died, probably from puerperal fever. She was wrapped in the winding sheet she had secretly bought for herself.[71]

Up to the mid-seventeenth century, the presence of any man at childbirth was rare, usually a signal of disaster. Male physicians were called only as a last resort. In general, midwives still delivered babies. The English countrywoman Catherine Schraders, born in 1655, delivered more than four thousand, for example, losing only ninety infants and fifteen mothers.[72] But Schraders's success rate was unusual. Midwives varied in competence. By this time, male midwives and physicians had been making inroads into the obstetrics business, and would eventually become the baby deliverers of choice. As we shall see, they initially made childbirth less safe before they made it better. They also made it less human, less sisterly, much to future feminists' chagrin.

Childbirth had been a social occasion enveloped in an aura of female ritual. Women delivered at home (in positions of their choosing; the sitting position was still popular) with a number of female friends in attendance. These women were known as "gossips," which did not have a pejorative connotation then but was a corruption of "God-sibs," meaning "God relatives." This was because they were charged with baptizing the child, as well as with providing moral support to the delivering mother. Childbirth was followed by "lying-in," during which the mother rested for about a month. Those who oppose parental leave time should take note! Before she re-entered the world, the mother underwent "churching," a custom that was built on the ruins of a Jewish purification rite making women fit to enter the sanctuary. The ritual was obviously tainted by misogynistic thinking. But by the early modern period, churching had evolved into a gesture of thanksgiving by the mother, if not for her child, then for surviving the ordeal of delivering it. Once delivered, the child was licked with the "basting tongue," scoured with salt, and purged. This molestation over, the child was swaddled.[73]

Swaddling persisted for a while. It was still thought to prevent the deformities of rickets and to keep babies warm. And, as always, it was a convenience. While the half-strangled baby hung from a nail, the person minding it could get on with other tasks without feeling guilty. The current baby expert Burton White, who advises against even such mild confinement as playpens, would not have been pleased. Full swaddling for the infant was stopped at six weeks in England, though mothers on the continent continued the practice longer. Yet even when the English mom liberated her baby from its wrappings, she insisted on broad bands or binders around the child's trunk and stays under the shift. Clearly, the idea was to restrict the child, a practice diametrically opposed to today's ideas about infant garments, which are designed to allow complete freedom of movement; hence the ubiquitous stretch suit. It is interesting to note that John Locke disapproved of swaddling, but not on account of its restrictiveness. He felt it was too protective, like a suit of armor. Children needed to be exposed to the elements lest they become spoiled and mollycoddled.[74]

The vast exchange of children during the Middle Ages that was typical of all except the poor continued into these centuries as well. In the upper classes, youngsters were sent to school and often boarded in a household near the educational institution. Apprenticeship was still a rite of passage for pre-teens in the middling ranks. The very poorest children became charges of their parish in sixteenth-century England and were apprenticed out by them. This is when the most flagrant child abuse occurred, because monitoring by parish officials of the children's situations was haphazard. It was only the garden variety poor children who stayed home. They were expected to contribute to household work from about the age of eight on — weeding, gathering wood, minding babies, and, later, ploughing, knitting, making hay. If middle- and upper-class teens were damaged by their culturally ordained banishment from the home, it is not apparent in the many surviving letters between them and their parents (usually the father), which also testify to the fact that, though physically absent from home, they were not absent from parents' thoughts.[75]

The curious business of wet-nursing actually increased in the seventeenth century, peaking in the eighteenth. So did the polemics against it — to little avail. The practice finally started petering out in England in the late eighteenth century, when maternal breast-feeding became the "in" thing among the upper classes (as it is today, though the trajectory from then until now is not a straight one). Foster nursing did not die out completely until the nineteenth century. In France, where the boarding of children with nurses was a highly organized cottage industry, the habit took even longer to disappear. And German parents continued to farm out babies well into the twentieth century.[76]

By the early modern period, the practice of putting out one's child to nurse had trickled down to the middle classes. Taking their cues from their social betters, the families of small tradesmen used a wet nurse to feed and mind their babies. All economic classes became involved in the business: the wealthy and middle classes as consumers, the lower class as providers.[77] It was rare for a nurse to be employed in the child's own home except in the case of higher aristocracy, like Shakespeare's Juliet, whose beloved nurse stayed on throughout her childhood. Usually, children were sent away for about one and a half years from cities to county parishes and from families in the country to nearby villages.

While the idea of exiling one's baby to a stranger's breast does not cohere with the modern notion of good mothering, it may seem particularly extraordinary to discover its popularity in this period. After all, people now clustered in nuclear families, married for love, and wanted babies. We can recognize ourselves in these social arrangements. Why would a mother (so like us) dispatch her child to nurse with another woman in a faraway household, in a home invariably poorer than her own, and then rarely visit it — something we find reprehensible?

The use of a surrogate nurse to breast-feed a child would, of course, be understandable in situations where the biological mother was unable to lactate. People were now very aware that feeding by hand was practically a death sentence (though they still did not know why), so the use of a wet nurse was the only viable option. In hindsight, we know that the high death rate was due to a culture-wide misunderstanding of the principles of nutrition and sterilization. The most common baby food at the time was unsupplemented pap or panada (basically, starch and water mixed to a paste); food pre-chewed by the caretaker; and, for pacification, sweetened alcoholic drinks, particularly gin or brandy. Feeding vessels were not washed. Babies developed rickets, scurvy, bladder stones, and other diseases, often failing to survive.

But wet-nursing in ordinary circumstances, where the biological mother was able to nurse, may have been popular simply because people did not perceive any harm in putting their babies out.[78] Indeed, country air and a robust wet nurse were considered excellent for infants. Besides, wet-nursing was not the path of least resistance; it was not the course of action for the lazy or unconcerned. Mother had to face the censure of preachers, moralists, and physicians, all of whom advised against it. Then, too, a good wet nurse was hard to find: she had to be healthy, strong, kind, sexually abstemious, and of an appropriate complexion (red hair and freckles wouldn't do). Moreover, her own child had to be duly disposed of; in other words, weaned or relegated to another, cheaper wet nurse, lower in the pecking order. In the 1640s in England, wartime conditions made the search even more difficult. Mary Lady Verney reluctantly decided to employ a woman whom she clearly found unsatisfactory. She wrote to her husband, Sir Ralph, "She looks like a slattern, but she sayeth, if she takes the child, she will have a mighty care of it . . . poor child, I pray God bless him and make him a happy man, for he hath but a troublesome beginning."[79] Apparently it never occurred to her to keep the baby home and feed him herself.

Probably the most famous search for a wet nurse was that conducted by England's Princess Anne in 1689. By then she had had twelve miscarriages, and three of her infant girls had died. Though a semi-invalid, she continued to do her duty, and in that year a son was born — the Duke of Gloucester. The choice of a wet nurse was clearly a matter of state importance. The young duke was first fed by a Mrs. Sharman, but he failed to thrive and had a convulsion. Immediately the court began to panic. Further attempts to find a nurse met with no success until a large reward was publicly advertised. At this, newly delivered countrywomen converged on the palace in droves. Among them was Mrs. Pack, with her one-month-old son. She was plain and very dirty, had a ruddy complexion and gigantic breasts, but Prince George (the duke's father) saw Mrs. Pack and immediately took her to feed his son. Almost at once, the baby recovered. Mrs. Pack was now in an extremely powerful position, since the life of the heir to the throne seemed to depend on her milk. Orders were given that she was never to be contradicted in any circumstances — an arrangement of which Mrs. Pack reportedly took full advantage.[80]

The choice of a wet nurse, high-born or low-born, was not a careless one, and parents' serious concern in the matter at this period does not suggest a lack of regard for the child. The questionable issue to my mind is that farmed-out babies were rarely visited. We know from diaries that sometimes parents did not even attend their children's funerals. Medical writers and moralists were forever urging parents to supervise their children at nurse, which suggests that many did not do so. Moreover, the literature of the time was filled with stories of changelings, of a child's discovery of his or her parentage, of mistaken identities (Shakespeare is full of them). What these signify is a culture-wide genealogical bewilderment. It was, no doubt, a product of how children were raised. The discontinuity in their caretakers, the abrupt transfer from nurse to biological mother, understandably would have fueled fantasies in children about their origins and prompted questions about the true identity of their parents. Some of the fantasies may have been based on reality. It is not outrageous to suppose that if an infant of wealthy parents were to die in the care of a wet nurse, she might be tempted to conceal the death by substituting another baby. Had parents visited more, these stories might have lost their punch.[81]

Yet it would be inaccurate to assume that the displacement of an infant for a long period into another environment always led to disaster. The nurse-child bond turned out to be a positive experience for many people.[82] Whether the nurse lived in or out, the child often remembered the old nurse, in addition to the biological mother, in its will. Over the course of his or her life, the child, aided by the mother, continued to visit the former nurse and sometimes undertook her welfare and that of her family, providing housing and comforts in her old age. The poet Alexander Pope erected a memorial to his wet nurse:

> *To the memory of Mary Beach*
> *who died November 25, 1725, aged 78*
> *Alex. Pope, whom she nursed in his infancy*
> *and constantly attended for twenty-eight years*
> *in gratitude to a faithful old servant erected this stone*

Apparently children were able to transfer their affection from one mother figure to another. Perhaps Drs. Spock, Brazelton, Leach, and other baby gurus who hold the mother-child bond sacrosanct, should take heed.

At the same time that some women refused to nurse, there

seems to have been a number of mothers who felt strongly that it was important to suckle their own children, and who, in spite of opportunities to do so, refused to employ a wet nurse. James I's queen, Anne of Denmark, breast-fed her son out of sheer snobbery. It would have been unseemly, she felt, for the child of a king to suck the milk of a servant. Puritan mothers felt breast-feeding was a religious duty. But for all the Puritan preaching about the evils of wet-nursing, the ideal was seldom realized: the wife of William Gouge, one of the most vociferous anti–wet nurse protestors, for example, nursed only seven of her thirteen children.[83]

There is little evidence at this time, unlike the Middle Ages, that privately employed wet nurses neglected their charges. There would have been no real motive for such behavior; private wet nurses were well paid. The nurslings were these women's bread and butter. If a baby died, there was no guarantee that another child of solvent parentage could be readily found. The picture may have been less rosy in France, however, where death rates for wet-nursed babies were high.[84]

But private wet nurses serving the middle and upper classes are only part of the story. A vast number of lactating women were employed by public institutions, such as foundling homes or parishes. These women either lived in the institution or took children into their homes. Unlike privately employed nurses, they were destitute and usually from the lowest social classes. Moreover, they had to nurse numerous charges — up to as many as forty! Their salary was low and, on top of that, civic employers were sometimes negligent about paying what was owed. Abuses abounded. There were simply too many nurses to be policed adequately. Often the little charges brought syphilis with them, infecting the nurse and her family, a situation that would hardly endear the child to its nurse. Infanticide occurred. Parish officials did not ask questions.[85]

Foundling homes had already devolved into holding pens at best and death camps at worst. Now, England joined the foundling institution business. Initially the British homes were run by a genuinely concerned administration. Christ's Hospital, in London, for example, provided its early charges with featherbeds and good food, unheard-of luxuries in 1552. So confident were the city fathers of eradicating the abandoned-baby problem within a few years that no expense was spared to make the venture a success. But soon there was a flood of applicants, so many that Christ's Hospital was forced to close its doors to foundlings. Indeed, all of England's institutions suffered the same fate, as had most foundling homes across Europe — serious overcrowding, a shortage of wet nurses, appalling hygiene — or they would have had to drastically limit their intake of children. Good care among those institutions which could not restrict admission crumbled under the crushing numbers of abandoned babies they were obliged to take in. By the nineteenth century, for example, the hospice in Moscow was admitting fourteen thousand abandoned nurslings a year. Thousands of babies died in transit to the hospitals. Inevitably, the institutions, exhausted by the utter impossibility of their mission and ignored by an uncaring public, became germ-filled warehouses with a general disregard for the lives of the infants entrusted to them. In the early modern period, the mortality rate fluctuated between 80 and 90 percent. In the Dublin institution, virtually all the inmates died. Things were not much better in the countryside. More and more babies perished under the neglectful "care" of overworked, underpaid nurses.[86]

Most foundlings in this period, unlike those in the centuries before, were bastards,[87] which testifies to the desperate plight of unmarried mothers. As we have seen, the religious changes brought with them an aggressive prudery about sexual matters. There was a quantum change in attitudes about moral conduct. The definition of "good mother" hardened, and most certainly did not embrace women who produced babies out of wedlock. Before this time, an unmarried mother could be absorbed into a household as a servant. Prostitutes were tolerated in a community, and illegitimate children were not especially ostracized. Now, an "immoral" woman was threatened with hellfire and damnation. She was barred from employment; she had no social role. A woman who strayed — the unmarried mother — inspired the same virulent scorn as her older counterpart, the witch.

Facing material privation and social censure, with no way to survive, she had no option but to abandon her child. Even as a wet nurse in a respectable situation, she would have had to relinquish her baby. That the abandonment was a heart-rending decision is apparent from the notes sometimes left with the child:

"I am not able to subsist any longer," or "I am render'd most miserable."[88] These are *cris de coeur,* not Hallmark whimpers. ❍

AS WE PROGRESS along the timeline, we see that parents abandoned their children for a multitude of reasons whose moral acceptability varies when measured by a modern moral compass. In Classical Greece and Rome, the reasons for exposure appear frivolous, given the abundance of food; during the Early and High Middle Ages, the practice was clearly driven by economic need. Most of the abandoned babies in medieval times seemed to have survived (in contrast to those in antiquity), disposed of as they were by the church, which dealt with these babies on an *ad hoc* basis. But the good news did not persist into the Late Middle Ages. The rate of abandonment seems to have accelerated in the Renaissance for reasons that remain puzzling. By then, babies were dying in droves in foundling hospitals, which now bore the responsibility for abandoned infants. By the early modern period, however, the causes for neglect were less obscure. One reason for abandonment stands out above all others — enmity toward "immoral" women. Society focused its hostility on the unwed mother who was compelled to abandon her child out of desperation. She had no recourse.

There are levels of human misery that displace sympathetic human response. Sometimes — infrequently — mothers murdered their newborns. Perhaps they were too enervated to go through the motions of abandonment. Perhaps they viewed the murder as mercy killing, in light of the bleak prospects for a bastard.

Unlike the infanticide of earlier times (ancient Phoenicia or Greece), this infanticide was not a social act but a desperate, personal one. However, there is no good evidence of increasing neglect or infanticide in early modern Europe. What did change — dramatically — was the ways in which infanticide was prosecuted. In the medieval world, the church punished *both* parents, and justice was mild — a few days in the stocks, perhaps. Apparently, the church was sympathetic to the plight of the parents who may have been negligent or were driven to abuse by circumstance. These parents were not viewed as evil. But now investigations were narrowly focused on the mother. Prosecution was taken over from the church by the state, which proceeded with unprecedented vengeance to zero in on the "lewd" unwed mother. The zeal to punish unmarried mothers was equalled only by the assault on witches, which was occurring at the same time. Any concealed pregnancy that ended with death of the child was presumed to be murder — this in an age when a third of children died of natural causes before the age of five. Punishment was often death, sometimes by torture: in Denmark the woman was beheaded; in Sweden she was cast into a fire; in Prussia she was buried alive with a stake driven through her chest. Numerous women were executed merely because their baby had died. Countless others were killed for being the starving, desperate victims of an unsympathetic society. In 1692, for example, Mary Goodenough was convicted of infanticide. She had allowed a neighbor sexual favors in return for "necessary maintenance" for herself and her two children. When her illegitimate baby was born, she did not struggle to save its life. "It was for want of Bread," she said. For this, she was executed.[89]

In France in this period, between 10 and 20 percent of all executions were for infanticide.[90] The flurry of executions appears to be a result not of an increase in child murders, or even an eruption of sympathy for the deceased child, but the product of a new, compelling hatred for the mother. ❍

AMID THE VAST changes in religion that characterized the sixteenth and seventeenth centuries, ideologies of motherhood were drastically revised — indeed, overturned. Motherhood became a necessary component of a woman's virtue and an essential ingredient in the good patriarchal order. Women were confined to the home, but if they were properly married and fertile, as well as obedient, quiet, pious, and chaste, they were valued. They were not exalted in literature or art, but at least they had a role. On the other hand, if they were not "good," if they were nonconforming, like the witch and the unmarried mother, then they were criminalized and punished.

A majority of women, comfortably ensconced in this scheme, benefited from their newly acquired status of good mother, and took child rearing seriously. Understandably, they conducted themselves differently from their modern counterparts. They were far more God-fearing and restrictive and psychologically insensitive. And they certainly did not value proximity to their children; they sent them away to nurse and to become apprentices. But they seemed to raise their children with the children's best interests in mind. This was mother love — the early modern version.

And the women of the under class who abandoned and killed their babies did so *in extremis*. Victims of a culture that accorded them no role, the objects of misogyny, they had no other option.

Compared to the exotic terrain of the Middle Ages, the early modern period looks remarkably familiar, in part because many of its attitudes and assumptions linger in the background of our own domestic arrangements.[91] It is in this era that there developed the job description of good mother: the mother at home, installed in a patriarchal household and naturally inclined toward subservience. Her image is so familiar that we may fail to realize she was invented. We see her as eternal.

Once again, it seems hardly coincidental that the neglected and abused children of the era were the offspring of a subset of women who were themselves neglected and abused. The conventional mother was able to provide conventional nurturance to her offspring. It was the "bad mother," the unwed, sexually active mother, who triggered virulent hatred in her society, and who, unable to satisfy her own or her child's basic needs for food and shelter, sacrificed her child. Child abuse, once again, was fueled by misogyny, not by a character flaw in the mother.

SIX

The Exaltation of Mother: Eighteenth- and Nineteenth-Century Mom

From Devil's Consort to "Angel of the House"

In twentieth-century terms, the world's most infamous monster, the fiend known today as Frankenstein (after his creator), was a product of a dysfunctional family. In the original version, written by Mary Shelley in 1818, the monster, like all children of his age, was born innocent. He was driven to monstrosity by parental rejection, for as soon as he was constructed, he was suddenly and inexplicably abandoned by his creator. Spurned by a deadbeat dad, the monster roamed the earth, suffering excruciating loneliness, wistfully observing loving families to which he could never belong. Though Frankenstein has had many successors — E.T. looking for home is one — he did not have too many predecessors. How could he? Until the eighteenth century, the concept of home as sanctuary had not been invented.

Though the rudiments of "nesting" had been contrived two centuries before, the idea of a home as a safe haven in a heartless world had its quintessential moment during the Victorian era. Domesticity was sentimentalized, assigned redemptive qualities, even made into a fetish. A mother — she who presided over the sacred temple of the hearth — became the repository of all that was decent and good. Previously considered morally vulnerable, sexually voracious, emotionally inconsistent, and intellectually inferior, she metamorphosed into the True Woman — virtuous, gentle, devoted, asexual, limited in interests to creating a proper refuge for her family and to tenderly guiding her children along appointed ways. Mother inspired outbursts of insipid rhapsody. No longer mere flesh, but a glorified substance, a glow, she was idealized to the point of parody. Indeed, she became a secular version of the Virgin. Thackeray, in fact, placed her a notch higher. He said, "Mother is the name for God." Woman, who only a century earlier could be condemned as a consort of the devil, had become the Angel of the House.[1]

Why did mother undergo this remarkable personality enhancement from devil to angel? It's a two-hundred-year-long story, stretching from the French Enlightenment, in the early eighteenth century, to the death of Queen Victoria, in 1901, spanning revolutions in England, America, and France, and political unrest in Russia. But the most cataclysmic of all the social upheavals for mother was the Industrial Revolution. It shattered the traditional structure of the family by splitting apart what had been an indivisible whole — the home and workplace — never to be reunited.

From the Rhineland to the Mississippi, whole villages were emptied to feed the factory system with human labor. A settled agrarian life based on community, which had persisted for centuries, was destroyed, and in its wake came "dark, Satanic mills."[2] This extraordinary social dislocation entailed the transformation of the family as an economically productive unit into a consumer unit, one in which dad was exiled daily to earn money via hard work in distant factories and mom was cloistered in the home, trying to make ends meet on the household allotment doled out by dad. Until that time both sexes, indeed, all members of a household, young and old (except infants in wealthier homes), servants, apprentices, and hired hands, all worked in close proximity. Living was an interactive enterprise. There was plenty to do — growing crops, baking bread, spinning cloth, making furniture and soap, preparing medicines. But with the advent of industrialization such products were manufactured and had to be purchased with wages. Wages had to be earned outside, in the cold, cruel world. Life henceforth would be divided into two spheres: dad's, a "public" arena of dog-eat-dog competition and survival of the fittest; and mom's, a "private" sphere, the home, in every feature a counterpoint to the former.

To go from a society organized around household production to one organized around large-scale factory production, from a society ruled by God, father, communal obligations, small-town gossip, and the seasons to one ruled by an impersonal market, was to deconstruct the family and to scramble its characteristics and values. The result was not unlike a Picasso painting. The essence of family remained recognizable — nuclear loyalties, love (ideally) between husband and wife, the definition of good mother — but different features were highlighted. Internal and external dynamics changed. Sex roles became exaggerated.

As the family moved from farm or small town to the city, the grip of the community eased, and the family came to be a separate, private entity. Family members developed much fiercer loyalties to one another than to anyone outside their unit. Unrelated women became isolated from each other, no longer gathering in sewing circles, at the well on washdays, or at the home of a delivering woman. The family, ceasing to produce goods, tended to concentrate on its remaining functions — eating, sleeping, sex, the socialization of children, and (until the early twentieth century, when public institutions took over) birth, death, educating youth, and the care of the sick and aged. Dad lost some of his authority within the home as he became remote from daily activities. At the same time, home was imbued with sentiment; it became a place "where the heart is" as well as, in its ideal manifestation, the locus of intimacy, peace, spontaneity, and unwavering devotion to people and principles beyond the self. Home was transformed from a mere four walls into a refuge, a haven where one might retreat for repose or renewal or inner fortification. These ideas, even today, are central to the bourgeois Western dream.

Into this new model of domesticity was insinuated the new model child — the Romantic child of the poets and philosophers. In contrast to a preindustrial youngster, who might have been welcomed as a future laborer, this child was regarded as "economically worthless" but "emotionally priceless."[3] Children tended to stay around the domestic scene a lot longer, as they were no longer apprenticed. Previously an object of utility, the child mutated into an object of sentiment.

In the early modern world, the father was the central figure in the lives of his children. Motherhood was singularly underidealized. Child care was not regarded as a predominantly maternal responsibility (recall that advice tracts were written for men); neither was motherhood a woman's primary occupation, since she had so much else to do.[4] But that all changed.

So stridently did this new "cult of domesticity" cry out for an appropriate mistress to oversee things that it would have been impossible not to upgrade mother's status. In the reflected glory of her exalted home, she could no longer be seen as a mere functionary. Motherhood became a "noble calling."[5] Dad's importance in the family waned as mom's waxed. The specifically maternal duties of child care, once defined haphazardly by her round of daily tasks, became a self-conscious enterprise, one that was assigned exclusively to mother, complicated and time-consuming.

The mother defined by this setting is precisely what people have in mind today when they speak of "traditional" mother (conveniently forgetting that she was only one model in a long series). What we have constructed as the good mother in our collective psyche — the stay-at-home arrangement, where mom's needs are never considered, and where father is assumed to be the primary breadwinner, whose cameo appearance is wonderful if it occasionally graces the holy mother-child tableau — is none other than the Victorian mother. Nowadays we may catch glimpses of her in debates about family values. Her image lurked behind the brouhaha over Hillary Rodham Clinton's chocolate chip cookies, and supports the continual refusal by the American public to provide universal free child care so that mothers of young children can go to work. (We seem to prefer that welfare mothers stay home to mind their children, for we have never funded programs that would enable them to do otherwise.) The Victorian mother has retained a tenacious hold over our minds.

In her late nineteenth-century heyday, the clergy, poets, politicians, and just about everyone put mother on a pedestal. She was a balm for every wound inflicted by the hostile outside world. Within the walls of her garden, mother taught virtue to children who would grow up and say, "All that I am, I owe to my angel mother." It is not surprising that to Madame de Staël's question "Who is the greatest woman alive or dead," Napoleon answered, unhesitatingly, "The one who has the most children."[6]

Human mothers had been honored before, but not in such an inflated manner. Flesh-and-blood mothers had never been held to standards of the Virgin Mary. Even the Virgin Mary had not been held to her own standards. Over the course of history, the Virgin Mary had actually been granted some erotic license: folk tales developed since the Middle Ages had her delivering the baby of a reverend abbess; substituting for a nun who went off to live it up as a prostitute; a few tales even hinted at her own promiscuity.[7] It was not until the middle of the nineteenth century that the Madonna was completely redomesticated into a Victorian mother.

The doctrine of "separate spheres" — that is, the blessed home versus the cruel outside — created a division of the world according to gender, not seen since the Italian Renaissance. Once again, it behooved the bourgeois woman to appear as idle and decorative as possible as a measure of her husband's affluence. Once again, her code of conduct emphasized ornamental refinement. Of course a distinction had long existed between women's and men's roles, but in early modern times, the two sexes at least worked in the same physical space, often side by side. One got the feeling, for example, that Martin and Katharina Luther could talk to each other and that each knew what the other was doing.[8] Now husbands and wives were set apart, a situation that, as we shall see, fed hyperbolic fantasies of gender difference.

The impact of the separate spheres was double-edged for the mother. On the positive side, it removed father from the home, which served to unravel some of the constraints of patriarchal control. It gave the middle-class woman her own domain, albeit a limited one, which enabled her to develop skills in the domestic arts, caring and communication, altruism and connection — qualities extolled by the present-day psychologists Carol Gilligan and Nancy Chodorow and the psychiatrist Jean Baker Miller. Mother's confinement freed her from the corrupt world of cash calculations and competition. Idealization and paternalistic subjection are certainly not the worst of fates, as any modern, beaten-down mother from Russia or Soweto will tell you; she looks on Western feminists' grievances with incredulity. And it would be naïve to assume that the Victorian mother was wholly without influence. She could often use the powerful lever of her dependence and self-sacrifice to prod her husband into good behavior. Man is not totally without conscience. The thought of the little woman at home was a powerful reproach to the man who slacked off. And in the words of the playwright Lillian Hellman, "There were always a great many mink coats to be earned." Though she was speaking of the twentieth century, her observation could easily be applied to the eighteenth and nineteenth centuries. Some women in every generation have been able to turn the liability of their subordinate status to their advantage.[9]

Nevertheless, the bifurcation of the bourgeois world made woman's work invisible. (No one would have asked a *hausfrau* whether she worked; nearly everyone has asked the contemporary mother that question.[10]) The "privacy" of mother's work served to mask her economic significance to the household. Unpaid work does not show up in the Gross National Product. Excluded from direct participation in the world, devalued for the nature of her contribution, she became utterly dependent on her husband's good will and earning power for survival. Many women found the situation less than ideal; it defined all women by a single standard, one developed by a sexist society. Bourgeois women were obliged to develop such "feminine" accomplishments as charm, musical performance, drawing, and speaking French, skills for which they may have felt little inclination or for which they had no aptitude. Life in the Gilded Age was life in a gilded cage.

To live the ideology of True Womanhood required a certain amount of economic wherewithal, clearly out of reach for the growing under class. With the doctrine of separate spheres, mothers who were not bourgeois lost the previous flexibility, status, and control of their work. Instead, they were granted the privilege of low-grade, exploited occupations, the double burden of waged and domestic labor, and the sole responsibility for child care that has weighed them down ever since.[11] Also, Victorian notions about domesticity and gender placed them well beyond the pale of respectability. Naturally, such a value system encouraged the working-class woman to aspire to the ideal of woman as full-time homemaker, which, from her perspective, looked like a good deal. This sharpened class differences among mothers.

The bourgeois mother paid dearly for her beatified status. The standards to which she was held — moral superiority, passionlessness, selflessness, domesticity — turned her into such a wet blanket that nineteenth-century male authors were forever inventing characters fleeing from her clutches; Huck Finn and Tom Sawyer are prime examples.[12] Even her clothing was confining, her corsets exerting as much as twenty-one pounds of pressure on her inner organs, her crinolines and petticoats hampering normal movement. Fasting and vinegar potions were part of her regimen. Many taboos were laid upon this totem.

The very perfection of True Womanhood carried within it the seeds of its own destruction. The impossibility of its standards exacted a high toll on woman — frustration, guilt, discontent. But because the mother was idealized, it was difficult for her to see what was going on, and still more difficult to alter it. Her suppression was disguised as kindness, which served to blur mother's insight into her predicament. And while women were no longer burned at the stake, many smoldered in quiet desperation, chafed by a set of social restraints and domestic provisos that corroded their spirit. At the bottom rung of the social ladder was the unwed mother (the "fallen woman"), for whom society provided no options. Her destitution forced her into the kind of basic strangeness that made her unfit for parenting. As in the early modern period, she was compelled to dispose of her baby.

Since the Victorian ideal of womanhood discouraged the recognition and display of discontent, for which it was partly responsible in the first place, the dissatisfied woman was in a no-win situation. In hindsight it is apparent that many women resorted to two antidotes, neither of which was satisfactory in the short term but turned out to be felicitous to future generations: repression and protest.

In regard to repression, these women were the spawning ground for the young science of psychoanalysis. Prevented from expressing their conflicted feelings, many unconsciously turned their psychic pain into physical pain. Their conversion reactions, neurasthenias, and headaches were the subject matter of Freud's early speculation. Their pain paved the way for future cures, and their discontent fueled the birth of the first organized women's liberation movement. Both trends combined, for example, in the figure of Anna O, whose early "talking cure" (psychoanalysis) enabled her to develop into Bertha Pappenheim, the head of the German Jewish Women's Organization and leading feminist in twentieth-century Germany.[13] ❍

TWO POTENT SYMBOLS of "home" bracket and reveal much about the nature and range of mothering practices. One is from a nursery rhyme, the other from a classic American novel by Nathaniel Hawthorne.

The first, a shoe, was the domicile of an old woman who had so many children she didn't know what to do. This nursery rhyme is a story of maternal desperation and child abuse, and is, sadly, an accurate reflection of eighteenth-century social reality. The new urban poverty created by industrialization was even more stressful than the agrarian poverty of previous centuries: the overcrowding, filth, inadequacy of facilities for disposing of waste, polluted water, and adulterated foods from the markets were unprecedented. The problems must have seemed insoluble, yet this does not excuse the callousness with which prosperous people ignored life among the poor, on whom, to a large extent, their prosperity depended. The growing division between the "haves" and the "have-nots" paved the way, of course, for the revolutionary ideas of Marx and Engels. Given the plight of single mothers (and many poor married ones), it is no wonder that they resorted to desperate means to deal with their children, as had unwed mothers in the two centuries before them.

For the fortunate bourgeois sector of the population, the House of the Seven Gables, though outsized, was in many ways typical. Unlike houses in the previous age, it was indisputably Home, perfectly suited for showcasing the Angel of the House and her romanticized offspring, with plenty of private space to bond and teach virtue, and public space to carry on a myriad of social rituals. The Victorian house, to be distinguished from its predecessors, was strictly zoned; that is, it was divided into private and public spaces, male and female spaces, children's and servants' areas — which conveys something about the compartmentalization of the nineteenth-century mind.

In the parlor, mother established her respectability by displaying herself, her bric-à-brac, and "feminine" skills, as noted. This was the period of calling cards and receiving hours.[14] Appearances mattered. All utilitarian objects used to maintain the family's exalted status — cleaning implements, kitchens, servants, servants' stairways, serving machines — were hidden from view. An aptly named device, the dumbwaiter, invented at this time, served to keep servants out of sight. In effect, the parlor restricted visitors to a carefully controlled reception area in which proper decorum could be observed.

By limiting the intrusion of nonrelatives into family space, the parlor may have served to enhance intimacy[15] and heighten sentiment among family members. In the private recesses of their domains, families wrote letters, read aloud, played "parlor" games, and talked about the weather. It was an age of conversation and gossip; the novel became popular.

On formal occasions, in wealthy households, men would retreat into a male zone, the smoking room, and women into a female one, the drawing room, so named because it was the place to which women "withdrew" after dinner. The division of rooms according to gender was an artifact of this period and indicates just how patriarchal Victorians could be: women were considered too delicate to tolerate cigar smoke, too scatterbrained to engage in male conversation.

In wealthier homes, the elevated status of children was reflected in the creation of a zone specifically designed for them — the nursery. In this room (or rooms) were elegant cradles festooned with lace, elaborate prams, and child-sized furniture, often decorated with pictures of animals or figures from nursery rhymes. Children's books illustrated by Kate Greenaway shaped the decorative arts of the nursery, and children's fashions, both then . . . and now, for that matter. People today are still quite taken with children's Victoriana. But it may be a mistake to be overly nostalgic for the charm of this period. Beatrix Potter, author of *The Tale of Peter Rabbit,* experienced her own nursery years as excruciatingly confining, and it is probably not an accident that she imbued her little animal characters with the rebelliousness and frustration that echoed her own feelings of childhood, during which she was kept by her father as a virtual recluse.

The Victorian home represented the height of domestication — and so did the Victorian mother. Both were elaborately constructed, highly complicated, and, as we shall see, increasingly unworkable.

The Romantic Tableau: Maternal Images in the Eighteenth Century

Before woman can write, declared Virginia Woolf fifty years ago, she must kill the "Angel of the House."[16] The role assigned to women, Woolf implied, is so restrictive that it is incompatible with artistic endeavor or virtually anything outside itself: women are held hostage to an impossible ideal. She went on rather famously to say that a woman needs a "room of her own." Despite Woolf's call to murder, reports of the Angel's demise are greatly exaggerated, as noted by her continued sightings today. But we are getting ahead of ourselves. Let us look at the Angel's rise.

The morally enhanced mother arrived in the eighteenth century in the wake of Romanticism, a sort of fever that afflicted Western Europe and North America in reaction to the aesthetic and humanistic tragedy of the Industrial Revolution. As green pastures gave way to factories, and community life was supplanted by the impersonal world of the Almighty Dollar, man looked with nostalgia to vanished cultures. God went on a leave of absence in some circles, replaced by a worship of Nature. The check provided by religion was therefore relaxed; the Puritan conviction of Original Sin modulated into a sense of goodness of the individual; the instinctive side of personality was acclaimed. The Romantic temperament characterized America as a "brave new world," and early men and women as "noble savages." It also bequeathed to us groundless theories about a prehistoric Golden Age in which peaceable matriarchy was overthrown by warmonger men (recall Bachofen). And Romanticism gave us the innocent child, the home as sanctuary, and mother as presiding angel.

The Romantic man *par excellence* was the philosopher Jean Jacques Rousseau. Late in life, the eccentric Rousseau liked to let his boat drift in a Swiss lake. "Sometimes I cried out with emotion — 'O nature. O my mother! I am here under your sole protection.' "[17] Rousseau's pastoral retreats started a trend, not only for Switzerland, but for the equation of nature with motherhood, an association that is reminiscent of the prehistoric Great Mother, and one that pops up time and again throughout history.

Poets, theologians, critics, and ordinary sons joined the chorus in praise of mother — John Ruskin, Sir Edwin Arnold, Alfred Lord Tennyson. As she was idealized and associated with altruism and self-sacrifice, mother became, in time, a caricature. Can we take seriously the poet Jean Richepin's contribution to this literary genre?

There was a young man loved a maid
Who taunted him. "Are you afraid,"
She asked, "to bring me today
Your mother's head upon a tray?"

He went and slew his mother dead
Tore from her breast her heart so red
Then towards his lady love he raced
But tripped and fell in all his haste.

As the heart rolled on the ground
It gave forth a plaintive sound.
And it spoke, in accents mild:
"Did you hurt yourself, my child?"[18]

Maternal ecstasy re-invaded the canvas, this time in secular form. Even the fanciest ladies wished to be painted in blissful maternal reverie. Britain's Lady Cockburn, the cream of eighteenth-century nobility, may be found in Joshua Reynolds's brilliant portrait, where she is shown ignominiously engulfed by her three little boys. The inclusion of these rambunctious babies clinging and climbing over their tolerant mother like so many Italian *putti* is in distinct contrast to seventeenth-century portraits, where children, if they appear at all, were depicted as still, well-behaved little adults. This break in convention corresponded to the eighteenth century's dramatically different view of domesticity.[19]

From the ateliers of eighteenth-century France came a multitude of happy mothers, many of them familiar to us from upscale notecards.[20] The names of the paintings — Fragonard's *The Joys of Motherhood* and *Mother's Kisses* and Greuze's *The Beloved Mother* — only hint at the rococo exuberance with which the pleasures of mothering are conveyed. In de Saint-Aubin's *Happy Mother,* the subject's maternal bosom is bounteously displayed with the clarity and frontality of an archaic goddess, along with two babies in her lap, both looking drunkenly sated on mother's milk.

The stunning young artist Marie Élisabeth Vigée-Lebrun, a favorite of the French court, continually painted Marie Antoinette *en famille,* in a fruitless attempt to popularize her. Lest anyone doubt the artist's own maternal devotion, Madame Vigée-Lebrun, in an outrageously flattering portrait, *The Artist and Her Daughter,* pictures herself protectively embracing her child, who was five or six at the time. A mother's blind love shines through in every stroke. Though sentimental, it is a masterpiece. Reportedly, the artist indulged her daughter excessively, and the child was difficult and spoiled.[21] A viewer of this painting would not be surprised.

In literature, too, mother was now idealized: Samuel Richardson's *Pamela* (1741) heralded the change. The ex-servant Pamela settles into her married life with the squire Mr. B. and takes on the serious but pleasurable task of rearing their children. Though the plot actually revolves around spicier themes, no doubt accounting for its popularity, it does dwell periodically on Mrs. B.'s maternal virtue. It shows her unsuccessfully pleading with her husband to allow her to breast-feed her baby; she jeopardizes her own health to nurse her son when he contracts smallpox (probably a consequence of using a wet nurse); she reads Locke's *Thoughts on Education;* and, in the closing scene of the novel, she recounts moral tales to enraptured children clustered about her in the nursery.[22]

This lovely image of a seated, benign maternal figure reading to children grouped at her feet took on a life of its own in the eighteenth century in the persona of Mother Goose. Somehow, the popular collection of fairy tales by the previous century's Charles Perrault came to be ascribed to this saintly figure. Just who was Mother Goose and why did she capture the public imagination? No one knows for sure. Contrary to popular New England belief, she is not buried in Boston. She probably was just another Romantic conceit. But Mother Goose has persisted; she is featured on the frontispiece of many storybooks today,[23] though she has been cosmetically and financially enhanced over the years.

While we do not know Mother Goose's precise identity, we may reasonably speculate that she is a variant of the Virgin Mary (or, more likely, Mary's mother, Saint Anne), yet another sacrificing mother figure. The Virgin had always been more popular with women than with men, but what becomes obvious in the eighteenth century is that the "egoless" mother figure is especially popular with a *female* audience, for in that century she became a fixture in *women's* literature. Henceforth, the maternal martyr became a staple of melodrama, a genre addressed specifically to women, which has evolved over time from lowbrow Victorian novels and the writings of "scribbling ladies" to today's TV soaps. This is a curious thing. Why would women take such obvious interest in seeing themselves portrayed in this self-denying manner? Why are sacrificing mothers part of mothers' fantasy lives? What sort of wish does this gratify? What, after all, is the appeal of self-sacrifice?

On the psychological level, a partial explanation might suggest that women do not really identify with maternal martyrs much; rather, they identify with the children of those beneficent creatures. After all, in our unconscious, we never grow up. On a cultural level, if self-sacrifice is valued above all, one begins to understand how it becomes the collective goal or fantasy. That is, if the dominant culture wants mothers to be self-sacrificing, mothers want to be self-sacrificing. Mothers do not (or perhaps cannot) distinguish their own "want" from that which is imposed on them.[24]

The power of the moral-mother paradigm can be seen in its inversion. Even today, to accuse one's mother of immorality is to invite outrage — hence, the affront in the term "motherfucker." In revolutionary France, what better way to discredit the aristocracy than to impugn the reputation of its symbolic mother, the queen? Hapless Queen Marie Antoinette was the subject of a substantial pornographic literature (one pamphlet alone sold twenty to thirty thousand copies). These documents portray the queen engaging in homosexual practices, bestiality, prostitution, every imaginable sort of lewdness, much of which is physiologically impossible. Arraigned before the revolutionary tribunal, the hated

Marie Antoinette was accused of sexually abusing her son. Her retort was, "I appeal to all mothers who are present in this room — is such a crime possible?" Her pleas for maternal consideration didn't work. The common people could not associate her with maternal devotion, and they beheaded her.[25]

Just a century earlier, a child arrived on earth tainted by Original Sin, or at least readily vulnerable to corruption. But by the late eighteenth century, the Angel of the House could produce nothing less than a cherub. Indeed, the Romantic child was born "trailing clouds of glory," to quote William Wordsworth. John Locke, whose political writings had influenced the American Revolution, inadvertently set the stage for this sentimental view of the child. In his long, rambling *Some Thoughts Concerning Education* (1693), he had concluded that children arrived on earth without any preconceived ideas. They were *tabulae rasae,* empty slates, on which could be written anything the parents chose. They were not innately good, but neither were they innately bad. Rather, children were morally neutral.

Locke advocated the use of reason (he was a son of the Enlightenment, after all) to train a child out of his or her childish ways into the moral and rational perfection of adulthood. He was a great fan of a controlled environment, a philosophy that has informed a whole tradition of educational and psychological theory. Many people misinterpret Locke, however, and incorrectly assume that he said that children are naturally good, since he had denied the opposite.

It was the unconventional Rousseau who proclaimed the goodness of children: children begin as noble and unselfish creatures until society corrupts them. This philosophy was enunciated in his novel *Émile* (1762), an account of how Rousseau would have educated an imaginary boy. Rousseau opposed Locke's view that children should be reasoned with; instead, he insisted that they be given no academic training. Children were to learn their lessons as nature presented them. All actions were to spring from necessity, not from obedience. The supreme good was freedom. His theory was a call to the wild . . . but not for girls. Rousseau was not much interested in educating females, whose minds, he felt, should not be awakened, except to think what other people want them to.[26] If we put aside the points of difference between Rousseau and Locke, and Rousseau's outrageous sexism, we find an overall movement toward concern and sympathy with the child.

However much Rousseau may have approved of a free child in theory, he could not abide one in practice. He solved his own child-raising problems by abandoning five illegitimate children to a foundling home. As a tutor, too, he had been a failure, frequently becoming enraged at his pupils' insubordination and ignorance.

Nevertheless, performing child care "à la Jacques" became quite the vogue in the eighteenth century. Just as Original Sin had informed the attitude of the preceding centuries toward childhood, Rousseau's *Émile* dominated the eighteenth and nineteenth until Freud. In vain did rational minds fight a rearguard action, as did Voltaire in a letter to Rousseau: "No one has ever used so much intelligence to persuade us to be stupid. After reading your book one feels that one ought to walk on all fours. Unfortunately during the last sixty years I have lost the habit."[27] Voltaire's was a dialectical triumph, but no more, because belief in childhood innocence resonated with the times. Rousseaumania flourished.

Poetic counterparts to Rousseau include William Wordsworth, whose "Ode: Intimations of Immortality" portrays young babies being dragged away from the happiness of Heaven, and William Blake's "The Chimney Sweeper," about the sorry plight of little boys blackened with soot who are slaves of a corrupt new industrial society. In painting there was Joshua Reynolds in England and Philipp Runge in Germany (an obvious inspiration for the contemporary children's book illustrator Maurice Sendak). Their children squirm and wriggle, and caress their mamas. Even in portraits of ordinary American children by lesser luminaries, there is a sense of playfulness and affection for the younger generation. Kids had become more likable.[28]

Though he disdained sentimentality, the cantankerous writer Jonathan Swift also betrayed a covert sympathy for children. Taken at face value, Swift's "Modest Proposal" was a proposal for relieving the food shortage in Ireland: he suggested that children be killed for eating. But of course Swift was being satirical; his irony presupposed parental love of children, without which his absurd proposal would have failed to shock. His goal was social reform.

Reform was also the mission of the brilliant painter William Hogarth. His satiric drawings of ravaged children were used to expose the vices of a corrupt city life. In Hogarth's most famous print, *Gin Lane,* the London street is a madhouse where gin is fed to babies. A drunken and diseased mother lets a child fall to its death, and an insanely dancing man has skewered a baby with a cane.[29]

The Calm Before the Repressive Storm: Maternal Reality in the Eighteenth Century

Recall Little Buttercup's profession (in Gilbert and Sullivan's *H.M.S. Pinafore*), when she was "young and charming." It was "baby farming." This was a newly invented atrocity, or, rather, a new label for the old atrocity of putting children away by paying someone to be a foster parent. In the eighteenth- and nineteenth-century version, advertisements in newspapers euphemistically conveyed that children could be boarded — and in a style that meant that the patron need never hear from the infant again.[30] As a neighbor of one such establishment in London observed, pregnant women and babies entered, but no babies seemed to leave. Here was organized infanticide in the age of Little Lord Fauntleroy. One did not have to be a muckraker to notice.

This was a time when love for one's offspring was considered normal, average, and respectable, as it had in the early modern period and continued to be in contemporary times. But good nurturing required food in the cupboard. With industrialization, urbanization, and a soaring birthrate, even the most basic requirements for living eventually became unattainable by the growing under class in Europe. For our purposes, we can discern in the eighteenth century a love of children, but perhaps not a love of children not one's own, a situation that was to worsen in the next century, as would sexism.[31] ❍

THE NEW EMPHASIS on the joys of domesticity were not yet strangulating, as they would become for some women in the next hundred years, but in the meantime served as a new source of female authority.[32] At this time, a mother's obligations to instruct the young provided her with a platform to express her ideas on a broad range of subjects. Armed with such a duty, she could give advice, teach morals, even proselytize a captive audience.

With the Enlightenment, a rational approach to religion gained acceptance; the bite of seventeenth-century Puritanism was gone. Reliance on God gradually gave way to the secular belief that a child's welfare lay primarily in the hands of loving, watchful mothers.[33] Motherhood was revamped. Duties that once belonged to mother and father, or to father alone, were now the exclusive province of mother. Her additional responsibilities came at a price: additional anxiety. True, the eighteenth-century mother was aided in the fulfillment of her job description by an outpouring of child-rearing advice written for her, but it provided little solace when things went wrong. It is perhaps worse to feel that a child's death or depravity results from your own mismanagement than from your husband's or from divine providence.

Although some Evangelicals still clung to ideas of Original Sin, fire and brimstone, and will crushing, more moderate views toward children prevailed among the literate and genteel of Yankee North America and Europe. On the whole, child rearing seemed to take place with less moralizing and more acceptance of children and childishness. A story circulated in England that when young Charles James Fox announced he intended to smash a watch, his father, Lord Holland, said, "Well, if you must, I suppose you must." And another one about the same little Charles, whose father permitted him to ride into the dining room seated on a saddle of mutton, his feet trailing in the gravy.[34]

What was once considered indulgent now became ordinary: parents began purchasing books, toys, and games aimed specifically at children. They adopted naming practices that suggested closeness — the sharing of first names by fathers and sons, mothers and daughters — and were more reluctant to apprentice out their offspring.[35] Newspapers regularly featured a "woman's page," which often contained maudlin stories and poems about the deaths of children. Mother love was a touchstone of the bourgeoisie.

The eighteenth century added its contingent of highly principled men who condemned women who refused to breast-feed. The most prominent was Rousseau (whose Émile was nursed by his mother), but he was supported by nearly all the early great writers in the relatively new field of pediatric medicine — Hugh Smith, William Buchan, and William Cadogan. Their arguments in favor of breast-feeding differed from their predecessors'. Whereas earlier commentators condemned the practice of wet-nursing because the child was thought to imbibe something of both the physical appearance and the character of the nurse along with her milk, the newer protesters emphasized the healthful aspects of maternal nursing for the child and the pleasures of suckling for the mother. Perhaps more important, they were not as dogmatic as their forerunners about the evil effects on milk of sexual activity.[36] It was now thought that mothers could safely engage in sexual relations and become pregnant without impairing their milk supply.

Finally, all the inveighing against the use of wet nurses had some effect, at least in England. By the second half of the eighteenth century, the practice at long last began to conform to the propaganda, and wet-nursing rapidly went out of fashion among the wealthier classes. But the use of wet nurses continued in Rousseau's homeland, France, until the late nineteenth century. At the time Rousseau was writing, wet-nursing was rampant. In the 1780s, over 80 percent of the twenty-one thousand babies born in Paris were shipped out to be nursed in the country, even though the rate of death of babies sent to wet nurses was double that of babies nursed by their mothers. Whether mothers knew of the risk to their children or not, they insisted on using foster nurses. France had the highest infant mortality in Europe at the time, and the trickle of children deposited in foundling homes had turned into a flood.[37]

So why did French parents persist in using wet nurses? Perhaps because the demands of the French domestic economy placed great pressure on women to work outside the home. Apart from that, no one knows for certain. We are faced here with the conundrum we encountered in Renaissance Italy and Classical Athens: middle-class parents, who could have done otherwise, seemed willfully to put their newborn babies at grave risk. Again, historians disagree about explanations and the extent of the problem. What is interesting to observe is that, during this century, France's birthrate began to decline. France led all countries in a fall in the fertility rate. It is likely that French couples were among the first to practice birth control as a way to lower the murderously high infant mortality rate. In the next century, France would lead all nations in creating social programs to protect mothers and their babies. So if France was worse to its mothers and babies than other Western European nations in the eighteenth century, it redeemed itself in the nineteenth. ❍

BY THE LATE EIGHTEENTH CENTURY, male doctors had largely displaced midwives, especially among the bourgeoisie.[38] This was not because they had anything to offer that was superior to midwives, nor would things change until the 1870s, with the development of asepsis, surgical techniques, and anesthesia. Their mediocrity notwithstanding, obstetricians became all the rage. Perhaps it was the allure of the "scientific" that heightened their credibility. This was the Enlightenment, and people were enamored of anything that smacked of science.

The "secret" of forceps, having been sold for profit too many times, finally leaked out. Medical men, who had cleverly commandeered the blueprint for their manufacture, became specialists in their use, and established formal training programs from which women were excluded. In effect, they created a male monopoly on technical training in obstetrics. Women, believing these physicians to have superior expertise, began to insist that they attend their deliveries. In fact, we now know that the use of forceps and other techniques were highly primitive at this time, not much of an advantage. And obstetricians, more than midwives, lacked empirical experience and carried puerperal fever. Nevertheless, midwives fell out of fashion and were forced to limit their practice to the poor. Feminists point out that as a result of midwifery's demise, a healthy event became a medical procedure. Women who were delivering came to be treated as diseased objects and lost control of the whole birth process. While it is easy to blame men for this outcome, it is well to remember that women were co-conspirators.

Whether by midwife or obstetrician, the delivery of a baby was still a hit-or-miss proposition in the eighteenth century. In 1797, Mary Wollstonecraft, founding mother of Anglo-American feminism, died of puerperal fever, not long after delivering her child. She had relied on a midwife. Twenty years later, Princess Charlotte died in childbirth, along with her baby. She had been delivered by an obstetrician . . . who subsequently killed himself in embarrassment. Death was no stranger to the eighteenth-century mother, regardless of social class, political persuasion, or gender of deliverer.[39]

THUS FAR we have been talking about the attitudes and habits of the well-fed. That was only half the story. The historian Simon Schama described the other half: armies of emaciated beggars dying on the roads; prisoners rotting in hulks for stealing a loaf of bread; filthy bundles of rags deposited every morning on the steps of Paris churches containing newborn babies with pathetic notes claiming baptism. The problem of foundlings was so acute, and the number of wet nurses so inadequate, that foundling homes desperately experimented with feeding their little charges by bottle. The results were disastrous. Indeed, bottle-feeding remained unworkable until the end of the nineteenth century, when people finally understood bacteriology and the need to purify milk. These were the centuries in which foundling homes had near-total death rates.[40]

England had its own set of problems and its own solutions, a number of which worsened its problems. Over the hundred years following the noble failure of Christ's Hospital, there was a change in attitude toward philanthropy. One of the legacies of the Puritans was a sneaking feeling that if the poor were given charity, they would be less inclined to work. And idleness had become a sin . . . which gave rise to the workhouse, made famous by Dickens. There was no such thing as a free lunch.

On admission to a workhouse, an individual was given food and shelter in return for work, which presumably was to offset the cost of running the institution. Workhouses were not only for indigent mothers; parishes forced the destitute to move whole families into them. Conditions were Spartan. All able-bodied people were expected to work, and three years of age was not considered too young to start. It may come as a shock to realize that men like Locke, Voltaire, and Daniel Defoe, ordinarily regarded as humanitarians, all opposed generosity toward needy children, and basically felt that even toddlers should earn their keep.[41] Over the course of the century, as the census of these institutions rose, their conditions deteriorated until they became squalid hovels.

In England, abandoned infants and orphans were the responsibility of their parish. Hundreds of older children were exiled by parish officials to labor-hungry America. Most were sent to live with foster families, who were reimbursed by the parish, a situation that evolved into baby farming. Naturally, no overseer would be popular if the rates he levied to pay for this relief were high, so he kept the costs of such maintenance to a bare minimum. Having found a willing wet nurse or foster family, the parish officer felt he had discharged his duty, and he tended not to follow up on his placement. The smaller the sum, the less likely was the child to survive . . . but no questions were asked.[42]

Poor children, even when they had parents, may not have been much better off. Because mothers had to work, children were often left unattended. Many suffered from malnutrition. Many were dosed with opiates, a practice popular among baby farmers as well. Laudanum, or morphia, was freely available over the counter. One of the most popular was Godfrey's Cordial, also cynically called "mother's helper." In a sense it replaced swaddling as a means of controlling children. Not surprisingly, the use of opiates as a sedative for children was abused — so much so that in 1776 Dr. William Buchan, the author of *Domestic Medicine,* claimed that thousands of children died each year from its effects.[43]

The practice of abandoning children, so common in Europe, was practically unknown in America, especially in the eighteenth century. (Institutions for orphans had to be created in the nineteenth century to deal with the effects of immigration and urbanization. These were not repositories for abandoned newborns, but for older children from homes deemed "inadequate" by the state.) There was so much land, movement, and opportunity that people tended to take care of any baby that was needy. A 1775 article in the *Virginia Gazette* is illustrative: it reported that a surprised messenger found an infant carefully placed in a box on a road, along with some cash. He promptly adopted the baby himself. The fact that the abandonment of a baby was considered newsworthy testifies to its rarity.[44]

While the eighteenth century contained much human misery, there were notable pockets of "enlightened" sentimentality. In fact, in some ways the eighteenth century was more progressive than the nineteenth. After the witchcraft hysteria of the early modern era, the harsh persecution of deviant women spent its force, and the eighteenth century saw fewer indictments and convictions for infanticide. The actual number of child murders probably remained much the same, but people were more sympathetic toward the murderous mother, who was now seen as driven to her heinous act out of desperation. The enlightened monarch Frederick II of Prussia spearheaded a revolt against the persecution of unwed mothers, recognizing that many of these women had been raped or had prostituted themselves as a means of staying alive, and had no way of supporting themselves and a baby. Women who were in domestic service (by far the greatest form of employment for females) were especially vulnerable, as pregnancy was grounds for dismissal; and even concealment of pregnancy, prior to the reforms, was punishable by death if there was no live baby present at the time of inquiry. The poet Goethe, by the way, was a great supporter of these reforms. His character Gretchen in the *Faust* drama embodies the desperate plight of a mother driven to infanticide.[45]

A number of other people were concerned with the downtrodden and sought humane remedies for the growing population of unwanted children. Touched by the abandoned babies he encountered on his frequent walks through East London, Captain Thomas Coram enlisted support from the wealthy, and in 1741 founded the London Foundling Hospital. It became a favorite "cause" of the day's socialites. Handel gave concerts to help raise funds, and the painters Hogarth and Reynolds donated works. Compared to that of its continental counterparts, the London institution's mortality rate was impressively low. But it is important to understand that the death rate decreased *only* during those periods in which the hospital radically limited its intake. The London Foundling Hospital did not have a *tour*, the turnstile that facilitated the anonymous depositing of babies, but, instead, held a thoroughgoing interview with the mother, during which she was forced to present herself as "rehabilitable" — that is, either seduced and abandoned or a first-time offender. In other words, she could not be a prostitute. The system was designed to avoid giving unwitting encouragement to women who were selling their bodies. The assumption was, I suppose, that the tens of thousands of prostitutes in London engaged in such activities because they wished to. These women were still left with no option for their offspring but the trash heap or baby farm. Here, one sees how the best of intentions can go awry, especially when it is infused with sexism.[46]

A philanthropic gesture of this era that strikes me as particularly inspired was devised by Jonas Hanway, who, for a time, was a director of the London Foundling Hospital. He had investigated and published the dismal outcome of parish placements of babies, and as an antidote suggested that wet nurses and foster mothers be paid over intervals instead of in a lump sum, and be offered a *bonus* if their charges survived. His idea was taken up by a number of parishes, and it worked! But this was a drop in the bucket; the problem was massive.[47]

Sweeping reform was advocated by First Feminist Mary Wollstonecraft, in her *Vindication of the Rights of Women* (1792). She argued, sensibly enough, that better child care would result from better treatment of women — from providing women with, for example, education and equal rights. It is painfully ironic that she died shortly after giving birth to the child who became Mary Shelley. It was she, the author of *Frankenstein,* with whom we began this chapter. Perhaps we can now understand the monster's search for a home as a reflection of Mary's search for a mother.

Upstairs, Downstairs: Maternal Images in the Nineteenth Century

The nineteenth-century heir of Blake's protest poems about exploited chimney sweeps and Hogarth's paintings of battered children was Charles Dickens. His *Oliver Twist* is probably the most famous case of child abuse found in literature. Oliver, a foundling, is born in a workhouse, where he commits the unspeakable crime of asking for more gruel. En route to the obligatory happy end, Oliver is variously brutalized, starved, exploited by unethical employers, kidnaped by a gang of thieves, and wounded. But his pathos pales in comparison with that of Little Nell. The fate of Dickens's Little Nell was a matter of such grave public concern that throngs lined the pier in New York awaiting the final installment of *The Old Curiosity Shop* to learn if she had lived or died, while in England her demise unleashed an anguished furor.[48]

Everybody read Dickens. No living author has ever been more

hysterically beloved by a larger cross-section of the population. His novels produced reform in a dozen directions in law, in magistrates' courts; he was influential in the prevention of public hanging. But because of his popularity, authors began killing off their child characters in record numbers. The deaths became more and more gruesome. Some historians[49] see a kind of sadism, a sadism masquerading as morality, in all this child sacrifice. It was as if the authors, for all their avowed generosity of spirit, enjoyed abusing their own creations and their audience took pleasure in reading about the horrors.

By the Victorian era, the veneration of mothers had become a thinly veiled guise for their exploitation. Dickens was merciless to mothers who failed to give up their lives to their family's domestic happiness. Mrs. Jellyby, the philanthropist-mother in *Bleak House,* was a conspicuous victim of his satiric pen. While she calmly pursued the affairs of an African tribe on the left bank of the Niger, her household was in chaos: her unwashed children bumped downstairs on their heads, her own dress gaped open in the back, there was no hot water because the boiler was out of order and the kettle was not to be found, and the codfish served for dinner was half raw.[50] Clearly Dickens disapproved of Mrs. Jellyby's nondomestic interests and felt she should devote herself to matters closer at hand.

It doesn't take ingenious psychological sleuthing to realize that Dickens probably conveyed his ambivalence toward his own mother in the character of Dora in *David Copperfield,* an admittedly autobiographical novel. Dora is David Copperfield's first wife. Like David's mother, she is weak, pretty, and brainless, and is thought by critics to be the scapegoat for David's repressed hatred for his mother, who abandoned him in the novel by dying — all of which may echo Dickens's own feelings.[51] In a time when hatred of mother could not be acknowledged directly, Dickens gave us, as readers, ample evidence to reconstruct. His dark feelings broke through the thin veneer of the Victorian glorification of mother.

Dickens was not alone. The nineteenth century is particularly problematic for its maternal representations, or, more accurately, its lack of them. This is not to say that mothers were well portrayed before — they were not — but that the disparity in the sympathy conveyed for mothers and that displayed toward other members of the family was now greater. Consider this: in the nineteenth-century novel, daughters finally begin to speak. But in the typical novel, the daughter makes her way alone in the world in the hope of *avoiding* her mother's fate (like Emma in Austen, Tess in Hardy, Evelina in Burney, Maggie in Eliot, and Catherine and Jane in the Brontës). Often these daughters do not become mothers themselves; indeed, they try to evade motherhood at all costs. The novels are inherently flattering to daughters at the expense of their mothers.[52]

The marginality of maternal characters in the Victorian age is especially paradoxical because by this time female authors were no longer an anomaly and novels were often domestic. Yet even in her own sphere mother was nowhere to be seen. Novels were brimming with orphans whose parentlessness was resolved by a surrogate father. Oliver Twist, Cosette, Little Nell, and Little Eppie all get "fairy godfathers." What happened to fairy godmothers? When a mother does appear, like Mrs. Bennet in *Pride and Prejudice,* her presence creates more problems than her absence.

It is probably not coincidental, as Virginia Woolf noted in *A Room of One's Own,* that many nineteenth-century women writers were themselves childless — the Brontës, Austen, Eliot, among others. Woolf knew her Freud. "Did they write out of a thwarted need to give birth," she asked, thereby "making substitute dream children out of their novels?" a speculation that echoed her contemporary, the Freudian analyst Helene Deutsch. This "books or babies" myth still preoccupies people, probably because the sheer number of childless women authors is hard to ignore — Woolf herself, Cather, Wharton, Hellman, Porter, Moore, Welty, Oates, for example. "Almost no mothers — as almost no part-time, part-self persons — have created enduring literature . . . so far." That was the poet and story writer Tillie Olsen in 1972. In my view, the novelist Ursula LeGuin put the matter to rest when she wrote recently that the "books or babies" myth "is just a flipside of the theory that books came from the scrotum." The real issue is four thousand years of social conditioning and the absence of child care.[53]

Another remarkable fact about nineteenth-century women authors is that so many of them had lost their mothers at birth or in early childhood — Browning, Shelley, Eliot, and Gaskell, for example. "I never had a mother," wrote Emily Dickinson, but, in fact, she did, one who was alive and well when Dickinson cryptically wrote those words.[54]

What can we say about all this maternal absence? This topic has generated reams of computer printouts on both sides of the Atlantic. Some have pointed to the advantages of motherless protagonists — the arrangement gave authors the freedom to revise standard patriarchal plots, to prioritize bonds among women, for instance; or gave the heroine the freedom necesssary to develop her own script. The presence of Marmee in *Little Women,* one of a very few live maternal protagonists in nineteenth-century literature, for example, served only to coerce her daughters into conformity. She was the voice of patriarchy. How many decades of girls have wept when intense, active, creative Jo March succumbed to convention and married the docile, elderly German professor and thereafter wrote silly thrillers?[55]

Others have ransacked the literature trying to prove that mothers did indeed manage to tell their stories, but that their accounts were, more often than not, in the gaps, in the contradictions and omissions of the novel.[56] Women authors, they argue, have had to use subversive strategies to inscribe their subjectivity into what is a "male" narrative frame. Because the traditional narrative structure is unwelcoming to the female experience, women have been forced to devise creative and unconventional ways to tell their stories. To recover an author's subjectivity, the reader must read subversively, that is, attend to silences and absences, the unspoken and encoded, to look for repressed mother-daughter relationships, to foreground subplots. Such a reading might interpret the typical Victorian daughter's struggle against maternal identification, for example, to represent a profound if ambivalent *connection* between mother and daughter. So, from this perspective, Elizabeth and Mrs. Bennet, who ordinarily are viewed as mutually remote, might be considered highly enmeshed. Elizabeth needs her mother to butt up against. She uses her mother as a standard against which to distinguish her own personality. Her purposeful distance is a form of connection. A true lack of attachment between mother and daughter would be indifference, and Elizabeth is not indifferent.

What feminist critics have come up with is a distinctive female literary tradition. They have recovered neglected female authors and reinterpreted female characters in new ways. They have discovered some common feminine plot structures. (The search for affiliation is a popular one — to be distinguished from the male search for autonomy.) They have highlighted relations between female characters, especially mothers and daughters, which earlier had been trivialized. And while some feminist critics have focused a bit too much, in my view, on what texts do *not* say, on the whole they have shown us what women have accomplished *in spite* of social constraints.

The literary critics who have been most vocal about maternal absence are the French feminist revisionists of the psychoanalyst Jacques Lacan, known by some as the "French Freud." Lacan's explanation for maternal absence in nineteenth-century fiction — that maternal absence was inevitable because mothers could not and cannot speak for and about themselves — is derived from the idea that women do not have the language with which to express themselves. Lacan's feminist revisionists — Hélène Cixous, Luce Iragary, and Julia Kristeva — counter by offering up a specifically feminine language, *"écriture feminine,"* a language "written through the white ink of mother's milk," to paraphrase Cixous.[57] These women tend to get elemental in their metaphors. But they are supplying what, in their view, is a mother's voice.

According to Lacan's revisionists, women have two options: they can employ strategies to speak with their own voices even while using the "language of the Father," much as the Anglo-American critics have described women authors as already doing; or they can revolutionize language. They can create a mother-language, a language that approximates the presymbolic, early communication that goes on between baby and mother. Such a language, the aforementioned *écriture feminine,* would be characterized by play, disruptions, excess, gaps, grammatical and syntactical subversion, ambiguities; by generic transgressions; by fluidity. Cixous's "Laugh of the Medusa" and Kristeva's "Stabat Mater" are offered as examples.

This writing, while it celebrates the maternal body, often tends to stretch metaphors to a point of absurdity, and may collapse into undecipherable solipsism. More important, the French revisionists play off Lacan's insights rather than refute them. They fail to challenge, for instance, his concept of language as masculine. While it is true that Western language is full of patriarchal habits — the use of the male pronoun "he" to indicate the generic is an obvious example — I doubt that our linguistic structure precludes female expression. Throughout history certain women have managed to get their point across. The Abbess Hildegarde of Bingen, despite her exclusion from Lacan's "symbolic order," described female orgasm quite adequately in the Middle Ages, as did Emily Dickinson, using metaphysical symbolism (yes, symbolism — sorry, Lacan!) in the nineteenth century and Adrienne Rich in the twentieth. All of them did quite well with ordinary ink, not mother's milk.

In the middle of this absence, there is at least one extraordinary mother-saturated nineteenth-century presence. It was in a novel written by a woman — "whose course and employments have always been," as she reported, "retired and domestic . . . I have been mother to seven children." The author was Harriet Beecher Stowe; the novel, *Uncle Tom's Cabin*. From a modern perspective, it is a bad book. It is melodramatic, condescending to blacks, and it deifies motherliness as a woman's true destiny to such an extent that (black, white, male, or female) all her characters are rated on a scale according to their maternal virtue. But it was a masterpiece of transgression, probably in ways unsuspected by the author. Not only did it break the silence about slavery in the United States and galvanize public opinion on behalf of abolition in a manner that would be hard to overstate, but it reorganized culture from a mother's point of view. Yet it did the latter while remaining basically within the sentimental tradition of the popular woman's novel.[58]

In a remarkable turnaround from the typical novel, *Uncle Tom's Cabin* is propelled by the mother's fear of losing her child. (The usual plot, like that of *Peter Pan,* is the search for a mother, which is, of course, a plot triggered by the child's, not the mother's, wish.) The story begins as Eliza, a young slave mother, is escaping across the frozen Ohio River to free territory with her small son to prevent his being sold away from her. Motherly women (and men) help Eliza every step of the way, from the woman in a public house who gets her a ferry, to the wife of a senator who provides her with clothes for herself and the child. These characters, though unimpeachable Angels of the House, nonetheless defy their husbands and advocate strongly what they believe to be right. Here we have mothers speaking with their own voice. The bonds of motherhood are, for Stowe, a measure of morality, a model of what an ethical social community should be. Not only are all the characters in *Uncle Tom's Cabin* judged by their attitude toward this bond, but the author makes clear, in her "Concluding Remarks," that she is writing to "you, Mothers of America," who pity "those mothers that are constantly made childless by the American slave trade!"[59]

What Stowe achieved in literature, Mary Cassatt achieved in paint more subtly and with more appeal to a modern audience at the end of the century. Her exquisite portraits of mother and child are widely admired. She was part of a revolutionary group of Impressionist painters, including Edouard Manet, Berthe Morrisot, and Edgar Degas, that rescued the mother-child relationship from its role as sterile icon of redemption and fertility and made it three-dimensional. Cassatt's paintings are direct and unsentimental. In her canvases, she repeatedly emphasized women's thoughtfulness, their self-absorption, and, most of all, their dignity. *The Child's Caress* is a good example of Cassatt's refusal to prettify or typecast. Mother and child here are ordinary, even plain, with rounded features, unsmiling faces, and a somewhat leaden mien. Yet the painting's true subject — the pair's special connection and shared private sphere — is elegantly expressed. This is a prosaic moment, wonderful to be sure, but not ecstatic. One senses that this mother could lose her temper; she is no Angel.[60]

The Repressive Storm: Maternal Reality in the Nineteenth Century

It is not that the eighteenth century in Europe was an erotic paradise, but during the nineteenth the pursuit of pleasure fell under deep suspicion. The poet Byron described the transformation as going "from cunt to cant."[61] The cant of the Victorian period was particularly unfortunate for the Victorian woman, especially when she bore a child.

Patriarchal attitudes, somewhat muted in the last century, were recharged. This time around, male superiority was authorized not so much by the Bible as by science, the new orthodoxy. Charles Darwin's radical new theory of evolution did not appear to operate in women's favor, and certain of its distortions linger on today. Darwin dismissed women as biologically inferior. Men were more evolved; that is, more evolved on the important criteria. In his *Descent of Man* (1871), Darwin theorized that man's struggle for a mate accounts for his superiority. According to the laws of natural selection, qualities of courage, perseverance, and intelligence in the male — qualities necessary to get a girl — would be passed on to men. Evolutionary success for woman, on the other hand, meant reproductive success. Women's breeding capacity was the criterion of female excellence. Clearly, "science" suggested that women were made to be pregnant. Biology is destiny. The social order was grounded in the natural order.

Taking this a bit further, evolutionists have argued that women, for genetic reasons, have a greater and more inherent interest in childbearing than men, and that mothers are better equipped biologically to take care of babies than are fathers, or anyone else for that matter. In modern sociobiological terms (from the field popularized recently by Edward O. Wilson in *Sociobiology* and Richard Dawkins in *The Selfish Gene*), the mother has already invested so much in her offspring via pregnancy that she will continue to invest in a particular child in order to protect her initial investment. This distinguishes her from the "promiscuous" father, who has invested little.[62] Scientists still only imperfectly understand how natural selection operates, let alone sexual selection. But that hasn't stopped people from seizing on the idea that mothering is natural for a woman, and they have convoluted that into an imperative. Just a few years ago, married women who made a voluntary decision not to have children were considered selfish and odd. And if you asked a man to help you with the diapering, he might respond that he didn't have a uterus (an obvious prerequisite). His logic was as follows: biology is destiny, and his biology did not provide him with the ability to bear a child; therefore he did not have a "maternal instinct"; therefore he was unsuited to diaper. Q.E.D. Somehow the notion of "maternal instinct" became infused with the nature of one's reproductive equipment.

The so-called maternal instinct is a political hot potato. Derived from Darwinian thinking, it is one of those terms in common use whose meaning seems to vary with the user. Technically, the maternal instinct would imply that women are *biologically* wired to be mothers. Most people use the term loosely, however, to describe those inner promptings which induce women to care for their children. These are feelings mothers have, or think they should have, but they rarely think about the source of the promptings, whether they are biologically or socially derived. Feminists, interpreting the term narrowly, tend to bristle at the concept because it is reductionist and seems to imply that nonmotherhood is deviant and that fathers are not programmed to care for children.

A host of current arguments about maternal instinct rely heavily on analogy with animal behavior. There is an assumption that the skills we share with "lower" orders are somehow more fundamental, essential, and important, thereby rendering of consuming human interest the reactions of monkeys to surrogate mothers and the evasive actions of pregnant rats. Be that as it may, an honest review of the scientific literature is utterly inconclusive — Konrad Lorenz's female geese may have mothered, for example, but so do male marmosets, indicating that nurturing is not necessarily female. Furthermore, the innate universality of a maternal instinct in animals has never been demonstrated. In lower mammals, development of maternal behaviors may depend on specific circumstances without which they will not occur (for example, rats require certain olfactory cues; if absent, the rats may eat their young). Taken as a whole, the message from ethology is that if we have inherited any pattern from a primeval primate ancestor, it is probably one of flexibility.

Apart from the fact that women possess the equipment for lactation, mothers seem no more predisposed to, or innately skilled at, child care than are fathers, siblings, or nonparents. Besides, women obviously come in a variety of shapes, colors, sizes, talents, and temperaments. Why shouldn't they vary in degrees of "motherliness"? There is no biological necessity for any one particular woman to mother, and more than four thousand years of social pressure exerted on women may explain motherhood's popularity. The fact that babies are a product of sexual passion could also account for their prevalence.[63]

The popular but bogus science of craniology in the nineteenth century conveniently supported the conclusions of the early Darwinists. Presumably men were smarter than women because their brains are almost always larger. In the flurry of false scientism, apparently no one addressed the obvious question: If the possession of an outsized brain was the distinguishing feature of the master species, why was the world not ruled by whales? And craniology was not the only questionable science in this century. People still had lopsided views of conception — that the child originates in the father and merely grows in the mother, despite the fact that ova were discovered in 1845. This idea informs our language to this day: "to father" means "to generate"; "to mother" means "to nurture." But the maternal body could be a dangerous growth medium. Should mother think the wrong thoughts, especially at the point of conception, then the child could be branded for life — with a birthmark. Congenital malformations were understood to be proof of a mother's "illicit" thoughts (of another romantic interest perhaps?). It is notable that, though a mother could take no credit for producing a "normal" baby, she was blamed for producing an "abnormal" one.[64]

Ideologically speaking, women lost their sex drive in the nineteenth century; it seems to have been replaced by none other than the maternal instinct. From a Victorian perspective, women wanted babies and men wanted orgasms. The maternal instinct was the female analogue of the male sex instinct. Women were seen as dominated by their wombs. To the Victorian medical expert, it was "as if the Almighty, in creating the female sex, *had taken* the *uterus* and *built up around it*." We are back 350 years with Luther's contemptuous outburst: "That's what women are *for*."[65]

Respectable women were supposed to be as ignorant of sex as they were of business and politics. Sexual desire became the exclusive province of men and lower-class women. One prominent medical doctor dismissed the subject entirely: "The majority of women are not very much troubled with sexual feelings of any kind." How reproduction occurred is anyone's guess. Presumably men snuck into a darkened room to perform their animal duty while wives were to "lie still and think of the Empire," which is what one mother instructed her daughter to do on her wedding night. Even pregnancy, an all-too-obvious result of sexual intercourse, was cast in an ambivalent light. While pregnancy was a woman's glory, the proper pregnant woman stayed indoors. Scarlett O'Hara, the heroine of *Gone With the Wind,* lost her reputation in postbellum Atlanta for showing herself.[66]

This purported passionlessness of women is especially amusing because women's lust was alive and well just one century earlier. In the 1700s, the fictional Fanny Hill was happily plying her trade; Havelock Ellis could not find a single case of frigidity; and promiscuity was at an all-time high. Traditionally women have been regarded as more demanding than men: recall that the *Malleus Maleficarum* (the fifteenth-century witch-hunter's guide) warned that "carnal lust . . . in women is insatiable"; the writings of Chaucer, Boccaccio, and Montaigne are filled with hapless men who cannot satisfy their wives; the Song of Songs in the Bible has a "his" and "hers" section. All of which goes to prove how much ideology shapes thinking and feeling.[67]

But ideology is not fact, and historians sensibly point out that many married women probably enjoyed sexuality in the Victorian era but just didn't talk about it. Nevertheless, some medical doctors took the idea so seriously that they proceeded to define the presence of sexual desire in a woman as a disease, and they performed clitoridectomies (the surgical removal of the clitoris) to "cure" it. This procedure was also thought to reduce hallucinations, "vaginal catarrh," hysteria, mania, and epilepsy.[68]

If the myth that males are more sexual than females was not influential in the nineteenth century, it seems to be so in this one. What young woman hasn't been subjected to a barrage of arguments for sexual "favors" based on the male's more imperative "needs"? Such thinking was embedded in the rhetoric around the 1993 Spur Posse escapade in Lakewood, California, which concerned a clique of teenage boys accused of coercing girls into sex. The boys competed with each other for "scores," behavior casually dismissed by some of their parents as "boys will be boys." The cultural critic Camille Paglia might agree: the male homosexual has *more* sex than his straight male counterpart; the female homosexual has sex *less* often than hers. This proves, in her mind, that males naturally tend toward satyriasis and females naturally tend toward nesting, even when they are functioning outside social convention. Regardless of the respective strength of the male and female sexual drives, Freud was prescient in recognizing that both genders had them. But while he allowed women a sex instinct, he also, as we shall see, ascribed to them a maternal instinct of sorts. He was half right.[69]

Given the exalted status of motherhood in the nineteenth century, it is not surprising that the main argument early feminists advanced in favor of their claim for equality was based on motherhood. Elizabeth Cady Stanton, who organized the first woman's rights convention at Seneca Falls, New York, in July 1848, had seven children. She wrote to Susan B. Anthony, another feminist, "I would not have one less than seven, in spite of all the abuse heaped upon me for such extravagance." The first wave of Anglo-American feminists focused their energy on formal equality with men and the right to vote, but they argued for this agenda on the grounds of their common experience as mothers. In England and the United States, the claim of women's moral superiority over men because they were concerned with the welfare of children (and therefore with the welfare of the community) was long used to justify women's claim to the ballot. Women deserved the vote because they were virtuous, sober, devout, respectable, and *maternal*. The "mother heart" argument has been used as an excuse for almost every area of female activism. We see it today in Mothers Against Drunk Driving and in Sara Ruddick's peace politics based on what she calls "maternal thinking."[70]

The early Anglo-American activists did not feel the need to focus on motherhood as a feminist issue. They tended to take their maternal duties for granted, an attitude facilitated by their standing as privileged women in an era when affluent households had servants.[71] Ms. Stanton, for example, had an excellent housekeeper in Amy Willard, and did not experience motherhood as a burden that needed to be lightened.

On the continent, however, where early feminists were less bourgeois, the vote never took center stage. The emphasis was always on the need for support structures for mothers to facilitate their double burden in the home and in the workplace. In Germany, for example, where the early movement was called *Mutterschutz* (protection of motherhood), the priority was the improvement of the horrendous plight of unpartnered women with children. The essence of the female problem, to this movement, was the need for special concessions to mothers to give them a chance for a reasonable life.

Neither group of early feminists questioned women's maternal role. Both assumed that it was women's exclusive right (or burden) to mother. Neither group opted for fathers' involvement or the redistribution of domestic work. Perhaps this is understandable in light of the romantic attitude toward motherhood at the time. What is less understandable, even astounding, is the early feminists' opposition to birth control.

In this the feminists had strange bedfellows — the church (obviously), the medical profession (to its everlasting discredit), and "Malthusians." Thomas Malthus was an eighteenth-century political economist who predicted catastrophe for the world. Stating that the world's food supply increases arithmetically while the population increases geometrically, he concluded that the population will inevitably exceed the means of subsistence. Yet even he opposed contraception. He preferred benign neglect of the masses (the greatest source of population increase) and "moral" restraint.

Indeed, all these groups promoted abstinence, or, rather, male self-control. (No wonder prostitution flourished!) Contraception was not considered respectable. It was associated with sexual excess, with sex for its own sake, a Victorian taboo. Feminists felt that birth control might make women sexual playthings, more, rather than less, dependent on men.[72] Physicians on both sides of the Atlantic were too concerned with their professional image to dare involve themselves with so controversial an issue. The nineteenth century drew to a close without any significant medical involvement in family planning. When one realizes that cheap rubber condoms were available in the 1850s but that the American Medical Association did not make information available to patients until 1937, it becomes clear how conservative these men were. Anything that prevented women from fulfilling their maternal role was considered *verboten* by the eminent Victorians.

It is not as if every mother enjoyed all aspects of mothering all the time. Was that, perhaps, Victoria's secret? The queen, who had nine children, wrote to her daughter in 1859 that childbearing "is indeed hard and dreadful." Sophie Tolstoy, wife of the Russian novelist and mother of thirteen, complained bitterly in her diary of her pregnancies. About her husband, the source of her bounteous fertility, she resolved, "Gradually I shall retreat in myself and poison his life." Charlotte Perkins Gilman, author of the novella *The Yellow Wallpaper,* a fictionalized account of her postpartum depression and the botched Victorian attempt to treat it, was one of the few American feminist voices to speak out in the nineteenth century against mothers raising children in isolation. She argued for the abolition of private nurseries (and also private kitchens) and proposed, instead, the communal raising of babies in centralized day nurseries architecturally designed to meet their needs and staffed by trained professionals. The child would benefit from the professionalism of the caretakers and, she felt, would learn that he or she is not the center of the world but just one person among many, a characteristic that would facilitate socialization. As for mother, she would be free from her parasitic dependence on man, and she "will love her child as well, perhaps better, when she is not in hourly contact with it." Gilman found few supporters for her ideas among Anglo-American feminists because these early feminists held motherhood in great esteem and, given their middle-class status and the plenitude of servants, did not feel particularly oppressed by their "natural" roles. Communal child care was associated with the lower classes.[73]

In spite of all the rhetoric against birth control, the birthrate plummeted in the late nineteenth century in America and Western Europe (as it had in France the century before); family size was halved by the time of World War I. The upper classes started the trend, and by the 1880s the swarms of ragged children produced by the poor were regarded by the bourgeoisie, so Émile Zola's novels inform us, as evidence of the lower order's ignorance and brutality. The drop in birthrate was probably due to the use of contraception (even though no one was talking about it), because it occurred as a result of women ceasing to have children at an early age. Or, perhaps, it may be attributed to abstinence. Jane Austen's letters, for example, contain the advice to a friend that to avoid continual childbearing she should adopt "the simple regimen of separate rooms." Perhaps all that Victorian prudery served to reduce passion after all . . . but I doubt it.[74]

Why did people choose to have fewer children just then? There was no new birth control technology available to encourage the trend. Was it a protest against motherhood, as some Victorians feared? Was the motive primarily economic — an attempt to escape poverty or to protect newfound wealth? Or did the wish for a smaller family result from greater attachment to children and a desire to provide better care for the ones already born? I suspect that the answer is "all of the above." In light of centuries of excess children, infanticide, and abandonment, one would expect the falling birthrate to have been celebrated. Ironically, it was not. Once the trend was discerned, it fueled fears of depopulation and "race suicide," and later resulted in horrendous abuses of the lower classes and non–Anglo-Saxon ethnic groups in an attempt to reduce their reproduction. ❍

AT LONG LAST, by the end of the nineteenth century both mother and baby could be expected to survive the delivery process. Finally, people understood the principles of asepsis, and that knowledge, plus new surgical techniques, improved mortality rates. Anesthesia revolutionized the experience. Women were so fond of the painkiller that a few named their children after it. At first, the use of anesthesia during childbirth was resisted by physicians, who felt that women *should* suffer in delivery, like Eve. But they eventually gave in to the demand. In a truly radical act, Queen Victoria had anesthesia by chloroform for the birth of her seventh child, and that paved the way for its acceptance.

These exciting developments in the history of childbirth came at the expense of traditional midwives. Excluded both formally and informally from a scientific education, midwives were doomed to fall further behind as technology developed. Well-off women were the first to benefit from the new obstetric techniques. By and large, they still gave birth at home and therefore did not risk exposure to the infections prevalent in hospitals. Indigent women still relied on midwives, or, sadly, hospital clinics, where their chance of dying was seven times greater than if they delivered at home.[75] While medical men understood bacteriology, they still had no good tool for preventing the spread of bacteria until the advent of the "magic bullets" — the sulfa drugs and penicillin, after the late 1920s and 1930s.

Bourgeois women may have had fewer children in the later

nineteenth century, but they devoted more time to caring for them. Thanks to Locke and Rousseau, children were regarded as delicate persons who evolved through developmental stages and needed constant loving care. True, middle-class women were often helped in the performance of their domestic tasks by servants, but the standards of child rearing were so exacting, and etiquette so elaborate, that their net workload was not lightened. All that rococo ornamentation needed constant cleaning, and the newfangled flummery associated with the domestic arts of Mrs. Beeton (the Martha Stewart of Victorian England) took all day.

Hand feeding, that is, the use of the bottle, had finally become safe at the end of the nineteenth century, due to Pasteur's techniques for ridding milk of disease-producing micro-organisms. This was the final nail in the coffin for wet-nursing, even in France. Some cynical historians have pointed out that the employment of wet nurses fell only when artificial methods of feeding improved sufficiently to become a reasonable alternative.[76] The arrival of safer methods of artificial feeding may have ensured the survival of those babies in a foundling home who would have perished for want of a wet nurse.

This, too, was the heyday of the nanny in England, a peculiar institution that appears to have been limited to that island and its colonies. The British nanny, most assuredly, was not a wet nurse. She was a specialized servant, very proper, and she presided over the nursery. Upper-middle-class parents routinely surrendered their children to her and may have seen very little of them. Undoubtedly there were bad nannies, Draconian nannies, eccentric nannies, as well as loving and cuddly nannies. At its best, the English system created lifelong devotion between children and their nurses, as between Winston Churchill and his beloved Mrs. Everest. Sir Winston wrote, after her death, "She had been my dearest and most intimate friend during the whole of the twenty years that I had lived."[77] Though, of course, the system had its abuses. But the few people who have studied the use of governesses for raising children have concluded that the process was benign and relatively orderly. This is probably a good point for the modern conflicted mom to keep in mind when she guiltily places the fate of her child in someone else's hands. Multiple mothering is not inherently harmful.

To the poor child, the life of his or her bourgeois counterpart might have seemed pleasant. But it had its downside. Victorian children (as well as their mothers) were subject to a great deal of social control, especially on moral and sexual matters. Parents in the nineteenth century did avoid the use of physical punishment, preferring instead the "gentler" shaping of moral character through reason and the laying on of guilt. In America, spanking replaced horsewhipping, though evidently Davy Crockett's and Abraham Lincoln's parents failed to hear about the change; both men were whipped soundly as children. Nevertheless, there were two subjects about which Victorian parents were obsessional — constipation and masturbation. Regularity of the bowels was the first rule of health, and there were laxatives and other procedures to ensure it. Sometimes bowel training took place before the age of one.[78]

Masturbation was not tolerated. One quirky bit of history concerns a sinister figure, a prominent German doctor who deemed himself a child-rearing expert — Dr. Daniel Schreber. In his best-selling books he advocated enforced discomforts for children. He never mentioned masturbation as such, but many of the measures he recommended, from cold baths to an elaborate system of harnesses and braces, ostensibly to make the child grow straight, suggest that he may have had the practice in mind. Not surprisingly, his son went mad; but, to historians' eternal delight, the young man's memoirs were analyzed by Sigmund Freud. In fact, Schreber *fils* turned out to be one of Freud's major cases. What is odd from our perspective is that Freud did not connect Dr. Schreber's rearing methods with the problems of his son, which shows how little Freud was interested in actual parenting![79]

One can uncover sexual exploitation of children in any era, but because the Victorians portrayed themselves as such prudes, it is all the more striking that we find such an abundance of the perversion in their time. The scale of female child prostitution was mind-boggling. Speaking of a certain publisher of erotica, Oscar Wilde said, matter-of-factly, "He loves first editions, especially of women: little girls are his passion." There were at least two brothels in London that specialized in breaking in young virgins. In understanding this tragic aspect of Victorianism, it is sobering to realize that there was a Cult of the Little Girl, in which adult males photographed preadolescent females, sometimes with a bare shoulder evident, and always insisting on a higher, nonmaterial interest in their ethereal qualities. Lewis Carroll and John Ruskin were two votaries of the cult. Between child prostitution at one extreme and the simpering over nymphs at the other, the Victorian manner of child rearing seems less than generous.[80]

Revelations about Victorian child molestation have been in the news in the last decade because of a recent controversy in psychoanalytic circles. Freud has been accused of covering up (perhaps unwittingly) the childhood sexual abuse of some of his patients in the service of developing his theory of neuroses. Presumably, he denied that any sexual abuse had occurred, and instead insisted that reported "seductions" by patients were nothing more than fantasies. In point of fact, Freud may have misinterpreted a few cases (psychoanalysts are not clairvoyant), but he was certainly aware that in many instances the abuse was real, and he stated this. Despite the unpleasantness of the controversy, it did serve to spotlight the under side of Victorian life.[81]

So it should not surprise us that one of the greatest writers at the turn of the century had been sexually abused as a child. In a recent detailed biography of Virginia Woolf, it was revealed that at about the age of six, Virginia fell prey to the intrusive attentions of her two half brothers, George and Gerald Duckworth, both of whom became icons of British society.[82] Family incest seemed to have spanned all social classes.

While the children of the middle classes were forced to behave "respectably," often with considerable cruelty, the children of the poor were beasts of burden. It was soon apparent that the industrial enterprise had a need for unskilled workers, lots of them. Since children were cheaper than their parents, they became the more attractive source of labor. By the 1830s, the cotton mills, the great symbol of English economic dominance, depended on children for nearly half of their labor force. In America, before the turn of the century, an estimated 2,250,000 children under fifteen were full-time workers — in coal mines, glass factories, textile mills, canning factories, in the cigar industry, and in the homes of the wealthy — in short, wherever they could be used. Four-year-old boys worked sixteen-hour days sorting beads or rolling cigars in New York City tenements; five-year-old girls worked the night shift in Southern cotton mills; little children worked unbearably long hours making lace on the continent. There is no comparison between conditions of work for a preindustrial child and the conditions of work for a child on a production line. These children grew up hunched and rickety, sometimes blinded by fine work or the intense heat of furnaces, their lungs ruined by coal dust or cotton dust — if they grew up at all.[83]

After a benign period in the eighteenth century, sexism returned in the nineteenth, though, as we have seen, it was couched in paternalism. Bourgeois mothers were so pure and delicate that they required chivalrous protection by men, which, of course, meant their subjection. If poor women could not marry, they were forced to sell their bodies in order to survive. (A famous example is Fantine in the novel and now musical *Les Misérables*.) Prostitution surged. By the mid-1800s, it is estimated, there were between twenty thousand and eighty thousand prostitutes in London. These were not fancy courtesans, but streetwalkers and vagrants, the very bottom of the pit of social suffering for women. It was mostly their offspring who sadly littered the gutters of London, or who were harvested by baby farmers, though sometimes even properly married women had to abandon their infants for self-preservation or to provide for their older children. When reform did occur it did not apply to all needy mothers (except in France), but only to those who could return to a respectable life. Prostitutes still had no options for their babies.

Equal in horror to the fate of the poor child was that of the unwed mother. While her position had improved somewhat in the eighteenth century, it worsened in the nineteenth, largely due to the passage of the 1834 Poor Law in England. Prior to this a woman could file a paternity suit and sometimes receive financial assistance from the father of her child. Now the burden of responsibility for the child was placed exclusively on her shoulders. Even deserted wives could no longer sue their husbands. It was mother and child against the world: the workhouse or nothing. Understandably, there was an increase in abandonment and infanticide in the nineteenth century.[84]

Although privileged women generally discontinued the use of wet nurses at this time, poor urban women used them in greater numbers. This was certainly true in France. The sale of Godfrey's

Cordial flourished, as did Little Buttercup's profession. The Germans dubbed baby farmers the "angel makers." In 1870 there were 276 dead babies found in the streets of London, many left by baby farmers who did not wish to pay funeral expenses.[85] Worse yet, a number of these baby farmers were involved in a wide-ranging scam in which they purchased insurance on their charges for burial expenses. The insurance schemes were called "burial clubs," though they could more accurately be labeled "death clubs." The mortality rate of children insured by burial clubs was almost double that of children in general.[86]

Such practices died out at the end of the third quarter of the nineteenth century, when the acceptability of contraception made such desperate methods unnecessary. It was only then that infanticide disappeared for the first time in European history.[87] Ironically, it was the acceptability of birth control that made mother love — on a macroscopic level — possible.

Having looked at the widespread misery among poorer women and children in the nineteenth century, let us remember that this was also the age that witnessed the rise of the welfare state and of various philanthropic organizations (however ineffective they were in their fledgling forms). Countries in Western Europe and, a bit later, in the United States began to provide clean milk for babies, education in infant care for mothers, and routine medical supervision. France, the country with the worst child-mortality rate in the eighteenth century, embarked on a program of aid to unwed mothers that reduced the abandonment rate by half![88] In 1874, France began to regulate its huge wet-nursing industry, and it, too, was revolutionized. To the French, it was more important that poor children be nurtured than that their mothers be punished for immorality. Their policies may have been motivated less by civic virtue and open-mindedness than by a xenophobic fear of depopulation (which had begun in France a century before it showed up in the other Western European countries), combined with a heightened national awareness of German militarism. Nevertheless, France's social policy must be commended for its generosity to unattached mothers at a time when other countries ignored them.

In England and America, revelations of the plight of small children in the mills and mines and rural labor gangs led to some piecemeal reforms. Thomas Barnado sent thousands of indigent British youngsters to Australia and Canada; Charles Loring Brace sent American slum children to farm homes in the Midwest. History has not been kind to these originators of "foster care." Many of their charges regarded enforced removal from their homes as a form of banishment and indentured servitude. Nevertheless, the reformers' motives were undoubtedly philanthropic. Finally, in the late 1800s, societies for the prevention of cruelty to children were founded. In the United States, the child rescue society evolved out of the Society for the Prevention of Cruelty to Animals, since, ironically, the animal agency had been the only resource available to protect a little girl named Mary Ellen who was being physically abused. ❍

ONE OF THE GREAT PUZZLES of our history is that in the eighteenth and nineteenth centuries a blatant disregard of women and children coincided with the greatest glorification of mother and child. Obviously we have to consider a class division between those who form the backbone of industrialization and those whose pampered lives rested on that labor. But there is a sense in which even the idolization of mothers and children among the bourgeoisie was shallow, perhaps exploitative, sometimes cruel.

However, there were indications of positive change. Mothers were beginning to take charge of their maternal lives by the end of the nineteenth century: they had fewer children by design, they demanded anesthesia, they used motherhood to justify their participation in public decisions, they underwent psychoanalysis, and they read Harriet Beecher Stowe. In 1879, Ibsen's Nora, in *A Doll's House,* responded, to her husband's dictum that "before all else" she was a wife and mother: "That I no longer believe. I believe that before all else I am a human being." Nora was ahead of *our* time.[89]

SEVEN

Fall from Grace: Twentieth-Century Mom

Scientific Mom: 1900–1940

Mom got her sex drive back in the early decades of the twentieth century, and she got the vote . . . but she lost her poetry. No one wrote paeans to her anymore. Both her hair and her skirts got clipped, but so did her Angel's wings. She was cast down from her pinnacle of irreproachable purity along with the epic style of domesticity. Of course, a few stalwart men clung to romantic notions of motherhood, especially those who had been their mothers' favorite: Adolf Hitler in 1935 changed Mother's Day to his own mother's birthday, August 12, and made it a national holiday;[1] and Sigmund Freud, a true Victorian gentleman, could never quite believe that mothers could be harmful to their children. But to most men, mother was no longer quite so exalted. Novelists wrote of cowboys and adventure, anything to escape mom's domain. Masculine humor, like that of H. L. Mencken, made fun of her. "The average home is a horribly dull place," wrote F. Scott Fitzgerald, prophet of the Jazz Age. Mom had become dull as dishwater, as ho-hum as a household appliance, of which there were now many to choose from.

The impetus for mother's fall from grace was the rise of science. That which had endowed her with a maternal instinct now told her that her instinct alone was no longer sufficient for raising a happy and healthy child. An astonishing range of scientific discoveries and inventions appeared during these years — electricity, x-rays, sulfa drugs, the telephone, the automobile, movies — along with a dazzling array of "labor-saving" devices (much needed, since servants were no longer readily available). They seduced people into thinking that the possibilities for life improvement were endless if only one followed the dictates of science. If science and technology could produce all these wonderful things, couldn't it also guarantee the production of consistently wonderful children? It followed then that mothers *must* make use of the latest expertise in raising babies. Motherhood underwent a technological face-lift. Borrowing techniques from recently developed and improved industrial production, as well as from the new fields of psychology and child study, which proclaimed themselves to be scientific disciplines, mothers sought to reorganize child rearing along rational, standardized lines. All of a sudden mothers employed thermometers, formulas, milestone charts, and schedules, and they consulted numerous treatises on appropriate courses of action in their endeavors. They bandied about new, impressive-sounding terminology — vitamins, proteins, bacteria — intimidating the uninitiated. The Victorian mother would have been lost.

The good news was that "scientific" motherhood upgraded mothers' domestic tasks and endowed them with an aura of professionalism, like calling a janitor a sanitation engineer. The bad news was that much of the science was questionable; it undermined mothers' confidence in themselves; and it placed mothers under the thumb of self-appointed — usually male — experts.[2] It also needlessly complicated inherently simple tasks — feeding, for example, became clock-bound; burping a baby was elevated to a fine art; providing fresh air became a complex exercise — all of which may have enhanced motherhood's mystique, but was pedantic, superfluous, and sometimes just plain silly. No one seemed to question the efficacy of all the new techniques. Nevertheless, on the whole, the ideology of scientific motherhood was benign. The associated technologies of hygiene, sanitation, and nutrition actually improved child survival rates. And even the "bad news" was mostly harmless. Scientific motherhood was performable; while it was labor-intensive, it was concrete and had a defined endpoint. It was, therefore, not nearly so guilt-inducing as child rearing was to become in the second half of the twentieth century, when the rules changed and the instructions became much more ambiguous.

The excessively idealized and repressed nineteenth-century mother was bound to give way. The Victorian True Woman became the twentieth-century New Woman, an image that thrived until the Depression and that was personified by such heroines as Amelia Earhart, who flew across the Atlantic; Margaret Sanger, the American pioneer of birth control; and Rosa Luxemburg, the German Socialist leader. In her most frivolous form, she was the flapper — the independent, assertive, pleasure-hungry, fox-trotting young woman with a cigarette in one hand and a man in the other. She stood for a kind of autonomy that challenged traditional Victorian gender roles. The New Woman's growing numbers filled the ranks of reform movements, particularly the suffrage movement, which finally won the vote for women in 1920, a century after it had begun.[3]

The New Woman had fewer children than her mother had, and did things besides homemaking, though her "liberation" was short-lived. She would revert back to a semi-Victorian mode by mid-century (history is never unidirectional). In the meantime, the New Woman was much more likely than her mother or grandmother to have attended college, to be a member of a woman's organization, or to hold a job, often in the newly expanding female occupations of teaching, nursing, and social work.[4] Child rearing was still a woman's principal responsibility, and exclusively hers, but now other activities were permissible. Because a New Woman had fewer children and lived longer than her mother, half her life lay ahead of her after her last child left the nest. Clearly, mothering was no longer enough to fill a life span.

Even though women in record numbers were attending college and working, marriage was more popular than ever. The average age of marriage *dropped* (except for women who had graduated from college). The trend may have had to do with the rediscovery of female passion and the designation of the marital arena as the site for its occurrence.[5] "Passionlessness" was reclassified as "frigidity." Marital sex was not only tolerated; it became downright obligatory. This is not to say that there was no longer a double standard — indeed, newly proliferating sex manuals urged women to "fake" orgasm — but that sexual expression was considered central to the happiness of both genders and was separate from reproduction. Something must have been going right in marriage, for not only were women marrying at a younger age, but after 1900 men's patronage of prostitutes was dramatically reduced.

Husbands and wives were to be not only lovers, but friends.[6] Families were not quite the "encounter groups" they would become in our age, but they were saddled with the responsibility for fulfilling the emotional and psychological needs of their members. Compatibility became a big deal. Because families were relieved of some burdensome functions, like education and health care, and traditional roles were softening, perhaps they were primed to become cauldrons of sentiment. However, it would be wrong to think of this transition as seamless. Important differences existed, for example, between social classes. In the tenements, women expected little emotional intimacy from their husbands. Marriage was still a straightforward food-for-sex transaction.

The gender gap certainly existed in the early twentieth century, but perhaps a bigger source of conflict for the family was the generation gap, the newfound opposition of youth to age. Adolescence was becoming a sharply defined life period, replete with peer group consciousness, behavioral codes, and normative rebelliousness. Identity, no longer assigned at birth, was something that had to be worked out.[7] The chances for downward mobility were great. Teenagers became a source of worry to their parents and quickly developed proficiency in challenging authority.

This imposed new difficulties on both parents, but especially on dad, who was already suffering a partial loss of dominance resulting from mom's "emancipation." With a boom in suburban living at the turn of the century, dad spent even less time at home, because he spent more time commuting. Father was fast becoming irrelevant to everyday family life. His absence led, in some instances, to estrangement. Expressing emotion was probably not his strong suit anyway, since it was discouraged in his sphere. To his children, dad became more of a paycheck than a person in charge. He was someone to be humored, cajoled, and implicitly patronized by long-suffering wives and clever children. Dagwood Bumstead (of the 1930s' "Blondie" comic strip) and the faintly ridiculous hero of Clarence Day's memoir (later a Broadway play) *Life with Father* were well-known variants on the general type (father as incompetent). To an extent, dad was kicked upstairs in his house. With regard to child rearing, he was replaced by the medical or psychological expert, who was installed in the home as the new source of patriarchal authority.[8] Public patriarchy, however, remained intact.

The most poignant shift away from the patriarchal father occurred among immigrant families in the United States, where once proud men from Italy, Russia, Greece, Ireland, were reduced to being sweatshop laborers and members of stigmatized minorities. With their marginal status — they were neither part of the Old World nor part of the New — came an inevitable sense of loss. Their wives suffered too, but females were second-class citizens to begin with, so perhaps their decline in status was less painful. Then, too, their job description mostly remained the same. Having brought from the Old Country the patriarchal ideal for family relationships, these women at first humbly accepted the male prerogative and sought to bolster their husbands' self-esteem. Long trained in the practical art of making ends meet, they took in piecework and boarders and somehow ran the household. This wave of immigrants tended to remain, in attitude and language, uprooted peasants, and they became dependent on their sons and daughters, who attended American schools, knew English, and understood the ways of the big city. But while mother tended to respect father's waning authority, his children were often embarrassed by both parents' traditional ways and weak position in society.[9] Painful conflicts among all members of the family spawned guilt, identity crises, and a rich literature of assimilation.

In the earlier literature — the novels and stories written before the 1930s — the author's hostility, if expressed at all, was directed at the "old man." In Samuel Raphaelson's Broadway play *The Jazz Singer,* for example, Jack's Old World Jewish father is the heavy and his mother is heroic. Similarly, the sentimental hit song "My Yiddishe Mamma," introduced by Sophie Tucker in 1925, is a no-holds-barred tribute to the Jewish mother's virtue and self-sacrifice, as are Anzia Yezierska's *Bread Givers* (1925) and Sholem Asch's *The Mother* (1930). All portray the Jewish mother as wholly dedicated to the needs of others, self-denying, and able to coax forth meals from her "magic pots." The father, typically a devout man, is unfit for the labor market and unable to adapt to modern life. The mother, this literature tells us, was the emotional, if not the economic, backbone of the family. It is hard to believe that such feelings would turn rancid at midcentury, when the Jewish mother became a vampire.[10]

The astonishing metamorphosis in the perception of the immigrant mother, and the Jewish mother in particular, was, as we shall see, part of a drift toward mother-bashing in the decades after World War II. Perhaps these first-generation Jewish sons — Dan Greenburg (*How to Be a Jewish Mother*), Bruce Jay Friedman (*A Mother's Kisses*), Philip Roth (*Portnoy's Complaint*) — resented the real or imagined pressure placed on them to achieve material success and thereby garner respect for their immigrant families. Perhaps they felt guilty about surpassing their fathers and unconsciously chose to direct their hostility against a less vulnerable target, their mothers, who were no longer taking in piecework and behaving subserviently. Perhaps they blamed their mothers for their fathers' humiliating predicament. By the 1950s, "Jewish mother" became pejorative for *she who eats her sons*. But we are getting ahead of ourselves. In the meantime, it was father who took the heat, when there was any.

PATRIOTIC MOTHERHOOD AND POPULATION CONTROL

As the prestige of dad fell, that of the child rose. Children represented, as they had for decades, a romanticized past, but now they also became a symbol of the future. This was true not only for immigrant families who saw their Americanized children as a ticket to a better life, but for the general population as well, who exalted the child for "teachableness" and pliancy. There was a growing feeling that children might be *better* suited than adults for the industrial world.[11] The Swedish writer Ellen Key declared the twentieth century to be *The Century of the Child* in a book by that title, which first appeared in English in 1909 and became a best seller in America. In the overblown rhetoric of the day, every child was a potential president or messiah. Perhaps some of the reverence had to do with children's increasing *rarity*.

By the twentieth century, the fertility rate in all of Western Europe was declining. It was a period of intense national rivalry and imperialistic competition. Just as colonies, armies, and industries were absorbing more people than ever, the supply appeared to be dwindling.[12] With Europe fast moving toward military confrontation, a nation's heirs acquired political significance.

It was not only the quantity of the heirs that caused concern, but their so-called quality. The eugenics movement — the science of "improving" the human race by the careful selection of parents — had captured the public imagination (another legacy of Darwinism). People feared racial extinction and a takeover by lower (non-WASP) orders. The extent to which such talk was in the air was reflected later by Aldous Huxley's satire *Brave New World.*[13]

Even polyglot America cried "race suicide" as the conviction grew that immigrants and the poor would outproduce the native-born middle class. President Theodore Roosevelt went around the country exhorting white native-born Americans to have more children in order to preserve the national character.[14] By 1900 abortion had been outlawed in every state of the Union, and federal laws limited the availability of contraceptives. The poor, on the other hand, were welcome to limit their families as much as they could. Even child-rearing manuals in this era began with advice on the selection of the *fittest* mate, genetically speaking. From our perspective, the eugenics movement was to be the *reductio ad absurdum* of political incorrectness.

On a more positive note, the exaltation of the child coincided with the Progressive Era, a period when Americans throughout the country, and at all levels of government, finally sought reform that would enable their society to deal with the new urban-industrial order. A parallel movement occurred in England. Reformers launched ambitious federal programs to provide health services and welfare to mothers and infants, and to train mothers in the new science of parenting. Inspired by faith in reform, they transformed the processes of childbirth, child rearing, and housework for poor women, but, in the process, assigned the government new authority to intervene in family problems.[15] The sincere desire to improve social conditions coexisted with a disdain for ordinary people in the minds of Progressives, whose methods were sometimes insulting to the traditions, tastes, and sensibilities of the lower classes.

Day-care centers were a case in point. On the surface, the motive behind the creation of these nurseries was benevolent — to create a familylike alternative to "unacceptable" home conditions for children. But the government had the power to determine what was "unacceptable," and its decisions were influenced by a prevalent fear that without such nurseries, children from poor and immigrant homes would fail to become Americanized or, worse, would become delinquents. On top of its cultural insensitivity, the legacy of day care was also contaminated by its historical association with "inadequate" mothers.[16] Government-run child care was considered a placement of last resort for poor children, and certainly no place at all for offspring of the middle class. This stigma persisted until World War II, when the middle-class woman, on entering the labor force to support the war effort (she was dubbed "Rosie the Riveter"), placed her children in day care. All of a sudden, public day care underwent a remarkable change and became patriotic and good. Once again, we see the fickleness of the ideology of good parenting.

The efforts by the United States to increase its native birthrate paled in comparison to the countries of Europe, a number of which feared national extinction. France gave out bronze medals to mothers of five, silver medals to mothers of eight, and vermeil medals to mothers of eleven or more.[17] Italian mothers of fourteen could meet Mussolini. German mothers of four, in addition to receiving a medal and a family allowance, were saluted by the Hitler Youth and armed forces. As patriotic duty was added to the moral imperative for women to have children, the case for women's equality naturally had to be shelved.

After the huge losses of men in World War I, the already distorted emphasis on demographic planning gave way to a populationist obsession in Germany. Efforts to maintain racial purity became sinister. A massive propaganda campaign was employed to encourage breeding among people of the "master race." Images of radiant Aryan mothers and healthy children reminded women of their social obligation to reproduce. The message was enhanced by generous material incentives, and by punitive taxes for the unmarried. Meanwhile, those women who were "racially impure" (for example, Jews and Gypsies) were prevented from bearing children by compulsory sterilization, by abortion — or, later, by their extermination.[18]

The German cult of motherhood was coupled with a flagrant antifeminism. One of the earliest Nazi Party ordinances excluded women in perpetuity from holding any office. Women were to be "emancipated from emancipation," to paraphrase the Nazi ideologue Alfred Rosenberg. Instead, women were to revert to the old formula of *Kinder, Küche, Kirche* (children, kitchen, church).

Ironically, the Third Reich undermined its stated objective of creating strong families by demanding absolute loyalty to the Führer, Hitler. Children were encouraged to inform on the political attitudes of their parents. The socialization of children itself was concentrated outside the family in various youth organizations.[19] Queen Victoria would have been appalled.

THE NUTS AND BOLTS OF SCIENTIFIC MOTHERHOOD

Just as cookbooks began quantifying measurements — a "walnut-sized piece" of compressed yeast became, for example, a "tablespoon" — educated mothers in the early 1900s employed quantitative jargon (precise weights and measures; IQs) in referring to their children. Motherhood, as we have seen, was upgraded to a profession. It was now thought to be lawful, rule-bound, embodying a body of scientific knowledge that had to be mastered. In the late 1920s, Vassar College, one of the first women's colleges, offered courses in motherhood and the domestic arts, temporarily forgetting its mission: to supply the same educational opportunities for women as men. A writer in *Cosmopolitan* magazine urged that mothering be formally instituted as a career, open only to those who could demonstrate fitness. "Doctors and lawyers and clergymen fit themselves to have charge of human lives. Why should not mothers?"[20] Along this line, the writer Ellen Key endorsed a scheme to reimburse mothers for their important contribution to society. Nothing much came of it, but it does give one an idea of the tenor of the times.

At the turn of the century, women in America began to gather in groups to study and discuss child raising, which led in 1897 to the establishment of a National Congress of Mothers. The mothers' movement gained professional cachet by holding a White House conference, convened by Teddy Roosevelt, to establish a federal Children's Bureau, assign national holiday status to Mother's Day in 1914, and provide a nationwide apparatus for diffusing "expert" advice on child raising to the working classes. The profession of motherhood had arrived.

The professionalizing of parenting might have seemed flattering to women, since child raising was now thought to be a tricky business, even challenging enough, perhaps, for the odd brainy woman who might actually have a taste for "isms" and "ologies."[21] But the upgraded job description more likely served not to advance the status of women but to provide females with a calling in which they could excel without being threatening to males. Anyway, the upgrading had its downside. The idea that motherhood required training must have been unsettling to the average, uncredentialed mother (if not laughable to the more self-assured). It was hardly a step forward with regard to sexual symmetry and the equitable distribution of domestic labor: the assumption that mothering belonged uniquely to women had never been challenged. Besides, actual changes in mothering practice were more cosmetic than worthwhile, entailing a great deal more posturing than substance.

Moreover, it initiated, sad to say, the unprecedented attitude of deference by mothers to child-care authorities. So important and complicated was the molding of the child thought to be that the task could no longer be left to mere mothers. The child-care experts wielded far greater power than had their predecessors; their readers were the first generation of mothers to raise children "by the book."[22] The new technologies of mass distribution of media no doubt helped.

Most of these experts were trained in medicine or the new fields of psychology and child study. We see their influence in Mary McCarthy's novel *The Group,* where two mothers, Vassar class of '33, are following their toddlers through Central Park. "Have you heard about Gesell's studies at Yale?" one asks. "Finally we're going to have a scientific picture of the child."[23] Indeed, these were the years in which the American psychologist Arnold Gesell started recording the timetable of normal child development. Parents were now eager to fit their children into the pattern of the average, and the specter of the norm loomed large in mothers' psyches, providing yet another source of anxiety.

Though he is famous for inviting Freud to lecture in the United States, the psychologist G. Stanley Hall was one of the founders of the child study movement. Eager to establish child study as a sound scientific discipline, he sought to make it as rigorous and quantitative as, say, physics.[24] Darwin had already published a detailed record of the earliest months of one of his own children, and Hall encouraged ordinary mothers to do the same. He had mothers track their babies' character traits, habits, speech, and so forth and mail their data to experts for them to use in developing his new science. The mothers' movement adored Hall. His presence at meetings added the aura of the laboratory and seemed to promise a glorious future for motherhood.

Truly scientific motherhood, however, required that mothers not merely monitor their children, but read and follow the advice of scientifically trained experts. The most popular guru of the nursery in the first half of the twentieth century was the American pediatrician Luther Emmett Holt (his counterpart in Europe was Dr. Truby King), whose book *The Care and Feeding of Children,* published in 1894, was reprinted twelve times in his lifetime. It was a dry, formal little work, appealing to the new fashion for scientific precision.[25] His advice reflected the contemporary preoccupations with feeding and cleanliness, advice much needed at the time. Much of the book concerned nipples, bottles, and getting rid of germs. He was adamantly opposed to the "promiscuous" kissing of babies lest it spread infection.

The mothers who read Holt's book, and the even more popular *Infant Care,* a publication of the American Children's Bureau (which derived many of its precepts from Holt), learned that babies must be highly scheduled and disciplined at an early age. The key was regularity. The worst mistake parents could make was to encourage too much camaraderie with their offspring. Young babies were not to be played with or overly stimulated. Inciting a baby to laugh in apparent delight was to impose a dangerous strain on its nervous system. Toilet training was to begin at two to three months! Bad habits (thumb-sucking, masturbation) were to be explicitly discouraged.[26] Mother was, first and foremost, a promulgator of sound habits.

Out of the reverence for scientific child rearing came, crazily enough, the vogue for bottle-feeding, a fashion that has not abated, except among educated, bourgeois women only about twenty-five years ago. (It also became customary for women of all social classes to give birth in hospitals, which had become safely sterile.) It was not that physicians or manufacturers forced women to bottle-feed. But the fact that the new, artificial foods for infants were "scientifically" constructed lent prestige to their use, and the formula-feeding regimen at the time was so complicated that it seemed to require a degree in chemistry, which also elevated its mystique. Mothers began to look to the specialists in pediatrics to direct their infants' feedings, and that group was not about to undermine itself by enthusiastically promoting breast-feeding. The manufacturers of infant food shrewdly capitalized on these tendencies, creating an industry that is still lucrative. The epitome of the anti-breast-feeding trend was an "anti-embarrassment" device, a harnesslike contraption with a tube that came through the blouse and enabled mothers to breast-feed while they seemed to be bottle-feeding.[27] In this way, a mother could look up-to-date.

The regulatory approach to child raising achieved the scientific seal of approval in the late teens with the development of behaviorism, the school of psychology that jettisoned the mind entirely, and instead studied behavior, pure and simple. According to behaviorism, there was no need to speculate on mental states. All psychologists needed to consider were responses to stimuli, and conditioning by repetition and reinforcement. John B. Watson, one of the first of many behavioral psychologists to generalize about human behavior by studying rats in mazes, claimed that children are made, not born. (Here we see the influence of John Locke.) "Give me a dozen healthy infants . . . and I'll guarantee to take any one at random and train him to become any type of specialist I might select — into a doctor, a lawyer . . . even into a beggar man or thief."[28] It is not surprising to learn that Watson, in later life, embarked on a successful second career in advertising.

Watson is infamous today for finding that he could make a small child terrified of a bunny by banging loudly near the child's head whenever the bunny was put near it. To Watson's triumph, he discovered that he could reverse this conditioned response by reintroducing the bunny gradually, and at a distance, under more soothing circumstances. The seeds of "behavior therapy" were sown.[29] He advocated raising children in accordance with these principles.

Watson's *magnum opus* was *The Psychological Care of Infant and Child,* published in 1928. Reading it is a bit like stepping into *A Clockwork Orange,* though the *Atlantic Monthly* hailed it as a "godsend to parents." It was even more rigid than Holt, positively fulminating against cuddling and affection. Watson's reason for astringency was not germs, however, but "spoiling." Picking up a baby between scheduled feedings, for example, was to invite future moral laxity. Again, there was much stress on regularity, punctuality, discipline, and cleanliness. Toilet training was now to start at — believe it or not — one month. Toward the end of this era, a *New Yorker* cartoon showed a young mother, bottle in hand, hovering over an infant shrieking in its crib while she counted the minutes on her watch until feeding time.[30]

Watson confounded tenderhearted critics by bringing up his two little boys by behavioristic methods. Neither child could ever remember any demonstrations of affection from their father, although their mother sneaked in a kiss and a hug once in a while. Newspapers photographed Billy and Johnny as "happy children, free from fear and temper tantrums." The little boys never obliged hopeful psychoanalysts by going crazy. According to a biography of Watson, they apparently remained "well-built, healthy, bright, and good advertisements for behaviorism."[31] All of which proves that many children survive their parents' idiosyncrasies quite well.

Now that behaviorism had been found, there seemed little room in it for red-blooded mothers.[32] In Watson's system, mother became irrelevant. She was to be so robotic that she was eminently replaceable. In fact, in the preface to *The Psychological Care of Infant and Child,* Watson wondered whether children should know their parents at all. Much later, B. F. Skinner also toyed with doing away with parents in his provocative utopian novel *Walden Two.*

Oddly enough, scientific child rearing, despite its mechanical character, turned out to be congenial to anti-establishment thinking and lifestyles. After all, behaviorism is well suited to an egalitarian ideal, and it promises endless possibilities for transforming a child into a desired personality type, if only one were to figure out the appropriate stimulus-response connection. Because a baby's personal mother is irrelevant, such a system could promote collective child rearing, a practice that might serve many political or ideological purposes. So, ironically, Watson and Skinner, however rigid and antiseptic they themselves were in their techniques, set the stage for the "touchy-feely" communal child rearing that was briefly popular in the countercultural living arrangements of the 1960s. And they cleared the ground for raising children the "government" way in the great social experiments of the early twentieth century.

The revolutionary founders of Soviet Russia attempted, for example, to do away with maternal child rearing altogether. In their view, the nuclear family arrangement was bourgeois, artificial, and, according to Marx and Engels, a product of capitalism.[33] The more radical revolutionaries fulminated against the coziness of the domestic hearth, and advocated, as an alternative, "free" love, communal living arrangements, and the near total institutionalization of children's upbringing (the better to indoctrinate them with "proper" values). A leading Bolshevik feminist, Alexandra Kollantai, added that communal child rearing would free women to contribute to society by participating side by side with men in productive labor and Communist Party activity.[34]

As it turned out, the Bolsheviks had seized power with no blueprint for the society they hoped to build. The 1920s became a period of social experimentation, including various revolutionary programs for bringing up children, but none of the schemes gained wide support. Lenin had more pressing issues on his mind. The economic disasters of the 1920s and 1930s gave the death blow to these experiments, reducing Russia to a state of social collapse, epidemics, and famine. The countryside was blighted with abandoned, starving youngsters. Millions of shocked and puzzled peasants, particularly women, blamed the Communists' attacks on the family for the widespread misery.[35]

With consummate hypocrisy, Stalin completely reversed gears and co-opted the traditional nuclear family, glorifying it as a specifically Russian institution. Women's emancipation was henceforth subordinated to economic, political, and military goals. The Soviet state mounted a fascist-style glorification of motherhood in the manner of Germany, and tightened divorce laws. The Russian woman found herself worse off than ever. Now she was an economic tool of the regime, compelled to work all day *and* carry the entire burden of child care and domestic work in her "leisure" hours at night.[36]

Before the debacle of Stalin, idealists everywhere looked to the new social experiments in Russia for inspiration. One derivative was the communal farm, the *kibbutz*, founded in Palestine in the 1920s. Though it is not popular at the moment, given the recent course of global events, it is an example of successful alternative mothering. The founders of modern Israel, having experienced a real threat of annihilation, were imbued with missionary zeal and a sense of high purpose in establishing a safe home for Jewish people. As in the Soviet Union, personalized maternal child rearing was discouraged in the interest of wider community.

The early settlers, much like the Bolsheviks, wished to fashion the young into people who were dedicated to the land and their people, and were prepared to devote themselves to collective, national goals. It was thought that communal child rearing would be the most effective means of achieving this transformation, and would allow mothers to take their places in the work schedule.

Early on, children on a *kibbutz* lived apart from their parents, a practice abandoned in recent years. The communal dining hall, symbolic of the common interests of the whole *kibbutz*, is less used nowadays and serves mostly as a "take-out" kitchen. Nevertheless, the children are in collective day care all day, and qualities of good parenting are expected in every adult for every child, though, understandably, parents prefer and identify mostly with their own offspring, with whom they now live. Despite multiple mothering, disaster did not befall those raised on communal farms, even during the period when children lived apart from their parents. Children from the *kibbutzim* (only 2 to 4 percent of the population of Israel, and falling) account for a disproportionately large percentage of Israel's political, cultural, and economic elite. While studies have shown that some of these individuals are less individualistic than the norm, they are hardly social misfits.[37] If anything, they are more socialized than the average person, having lived in a group setting for so long. Communal child rearing may not be everyone's cup of tea, but it certainly can qualify as a form of good mothering.

THE GREAT PATRIARCH

It is interesting to realize that Sigmund Freud wrote his "Essay on Infant Sexuality" during the craze for assembly-line mothering. It was hardly a popular triumph. The world was not ready for the unconscious preoccupations of children and was appalled at the idea that infants were born with sexual urges. Parents had barely got used to the idea that grown women had sexual urges. All but an ultra-modern few dismissed the ideas and concentrated instead on mechanistic psychology.[38] They were short-sighted, indeed. For Freud set in motion ideas that would forever change the face of motherhood. This did not happen in his lifetime, however.

Freud, the man who brought sex out of the closet, had his sons sent to a family physician to learn the facts of life. Though he lived well into the age of the flappers and women's suffrage (he died in 1939), and revolutionized the way we think about ourselves, he was hardly a revolutionary in his personal life. To the end he remained an unreconstructed Victorian gentleman, bourgeois in his values, manners, tastes, cultural inclinations, and sartorial style. He welcomed women's contributions to his psychoanalytic project, and enjoyed their company, but Freud was openly opposed to the feminist movement of his time, and he saw women as genitally defective and morally inferior. His Oedipus complex gave pride of place to the father, thereby colluding with the institution of male dominance and a rigid division of labor according to gender.[39] Though his social behavior may seem patronizing or cloying to a modern woman, he was unfailingly gallant toward females; he called his young fiancée, Martha Bernays, his "delicate, sweet girl," whose fate was to be "an adored sweetheart in youth and a beloved wife in maturity."

Just as the major novels of his day suppressed the mother and instead placed the relation of father and son at the center of their plots, so did Freud move fathers to the fore in the drama of child development. This had the advantage of sparing mothers from blame for mental illness in their children, for which they would be relentlessly blamed in the decades following the world wars, but it also trivialized their contribution to their children's lives. Freud maintained a benign view of mothering; it was a modest activity, performed quietly in the background, one that did not figure importantly in the formation of personality. So while mothers did not "cause" psychopathology, they did not "cause" much of anything in their children.

Again and again, Freud found that his patients dwelled on their fathers in their associations, and the centerpiece of their psychodramas was invariably patriarchal repression of their incestuous wishes (the Oedipus complex). In all of his five major case histories, mothers are relegated to the sidelines. Dora's mother in the famous "Case of Hysteria" was breezily written off in a few quick sentences as an obsessional housewife, without reference, except in footnotes, to Dora's attachment to her and to Frau K., also a mother. With sublime male chauvinism, Freud seemed more intent on convincing eighteen-year-old Dora of her supposed wish to suck at her father's penis (as she recalled sucking her thumb as a child), and her erotic desire for Herr K., whose masculine good looks Freud presumed to be irresistible.[40] Feminists have rightly grasped that Dora was in despair because Freud, despite himself, seemed to acquiesce in the wish of Dora's father to, in effect, "pimp" her to his friend Herr K. so that he could continue his liaison with Herr K.'s wife. Ultimately Freud's dismissal of Dora's madly cleaning mother as a significant player in this soap opera renders the story incomplete, if not incoherent.

The beautiful mother of precocious Little Hans, who was afraid of horses, was also given short shrift. Though to her husband the wife's seductive behavior was the cause of the son's behavior, she appears only fleetingly in Freud's narrative, which emphasized instead the role of the boy's father, the auxiliary analyst who transmits Freud's interpretations. And the Wolf Man's biological mother figures insignificantly in Freud's account of his case, mainly as the passive partner in the primal scene (of anal intercourse) that the Wolf Man had observed, or fantasized, as a little boy.[41]

Freud's lack of interest in the Rat Man's mother is especially odd, in light of his process notes, which make numerous references to her.[42] In his published account, Freud formulated the case in exclusively Oedipal terms, viewing the patient's obsessional symptoms — his nagging worry, for example, that, were he to fail to pay a debt for having his glasses fixed, his father would be tortured by rats boring into his anus — as arising from his fear of castration by his father as punishment for his sexual desires. But most twentieth-century psychoanalysts and psychotherapists would not ignore the provocative fact (revealed in Freud's working notes) that the Rat Man's mother controlled the finances of her almost thirty-year-old son, and paid for his sessions with Freud, though he actually possessed independent means. Surely an explanation of the Rat Man's dependency on his mother would be important for an understanding of his problems.

Let me emphasize that while the "sins" of the mother are not visited upon her children, according to Freud, neither are the "sins" of the father. It is the father's symbolic value, his position in the Oedipal configuration, not his actual behavior, that counts. Mother's symbolic value, presumably, does not have a high enough valence to figure in the equation. In Freud's Oedipal triangle, mother is an object rather than a subject; she is the object of her son's sexual desire. Generally speaking, in Freud's view, children's psyches are almost hermetically sealed. Children are endowed with an inner core of individuality, which ensures them a measure of autonomy from external reality, including, presumably, bumbling parents. Children are not, as Watson thought, lumps of clay to be molded by their environment, but active little molders in their own right.

Contrary to the common misconception, Freud was not concerned with specific child-rearing practices. Barring seduction or castration, whatever parents did to their children did not matter all that much. Unlike the child experts of his era, he did not assign importance to the scientific, behavioristic methods then popular, nor did he advocate permissiveness, lax toilet training, or psychological attunement (all later child-rearing fashions for which he is sometimes erroneously credited). Once, when one of his daughters-in-law was, in his opinion, cuddling her infant too much, Freud chastised her. Years later, the daughter-in-law perceptively pointed out that nowadays doctors tell the mother the reverse. (Her baby at the time was three or four months old, too young to sit up.[43])

As antiquated as Freud's case studies seem to the modern reader for their dismissal of mother, they seem even more peculiar when we realize the extent to which Freud ignored actual mothering, that is, real-life parental behavior. This is especially apparent in

Freud's study, mentioned earlier, of the psychotic Daniel Paul Schreber, son of the Victorian child expert Daniel Gottlieb Moritz Schreber. Freud wrote his formulation of Schreber (son) from Schreber's own memoirs, and seems to have accepted without question the received opinion that his father was an admirable person. Yet the father's highly repressive child-raising techniques were readily identifiable in the son's paranoiac delusions. The idea of correlating Schreber's illness with the methods of the father apparently did not occur to Freud, even though many of the father's books describing his bizarre regimens were still in print in 1911.[44] Any modern interpretation of these data could not overlook the implications of such extreme parental involvement. As for Schreber's mother, she is hardly mentioned. ❍

FREUD'S OVERSIGHTS in his cases are consistent with his model of the mind, which is entirely understandable, because he was constructing his model with the clinical data gleaned from his patients. Of course, there is no single Freudian theory but a multiplicity of ideas that evolved, retreated, collided, and were subject to constant revision by himself and others. Even so, Freud never developed a model that entirely allowed for unadulterated reality. Reality was filtered and distorted by the mind itself. In other words, according to Freud, the child's image of its mother is always colored by the child's unconscious processes and fantasies. The mechanism for distorting reality — the dynamic unconscious — was probably Freud's most brilliant contribution to our understanding of human behavior. The working of the unconscious, the ever-present, very human tendency to remove disturbing ideas by means of rationalization, compromise, and repression, is known to us all, and helps to explain not only neurotic symptoms, dreams, art, literature, but even something so mundane as why our children may hate us when we are behaving perfectly decently. What they actually hate is their psychic representation of us, not the real thing.

Freud's affinity for reality in his theories was always in flux. In his earliest thinking, reality mattered.[45] Hysteria, for example, was thought to be caused by childhood sexual abuse by a governess, perhaps, or a family member. This was dubbed "seduction theory," as the child was presumed to be seduced. However, around the time of his father's death, in 1896, and Freud's self-analysis, he shifted his focus of causation of neurosis from reality to the inner life of drives and fantasies. Now, the patient was thought to have "wished" for the seduction, and no sexual encounter occurred. It was precisely this shift in focus — Freud's abandonment of "seduction theory" — that has angered many feminists, for it trivialized, in their view, the reality of sexual abuse, though Freud, in fact, never denied its sometime occurrence, nor did he minimize its traumatic effect.

After this reappraisal, Freud articulated what is known as "drive theory." Henceforth, mental life was understood to be fueled by the energy of instinctual drives, namely sex and aggression. And people (now called "objects") were the targets of drives: they could facilitate drives or inhibit them. The nature of the baby's drives, their imperiousness and gratifiability, determined the nature of their objects. In other words, if a baby was, by constitution, not very needy, it would likely experience its mother as "good" — and vice versa. So, within this framework, babies *invent* their mothers.[46]

The reorientation from what was done to children to what children did with what was done to them had major repercussions. The importance of actual events declined. The valence of power for determining the child's personality now lay with the child, not the parent. Broadly speaking, neurosis resulted from a "bad" child, not a "bad" mother. And mothers were fated to be maligned. After the perfection of life in the womb, children were bound to experience their external mothers as comparatively less gratifying.

While Freud's drive theory did not connect child-rearing techniques with neurosis, it did set the stage for the radical change in child rearing that took place after the world wars. By attributing unfolding impulses to the child that were natural, expectable, and amoral, he lay the framework for those impulses to be tolerated. And later, mothers did just that — under the banner of "permissiveness" — though, of course, Freud was never himself a practitioner. Indeed, he was a distant father who left the child rearing to his wife.

With drive theory, the status of mothers, and all real relationships, were at a low ebb. The objects of human passions were understood to be solipsistic creations, psychic images that did or did not resemble the real people who were their inspiration. Freud did not rigidly stick with these ideas, as did Melanie Klein, who built a psychological theory, still popular in England, around infants' impulses, which were simply there, and which exerted a vigorous and terrifying force, irrespective of how the child was treated. Indeed, Freud retreated from this implacable child concept with the development of his well-known trinity of personality — the id, ego, and superego.[47] These structures provided mechanisms by which the outside could get in; that is, reality could influence the psyche. The ego and superego evolved out of early relations with caretakers: the ego served as a mediator between the child and the world; the superego was a repository of social norms, and derived partly from parental identifications. With these structures, Freud's child was no longer an island unto itself. But Freud never fully developed this "structural" model; it was left to his followers to build on his framework. Reality as an explanation always remained subordinate to the instincts; and mothers, consequently, were curiously invisible, almost irrelevant.

Yet near the end of his life, he remarked that the very early years of a child's life, when mother reigns supreme, are of greater importance than he had originally thought, and are even more significant for a girl.[48] The intense attachment that characterizes this stage comes to an end with the discovery that she is born without a penis. (Here we see Freud's patriarchal bias.) The girl feels injured, blames her mother, and rejects her in favor of the father. Freud understood a woman's wish for a child as a compensation for the wish for a penis. The baby substitute is more nearly gratifying if, being male, it carries the prized object. Motherhood, Freud felt, was the goal of female development.

Freud always elaborated his ideas about femininity with abundant disclaimers, once admitting to Princess Marie Bonaparte, a colleague and analysand, that he had never been able to answer the question "What does a woman want?" Nevertheless, his speculations about women caused controversy almost immediately. Karen Horney initiated a lively debate in which she argued that if a woman envied man's penis, it was not for itself, but as a symbol of man's social and political power. Both she and Ernest Jones disagreed with the idea that a woman's desire for a baby is secondary to her frustrated wish for a penis. Rather, they saw the desire for motherhood as primary, having to do with identification with one's mother. Despite these early challenges, Freud's theories about femininity and motherhood were not hotly disputed again until the late 1960s. Meanwhile, in accordance with Freud (and his predecessors, from Aristotle to Darwin), women were *supposed* to want babies. It was part of the natural order. And she was *supposed* to find her own fulfillment in raising them.

Freud could never believe that there were cruel or rejecting or seductive mothers, a belief that may have been typical of the Victorian era in which he grew up but was atypically sentimental of him. Psychoanalytic theory, after all, tends to deconstruct sentimentalism. But women were a blind spot for Freud. Why did he never fully appreciate the power of the mother, for example? Turning the psychoanalytic method on Freud himself, we may perhaps understand his idealization of mothers (which is an implicit devaluation of them, in that idealization obscures the extent to which men and women are equals) as a defense against his ambivalence toward his own mother.[49]

On the surface, Sigmund and Amalie, his mother, appeared devoted. When Sigmund was born she declared he would be a great man, and when he was seventy, she was still addressing him as "*mein goldener Sigi.*" In a late essay, Freud described the bond between mother and son as "altogether the most perfect, the most free from ambivalence in all human relationships."[50] But perhaps Freud protested too much. Amalie was no shrinking violet. Other family members found her willful and tyrannical. As a grown man, Freud almost invariably had stomach cramps before he dutifully visited her each Sunday.

Freud's mother seems to have been the ruling figure in his nuclear family. In Freud's youth, his father was already an aging, passive man who had failed at business and was no doubt a disappointing figure to little Sigmund, especially compared with his young, forceful mother. But though Freud's father's fortunes and personal powers declined in real life, he was restored to a place of honor in his son's psychoanalytic theory. He was fashioned in the Oedipal configuration into a patriarchal power, fashioned, perhaps, out of the feared and admired characteristics of his mother. In other words, Freud's Oedipal invention may have been a wishful reversal of his own family's arrangement. In one bold stroke, Freud achieved an identification with a father who was strong and in control, and he removed from the maternal sphere those traits which aroused fear. His powerful, controlling, attractive mother was made into an approachable object of need and desire. He rendered her benign.[51] And, for better or worse, that is Freud's true legacy to mothers . . . their benignity.

Empathic Mom: 1940–1980

It began with a boom — a baby boom — and ended with a bust — the movement for "zero population growth" and "child-free by choice." Between the late 1940s and the late 1970s the birthrate in America plummeted from four children to two per woman. There is a story in those data, and it isn't only about the horrors of overpopulation, the fear of ecological disaster, or economic recession. It is about mothers' disillusionment. During those years, women were sold a bill of goods (which, by the way, they are still buying), a burdensome, unperformable, guilt-inducing myth of motherhood. Slowly awakened to their predicament, if not to the cause, women reacted, unsurprisingly, by having fewer children.

Freud's benign, ineffectual mother did not remain benign and ineffectual for long. For better or worse, following World War II, Freud's followers (including his daughter, Anna) replaced her with a far more powerful and potentially malevolent model. Suddenly mother was of great moment. Whatever she did during baby's first years became the strongest factor in its development. By the end of the decade, mother was held to be the cause of her children's miseries, and, indeed, of the ills that beset humankind. Given the magnitude of her responsibilities, it is no wonder that mother became self-conscious about her performance.

And the new rules of conduct for child rearing turned 180 degrees away from earlier prescriptions. The astringent, scientific techniques of the decade before World War II were abruptly jettisoned in favor of cuddly, twenty-four-hour "permissiveness." The change happened so fast, according to social critics, that it could make a mother's head spin. Many women in the late forties and early fifties found themselves changing their methods in the middle of their child-raising careers. One mother described her startling recognition, one evening at dinnertime, of the change in her ideas: "I was serving a new vegetable to the boys. Suddenly I realized that I expected Peter, the oldest, to clean his plate. Daniel, the middle one, didn't have to eat it but he had to taste it. And little Billy, as far as I was concerned, could do whatever he wanted."[52]

The goal of child care was no longer to stymie the natural inclinations of the infant, but to give them free rein. Gone were the wicked urges or bad habits that mothers sought assiduously to tame with Watson's behaviorism. Now, the child's spontaneous impulses were viewed as good, expectable, and sensible, and the child, instead of being a *tabula rasa,* actually knew, in some sense, what was right for itself.[53] Mother's job was to respond to baby's emotional needs (in effect, to read baby's mind), gratify its wants, tolerate its regressions, stimulate its cognitive development, and, above all, to feel personally fulfilled in carrying this out. The overriding emotion was (and is) empathy.

This new, determinedly gentle child-rearing philosophy was formulated in a world that was reinventing itself after totalitarian insurgence, a world that had become understandably suspicious of any ideology smacking of the Third Reich or Stalin's Soviet Union. The behavioristic approach, eugenics, and patriotic orderliness might have been suited to societies that saw their children as a generation with a military purpose, but now the free world wanted its children to be free. Subordinating the individual to the good of the whole became dramatically unfashionable. Besides, the old concerns of inculcating discipline and self-control seemed a little too ascetic in the booming postwar economy, which was at least partly dependent on self-indulgence and consumerism. And what better way to instill the urge to shop than by permissiveness during the earliest years? From now on, the child was to set the pace of child care, with mom in tow, loving, nurturing, sensing every need, seeking tactfully to guide it toward becoming a cooperative member of a happy family, and, all the while, "having fun." These ideas dovetailed nicely with various misreadings of Freud, whose ideas were finally infiltrating the mainstream. Freud was interpreted as having suggested that repression was bad. He had suggested nothing of the sort, and in fact felt that repression was a necessary component of civilization, and that conflict was inevitable. As we have seen, Freud was hardly a free spirit in personal matters. Nevertheless, because he wrote about conflicts that children faced in the course of growing up — oral, anal, phallic, Oedipal — on which neurotic people fixated, a generation of child experts seized on the idea of minimizing these conflicts for all children, presumably to forestall "Freudian" traumas and thereby avoid mental illness. I suspect that Freud would not have been pleased by the transactions carried out in his name.[54]

In the wake of repressive conflict writ large, *repression* and *conflict* had become dirty words. They were to be avoided not only in the nursery, but in education as well. The progressive school movement popularized by John Dewey in principle and by A. S. Neill, headmaster of the experimental school Summerhill, captured the public imagination. So did Clara Davis's experiments on children's food preferences, showing that, without parental instruction, children automatically chose a balanced diet; Carl Rogers's client-centered counseling; and Margaret Mead's research on the "carefree" Samoans. Her study indicated that many childhood conflicts were avoided in societies that took a relaxed approach to children's activities and demands. There is now considerable suspicion that Mead was the victim of a hoax by her Samoan informants.[55] But her message matched the mood of many intellectuals at that time, who seemed to favor peaceful, non-hierarchical arrangements for most human relationships, including that between parent and child (though, apparently, not between male and female). Perhaps gentleness toward children in the postwar era was healing; perhaps it made up for an "ungentle" past. ❍

THE EMPATHIC MOTHER was in her heyday during the cultural roller coaster of the "fifties" (shorthand for the period from the late 1940s to the early 1960s) and the "sixties" (from the mid-1960s to the mid-1970s), and she persists, in somewhat altered form, today. To many, whose memories of the fifties stem from faded magazine photographs, old movies, and television reruns, the period stands out as the golden age of the family, the most evolved version of the most perfect and timeless kinship arrangement, the nuclear family — the Nelsons, the Cleavers, the Rileys, the entourage around Donna Reed. In this era, mothers' self-sacrifice was celebrated daily on TV in "Queen for a Day," weekly in "I Remember Mama," while father's wisdom earned kudos in "Father Knows Best." It was an age of peace and prosperity — economic expansion, better housing, vocational opportunity, gentrification, and foreign travel, a time when higher education became a reality for the average person. And, indeed, compared with today, family life in the 1950s was, superficially, more stable. There was a low divorce rate, far fewer single-parent families, and half the illegitimacy rate. The birthrate approached that of India (only to take a nosedive in the 1960s). Evidently, to a generation economically strapped in the Depression and sacrificing for the war effort, the opportunity to have a family and buy a suburban house with a picture window, a backyard barbecue, and a living room teeming with children filled a deep emotional need.[56] People these days tend to regard the fifties nostalgically as a reference point for measuring recent changes in family life.

But the fifties were an aberration. Far from setting standards of normality, from which current trends are a deviation, the 1950s were characterized by deviant family patterns. Had the 1950s not happened, today's blended families, birthrates, and illegitimacy rates would look normal. And contrary to the prevalent notion, many women were *not* full-time mothers. Millions of middle-class wives entered the workforce in the fifties, though most of them worked part time. They were not so much pursuing careers as helping to pay for a mortgage, a second car, or a major appliance.[57] Had they been more vocationally ambitious, they would have been barred from advancement by rampant sexism. Despite the fact that women were employed outside the home in increasing numbers, the pretense was that they were not. A working wife was not something to brag about: she signaled her husband's inadequacy as a breadwinner. Indeed, working wives and child-care centers were denounced as Communist ideas. (Much political capital was made from contrasting the stereotypes of domestic life in the West and the Soviet Union. Some readers may recall the famous "kitchen debate" in 1959 between Vice President Nixon and Nikita Khrushchev at an American exhibition in Moscow.)

There was an underside to the fifties, made up of exaggerated conformity, homophobia, complacency, mass culture, racism, and consumerism. Brand names, installment buying, and advertising flourished and became habit-forming. And the period was almost a throwback to the Victorian era, with its polarized sex roles and its reverence for home and hearth. It was as if the New Woman, Rosie the Riveter, and women's suffrage had never happened. Feminism, if it was recalled at all, was part of a long-gone historical era, a dimly remembered movement of presumably disgruntled old maids. Not since the late nineteenth century had women's clothes so emphasized the wasp waist and been so constraining (tight girdles, pointed brassieres, spike heels). A reinvigorated sexual double standard divided girls into "nice" ones, who would "go all the way," and "good" ones, technical virgins, whom a respectable man might marry. But ill-timed sexual intercourse would not only reduce a fifties woman's marital prospects; it might result in unwanted pregnancy. As late as 1965 it was illegal in Connecticut for a druggist to sell contraceptives or for doctors to prescribe them. Unlike their mothers, young women who attended college in the 1950s had no career plans and dropped out in large numbers to marry. Indeed, people were rushing to the altar in record numbers and at younger ages. These were the parents of the baby boomers. In the home, the wife served as her husband's ego massager, sounding board, and housekeeper — which meant that she did all the household chores and child rearing with the exception of locking up at night, fixing broken things, and yard work, which the husband performed when duly nagged.[58]

The revival of a cult of domesticity in the fifties was Victorian domesticity with a twist — there was no romance. Domesticity was no longer an adequate prop for female self-esteem. Technological innovation along with the advent of experts sounded the death knell for housewifery as a skilled craft. In effect, science spoiled the home as an arena for the display of female prowess. The presence of evaporated milk, Crisco, Chef Boyardee spaghetti dinner, with sauce, pasta, and cheese all in one container, implied that it would be primitive to make, say, one's own soup when the manufactured product was so much more "advanced" than the homemade variety. This was surely the nadir of Euro-American cookery! What no one had foreseen was that while routine housework could continue to fill a woman's time, it starved her brain.[59]

The contours of what Betty Friedan would call "the feminine mystique" were now in place. Suburban housing patterns reinforced women's isolation from most of the world of adults. The portion of a woman's day spent chauffeuring other family members increased exponentially. The poet Anne Sexton, who later committed suicide, captured in the poem "Housewife" the revulsion that domesticity inspired in many women:

Some women marry houses.
It's another kind of skin; it has a heart;
a mouth, a liver and bowel movements.
The walls are permanent and pink.
See how she sits on her knees all day
faithfully washing herself down.
Men enter by force, drawn back like Jonah
into their fleshy mothers.
A woman is her mother.
That's the main thing.[60]

There was a poor fit between woman's expectations for happiness and her experience. For black women of the same period, paid work (which Friedan recommended for middle-class women) was usually drudgery; work in the home seemed far more satisfactory.[61] But for white women, the fifties were a time bomb waiting to explode. However, there was a brief lag between woman's discontent and her formal expression of it.

What happened in the meantime, and probably served as a trigger, was the sixties: the return of the repressed. In those tumultuous years came the civil rights movement, the antiwar movement, the student movement, rock and roll, the counterculture, and the sexual revolution.[62] Even people of a less "revolutionary" bent began to marry later and have fewer children. Most women college graduates were now in the workforce. A working wife was no longer an embarrassment to her husband.

The pill — a watershed for the changing sexual norms of the 1960s — was not only more effective than other methods of contraception but for the first time gave woman the sole and entire control of the process. Now she could use or take sex in exactly the way men had always been able to do — casually, spontaneously, or seriously, meaningfully, whatever. It was her choice.

There were no untoward consequences. Meanwhile, birth control itself had been transformed, at long last, from a "private vice" to a "public virtue," a mainstay of the social order.[63]

With women in charge of their own bodies, an epidemic of "the problem that has no name," and habits of rebellion in the air, the stage was set for the rebirth of a women's movement . . . and in September 1968 a group of women demonstrated against the Miss America Pageant in Atlantic City. They did not burn their bras, but they did fashion a means for the expression of women's unhappiness about gender norms. Of all the movements of the sixties, none had a more lasting effect on public and private life than this second wave of feminism. It initiated a profoundly new way of interpreting human experience: though men and women are "created" equal, women are unfairly subordinated socially, politically, and economically. Women's lib, as it was called, was as much an emotional and intellectual understanding as a political movement. For many women it was like a psychoanalytic insight or the "aha" experience in problem solving. It was called the "housewife's moment of truth" or "consciousness raising," and it spread like wildfire. The ideas passed from heresy to acceptance in a remarkably short time — the clitoral orgasm, equal pay, girls in Little League, women learning "masculine" skills — all entered the public domain.[64]

But even as Reagan appointed the first woman to the Supreme Court, and women were having fewer children, the forties' image of the good mother — she who emits endless waves of empathy — retained its hold on mom's superego. By the 1980s, the momentum of the women's liberation movement had slowed. Yet through it all — the shifts in gender relations, variations in economic conditions, and world events — the ideal of the permissive, all-giving, psychologically attuned, tenderhearted mother, like the Energizer bunny, just kept going and going. And she became a universal punching bag — the butt of every joke, the villain in every film, the destructive imago in every child's psyche.

SPOCK-MARKED PARENTING

Had Tom Sawyer run away from home in the twentieth century instead of in the nineteenth, Aunt Polly would have been taken to task. Back in the mid-1800s, it was generally agreed, by Tom's aunt and all the neighbors, that Tom was foolish to run away from such a good home; a century later the neighbors would likely have felt that Aunt Polly's home was not good enough. Psychologists and professional social workers would have evaluated her "mothering," probably found it wanting, and might even have suggested another placement for Tom. After all, children do not run away from good mothers. The dominant belief after the Second World War was that "there are no problem children, only problem parents." Child rearing had become a perilous endeavor, a virtual set-up for parental blame. It is no wonder that by the 1970s, women were having fewer babies, and when the popular columnist Ann Landers asked her readers to write about their experience as parents, 70 percent of the voluminous number who responded reported that their experience had been negative.[65] Part of the problem was the new, onerous myth of motherhood.

While the aim of child rearing in grandmother's day had been to produce well-behaved, polite children with regular habits, ever since the mid-twentieth century mothers have been saddled with the Sisyphean task of avoiding psychological distress. Grandma would never have thought to look into her baby's psyche; today's mother hardly looks anywhere else. Baby's state of mind largely determines mommy's state of mind.

Take potty training. In the years before permissiveness, Holt or Watson would have dealt with the issue by recommending that a baby a couple of months old (surely no more than eight) be strapped into a special toilet seat and left alone in the bathroom with the door closed for a half hour or however long it took. We'll never know how many children were actually subjected to this regimen, yet it was portrayed in the child-advice literature as ideal. But since the 1940s, toilet training has been resolutely left up to the child. It must not take place too soon or be taught too strictly. If parents were to engage in a tug-of-war for control over a youngster's sphincters, the child might be scarred for life and become a messy and disorderly adult (symbolically defecating all over the place) or a stubborn and stingy person (defiantly never "letting go" of its feces), with a strong aversion to dirt. (This is an example of how superficial a grasp popular thinkers had of Freud.) Selma Fraiberg spent fifteen — count them! — pages in her popular 1959 book, *Magic Years,* describing how mothers go wrong when training their children. She explained that the feces are seen by the child as an extension of itself, so that flushing them down the toilet is the height of insensitivity. One had to wait to flush until the child left the room. The next wave of baby gurus confirmed that training should take place entirely at the toddler's own pace, even if it is not accomplished until the child is four, and that bowel movements should be accompanied by a great deal of smiling orchestration.[66]

While child experts had become more sensitive to baby — who knows, maybe even forestalling anal fixations? — they were increasingly insensitive to mother. Their new recommendations meant more work: at the very least, five thousand additional diaper changes. Prewar methods of toilet training minimized laundry (these were pre-disposable days, after all), and old-fashioned strict scheduling spared a frayed mother from being on call all day, assuring her predictable time to recoup. But the newfangled advice was burdensome, ambiguous, and open-ended. Now, mother had to be constantly on duty, ready to serve her child's call of nature. And here we have been considering only toilet training — never mind the myriad other aspects of baby care! Permissive child rearing, as some historians have acidly noted, was permissive of everyone except mother.[67]

From then on, whatever baby wanted, baby got. No longer viewed as a fierce little animal whose instincts needed damming up or snuffing out, postwar baby was seen as a gentle and sensitive creature whose instincts were reasonable needs, requiring facilitation, free expression, and gratification. There was no such thing as spoiling an infant. Crying was no longer due to "fussiness"; it indicated a valid need for food or drink or attention.[68]

Now that the infant dictated its demands, mother's routine was determined by those requirements. The good postwar mother gave her child undivided attention lest she miss an opportunity to toilet train or "cognitively stimulate." Rather than pursue her own ends in life, she was to maneuver, pretend, and manipulate so that her child would become "well-adjusted." In effect, mother had to play a part, as in a play, in which she reconstructed reality so as to cushion her child against all insults, like sibling rivalry, boring tasks, and other hardships. Any missed cue or fumbled line on her part could spell both cognitive and psychological harm. Her obligations had expanded from the physical realm to the psychic, and to add insult to injury, the new advice made her more culpable when things went wrong.[69] In other words, she was assigned a Pygmalion-type role, and any failure, such as mental disturbance in the child, was considered the result of her own shortcomings.

On top of the prescribed additions to mom's job duties, there was a prescription for her inner state. From now on, she was expected to be fulfilled by mothering. (The corollary, of course, was that her not being fulfilled meant she was abnormal.) This had been implicit all along, but it had never been explicitly constructed in psychological terms. Now the child-expert establishment insisted that motherhood was women's "natural" biological destiny. Reflecting the psychology of the period, it suggested that motherhood was a necessary developmental stage for all women and should supplant other identities. It was understood that the baby's pleasure was the highest good, but this was not experienced as a burden by the unneurotic mother, because the baby's pleasure was her pleasure. Mother and child were a mutually pleasure-giving unit.[70] After all, the good mother has no needs of her own.

Child care was said to be like a game enjoyed by both mother and child. The psychologist Martha Wolfenstein, in a review of the government's *Infant Care Bulletin* from 1914 to 1942, called the new expectation "fun morality," for it obliged mothers to have a good time, as if mandating fun were possible. An important component of this account was love, which was said to grow inevitably between mother and child. To experts of the period, loving was a mother's *job.* Mother love was seen as essential for baby's mental health . . . and for mother's.[71]

Ironically, this hyperempathic ideology of mothering was foisted on women (perhaps on our own mothers) just as they were going slightly mad under the pressure of social isolation, routine chores, conformity, and circumscribed options, just as they were losing their status as skilled homemakers, having been made redundant by labor-saving technology. True, permissive child rearing arrived when mothers seemingly had time to perform it, but the intensity of its labor, and the sheer number of children women had in this period, ensured that they would perform nothing else. If mothers happened to feel conflict over their new role expectations, it was a nonissue. The media had no comfort to offer the average ambivalent mother. If mom turned on the TV, she would have seen sappy, happy maternal martyrs, June Cleaver or Mrs. Anderson types, saccharine images whose experience of motherhood probably did not match hers or anyone else's. At the movies, mom would have watched Lana Turner in *Imitation of Life* or Joan Crawford in *Mildred Pierce,* both classic melodramas about working mothers who dared to be ambitious, and who inadvertently sacrificed their daughters in the process. Those films, among many others of the period, are essentially cautionary tales of maternal deprivation, solemnly warning mothers to stay home and preserve the status quo.[72] Trivialized on the one hand for their domestic work (which even a machine could do), mothers were now also endowed with the awesome power to do harm. Never considered special when they performed mothering, they were regarded as social misfits when they did not. Even their own daughters (us?) eventually turned against them, blaming them for their own subordination and failure to supply their children with the support and encouragement to become autonomous . . . a fine thank-you to the first generation of women who had tried so hard to be psychologically correct!

There were countercurrents, of course, especially in the 1960s, from writers who spoke with raw honesty about the experience of mothering — Anne Sexton, Sylvia Plath, Tillie Olsen, Grace Paley — but no one was listening. In the poem "Lesbos," for example, Sylvia Plath wrote of the guilt that lacerates the mother when she feels herself responsible for everything that goes wrong with the children. The poem is about a mother being out of control yet having to be in control. It is filled with hatred of domesticity turned inward against the self, yet leaking out, spilling out; rage that cannot be contained. Kittens are puking; daughter is kicking "face down on the floor"; "There is a stink of cat and baby crap." The mother is "doped and thick from [her] last sleeping pill." Father/husband is "hugging his ball and chain," yet he is able to "slump out." The mad housewife has no options. She is left in the kitchen to care for the children. We all know that scene — the effect of bloodcurdling screams, so typical of toddlers, on overwrought nerve endings. The horror of "Lesbos" is that it was autobiographical: tragically, a mother of very young children could not cry out for help except through carefully wrought, exquisitely controlled poems — which no one read until after she killed herself.[73] ❍

THE HARBINGER and greatest popularizer of this child-centered view of child rearing was the pediatrician Dr. Benjamin Spock, who burst onto the scene in 1946 with *The Common Sense Book of Baby and Child Care* (rumored to be assisted by his first wife). Perhaps it was his kindly, reassuring tone, or his user-friendly index, which allowed mother to look up everything from "crying" to "whooping cough," or perhaps it was his timing (babies were proliferating after World War II), but Spock immediately became the standard reference on everyone's bookshelf. Since then, his manual has gone through hundreds of printings, scores of editions, and has sold millions of copies. By comparison, Watson's guide, the former best-selling manual, sold 100,000 copies in its first few years.

Spock is not nearly as "permissive" as some said. He is as moralistic in his way as his predecessors were in theirs. And, no, he did not single-handedly cause the student rebellions of the 1960s, for which he has been blamed. Indeed, he has become less "permissive" in successive editions of his original book. Nevertheless, in stark contrast to his forerunners, he does promote relaxed discipline and play as healthful; and he does advocate a heretofore unheard-of amount of autonomy for the child — on-demand feedings, for example, and lots of concessions in such matters as masturbation, choice of teething objects, and getting out of the playpen. Much of this advice is in the service of avoiding pitched battles of will with one's youngsters. It is expedient more than ideological, but the thrust of his sympathy is for the child, not the mother. In the end, he constructs a "good" mother who is ever-present, all-providing, inexhaustibly patient and tactful, and who anticipates her child's every need. Mother has become baby's servant.[74]

Though Spock revolutionized child rearing, he was no eccentric; he was, in fact, representative man of his era, acutely alive to its tendencies and tensions. He had a conventionally chilly Yankee upbringing. Looking back at his own childhood, Spock remembered his mother as very "tyrannical, very moralistic, very opinionated, although very dedicated to her children." He and his five brothers and sisters felt that "their mother had x-ray vision because she could always spot guiltiness." Perhaps that is why, when he came to write his book, Spock sought to eliminate "guiltiness" in all children (unwittingly transferring it to mothers).[75]

But it would be a mistake to assume that Spock advocated permissiveness merely to exorcise his own demons. His enthusiasm for benevolence was in keeping with the mood of the decade, which, as we have seen, was responding to the horrors of war, death camps, and poverty. His wish to improve the child by gentleness, thereby improving humanity, may be understood as a reaction formation, a defense mechanism in which ugly, aggressive feelings are converted into their opposite. Perhaps these ideas reached their *reductio ad absurdum* in the 1970s, in "birth without violence," wherein childbirth was viewed as a trauma foisted on the infant-victim by way of its helpless mother, who was herself forced to deliver under harsh operating-room lights by the male medical establishment. In order to undo the shock of birth, the newborn was to be immediately placed in body-temperature water and massaged, and then kept in a warm, darkened room. This was known as the Leboyer method, after the French obstetrician who devised it. Birth by Leboyer apparently caused no harm. Whether it did any good is questionable.

Spock's ideas about infant sexuality, the presence of the unconscious, and Oedipal conflicts, and his equation of motherhood with healthy femininity, are straight from Freud, whose thinking had by now penetrated academia and filtered down to the mass mentality. His presumption that early experiences with mother have a crucial influence on later personality and the ability to cope with life derives from the post-Freudians and from the observations of developmental psychologists. These "baby watchers," as they have been called, were then constructing "attachment theory," in which baby and mother are presumed to be connected by a kind of invisible umbilical cord that on no account must be severed by mother's absence.[76] (To be sure, these folks would have become apoplectic had they encountered wet-nursing.) Similarly, Spock's sections in his later editions on cognitive development are a reflection of psychologists' observations of children. In this case, it was a dilution of the theories of Jean Piaget, who had noted that children's thinking matured in stages, along with their central nervous system. A great many child-rearing experts, though not Spock, interpreted Piaget as suggesting that the child's cognitive development could be hastened by appropriate stimulation. A whole "science" has grown up suggesting ways for mother to talk to her baby, to play with it, and to encourage its precocious intellectual growth so that it will grow up to be as clever as possible. Thus was born the obsession with cognitive stimulation . . . and more work for mom.

The popularity of Spock's book spawned a how-to-raise-baby industry that is still thriving. In the 1970s, more than five hundred volumes were listed each year under child rearing and parenting in *Books in Print* (and the number has more than doubled since then). The paperback industry of America did not fail to recognize a captive audience when it saw one. There was, and continues to be, a media blitz — advice columns, TV programs, videos, magazines — all telling mother what to do. During this time, there was a vocal subset of experts advocating behaviorism, especially for deviant children. But except for a nod to limit-setting in the late 1960s and early 1970s (when even Spock suggested firmer handling of babies and admitted the possibility of spoiling), the emphasis has remained on permissiveness. Just a glance at some advice book titles will tell you who's the boss: *Stop Annoying Your Children, Parents, Behave!,* and *Every Child's Birthright.* Women who had babies in the 1970s wallowed in the aesthetics of it all — natural childbirth and nursing were maternal musts. The institutionalization of baby slings to keep baby close, the obsession with mother-infant bonding, "rooming-in" in obstetrical units, the videotaping of the birth experience for posterity, all attest to the continued infatuation with the concept of tender-hearted, empathic child rearing.

Not that any of these innovations were bad, but this child-rearing philosophy inadvertently heightened mother's sense of inadequacy, not only because of the sheer impossibility of completing the assigned tasks (and being fulfilled, no less!), but also because modern writers insistently reminded mother, directly or indirectly, of the portentousness of her responsibility. The underlying message was that she had the ominous power to shatter her child's mental health. While they reassured mother of her natural ability to carry out her tasks, their assurances rang hollow, rather like a coach telling his or her team before the big game not to be nervous.[77] Perhaps their aim was to reduce tension, but their effect was to create a degree of anxiety and guilt in mothers that is unparalleled in history.

Few women could read about their formidable power to harm their children without a pang of conscience. What mother hasn't momentarily failed to stimulate or pay attention or delight in all baby's little accomplishments? Who hasn't been provoked by her children or had a screaming fit or even, dare I suggest, slapped them . . . only to undergo a black period of agonizing guilt and self-recrimination? According to child experts, even unconscious hostility could plant the seeds of neurosis in her offspring (and, of course, simultaneously define a woman as mentally defective). Pretending to have a good time while diapering baby was not enough — you had to *really* enjoy it. A deficient mother (you!) could be exposed by the very symptoms of your child's pathology.[78] Crankiness in a baby, withdrawal, uncontrollable crying, school phobia, surliness — all betrayed mother's ineptness. This was a dangerous time to be a mother.

Adrienne Rich, who raised her own children in the 1950s and early 1960s, wrote of "the invisible violence of the institution of motherhood" to mothers: "the guilt, the powerless responsibility for human lives, the judgments and condemnations, the fear of her own power, the guilt, the guilt, the guilt."[79]

And Tillie Olsen poignantly captured mother's torment in her story "As I Stand Here Ironing." The beaten-down mother, a veritable Käthe Kollwitz image of mother — stricken, without color, her hands gnarled, her cheeks sunken — is called by a social worker and told that her daughter is "a youngster who needs help." This prompts a long, anguished interior monologue in which mother faces her failures as a parent. In her sad reverie, she pleads for forgiveness, telling painfully why she fears she has ruined her daughter's life. She feels worthless, exhausted, guilt-ridden — as though she may have deserved what she got, but please, help her daughter, save her from being like a dress on an ironing board, flattened, rendered helpless. Such breath-taking honesty reveals a terrible vulnerability.[80] This was one of the first pieces of fiction to speak so loudly and clearly of the victimization of the mother who is assigned exclusive responsibility for her child's mental health, even in the face of adverse social circumstances. ❍

DON'T GET ME WRONG: I am not against child-rearing manuals. They are an indispensable source of information about children's medical and behavioral issues. Parents nowadays probably cannot do without one sort of guide or another, especially as grandma is likely to be retired in Florida, Aunt Betty is remarried and out of the family loop, mom's best friend is busy getting her M.B.A., and there is no one around to tell her about splinters and the "terrible twos." Conception does not automatically instill in mother the necessary knowledge about teething and separation anxiety. When they are good, child-rearing books can be vividly descriptive of children and how they behave, which helps the parent put the child's development into comforting perspective. Where they fall down is in their prescriptions, in their suggested techniques for child raising. While the advice is usually humane enough, and sometimes even effective, it fails to convey its own biases and ephemerality. Largely impressionistic, these books are imbued with an aura of moral superiority and absolute science, persuasive enough to put fear in the hearts of most inexperienced young mothers.

In 1976, for example, thirty years after the initial publication of his classic, Spock reversed his original position and suggested that mothers could work outside the home (with various restrictions) without causing harm to their offspring. Of course he had neglected to mention in the earlier edition that his advice might be transient. Likewise, he left no option for women who *had* to work other than a feeling of guilt for their negligence — even if they were keeping their families alive. What about all the self-recriminations of those working mothers who had taken him seriously for thirty years? What about all those women who would have been better off working? It now appears that their anguish was needless. *Caveat emptor!*

And there are just too many books. Not only does the wide range of advice confuse parents, but the vast quantity of data suggests that mothering is far more complicated and awesome than ever suspected. The constant coinage of new terms and new materials may leave the mother wondering what "new facts" will be discovered, exploding the current theory and revealing that everything she has done so far is wrong. How does she sort through the glut of advice? Whose counsel should she trust? Never mind that a number of experts recognize her quandary and urge her to trust her instincts and to select from the material that feels right. Spock called his first edition *The Common Sense Book of Baby and Child Care,* after all. But surely I am not the only person who finds such advice paradoxical. If mother knew which of her impulses to trust, why would she have cracked the cover of these books in the first place? Their very existence encourages her to distrust her instincts and to rely on experts instead. While many of the writers may initially appear to play themselves down and to advocate flexibility, on closer examination they are promoting their "expert" version of good mothering as more valid than mother's. The writers' medical and psychology degrees lend credibility to their views, and tend to blur the fact that their advice has not been scientifically evaluated.[81]

By the 1970s, most baby gurus recognized the father as a parent and endorsed daddy for the role of caretaker, even as primary caretaker. (This was hardly innovative: Puritan child-rearing experts had written their treatises exclusively for fathers.) Writers also tended to be sex-blind when referring to the baby. But despite these advances in political correctness, they persisted in assuming that the reader was middle class, heterosexual, part of a duo, and was available to devote the better part of her or his day to child care. Father, if he chose, might now share in the dispensing of round-the-clock empathy, but no one challenged the necessity of round-the-clock empathy. Child experts persisted in failing to come to terms with the breathtaking transformation of motherhood during the second half of the twentieth century: that nearly 60 percent of mothers with young children worked and nearly a quarter of American children live in single-parent households.[82] Yet, with the exception of a few experts like T. Berry Brazelton, many writers — Burton White, Selma Fraiberg, Penelope Leach, Hugh Jolly — continued to portray full-time domesticity as the desired norm, thereby condemning about two thirds of all mothers. Even when they paid lip service to a mother with outside interests, the content of their advice was so all-consuming that it seemed to preclude any activity other than child raising. Given the intensity of the enterprise, one wonders how a mother could have reared two. The experts continued to set great store by the "Leave It to Beaver" mom whose 1950s home came equipped with the breadwinning husband and every modern appliance. The popularity of this myth, which as we have seen was even a myth back then, endures today despite the changing Euro-American family landscape.

Consumerism cannot be blamed on child-rearing experts, but the same performance anxiety that impelled parents to purchase advice manuals (and was enhanced by those manuals) has been a gold mine to the baby business, which has banked on (successfully, I might add) mothers' feelings of inadequacy, especially of those mothers who were suckered into buying their product. Advertising encouraged a view of good mothering as a continuous provision of toys, clothes, disposable diapers, and activities. There was an explosion in the upper end of the juvenile product market in the late 1970s as two-income professionals who had postponed having children finally reproduced. (This has continued, as we shall see, even into the lean late 1980s and 1990s.) For many of these parents there were to be only one or two children to lavish their paychecks on. Dubbed "gourmet" babies, the children were showered with expensive material goods and trips to Disneyworld.

In addition to costly clothing and toys, gourmet babies got a jump start in mental and physical training. Fitness centers taught mothers how to give massages to newborns. Flash cards and cassette tapes helped parents impart language and math skills. (Here can be seen an overzealous application of distorted Piagetian theory.) The grand master of better baby building is Glenn Doman, whose *How to Teach Your Baby to Read,* published in 1966, inaugurated a lucrative industry, including books, tapes, seminars, and classes that have spawned many imitators. Why have a merely "normal" baby when you can have an improved model?[83] In the world of baby care, good judgment gave way to intense competition and flagrant connoisseurship.

Lost in the pursuit of the perfect baby toy and all those baby improvement programs was mom. She was the one massaging her child's muscles and flashing all those cards, again and again and again. Whether these techniques increased America's output of geniuses is questionable, but they certainly added to mom's impressive load of maternal guilt. It takes a certain level of self-assurance to resist signing up your baby for swimming lessons when you are told that infancy is a "critical" period after which baby might develop fear of water. If baby does not get on the fast track, it is mom's fault.[84]

In light of the impossible psychic demands heaped upon mothers, it is not surprising that when the new wave of feminism exploded in the late 1960s, one of the first casualties was motherhood. While few feminists in the nineteenth century had felt that motherhood clashed with personhood, activist women in the early stages of the recent women's movement considered motherhood one of the major institutions that oppressed women and prevented them from taking more active control of their lives. Their newly awakened anger apparently caused feminists at first to take positions that were extreme. Among the most famous "antimotherhood" tracts of the period were Shulamith Firestone's *The Dialectic of Sex* (1970) and Ellen Peck's *The Baby Trap* (1971), which reflected the popular slogan of the day, "It is up to women to stop rocking the cradle and start rocking the boat," for which feminists have been apologizing ever since. In retrospect, the rhetoric of that decade (like all utopian writing) sounds thin, absurd, undigested.[85] Unfortunately, it led to an unfair caricature of feminism as motherhood hating, which has resulted in an ever sharper cultural anxiety.

By the end of the 1970s, the brief storm of antimotherhood sentiment had spent its force. In her passionate, ground-breaking book *Of Woman Born,* Adrienne Rich now understood patriarchy to be the oppressor, and not motherhood, which is only a product of patriarchy. Rich distinguished between the *institution* of motherhood under patriarchy — with all the distortion and pain that it wrought for women — and the *experience* of mothering, which implied new and feminist possibilities. Feminists embraced motherhood as an acceptable, potentially rich and rewarding option for even a "liberated" woman. Those advocating abortion in this period carefully portrayed themselves as pro-baby, that is, pro-choice, emphasizing the right to wait, to space, and to have each child wanted — *not* the idea *not* to have kids at all. Feminists wanted it known that they felt okay about motherhood.

These were heady days for activist women. The groundswell of support for the passage of the Equal Rights Amendment in the early 1970s, and the decision by the Supreme Court (in *Roe* v. *Wade*) to make abortion legal, suggested that the American government was willing to provide support to mothers in nontraditional situations. Landmark media images of women, like the acerbic matriarch in the TV sitcom "Maude," and the betrayed mother who reconstructs her life in the popular 1978 film *An Unmarried Woman,* lent credibility to a wider range of options for mothers than ever before. Many women felt newly empowered. Numerous self-help groups, the most famous being the Boston Women's Health Collective, spearheaded a movement to reinstitute "natural childbirth" and a more humane set of birth rituals. More women, in accord with their own wishes, gave birth "awake and aware," in the presence of "significant others," received fewer drugs, held their babies right after birth, and were likely to breastfeed, with the hospital's blessing. All things seemed possible.

But the renewed acceptance of motherhood brought its own set of problems. Women in the 1970s absorbed the baby *and* the bathwater, that is, the baby and the contemporary inflated ideology of good mothering (relentless tenderness, total availability, and so on). Given permission (in theory, anyway) to "have it all" — children *and* careers — these young American mothers attempted to become superwomen. Facing formidable problems — no federally backed maternity leave, day care, or hospitalization for childbirth (almost all other Western nations have government programs for mothers); a job market that discriminates against women and makes no concessions for the needs of mothers and children — they stumbled. Had they consulted women of color and immigrant women, many of whom had been struggling all along, they might have been forewarned. The *Wall Street Journal* captured the problem when it described the new working women: "Aglow with talent and self-confidence, young women who came of age in the early 1970s breezed through college, picked up their law degrees and MBA's and began sprinting up the corporate ladder." But there was a snag: these women found their careers "sabotaged by motherhood."[86] The growing prolife, protraditional family constituency of the New Right couldn't have been more delighted, and in the 1980s, as we shall see, they mounted an effective media campaign against these women, portraying them as greedy, ambitious ball busters, whom no one would want as mothers. Tragically, the conservative backlash added insult to injury for the skyrocketing number of women who *had* to work to support their families.

While in certain circles there was considerable interest in father's involvement with his children and his influence on child development, and parallel portrayals of the New Man (tender, child-caring) in the media, Mr. Mom never substantially happened in fact. Barring a newfound enjoyment in his children, father rarely engaged in the nitty-gritty of their daily care. Men claimed that this was because women were unwilling to share the baby; women claimed that men wished to participate only in the positive aspects of child care (like conception, of course, and birth and ball games), and that they devised ingenious ways to resist the onerous chores (like chauffeuring and cleaning up kids' messes). In any case, "shared parenting" remained a pipe dream in most households. Mothers were exhausted. But while they sometimes voiced their grievances about the unfair division of labor, they never thought to question old shibboleths about good mothering.[87] ❍

AS MOTHER CAME to be viewed as the primary agent in her child's development — and its primary obstacle — she went from an underwhelming presence in literature to an overwhelming one. Emerging from nineteenth-century obscurity, mother became fair game for insult, particularly by sons who had read a little Freud and thought they understood him. No longer bound by Victorian propriety, they felt free to express a hostility that heretofore was reserved for the wanton woman. By the mid-twentieth century, mother was identified as the source of all the misery besetting society. This was the heyday of mother bashing. In literature, media, sociology, psychology, even feminism, mother had become a monster.

The seeds were sown in the first half of the twentieth century. D. H. Lawrence, Ernest Hemingway, and William Faulkner all debunked the New Woman. Lawrence's frantic insistence that women be kept under control, Hemingway's representations of what happens when they are not, and Faulkner's enigmatic references to women's fearsomeness convey an unmistakable dread of the emancipated woman. The anxiety extended to mothers as well. The stifling, overinvested mother of Paul Morel in Lawrence's *Sons and Lovers,* a forerunner of the devouring, soul-destroying, emasculating mothers who stalk through the pages of so many later literary works, is typical. Lawrence is so disdainful of mothers that his most virile figures — Lilly (a man) in *Aaron's Rod,* and the groom in "St. Mawr" — spitefully abstain from fatherhood in order to deprive the female of motherhood. Hemingway's men are generally alienated from their bossy mothers, and Faulkner nastily described mother as "the supreme primal uterus." But important maternal figures are still relatively rare in these early decades, and when they appear — as in Virginia Woolf's *To the Lighthouse* and Lawrence's *Sons and Lovers* — they are invariably killed off or silenced so that the protagonist of the novel can develop, just as in nineteenth-century works.[88]

By the 1940s, literary mothers did not necessarily die, but the reader probably wishes they had. Mothers — mostly failed nurturers or intrusive manipulators — suddenly loomed large, and their malevolent hold was specifically *psychological,* mirroring, as we shall see, the psychoanalytic thinking of the day. Most notorious was the attack on "Mom" by Philip Wylie in his nonfiction best seller, *Generation of Vipers* (1942). This slash-and-burn collection of essays blamed mother for everything from the pasty look of American men to political corruption. His description of a society gone soft, ruined, and shriveled by hordes of predatory, castrating moms, became as much a part of the 1940s' and 1950s' discourse as happy homemakers and caretaking mothers. Wylie's conclusion: "Gentlemen, Mom is a jerk." The numerous printings suggest that Wylie's work had tapped a fund of inchoate rage in larger society.[89]

Why all the vitriol? Perhaps because men began to think that women were getting off too easily. The shift in the nature of housework, all those labor-saving devices, made domesticity seem less like real work.[90] Indeed, Wylie's diatribe mostly had to do with mom's idleness and her consequent attempts to bind her sons to her so as to fill her time. Also, men somehow made women responsible for the new materialism of contemporary society, casting them in the role of endless consumer. In fact, 80 percent of the family's needs *were* satisfied by purchases *by women!* Understandably, men began to feel that their work existed only to supply women with the goods and cash they craved. Men felt exploited. (I suspect that some projection was operating here, that men blamed mothers for the acquisitiveness they themselves felt ashamed of.) Perhaps, too, woman's real gains in power (the vote, contraception), and her recent foray into the labor force during the war, triggered man's atavistic fears of his dependence on her, anxiety about her sexuality and autonomy, which sparked defensive hostility and a wish to keep her safely ensconced in her tract house.

Mom became a scapegoat. She was accused of unmanning her sons (*Look Back in Anger, The Glass Menagerie*) and suffocating her daughters (*The Bell Jar, Lady Oracle*). In time she acquired an ethnic voice — Spanish in García Lorca's *The House of Bernarda Alba,* Southern in McMurtry's *Terms of Endearment,* Irish in [illegible] Edna O'Brien story. And with an eager assist from various Jew[illegible] writers, like Dan Greenburg, Bruce Jay Friedman, Harold B[illegible]key, and, of course, Philip Roth, the "Jewish mother" emerge[illegible] devourer of her children's soul with every spoonful of her chicken soup.[91] Gossipy, plump, overprotective, hungry, sh[illegible] came a familiar figure in novels, movies, and comedians' m[illegible] logues. The Borscht Belt couldn't have survived without [illegible] nor could Woody Allen, for that matter, though he seems [illegible] spent much of his adult life dragging her through the mu[illegible] his films *Annie Hall* and *Stardust Memories*). With her [illegible] ability to cultivate guilt, the Jewish mother became a [illegible] for all mothers — a sad irony, when it was mothers t[illegible] who were suffering under the guilt of their supposed ina[illegible]

Edward Albee's surrealist play *The American Dre*[illegible] s mom's predatory nature with particularly horrible [illegible] The heroine, Mommy, is sterile, so she buys a ba[illegible] n adoption agency and proceeds to mutilate him. Whe[illegible] ks only at daddy, she cuts out his eyes; when he ma[illegible] he cuts off his genitals and hands. Albee's animus again[illegible] vs no bounds, yet rage against mothers was not l[illegible] lle authors. Women, reflecting dominant assumption[illegible] in mother bashing. In Doris Lessing's *Children of V*[illegible] or example, Martha Quest struggles with dreams [illegible] is ultimately stunted by her mother, a woman so [illegible] ith the patriarchal order that she betrays her daugh[illegible] ok of the series, we see a maturing Martha still haunted by her mother — driven, in fact, to illness by a prospective visit from her.[92]

Among the greatest movies of the period, there are mothers of awe-inspiring destructive malevolence. In *Now, Voyager,* a fable of maternal ev; Bette Davis, the dominated daughter, struggles to overcome hr mother, a paragon of repression and sexual denial; in *Psycho,* Ms. Bates, having driven her son, Anthony Perkins, to matricid continues to live on inside him, murdering any woman to whom he feels an attraction; in *Rebel Without a Cause,* the Wylique Mom (James Dean's mother) denies her son the strong re model he needs through her dominance of her "henpecked husband; and in *The Manchurian Candidate,* the Communis mother, Angela Lansbury, forces her brainwashed son to kill bride and to attempt to assassinate a presidential candidate bef she gives him an incestuous kiss on the lips. The apotheosis f s genre can be seen in the 1949 film *White Heat.* In it, James agney, as a mother-fixated gangster, sits on his mother's lap, suf- s from crippling migraines only she can cure, has a psychotic akdown when he learns of her death, and meets a fiery end p an exploding gas tank while shouting, "Made it, Ma! Top of world!"[93]

)utside the realm of fiction, the 1965 report by Daniel Patrick nihan had the temerity to blame the so-called tangled pa- gy of the fatherless black family on mothers . . . as if black en didn't want another paycheck in the house. And the cure lestructive" black matriarchy, according to Moynihan? More for fathers! Moynihan eventually recognized that these ideas acist and sexist, and he apologized.

ther blaming took place in feminist circles as well. Too ccounts of mothering by activist women turned out to be y of their victimization by their mothers. The psychologists Chodorow and Susan Contratto examine this paradoxical of feminists to applaud women even while they "bash" (as if mothers weren't female).[94] They attribute the cause sts' debunking of mom to their belief — to everyone's n an all-powerful mother, who, because she is fully re- for how her children turn out, is blamed for everything, child's limitations to the crises of human existence.

Closely allied to this is the fantasy of maternal perfection — that if mom could only escape from patriarchy, she would be ideal. These ideas are embedded in the otherwise brilliant writings of Adrienne Rich and the sociologist Alice Rossi, who tend to romanticize maternal possibility and assume that children's needs are legitimate and must be met (shades of Spock here?).

The central premise of Nancy Friday's simplistic *My Mother/ My Self* is that mothers are noxious to daughters, and a daughter's subsequent unhappiness stems from this initial relationship. Mothers, she argues, make daughters in their image. As the mother, in becoming a mother, has denied her own sexuality, so she must deny sexuality to her daughter.[95] Perhaps one can dismiss Friday as merely a popular writer and a dubious feminist, but it is harder to ignore Judith Arcana in *Our Mothers' Daughters,* Jane Lazarre in *The Mother Knot,* and Dorothy Dinnerstein in *The Mermaid and the Minotaur,* all of whom give similar accounts. The only difference is that these writers claim that mother's destructive behavior is not her fault, but a product of her entrapment within patriarchy. None questions the appropriateness of the child's wish for perfect gratification (via mother), nor the advisability of mother's attempt to meet those "needs" (or, more accurately, "wants"). All assume that the good mother gratifies all the needs of children. All are written from a daughter's perspective, not a mother's. Clearly these feminists were reflecting the cultural patterning of the 1970s. I suspect they would alter the thrust of their accounts today, but as their work stands, it serves as a reminder of the virulent animosity directed toward mother less than twenty years ago. Much of the bitterness was fueled by the psychology of the period, which was obsessed with maternal pathology.

TERMS OF ENMESHMENT

Predatory moms suddenly appeared in the free associations of patients on the psychiatric couches of America and Europe in the 1940s, as did their alter egos, neglectful moms (code for "mothers who had outside interests"). Wylie's *Generation of Vipers* opened the floodgates to a tidal wave of mother bashing in popular psychology that is only now subsiding. Much of the sniping was the result of gross distortions of sound theoretical thinking and good science, but not quite all of it was. Sometimes it was the "good" science that was at fault.

The "overprotective" mom was the first to take a hit. In 1943, the psychoanalyst David Levy published *Maternal Overprotection,* and a new phrase was coined. Also known today as the "smothering mother," she is the one who presumably won't let go, who must intrude into every aspect of her child's life. After perusing two thousand case records at a clinic in New York that he directed, Levy concluded that the overprotected child becomes socially maladjusted because, later on, he or she tries to force every situation into the original pattern of its life, of being the beloved tyrant of an ever-responding mother.[96] Any sensible reading of Levy's book would suggest that his conclusions are speculations, not hard facts, and that they do not lend themselves to specific directives to mothers. Nevertheless, the psychiatric consultant to the U.S. Army and Navy, Edward Strecker, leveled the accusation of "overprotectiveness" at the mothers of America, whom he charged with mollycoddling the nation's potential soldiers. Three million men had been classified as too emotionally unstable to serve in the military during World War II, and Strecker attributed the cause to maternal apron strings.[97]

Now mothers were really in a bind. Told by Spock to love their baby, they had to be careful not to love too much. Even someone as formidable as the anthropologist Margaret Mead cowered after a telephone conversation with Dr. Levy: "I knew that I would have to work hard not to overprotect my child."[98]

Mother blaming reached a crescendo after the Second World War with the publication of *Modern Woman: The Lost Sex* by the sociologist Ferdinand Lundberg and the psychiatrist Marynia Farnham. They estimated that between 40 and 50 percent of all mothers were "rejecting, over-solicitous, or dominating." Afflicted with penis envy and an unwomanly drive to power, mother could potentially destroy all the people around her. One of the results, Lundberg and Farnham warned, was the extensive castration of the male. Only if woman was to re-establish her essential dependence on man, stay home, and not intrude on her son, could her family achieve contentment.[99]

Soon to be added to the hit list was the neglectful mother, she who did not cuddle her child enough. The animosity against this so-called depriving mother exceeded even that against the overprotective mother, and it is her specter that dominates the diatribes against day care even today. This time, the impetus for the attack came not only from the clinical impressions of psychoanalysts, but, at least initially, from actual observations of the pathetic little babies left to idle in wartime orphanages. The clarion call for better mothering was *The Rights of Infants,* written by the New York analyst Margaret Ribble in 1943. As the title of the book suggests, Ribble was championing the infant against its parents. An ardent supporter of warm human contact between mother and child, she advocated not only rocking, lullabies, and prolonged breast-feeding, but she went so far as to suggest that baby sleep beside mother in her bed, a rather maverick thought for a good Freudian. Ribble's central premise was that children need TLC (tender, loving care), a term for which she is famous; it is essential for their development, and without it they are irreversibly damaged. As evidence of the deleterious effects of maternal neglect, Ribble described a disease known as marasmus, a wasting away for want of loving attention, about which a spate of anecdotes circulated in medical circles. One was the story of Old Anna, at an institution in Düsseldorf, who wandered about with a baby on each hip. When a case looked hopeless, it was turned over to her. Presumably, she just cuddled the infants and usually succeeded in healing them, reminding me of the medieval miracle stories about the Virgin Mary.[100]

Shortly after World War II, the psychoanalyst René Spitz conducted a dramatic two-year experiment, demonstrating the lethal effects of maternal deficiency, which he captured in films that still shock students in Introductory Psych. In this famous study (which pioneered the practice of engaging in the close-up observation of infants), the amount of affection bestowed on two groups of institutionalized babies differed: in a "nursery," the children's mothers (who were delinquent girls, as the nursery was in a penal institution) took care of them; in the "foundling home," overworked nurses cared for the babies. The difference between the two groups was striking. In a matter of weeks, the children in the foundling home (with no mothers) became weepy and withdrawn, suffering weight loss and insomnia. They seemed to wither away, and within two years 37 percent had died. The babies in the other group developed normally.[101] After these findings were published in the 1940s, social agencies began to discontinue orphan asylums and to place motherless children in foster homes.

Meanwhile, new research was corroborating the importance of physical contact in the development of infants and small children. Inspired by Spitz, Harry Harlow, an animal-learning theorist, devised his famous experiments with rhesus monkeys. He took baby monkeys from their mothers shortly after birth and raised them with two surrogate mothers — one made of wire mesh, the other covered with terry cloth. While either dummy "mother" could be equipped with a feeding nipple, the infant monkeys bonded only with the terry cloth figure, snuggling against it and running to it when frightened. The conclusion: infant attachment, or at least monkey attachment, depends on tactile comfort. So what matters is not the hand that feeds you, nor even the heart that beats for you — but the cuddly arms that enfold you.

What a pleasing message! How life-affirming and commonsensical — that mothers and babies must be physically close. But soon that sensible idea was removed from its scientific context, however questionable to begin with, and was used as a means of driving mother back to the home so that she could be available twenty-four hours a day for continuous contact. Even respected researchers began going beyond their data in making pronouncements. Spitz, for example, led a generation of psychoanalysts in an absurd effort to trace each childhood disturbance to maternal deprivation. In 1965, he devoted a major part of his *magnum opus, The First Year of Life,* to connecting specific maternal attitudes with specific infant problems: "hostility in the guise of manifest anxiety" in the mother was said to produce eczema in her infant; "oscillation between pampering and hostility" would lead to rocking; and "primary anxious overpermissiveness" was thought to cause colic.[102]

At the same time, across the Atlantic, a most unusual British psychoanalyst, John Bowlby, an heir to a baronetcy who, as a child, had been looked after by a nanny, was thinking along the same lines. Bowlby's genealogy as a psychoanalyst was as impeccable as his familial lines: he had been supervised by Melanie Klein. Like his mentor, Bowlby felt that the mother-child tie — the infant's experience of feeding at the breast — was the prototype of all human relationships. This was one of the areas in which

Klein parted company with Freud, who, you may recall, had argued that later issues — namely, Oedipal conflicts — were more important in child development. But unlike Klein and Freud, Bowlby felt that real-life events — the way parents treat a child, especially in the first three or four years — were crucial. Klein would have none of it. To her, fantasies of mother, not actual mother, were the dominant factor. Some historians have sniped that Klein's need to justify real mothers in her writing stemmed from her painful and embarrassing, and very public, conflict with her daughter, the psychoanalyst Melitta Schmideberg. Be that as it may, Klein, in her psychoanalytic play therapy with children, would never agree to see the children's parents, a practice that seems very odd today.[103]

Bowlby was the original architect of "attachment theory," according to which all children are biologically biased to form an attachment to the person looking after them, a concept obviously reminiscent of "imprinting," which the ethologist Konrad Lorenz had developed to explain why goslings follow their mother. Like Lorenz, Bowlby viewed the mother-infant bond as an evolutionary adaptation, designed to prevent infants from straying too far from their caretakers and into the jaws of a hungry predator.

World War II had dislocated millions of people, leaving untold numbers of children homeless and in foster care. In 1948, the United Nations decided to study the needs of war orphans, many of whom had been institutionalized for long periods, and children who had been boarded in rural areas to protect them from air raids, and it entrusted the task to John Bowlby. The result was his *Maternal Care and Mental Health* (1951), republished in 1953 in simplified form as *Child Care and the Growth of Love,* which became a best seller.[104] His review makes grim reading. The war-ravaged children were severely damaged — emotionally withdrawn, likely to be physically stunted and sickly, much like Spitz's foundlings. And Bowlby's findings, like Spitz's, led to needed reforms. Bowlby concluded that when a young child does not experience a "warm, intimate, and continuous relationship with his mother," he may become emotionally crippled for life. He called this situation "maternal deprivation." According to Bowlby, maternal deprivation was as damaging in the first three years of life as German measles in the first three months of pregnancy: "mother love in infancy is as important for mental health as proteins and vitamins for physical health."[105]

Bowlby reasoned that many young children form an internal working model of themselves and others based on early ties with their mothers. The model is fixed at an early age. So if babies are deprived of mother love (due to separation or loss of mother), they will be unable to form human relationships. Hence, the quality of the mother-infant bond — which Bowlby termed "attachment" — is a crucial factor in mental health. And researching the quality of attachment between mother and baby was precisely what Bowlby's colleague, the American developmental psychologist Mary Ainsworth, attempted to do with her famous tool, the Strange Situation — a twenty-minute stress test for infants that classified them as either securely or insecurely attached. It has been said that the Strange Situation consists of "strange people doing strange things to little kids in strange rooms," which is not far from the truth. Briefly, a baby's responses are measured in increasingly stressful situations — placement in a strange room with mother, the arrival of a stranger, the departure of mother, and her return. It has been shown that, in the short term, "insecurely attached" babies are likely to see others as untrustworthy. But long-term results are inconclusive. Nevertheless, the Strange Situation became as popular in developmental psychology circles in the 1970s as the IQ test was in the 1950s. Both were erroneously thought to be reliable measures of children's functioning and to be predictive of the future.[106]

Attachment theory has proven to be immensely appealing, arriving, as it does, at such a cherished platitude — that mommies matter. Much of what Bowlby and Ainsworth demonstrated rang true. Mothers know that children may be anxious with strangers, that they can become clingy, and that they may retaliate against the caretaker on her return. So when Bowlby wrote in his 1951 monograph that the full-time employment of mother outside the home constituted maternal deprivation, on a par with, say, war or imprisonment of a parent, mothers were prepared to believe him.

Interpreted literally, attachment theory advocated that mother stay home. And that is exactly how it has been popularly construed. In England, under the guise of "Bowlbyism," nursery schools no longer accepted children under the age of three, and doctors, social workers, and teachers all advised women that they were putting their young children at risk by going to work.[107] In America, attachment theory became the cornerstone of child-rearing manuals from mid-Spock to Brazelton.

One of the more absurd outcomes of this interest in attachment has been the obsession with the mother-infant bond. Bonding, in the public's eyes, has become the Krazy Glue that instantly welds together mother and child. Should mom fritter away critical minutes after delivery by failing to cuddle baby, she will have forfeited her best and maybe only chance to cement a biologically based link to her child. These ideas, according to the psychologist Diane Eyer, are actually distortions of early 1970s' research findings of an instinctual process in women right after birth when they are hormonally primed to accept (or reject) infants — just as goats do. Although most of the scientific community over a decade ago dismissed that research as seriously flawed, pediatricians and child-care experts continue to preach maternal bonding as a reason for mother not to go back to work after having baby.[108]

On the positive side, these ideas have been used to humanize the childbirth experience and reform foster care. The flip side is that they have become unhinged from their scientific moorings (which were dubious in the first place) and have been used to justify exaggerated claims — that there are "critical" periods for bonding; that babies need stay-at-home mothers; that a properly bonded infant will enjoy lifelong emotional security. Ultimately, bonding has become a mandate, and mothers who delivered by caesarean or who adopted or who did not experience an immediate postpartum clutch of attachment to their newborns have been made to feel remiss . . . as if good mothering were that simple.

Even as Bowlby and his colleagues were writing about the importance of mother for child development, criticism was being leveled at them from a variety of quarters. The psychoanalyst Anna Freud sensibly pointed out that the way a child may react to the loss of its mother has something to do with the nature of the child, its ego strength. The experience is not always devastating. In experimental circles, Rutter gathered evidence to show that "maternal deprivation" was not the only factor, or even the most critical factor, in healthy development.[109] Rutter was not arguing that separation from mother was good, but that it was merely one element among many that may "cause" antisocial behavior, with discord in families and dysfunctional practices being far more powerful as determinants. (It should be noted that Spitz and Bowlby had collected their evidence from highly dysfunctional environments.) Other data showed that babies could recover from early traumas and that they are often extraordinarily resilient, thereby contradicting Bowlby's idea that damage from maternal deprivation is irreversible. Moreover, children were able to attach to multiple caretakers without untoward consequences.[110] And in longitudinal studies (of which there are, understandably, few), the strongest predictor of maladjustment appeared to be temperament of the child, not a bad mother.[111] Jerome Kagan, an influential psychologist at Harvard and a prolific researcher, has become one of Bowlby's and Ainsworth's most vocal detractors. His studies continually fail to confirm their findings about "maternal deprivation" and point, instead, to the role of genes in child development.

But even while a consensus of researchers concluded in the 1970s that mothers were not the sole cause of psychopathology, practicing clinicians and the dominant mother culture failed to notice. These were the years when Bruno Bettelheim, an elder statesman in the child psychology establishment, was blaming mothers for causing autism, and schizophrenia was thought to result from "refrigerator" moms, or mothers who gave their children mixed messages. These were the years, the psychologists Paula Caplan and Ian Hall-McCorquodale showed, when mothers were scapegoats for virtually every type of mental problem, when not a single mother of a patient was portrayed as mentally stable.[112] Child-care experts also remained out of touch. In 1977, just as mothers were returning to work in unprecedented numbers, Selma Fraiberg published *Every Child's Birthright: In Defense of Mothering,* in which she reiterated Bowlby's argument, that without the full-time attention of *one* mothering person, a child will be in jeopardy. It was a hot seller. ○

THE NAMES WERE CHANGED, but not to protect the innocent. The jargon may have been different, but between 1940 and 1980 the locus of blame for psychopathology was much the same in the psychoanalytic institutes as it was in developmental psychology and in popular psychology — Mom. True, the "overprotective" or "neglectful" mother was called "schizophrenogenic" or "narcissistic" or "nonempathic," but the nature of the grievances against her was indistinguishable. This makes perfect sense, given the cross-pollination among these groups; indeed, a few of the major players were the same. Bowlby, for instance, was a psychoanalyst, a researcher, and a popular writer; and Donald Winnicott, who was beloved by the British public for his wartime broadcasts, was a brilliantly original and respected psychoanalyst.

Toward the end of his life, Freud had devised a model of the mind — consisting of the id, the ego, and the superego — that would allow reality (hence, mother) into the child's psyche. Having gained entry, she took over, at least in the eyes of post-Freudians. Heretofore ignored, mother now became all-powerful, and whatever she did to her child underwent microscopic scrutiny. Good mothering became utterly critical and highly codified: in psychoanalytic terms, mother must be sure to offer timely and proper doses of "ordinary devotion," "mirroring," "empathy," "psychological attunement," and must allow herself to be "idealized," all the while making sure she provided "optimal frustrations." To do otherwise was to invite a pejorative diagnosis of herself, such as character disorder (briefly, a person who cannot form wholesome relationships), a condition so dire as to be often regarded as untreatable.

Midcentury psychoanalytic thinking colluded in the obliteration of mothers as persons. It assumed that motherhood was the child's drama, with mom in a supporting role. The plot was played out against, or with, a female parent whose job it was to service her child's needs and then disappear into the scenery. Though in practice psychoanalysts tried to be neutral and objective, their theory had become profoundly child-centered. Formulated from patients' reconstructions of their childhoods, and not mothers' reconstructions of their maternal experience, it looked at motherhood only from the baby's position.

In these years, both the theory and techniques of psychoanalysis were turned on their heads in all but the most conservative institutes. With psychopathology being understood as maternally induced, the practice of psychoanalysis became more "motherly," perhaps in compensation. Freud's aloof, rationalistic, "paternalistic" stance was slowly giving way among many analysts to a more empathic, warmer, "maternal" approach.[113]

To be sure, psychoanalysts are not wedded to literal interpretations of their texts. Besides, psychoanalytically oriented therapists, even more than psychotherapists of other persuasions, contend that real-life events, like abusive parents, matter less in a child's life than the child's interpretation of those events (for which they have been much criticized). Nevertheless, the pervasiveness of mother blaming in psychoanalytic theory after Freud is too extensive to be overlooked, even if it was not consciously meant as a blanket indictment of all mothers.[114]

It can hardly be regarded as coincidental that psychoanalysts at this time constructed an ideal of female behavior to go with the empathically raised child, wherein maternal self-sacrifice was considered normal and good. The proof of healthy femininity was now a woman's willingness to be a masochist, according to the Freudian psychoanalyst Helene Deutsch (who apparently did not meet her own requirements for femininity, since she hired baby sitters). Masochism is adaptive for a woman, Deutsch argued in her second volume on the psychology of women, *Motherhood*.[115] It represents an adjustment to the realities of her life, in which many of the normal female functions involve a combination of pain and pleasure, even joy, such as defloration and childbirth. What good fortune for a greedy child, whose every wish would now become masochist-mom's command.

Sexuality, for Deutsch, was in the service of reproduction, which, in turn, was in the service of healthy femininity. Here, her ideas did not differ from Freud's, and, accordingly, she has been dismissed by feminists and others as a "dutiful daughter." But in Deutsch's system, Freud's shadowy mother, rejected early on by the girl in favor of a robust father, is restored to full, powerful form. Deutsch also went a step beyond Freud when she attributed women's motives for having babies as not so much displaced penis envy as identification with mother.[116]

For thirty years after Freud's death, psychoanalysts did not write much about women's wish to procreate, and when they did, they tended, like Deutsch, not to focus on the idea of a baby as a substitute penis but on the notion that girls tend to identify with their moms. Indeed, psychoanalysts like Judith Kestenberg and

Henri Parens demonstrated experimentally that the wish for a child *precedes* penis envy, so a little girl's wish for a baby can hardly be viewed as a substitute for something she does not yet want.[117]

Still, almost all psychoanalysts persisted in equating healthy femininity with the desire to have a baby. Problems like infertility and postpartum depression were seen as evidence of women's poor adjustment. A woman *had* to have a child and be happy about it to prove her credentials. Therese Benedek in 1959 anticipated many other writers in viewing the woman's urge to procreate as an "organizer" of femininity.[118] She understood motherhood to be a developmental stage, in which women identify with their children, and also with themselves as children, which neatly serves to reactivate (and help resolve) earlier conflicts around their own experience of being mothered. Still missing in all this theorizing was the idea of reproduction as an *opportunity* rather than a *requirement.*

Yet it would be a mistake to dismiss completely the psychoanalytic writing on motherhood during this period as insensitive to women. The bulk of the literature dealt not with primary causes of the wish to have a baby, but with secondary elaborations of that wish, and offered many insights into women's motivations. There were important clinical studies of women revealing that some wanted a child so as to feel special through a relationship with the baby or the baby's father, or they wished to entrap the father. (At times, psychology coincides with common sense!) Other women wished to have a baby in order to identify with the child and feel loved, or to actively reverse or master unsatisfying experiences with their own parents. Others fancied a "perfect" loving relationship with the baby, and wished to experience themselves as being a virtuous, selfless caretaker.[119] The list could go on. There are almost as many "secondary" explanations for having babies as there are mothers. ❍

BY AND LARGE Freud took for granted the nurturing functions of a mother, as we have seen. The tie he interpreted repeatedly was that of the child to its father. Nevertheless, during Freud's lifetime a number of famous analysts, in defiance of him, attempted to emphasize "pre-Oedipal" ties to the mother. What they meant was early emotional relationship *preceding* the triangular conflict (occurring between ages three and five) in which the little girl longs for the love of the father and feels rivalry with the mother, or the little boy longs for the mother and feels rivalry with the father. Otto Rank, for example, made the newborn's mother the center of his system, an idea that followed inevitably from his conception of the trauma of birth. Only Ruth Mack Brunswick was able to stress the importance of the pre-Oedipal mother in the development of the child in a manner so tactful as not to seem a revolt against Freud's basic ideas.[120] She did this by assigning mother's importance specifically to the female child, an area in which Freud admitted some ignorance. For Brunswick, and many analysts today, the earlier tie to the mother is far more archaic and primitive than the Oedipal; when it goes awry, it can cause serious mental problems.

In the 1930s, a renegade tradition began to emerge, deriving in part from earlier Freudian defections, explicitly breaking with the drive model (wherein instincts from within, namely sex and aggression, propelled the human psychic apparatus). It was called interpersonal psychoanalysis, and its tenets feel strangely modern. Its main proponents were Harry Stack Sullivan, Erich Fromm, Karen Horney, Clara Thompson, and Frieda Fromm-Reichmann. They shared a belief that classical Freudian theory underemphasized the social context that must figure in any theory that accounts for the origins, development, and warping of personality.[121] They emphasized the role of the "other" in the development of psychopathology. It was a small step for "other" to become "mother." Unable to understand mental illness from a drive standpoint, both Sullivan and Fromm-Reichmann, for example, traced schizophrenia back to the relationship with a "bad" or "schizophrenogenic" mother.[122] This mother was seen as malevolent, restrictive, clinging, and more concerned with her own welfare than with the child's. Because of her rejection, the child was filled with anger and insecurity, and became mentally ill.

The advent of "ego psychology," which developed naturally from Freud's structural theory before he was cold in his grave, similarly paved the way for the prominence of "outside" influences on child development. As articulated by Anna Freud and Heinz Hartmann, an individual's ego was understood to be strong, partially autonomous, and conflict free, capable of enabling a person to adapt to reality. Presumably, such reality included mothers.[123] As a child analyst, who, unlike Klein, worked with both children and parents, Anna Freud could not help "seeing" the powerful influence of the primary caretaker (to be distinguished from analysts of adults who merely "hear about" the role of other persons).[124] From this, she concluded that mothers matter, though in her own life it was her father who reigned supreme.

In the postwar decades, new ideas were percolating within the psychoanalytic institutes about the importance of mothers, neatly corresponding to the observations of Ribble, Bowlby, Spitz, and Levy. They achieved prominence in the new theories of "object relations" and "self psychology."

Up to this point, Freud, Klein, and the ego psychologists had all stressed the importance of innate drives and the child's own psyche in determining personality. The interpersonal theorists took the opposing position, emphasizing the role of social influences on the child, and playing down the psyche. The baby in their view is like a sponge, absorbing reality without mediating it through fantasy, distortion, or any defense mechanism. Object-relations theory, in contrast, contends that it is not drives that are critical but objects (that is, persons). It is not quite so drive-ridden as Freud, Klein, and company, nor quite so environmentally deterministic as the interpersonalists, yet object-relations theory postulates an anemic psyche and does not, in my view, take sufficient account of the effects of the child's unconscious in distorting experience; it therefore ends up blaming mothers.

The object-relations theorist W. R. D. Fairbairn and, later, Harry Guntrip maintained that humans are motivated not so much by erotic desire but by a desire for a relationship. The content of the child's internal objects (its inner life) derives completely from real, external objects. As objects are internalized, they are fragmented and recombined, to be sure, but they always derive from the child's real experience of its actual parents. In other words, children do not invent them out of whole cloth. Fairbairn's clear implication is that parental deprivation is at the root of all evil. Although he does indicate at some points that such total parental availability is impossible, he does not say that baby's wishes, by their very nature, are ungratifiable. He suggests that parental failure to provide complete satisfaction is a product of the parents' own psychopathology, leading, I suppose, to an infinite regression of mother blaming ending presumably only with Eve.[125]

Fairbairn and Guntrip anticipated Margaret Mahler, the most important object-relations theorist in the United States, for whom the child at birth is psychologically fused with the mother. Her compelling ideas derived from her observational research project with mothers and babies at the Masters Children's Center in New York, and have strongly influenced a recent generation of psychotherapists, especially social workers. Mahler's unique contribution was her description of the baby's "psychological birth" as an individual — the slow course of its emergence from symbiosis with mother through a long "separation-individuation" process, including subphases of "hatching," the "practice" of independence, separation anxiety ("rapprochement"), and eventually true autonomy, all of this supposedly accomplished by the age of three. The requirements Mahler places on the mother during these years are formidable, subtle, and ever changing. At first mother must be available to act as a buffer between the child and the external world, to function as an auxiliary ego and stimulus barrier. Later, she must be willing to relinquish this closeness in favor of a high-level relationship with an increasingly independent individual. Mother's failure in this regard may result in "severe disturbance of individuation and psychotic disorganization."[126] In all fairness, Mahler did write about the child's contribution to its own mental problems with regard to constitutional factors, and its talent (or lack of talent) for eliciting tenderness from its caretakers, but the thrust of her writing emphasizes the responsibility of mother. And as her ideas filtered down to the general public, they were taken to mean that mothers must constantly tune in to their babies for three years. Hence, good mothers of young children were not to be otherwise engaged.

Donald Winnicott, the British psychoanalyst, came to psychoanalysis through pediatrics, and though he claimed theoretical allegiance to Freud and Klein, he bears much in common with the object-relations theorists in their emphasis on mothering. Winnicott often said, "There is no such thing as a baby; there is only a baby in a certain environment," implying that the baby and its mother must be considered as a unit. Many of his contributions concerned the conditions necessary for enabling children to separate from others and develop a "true self" while maintaining a capacity for intimacy. Even though Winnicott freed mothers from the requirement of perfection by asserting that mother merely had to be "good enough," a revolutionary concept at the time, he developed so daunting a list for being "good enough" that he left little room for mom to do anything else. First, mother must be exquisitely responsive to baby's needs and gestures. Then, she must provide a nonintrusive "holding" and mirroring environment (that is, be empathic). She must join with her child in respecting its "transitional objects" (in other words, schlep its security blanket around). Finally, she must survive and not retaliate against her baby's "usage" of her (that is, be a good sport about all this). Fortunately, Winnicott was careful to state that these tasks were well within the capabilities of the "ordinary devoted mother." In fact, he was as reassuring to mothers as he was condescending: "You do not have to be clever, and you do not even have to think if you do not want to. You may have been hopeless at arithmetic at school, or perhaps got scholarships but . . . you can be an ordinary devoted mother." These reassurances sound a bit hollow in light of his definition of psychosis as an "environmental deficiency disease." We all know what he meant by "environment."[127]

Probably the psychoanalyst who was hardest on mothers was Heinz Kohut, the architect of self psychology, though his insensitivity was undoubtedly inadvertent. For Kohut, the child's early experiences of relationships with others were as essential for its psychological survival as oxygen was for its physical survival. The basic constituent of Kohut's model of the psychic apparatus is the self. The infantile self is helpless, weak, and amorphous and needs a "selfobject" to provide cohesion, constancy, and resilience. Selfobjects are usually people (typically mothers) who perform the tasks that, if all goes well, will later be performed by the individual's own psychic structure. Kohut considered the empathic relation between the selfobject and the infant as essential to healthy child development.

The good selfobject, first of all, "mirrors" the child — admires its grandiosity and displays constancy, nurturance, respect, and general empathy.[128] Second, the selfobject must permit idealization by the child, so that the child can experience a sense of merger with a strong, valued figure. In time, the selfobject must slowly and incrementally provide "optimal frustrations" so that an internalization of the selfobject takes place. Kohut called this process "transmuting internalization." If completed successfully, it will give rise to a permanent psychic structure — a cohesive sense of self. Chronic failure in empathy, attributable to parental character pathology, undermines the healthy development of the child's self and leads to narcissistic psychopathology. In a late essay, Kohut wrote that the kind of struggles depicted by other theorists (Oedipal conflict) are in fact early breakdowns in self-organization, which in turn result from shortcomings in parental empathy.[129] So it's not conflict that causes mental problems, but deficits; that is, the mother's deficits.

Kohut cited as an ideal selfobject relationship that of Eugene O'Neill toward his third wife, and that of Proust to his housekeeper, Celestine. The biographies of both writers, however, suggest that they used these women as doormats. Apparently, Kohut advocated empathy for the child but had little for the selfobject.[130] ❍

IN THE DECADES after World War II, the hallowed halls of the psychoanalytic institutes echoed the blaming of mother for psychopathology, amplifying its acoustics, drowning out, ever more thoroughly, mother's voice. True, mother was empowered, but seemingly only to do harm. She was not yet a person in her own right. By the late 1970s, it was still only Portnoy's complaint that mattered, not his mother's.

Reinventing the Myth: 1980–1990s

After decades of sensory deprivation with regard to their palates, Americans in the late twentieth century developed a taste for gourmet food. Cuisinarts proliferated in upscale kitchens, along with a myriad of other gadgets for food preparation. Americans had rediscovered the craft tradition in cooking. Nature and all things natural were back in business. That was the good news. It was also the bad news. For along with their elevated palates came elevated expectations for women, who were still doing 84 percent of the housework, despite media depictions of participant husbands.[131] Ironically, while our mothers may have preferred to cook from scratch but were obliged to pry open a can of Campbell's soup, heat, and serve, in order to appear up-to-date, modern mothers would be considered slack for serving up canned food, if not downright malevolent for foisting chemical additives on their unsuspecting families. Standards for domestic excellence have *increased* since the appearance of labor-saving devices, and the aggregate time we spend on housework has remained much the same as that of our grandmothers, but, unlike our grandmothers, almost 70 percent of today's educated mothers with young children are in the labor force, most of them full time. At the moment, mothers are trapped in a cultural time warp. They have changed, but mainstream expectations have not.[132]

Thirty years after Friedan, many women are on the edge of a huge generational divide, and they are experiencing vertigo. We are the first cohort of women, who, whether by choice or necessity, work outside the home. We are the first generation of women among whom many dare to be ambitious. But there is no getting around the fact that ambition is not a maternal trait. Motherhood and ambition are still largely seen as opposing forces. More strongly expressed, a lack of ambition — or a professed lack of ambition, a sacrificial willingness to set personal ambition aside — is still the virtuous proof of good mothering. For many women, perhaps most, motherhood versus personal ambition represents the heart of the feminine dilemma.

Part of the problem is that we still do not know what to make of nurturance. When nurturance is given out of love, inclination, or a sense of responsibility, the assumption persists that whatever form it takes — dropping one's work to minister to a sick child, baking a tray of chocolate chip cookies — the behavior expresses a woman's biological nature. But when nurturing acts are performed by men, they are interpreted as extraordinary. When nurturance is provided by housekeepers, child-care workers, or kindergarten teachers, its value in the marketplace is low.[133] So, in performing nurturance, in becoming stay-at-home mothers (should we have the luxury of that option), we fear that we are turning into our own mothers, complete with their low status, self-sacrifices, and frustrations. And it feels politically incorrect to talk about how much many women want to stay home, at least part time, when they finally do have children.

But if we are ambitious, or even if we work outside our homes out of necessity, we are afraid of what our distraction will do to our children. Publishing, advertising, psychology, and the child-rearing establishment still conspire to convince women that their careers are at home. Today's steady rise of divorce and a recessionary economy (mandating a dual paycheck for a middle-class lifestyle) collide with our failure to get flexible work hours, maternity and paternity leaves, federal financial support and uniform standards for day care, reliable help from men, and, finally, a rational child-care ideology that is sensitive to both children *and* mothers. So where does this leave us? Either childless or very mixed up.

During the 1980s and the early 1990s, the "problem with no name" splintered into a multitude of problems with many names: the "superwoman syndrome," "deadbeat dads," "the mommy track," "surrogate motherhood," "the single mother." It was, and is, a complex and paradoxical time. On the one hand, we have seen certain feminist advances. Professor Anita Hill's testimony before a Senate committee that Supreme Court nominee Clarence Thomas sexually harassed her in the workplace had the nation glued to its television sets and permanently raised people's consciousness about harassment, rape, date rape, and women's protection under the law; mothers saying goodbye to their children and going off to battle in the Persian Gulf would have been unthinkable only two decades before. On the other hand, we undoubtedly are in the midst of a conservative backlash against the women's movement and civil and human rights of all sorts. The 1989 Supreme Court *Webster* decision, which sharply restricted *Roe* v. *Wade* and access to abortions for the poor, was only the final chapter in a decade-long conservative agenda, marked by the failure of the Equal Rights Amendment and a general whittling away of reproductive rights. How quickly we have forgotten that before they gained the right to terminate pregnancy, women had to resort to back-street abortions in this century, and abandonment and infanticide in preceding ones. From the dunghills of ancient

Greece to the baby farms of Victorian England, mothers have employed desperate measures to deal with infants for whom they could not care. History has shown us that mother love does not flourish when motherhood is mandatory.

A wave of cultural nostalgia swept Ronald Reagan into the White House and precipitated a vigorous attempt to turn back the clock and reinstate the traditional family (odd, because Reagan himself had been divorced). Perhaps it was anxiety over the oil shortage, or the hostage crisis, or double-digit inflation, but people wanted to restore a lost "golden" past of family, flag, neighborhood, and work. Many of these sentiments were stoked by a New Right, pro-life constituency, like the Reverend Jerry Falwell's Moral Majority. With its newspapers and daily radio time, and conservative-funded think tanks such as the Heritage Foundation, it was able to dominate much of the media.[134]

More babies were born in 1989 than in any other year of U.S. history. Bill Cosby's successful television series epitomized the idealized values of the age and spawned a swarm of warm family comedies on TV. Also reflecting the national bubble of pronatalism was a glut of nesting films like *Baby Boom, She's Having a Baby,* and *For Keeps,* in which gurgling, picture-perfect newborns arrived to rescue selfish, work-oriented men and women from the evils of feminism and the Me decade.[135] The late eighties blockbuster movie *Fatal Attraction* tells it all: the betrayed mother here was so warm and appealing, she embodied everything that must be saved from the evil, predatory career woman. Hollywood's heart was clearly beating for, and in, the maternal bosom in the backlash years.

In the political realm, the "family" became a buzzword, invoked, paradoxically, by politicians in both parties. Indeed, Republicans and Democrats spent much of the long 1992 campaign arguing about which owned the family. They meant different things by the term, of course. Conservatives used the word as a synonym for "traditional social values," while liberals used it to evoke compassion as a way of defending social programs for a proliferation of family forms.[136] The parties were deeply divided over specific issues like abortion, condoms for teens, mother-centered vs. public approaches to child care, parental leave, and more. The result was national deadlock on these maternally related issues.

Amidst the gush of baby love, organized feminism has been

strangely tongue-tied about the proper place of motherhood in a woman's life.[137] Feminists in the 1970s were concerned with equal rights, access to professions, and abortion rather than with protective legislation for women with babies. But now feminists themselves were having babies, and they wanted high-quality, affordable day care. However, when Betty Friedan, in *The Second Stage,* voiced the concerns of these women, and accused earlier women's rights proponents of going too far in rejecting family life, she was regarded by some feminists as a traitor.[138] Friedan was seen as playing into the hands of the New Right, who conveniently seized on her portrayal of feminists as anti-family. Similarly skewered was Felice Schwartz for her article in the *Harvard Business Review* suggesting a revised work trajectory that would include time for children. Schwartz had intended to enhance employment opportunities for both "career-primary" individuals and those who wanted "career and family," but she was interpreted as advocating the equivalent of gender apartheid — a fast track for men and a mommy track for women. One cannot speak blithely of solutions for working mothers without invoking an image that can be read as women needing help . . . not a happy thought for a feminist. Today, issues like child care and family leave have moved higher up on the feminist agenda. Still, building a supportive culture within the women's movement for both mothers and non-mothers has proved a difficult task, just as it has in the world at large. No wonder today's mothers are confused.[139]

Advice from the child-rearing gurus has not helped their confusion. Ask three different child experts today's burning question — How long, if at all, should a parent stay at home with a new baby? — and you will get three different answers. Dr. T. Berry Brazelton, who as recently as 1986, when his three grown daughters convinced him otherwise, believed that a mother's place was in the home, has tempered his view with economic reality. He now puts the minimum at four months. (But even that may be out of reach for many mothers; the United States still has no coherent maternity leave policy.) Spock hedges. In the latest edition of *Baby and Child Care,* he talks about parents' "rights" to outside careers but also suggests that they are the ones best suited to mold their children during the first two or three years of life. One senses that, despite great political tact, Spock fundamentally believes that mom (or dad) should stay home and raise the kids. The Harvard psychologist Burton White, author of *The First Three Years,* dispenses altogether with political niceties. He is against substitute child care during baby's waking hours for two and a half years.[140]

Child experts might as well be saying, "Let them eat cake." They remain stubbornly unaware that fewer than 7 percent of American families are composed of a breadwinner father and a homemaker mother.[141] Perhaps because they formulated their ideas in a period when few people wanted adult women to leave their homes, they are unable to conceive that women now need or want to go out to work. But we have passed the point in history when a stay-at-home-mother role is possible for most women, even if it is desired.

Furthermore, we have seen that motherhood as a full-time job can be questioned from a historical and cross-cultural perspective. If an intense, one-on-one, exclusive mother relationship were, in fact, essential, we would have to conclude that except for a brief period in the fifties, most cultures, past and present, in its absence, produced damaged people. Wet-nursing was popular in Europe until the nineteenth century, suggesting that many mothers did not even see their own children for two years. Certainly preindustrial mothers were too busy cultivating or preparing food to lavish round-the-clock attention on their offspring. And even bourgeois Victorian mamas relegated the task to servants. Clearly child rearing does not have to be a full-time maternal job unless it is deemed so by cultural fiat (which is not to say that stay-at-home mothering is bad; just that it is not necessary).[142]

Moreover, child-expert advice flies in the face of two decades of exhaustive research, which has failed to demonstrate the negative consequences of day care. This is not for want of effort. The psychological research to date continually looks for bad outcomes from maternal employment and other-than-mother care *instead* of looking for bad outcomes from the lack of societal supports to mothers. In other words, the way psychologists have been framing their research questions reflects the culture's idealized myth of motherhood. So, while research has failed to demonstrate the deleterious effects of day care, it has also failed to demonstrate the deleterious effects of *no* day care — because it did not set out to find them. The unfortunate result is that our psychological research has inadvertently contributed to the maintenance of the status quo, instead of stimulating questions about social change and help for mothers. Indeed, we have no day-care policy in this country in part because there is no consensus as to what is best for children.[143]

Meanwhile, day care continually gets debunked in the media. Recently, Jay Belsky, a Pennsylvania State University psychologist, in a review of a number of studies, tentatively concluded that more than twenty hours a week of nonparental day care during the first year of a baby's life may put the child at risk for an "insecure" attachment to its mother. Soon Belsky found himself making the network rounds — "Today," "CBS Morning News," and "Donahue" — and fielding dozens of press calls. Conservative politicians sought out his testimony for the *Congressional Record*. Yet even Belsky emphasized the flaws in his methodology and strongly advised against overreaction. But his caution "fell on deaf ears."[144] Instead, the media have focused on the dark side of day care, like fires and sexual abuse. When a major University of New Hampshire study revealed that there was *no* epidemic of child abuse at day-care centers, it was buried in the classifieds in the *New York Times*.[145] Day care has been made to seem, by the media, more dangerous than families, where, of course, the great preponderance of child abuse occurs.

New heights of mother bashing by the media were reached in the 1980s and early 1990s, matching in reverse the ludicrousness of the syrupy odes to mothers in the Victorian period. Various unsympathetic, tell-all biographies, of which *Mommie Dearest* by Joan Crawford's daughter is the most famous, became commonplace. Bette Davis's daughter, B. D. Hyman, also composed one (*My Mother's Keeper*), as did Cheryl Crane, daughter of Lana Turner. The genre was not limited to disgruntled daughters. Writing about his mother, Rebecca West, in 1984, Anthony West was determined to show that "she was minded to do me what hurt she could, and she remained set in that determination as long as there was breath in the body to sustain her malice."[146] In the first half of 1993 alone, we heard grievances from a long list of bitter offspring, including the choreographer-dancer Twyla Tharp and the daughters of Marlene Dietrich, and the feminist Alva Myrdal. Rarely are the mothers around to defend themselves. But First Daughter Patti Davis did not wait for Nancy Reagan's demise to impugn her in a thinly veiled novel, an exquisite irony, in light of the Reagans' profamily stance.

Supporting the mother bashing of these celebrity children is a vast contemporary "pop" psychology and self-help industry that sees pathology in everything mothers do. The recovery-movement sage John Bradshaw, for example, whose *Homecoming: Reclaiming and Championing Your Inner Child* has been the basis of a twelve-part PBS series, encourages his clients — whom he calls "adult children" — to compile a catalogue of parental (usually meaning maternal) flaws and failures. Grievances may include "nonphysical abuse," and just about any lapse of parental understanding, support, and attentiveness. The mother who has never been abusive, addictive, obsessive compulsive, or "co-dependent" may nonetheless corrupt her children by failing to attend to their dependency needs. Or mother may inadvertently pass on a legacy of "original pain" if her own parents or grandparents practiced obsessive and compulsive behavior because they themselves had the misfortune to be children of alcoholics, co-dependents, drug addicts, overeaters, gamblers, or workaholics. According to Bradshaw, if you've had a mother, she did it wrong.[147]

Parent blaming takes on a special color in women's books and magazines, where the mother-daughter relationship in particular is portrayed as perpetually adversarial. Just a glance at some titles conveys the gist: "How to Get Over Your Mother," or *Mothers and Daughters: Loving and Letting Go*, or *Mother Love, Mother Hate: Breaking Dependent Love Patterns in Family Relationships*. This literature suggests that mothers, because of their own emptiness, cling to their daughters. But while mothers try to fuse, daughters try to disengage. If you believe these books, mothers and daughters are locked in eternal combat.[148] Interestingly, some of the better novelists of the decade also conveyed this conflict. Maxine Hong Kingston's Chinese mother, Jamaica Kincaid's black Caribbean mother, and Louise Erdrich's Native American mother all tried to hold back their daughters, to bind them to their old ways and to themselves. Though the novels are compelling and highly nuanced works, they are written from a daughter's perspective. One's sympathy is directed toward the child, not the mother.

Meanwhile, mothers were getting a mixed press, at best, in the movies, even as parenthood and children were being extolled. The films *Kramer vs. Kramer* (1981), *Three Men and a Baby* (1988), and *Raising Arizona* (1987) all valorized fathers . . . though there are no data showing that large numbers of fathers are, in fact, fulfilled by making child care the center of their lives. And toxic movie mothers kept on coming. In 1980, Mary Tyler Moore, the controlling, uptight mom in *Ordinary People,* caused much misery as she unfairly blamed her lovable surviving son for the death of his brother, her favorite. In the 1990s' Hollywood saga *Postcards From the Edge,* a former movie queen virtually causes her daughter's drug overdose, presumably by stubbornly refusing to surrender the spotlight to her and fade quietly away. The archetype monster mother in *Like Water for Chocolate,* the 1993 contribution to the genre, is mythic in her near-destruction of her Cinderella-like daughter.

Furthermore, mothers are now being usurped in the public consciousness by their fetuses. Whether this is a conspiracy perpetrated by the New Right, which may want to portray the fetus as human so as to portray women who have abortions as murderers, is questionable. Nevertheless, there has been a new centrality given to the embryo in everyday culture: witness the 1990 comedy *Look Who's Talking;* the famous Lennart Nilsson photos of life in the womb in *Life* (most recently in August 1990); the use of ultrasound wherein a mother can see her fetus on a TV monitor. To doctors, the fetus is now an "unborn patient," and a mother a mere "fetal container," the empty place in the sonogram. Suits for "fetal abuse" are on the rise. All these representations portray the fetus as an entity in its own right, subtly shifting attention and sympathy away from mother. Some feminists worry that mothers are being marginalized in favor of their embryos in a regressive step back to the nineteenth-century view of women, defining their lives solely by their reproductive capacity.

The burgeoning interest in the fetus was probably enhanced by the explosion of new reproductive technologies in the 1980s — artificial insemination, *in vitro* fertilization, embryo transfer, and surrogate mothering — all of which raised troubling questions. Do egg and sperm donors have the right to know their children? May a surrogate mother change her mind about releasing for adoption the child she bears? Does biological maternity constitute motherhood? Thanks to new technologies, parents can detect fetal anomalies early on and choose to abort a defective baby, or even one of a less preferred gender. Indeed, female fetuses are being disproportionately aborted at this very moment, a practice reminiscent of the female infanticide of ancient Greece. The ratio of newborn children in China, for example, has reached 118.5 males for every 100 females. According to a recent *New York Times* article, as the ultrasound machine became more popular in China, and authorities began a tough crackdown on unauthorized pregnancies, the ratio became increasingly unbalanced in favor of boys. Last year, more than 12 percent of all female fetuses were aborted or otherwise unaccounted for.[149] Does this imply that mother love is operative only when a child is unblemished or the gender of choice? The fragmenting of the female sexual and reproductive body, through implantation or surrogacy, or through the removal of eggs, is a breaking-up of that object — Mom — which has been made to symbolize so much of the social order for so long. All this has triggered deep cultural anxiety.

Americans are transfixed by the custody battles played out before their eyes in the media, seemingly on a weekly basis. The feelings aroused are unprocessed and veer wildly. Mainstream society, usually the great conservator and romanticizer of fecundity, has been overwhelmingly on the side of *nonbiological* ties. When fourteen-year-old Kimberly Mays, swapped at birth, went to court in the summer of 1993 to divorce her genetic parents, Ernest and Regina Twigg, the public sympathized with Kimberly and argued that she and her legal father should be free from interference by her biological parents. In the same summer, the country witnessed with horror a tearful two-and-a-half-year-old Jessica DeBoers being forcibly transferred from her adoptive home to her biological parents. Yet feminists, who ordinarily bristle at the idea that "biology is destiny" and the sentimentalization of motherhood, paradoxically came out in support of surrogate mothers, that is, biological mothers, in child-custody battles with adoptive mothers. They feared that society's easy acceptance of surrogacy would make tolerable the leasing of women's uteruses, and would result in the exploitation of Third World women as wombs and the trivialization of women as people. These questions about maternity challenge everyone's cherished ideals, and we are a long way from a consensus. ❍

A RECENT *New York Times* article was entitled "It's a Boy! It's a Girl! It's Time to Shop."[150] Upscale 1990s' mothers continue to convert their parental anxiety into fevered consumerism. Today's baby invariably has an assortment of black-and-white toys, the all-important downward-staring mobile (to stimulate baby's brain), the *clear* rattle with (don't laugh) a Play and Learning TM (Guide) to instruct parents in its use, lots of Raffi records. The latest boom is magazines for toddlers.

These products did not exist twelve years ago when I was in the trenches of toddler-raising, nor, I suspect, will they persist beyond the next twelve. Perhaps as you read this they will already have gone the way of the hula hoop. If so, it is a fitting demise, their evanescence being a measure of their value. At best, these products do nothing more than shore up mom and dad's confidence. At worst, they are examples of status-seeking and narcissistic self-absorption.

There is a painful irony in educated parents' lavish outpouring of attention on their children. For while a certain minority of young children are receiving an abundance (arguably an overabundance) of gifts and training, it is becoming apparent that a growing number of American children live below the poverty line. One in eight actually goes hungry. Reports of child abuse and neglect have increased by 40 percent since 1985.[151] A nation filled with loving parents has somehow come to overlook crumbling schools, poor child health care, and deadly addiction. Every day, for example, 135,000 American children bring guns to school.[152] Where are their guardians?

Like the Victorians, we seem to be obsessed with our own children and to ignore everyone else's. The same parents who are in a frenzy about getting their child into the "right" kindergarten oppose child-care legislation. If we are to feel guilt about our performance as parents, let us derive that guilt from an appropriate source — our treatment of the nation's poor children. A more democratic allocation of our money, time, and concern across the population of children (and not just our own) would probably benefit everyone.

On the night in 1992 when Murphy Brown became an unwed mother, she gave birth to more than a baby. Thirty-four million Americans tuned in and CBS posted a 35 percent share of the audience. Despite Vice President Quayle's debunking, the show did not stir up significant grassroots protest nor lose any of its advertisers. By any standard, Murphy Brown — she who would have been stoned in Babylonia, or burned at the stake in early modern Europe — was a hit at the box office.[153] Brown had proudly and joyously borne an illegitimate baby, and the public obviously shared her maternal bliss. Her defiant act liberated women from the tyranny of mainstream domestic expectations, expectations that had long ceased to reflect reality, given the number of single mothers in this country. Of course, if Brown had been on welfare she would have been regarded as a "parasite," and if this were her second baby, she would have been seen as a "breeder," that is, unless she had been left by a man, in which case she would be a victim.[154] Nevertheless, Brown's insouciant motherhood has signaled a sea change in the unconscious sexism that once pervaded everyday life. She has forged new ways for women to mother.

We are living in a moment when women's identities are expanding. How else can we interpret the fact that women are marrying later, using contraceptives and abortion, having fewer children, and entering the labor force in ever greater percentages?[155] Despite a concerted effort to amplify a conservative backlash in public sentiment, the New Right coalition was unable to reverse the social and cultural transformations that had already taken place: women's new roles in the workplace; freer sexuality (despite AIDS); the mobilization of a powerful prochoice movement; the election of a president with a "liberated" wife; and the appointment of a mother with feminist sympathies to the Supreme Court.[156]

As new female icons Murphy Brown, Hillary Rodham Clinton, and Ruth Bader Ginsburg are freeing women to embrace formerly devalued ways of mothering, psychologists are finally beginning to exonerate women from blame for all psychopathology. Among a new generation of "baby watchers" and research-oriented psychoanalysts, it is now commonly thought that neurosis results not from a "bad" mother or a "bad" child, but from a "bad" match. The baby is now seen as a participant in, an activator of the mother-child dialogue, not simply a recipient. The bonding process is interactional.[157] Many recent studies suggest that the infant, even at birth, is a complex and capable young organism, differentially responsive to stimuli, and already anchored to reality.[158] But these data have not yet trickled down to all the psychology consulting rooms of America, and certainly not to those of the practitioners of "pop" psychology. Scientific information is slow to catch up with popular myth, particularly when it contradicts a cherished bias.

Meanwhile, a cohort of feminist thinkers is attempting to reformulate psychoanalytic explanations for gender difference and the urge to mother. The most famous is Nancy Chodorow, who, though lauded mostly outside psychoanalytic circles, is increasingly esteemed within. In her book *The Reproduction of Mothering,* Chodorow focuses on the problem of why women in nearly all societies, rather than men, are the primary caretakers of children. Her answer: in earliest childhood, the relations between a girl and her mother are, in mostly unconscious ways, different from those of a boy and his mother. In effect, girls and boys have different childhoods. Girls learn nurturance by virtue of their identification with their mothers; boys, in contrast, disidentify. Hence, women's mothering reproduces the existing division of labor. Chodorow says that fathers must take over half the parenting if the cycle is not to be repeated. The psychoanalyst Jessica Benjamin adds that both mothers and fathers should encourage their daughters' autonomy and sense of self.

To be sure, there are problems in Chodorow's and Benjamin's theorizing. Both, like their object-relations forebears, inadvertently blame mothers as they minimize the child's unconscious. Nevertheless, feminist psychoanalysts, however incomplete their speculations may be, have rightly emphasized the importance of identification and caretaking as determinants of the wish to have a baby. And in so doing, they have restored pre-Oedipal mother to her proper place in the formation of her child's personality. This thinking is a long way from the early psychoanalytic idea that a woman wanted a baby as a consolation prize for not having a penis! ❍

AT LONG LAST mothers have been allowed a voice in literature, and unlike their counterparts a decade earlier, they have an audience. We are beginning to see a new kind of mother in novels — the mentor, the one who guides her children to independent adulthood. She is no angel, however. She makes mistakes; she is not wholly fulfilled by her experience; she is ambivalent about her children. In sum, she is real. We can find her in Mary Gordon's *Men and Angels* and Gail Godwin's *A Mother and Two Daughters*. And she is all over the novels of the 1993 Nobel Prize winner Toni Morrison. In *Beloved,* for example, the black mother Sethe murders her child. Yet Morrison has the reader understand that the murder is an act not of barbarism, but of mother love — Sethe is protecting her daughter from slavery. Morrison avoids a simplistic maternal characterization. She pays careful attention to the maternal perspective. She does not blame Sethe, but applauds her endurance. Sethe is a latter-day Neolithic goddess. She is no one's bad mother. ❍

THIRTY THOUSAND YEARS after her birth, mother is leaving the realm of mythology and is joining the human race or, more accurately, rejoining it after the patriarchal takeover. It's about time.

For thousands of years, because of her awesome ability to spew forth a child, mother has been feared and revered. She has been the subject of taboos and witch hunts, mandatory pregnancy and confinement in a separate sphere. She has endured appalling insults and perpetual marginalization. She has also been the subject of glorious painting, chivalry, and idealization. Through it all, she has rarely been consulted. She is an object, not a subject.

As the primary caretaker of children during most of history, she has been variously obliged to nurse and not to nurse; to facilitate free expression and to suppress it; to cuddle and to avoid contact. During the Middle Ages, she might have overlaid her child in bed; in the eighteenth century she might have exiled the infant to a wet nurse in the country; in the late twentieth century she is probably cognitively stimulating *ad infinitum*. But by and large, when supported by her social milieu, she seems to have loved her babies.

Over the centuries, despite wild variations in child care, the incidence of mental illness among children, as best we can determine, seems to have been fairly constant. Whether children were empathized with or were the subject of Watson's behaviorism, whether they were sternly disciplined or spoiled, they managed to thrive. Apparently ordinary mothering does not cause psychological problems.

All this casts serious doubt on the validity of our current image of ideal mother. Perhaps she needn't be all-empathic, after all. Perhaps she can be personally ambitious without damaging her child. Perhaps she does not have unlimited power in the shaping of her offspring. Good mothering, history reminds us, is a cultural invention — something that is man-made, not a lawful force of nature.

As such, it is subject to human intervention. When mothers are able to see through the mythology, they may see that their "failures" stem not necessarily from personal defects, but from the way society is structured. They may stop blaming themselves. When mothers understand the biases inherent in our current conception of good mothering, they may learn to select among the rules and begin to create their own philosophy of child rearing, one that works for them and their children.

By unmasking the myths of motherhood, we can enlarge the possibility for taking control — through education, public policy, psychotherapy, even moral preachment — to achieve the climate we desire. In such a family climate, there would be personal sacrifice for a common good, but it would not be mother doing all of the sacrificing. It would be shared sacrifice. Such a family would not promote the self-fulfillment of any *one* member at the expense of another. At the societal level, child rearing would not be dismissed as an individual mother's problem, but one in which nurturance and the well-being of *all* children are a transcendent public priority. This society would accept changes in family structure as inevitable (and not necessarily bad) and would devise for them new forms of public and private support. I hope for a society that will tolerate and encourage a diversity of mothering styles and cohabiting groups. I hope for a society in which both women and men have the power of the world and the nurturant experience. I hope for a society that will, finally, listen to Mrs. Portnoy's complaint. As a mother, she has something to say.

ACKNOWLEDGMENTS

NOTES

BIBLIOGRAPHY

INDEX

ACKNOWLEDGMENTS

No one should have to live with a person who is writing a book. For this, I want to thank my daughter and husband, who, in the midst of it all, managed to thrive. If I were not Sally Thurer's mother, this book would not have been written, and, given our glorious, complicated relationship and her spunk, I suspect she has a book of her own in her, as well. To Bob Thurer, my loving companion in life, whose irrepressible calm, good sense, and belief in me have kept me from sinking into the abyss of self-doubt all these years, I am deeply grateful. His commitment to shared parenting has been indispensable. If in these pages I have occasionally taken an irreverent attitude toward the traditional family, it was not sparked by any real grievances with my own, for which my love is boundless.

I hail from a good mother, Lilly Lehrer, and a father, Sidney Lehrer (also a good mother), whose affectionate care animates me even today. I am enormously grateful to them, and to Gary Lehrer for his brotherly pride in my work, and to my supportive extended family. I owe special appreciation to Olibh Murphy, who has been a good mother to both our daughter and me. Olibh has been enormously protective of my need for time to work, and without her sensitivity I would not have been able to continue. I am deeply grateful to Leston Havens, who inspired — no, incited — me to write. His sensitivity, patience, and brilliant, quirky mind embody the ideal of psychoanalysis.

I have been fortunate to work in a community at Boston University that is an oasis of good values and humanity. One could not invent a more empathic or enthusiastic department chairman than

Arthur Dell Orto, who is always there when I need him. I am indebted, also, to Ken Paruti, our department coordinator, whose irreverent humor and concrete help kept me going, and to my colleagues in the Department of Rehabilitation Counseling, who have uncomplainingly done more than their share when I have been unavailable because of my involvement in this project.

I owe particular thanks to Ken Shefsiek for showing much grace under pressure as he expertly typed my manuscript. His unfailingly cheerful nature, reasonableness, and dependability helped assuage the anxieties of authorship. My thanks also to Susan Cannata, Ken's predecessor, and Nan Borod, who compiled my bibliography, for their assistance and critical intelligence.

I am grateful to my patients, from whom I have learned so much, and who managed to put up with the intrusive presence of this book in their treatment. Thanks are also due to my bright, creative, good friends — Kathleen Miller, Beth Wharff, and Susan Kay — a veritable Greek chorus of positive reinforcement. Over the years, I have constantly bounced my ideas off them, and their penetrating comments have been invaluable. And to Terry Hill, thanks especially for the steady supply of wit and willingness to tolerate my distractedness during the long gestation of these pages. Her incisive input and encouragement meant a great deal.

This book grew out of a paper submitted to the Advanced Training Program in Psychoanalytic Psychotherapy at the Boston Psychoanalytic Society and Institute (BPSI), to which I am grateful for creating an intellectually stimulating atmosphere in which it was possible to ask peculiar questions. Appreciation is owed my preceptors at BPSI, Sherry Turkle and Howard Levine, for their critical reading of my original paper, and to Ann Menashi, the librarian at BPSI, for her energetic assistance in procuring materials.

Above all, I thank my agent Doe Coover for "discovering" me; my editor, Betsy Lerner; copyeditor Frances Apt; the jacket illustrator, Amy Guip; and photographer Lorin Klaris.

If this book appears tall, it is because it stands on the shoulders of giants, the writings of others whose ideas helped shape the story I tell — Adrienne Rich, Gerda Lerner, Barbara Ehrenreich and Deirdre English, Arlene Skolnick, Christina Hardyment, John Sommerville, Lawrence Stone, and many others. To them, I am grateful. In the end, of course, the synthesis is my own. The one patient referred to in the text is a composite of three, and has been disguised in such a way as to be unidentifiable.

The portrait I have painted of motherhood is ultimately Impressionistic and I have used a broad brush. I do not mean to project my particular interpretation of events as the final word. I offer this book as a step toward awareness in the hope that one day finer strokes will be added. As I was writing I was painfully conscious of my own white, Western, middle-class cultural perspective — and of the similar bias of most of the available sources. Certainly welfare mothers, male mothers, immigrant mothers, lesbian mothers, working-class mothers, black, Chicana, and Native American mothers, and others, all deserve their own interpreters and, it is hoped, at some point will have them.

NOTES

Introduction

1. Sommerville, 1982, 1990, p. 6.
2. Ruddick, 1989, pp. 29–31.
3. Ibid., p. 30.
4. Ehrenreich and English, 1979, ch. 7.
5. Demos, 1986, p. 64.
6. Clarke and Clarke, 1976, p. ix.
7. Weiss, 1977.
8. Spock, 1945, 1968, 1976.
9. Weiss, 1977.
10. Cowan, 1983, p. 126.
11. Coontz, 1991, p. 215.
12. Davis, 1988.
13. Polatnick in Treblicot (ed.), 1983, pp. 21–41.
14. Gilbert and Gubar, 1979, 1984, p. 38; Barzilai, 1990.
15. Heilbrun, 1990, p. 15.
16. Smith, 1990, p. 32.
17. Barron, James, and Mary Tabor, "17 Killed and Life Is Searched for Clues," *New York Times,* August 4, 1991.
18. Smith, 1990, p. 32.
19. Dally, 1983, p. 19.
20. Anderson and Zinsser, 1988, v. 2, p. 247.
21. Boswell, 1988, p. 418; Klapisch-Zuber, 1985, p. 1357; Golden, 1981; French in Grant, 1988, 1989, p. 1357.
22. Badinter, 1980, p. x; Sussman, 1982, p. 20.
23. Balint, 1949.

1. Mothering — The Old-Fashioned Way

1. 50,000 B.C. to 10,000 B.C., also known as the Paleolithic. This is the earliest phase of human history. The story of Abraham (of the Old Testament) is believed to have occurred no later than 1800 B.C. Writing was developed about 3000 B.C.
2. Patriarchy refers to rule by the father in both family and society. Matriarchy refers to rule by mothers. To date, matriarchy has not been found in any culture, at any time. By contrast, matriliny, which refers to descent (kin, birth, inheritance) reckoned through the female rather than the male line, is thought to characterize numerous cultures, notably, in prehistory. Matrilocality, wherein the husband moves into the wife's clan, has also been found. But matriliny and matrilocality are not matriarchy. In both cases, the woman's brother, not her husband, wields power — and he is a man.
3. Miles, R., 1989, p. 27.
4. Sjoo and Mor, 1987, p. 8.
5. Ehrenberg, 1989, p. 11.
6. Miles, R., 1989, p. 7.
7. Boulding, 1976, p. 11.
8. Leacock, 1977.
9. The importance of the container has been given short shrift. One need only pause for a second to appreciate the monumental significance of the bag to civilization, without which we would be utterly immobilized. Just as the container has been denigrated or overlooked, so has the mother, which it has come to symbolize.
10. Tanner and Zihlman, 1981; Ehrenberg, 1989, p. 66.
11. Lee and Devore, 1968; Turnbull, 1968.
12. Ehrenberg, 1989, p. 62.
13. Davies, 1981, 1990, p. 32; Shackley, 1980, p. 49.
14. Eisler, 1987, p. 7; Gadon, 1989, p. xii.
15. Ehrenberg, 1989, p. 66; Barstow, 1983, p. 7.
16. The Neolithic followed the Paleolithic. The period in which mother-child figures were produced was around 6000 to 5000 B.C.
17. Sjoo and Mor, 1987, p. 71.
18. Gadon, 1989, pp. 6, 10; Eisler, 1987, p. 4; Miles, R., 1989, p. 21.
19. Miles, R., 1989, p. 27.
20. Roughly 10,000 to 5000 B.C.
21. Most scholars who argue for female-centered religion place it in the Paleolithic, the Neolithic (10,000 to 5000 B.C.) as well as the Choleolithic (5000–3000 B.C.) and Bronze Ages (3000 to 1200 B.C.) in the area that Marija Gimbutas has designated Old Europe (Southeast Europe). Others also include the prehistoric periods of the Ancient Near Eastern cultures (Egypt, Sumeria, and Palestine), while others stretch it to cover

the historical period until the triumph of Christianity in A.D. 500.

22. See, for example: Eisler, 1988; Gimbutas, 1982; Gadon, 1989; Sjoo and Mor, 1987. Past celebrants include Bachofen and 1861, tr. 1967; Briffault, 1931, tr. 1969; Diner, 1965; Davis, 1971.
23. Plant cultivators, who used simple techniques like slash-and-burn, and hand tools, like the hoe. Horticulture is thought to have been invented and carried out by women, aided by children.
24. High-yield plant cultivators, who make use of the plough, traction animals, and irrigation. Agriculture is thought to have been carried out by males, with auxiliary tasks assigned to women and children.
25. Eisler, 1987, p. 10.
26. For example, de Riencourt, 1974; Fisher, 1979; and Miles, R., 1989.
27. Lerner, 1986, p. 46.
28. Gimbutas, 1982, p. 11.
29. Excavated by James Mellaart, a British archeologist, in 1961–63.
30. 3000 to 1500 B.C. (the Bronze Age).
31. Sjoo and Mor, 1987, p. 71.
32. Boulding, 1976, p. 14; Ehrenberg, 1989, p. 89; Gordon, 1976, p. 4; Kolata, 1974.
33. Boulding, 1976, p. 117.
34. For example: Boulding, 1976; Ehrenberg, 1989; Gimbutas, 1982; Mellaart, 1967; Gadon, 1989; Barstow, 1983; Rohrlich-Leavitt, 1977.
35. Boulding, 1976, p. 139. This contradicts Jensen, 1963, pp. 162–206, who feels that human sacrifice increased among crop cultivators.
36. Gadon, 1989, p. 28.
37. Leacock, 1977; Fromm, 1973, p. 155.
38. Lerner, 1986, p. 148; Eisler, 1987, pp. 18–19.
39. An area in Southeastern Europe where Neolithic civilization existed. It was named "Old Europe" by Marija Gimbutas, its most important archeologist.
40. Ortner, 1974, p. 45.
41. Dinnerstein, 1976, p. 108.
42. Eisler, 1987, p. 22; Stone, M., 1976, p. 199.
43. Erikson, 1968.
44. Xenophon, *The Economist,* tr. 1867, p. 42.
45. Joseph Campbell, the mythologist, wrote about this in *Hero with a Thousand Faces.*
46. Rabuzzi, 1988, p. 95.
47. Rich, 1976, 1986, p. 96; Neumann, 1955.
48. Gadon, 1989, p. 226.
49. Davis, 1971, p. 35.
50. Rich, 1976, 1986, p. 91.

2. History Begins, Herstory Ends

1. Corresponding loosely to the Bronze and Iron Ages.
2. Boulding, 1976, p. 241.
3. Lerner, 1986, p. 8.
4. Miles, R., 1989, p. xiii.
5. Miles, R., 1989, p. xiii.
6. Chodorow, 1978; Miller, J. B., 1976; Benjamin, 1988.
7. Rich, 1976, 1986, p. 120.
8. Rich, 1976, 1986, p. 100; Davis, E., 1971, p. 97; Miles, R., 1989, p. 40.
9. Olivier, 1989, p. 115.
10. Lerner, 1986, p. 145.
11. Miles, R., 1989, p. 26.
12. Lerner, 1986, p. 127; Campbell, 1972, p. 55.
13. Lévi-Strauss, 1969, p. 481; Gimbutas in Spretnak, 1982; Boulding, 1976, pp. 191–92; Kingsley, 1989, p. xiii.
14. Anderson and Zinsser, 1988, p. 12.
15. Dinnerstein is the intellectual heir of Simone de Beauvoir, 1952; Margaret Mead, 1949; and H. R. Hays, 1964; all of whom documented men's fear and hatred of women.
16. Dinnerstein, 1976, p. 67.
17. Klein, 1932, 1960, p. 338.
18. I read of a recent California group that resurrected this rite and offered a recipe for placenta stew (Kitzinger, 1978, p. 222.
19. Miles, R., 1989, p. 81; Olivier, 1989, p. 15.
20. de Beauvoir, 1952, p. 169; Horney, 1926, 1974, pp. 171–86; Montagu, 1953, p. 35.
21. Davis, E., 1971, p. 98; Kittay in Treblicot, 1983, p. 110.
22. Kittay in Treblicot, 1983, p. 113; Grahn, 1982, p. 274.
23. Fildes, 1986, p. 6; Kramer, S. N., 1959.
24. Fildes, 1986, p. 6.
25. Harrison, R. K., 1970, pp. 45, 51; Stone, M., 1976, p. 222.
26. Sommerville, 1982, 1990, p. 15.
27. Kramer, S. N., 1959, pp. 13–14.
28. Rohrlich-Leavitt, 1977, p. 54.
29. Sommerville, 1982, 1990, pp. 18–19.
30. Boulding, 1976, p. 228.
31. As quoted in Breiner, 1990, p. 15.
32. Fildes, 1986, p. 5; Sommerville, 1982, 1990, p. 18; Breiner, 1990, p. 16.
33. Breiner, 1990, p. 20.
34. Sommerville, 1982, 1990, p. 19.
35. Breiner, 1990, pp. 31, 32; Bleeker in Olson, 1990, p. 29.
36. Davis, E. B., 1971, p. 138; Boulding, 1976, p. 231; Stone, M., 1976, p. 37.

37. Stone, 1976, p. 38.
38. Fildes, 1986, p. 8.
39. Soren et al., 1990, pp. 25, 135.
40. For example, Merlin Stone (p. 188 and Elise Boulding (pp. 236–38).
41. Meyers, 1988, p. 52.
42. Soren et al., 1990, p. 42; Massa, 1977.
43. Stager and Wolff, 1984.
44. William Albright (p. 298); Alberto Green (p. 182); Paul Mosca (in entirety); Stager and Wolff, 1984.
45. Grant, 1989, p. 25.
46. For example, Raphael Patai, Steve Davies, and Eliner Gadon, pp. 167–89. The timing for the "syncretism" is the latter part of the second millennium B.C., roughly contemporaneous with the Babylonian conquest of Sumeria and the New Kingdom in Egypt.
47. As quoted in Lerner, 1986, p. 129.
48. Though the Hebrew God is not personified, He is constantly referred to as "He." The Bible and Talmud consistently use male anthropomorphisms; God is a "Man of War," a "Hero," "Lord of Hosts," "King," "Master of the Universe," etc. (Patai, 1967, p. 22.)
49. For example, Carol Meyers, 1988; Gerda Lerner, 1986.
50. Also known as the Old Testament (to be distinguished from the New Testament, both of which constitute the Christian Bible). The Hebrew Bible contains the Five Books of Moses (including the Ten Commandments), the Prophets, and the Writings.
51. Fildes, 1986, p. 3.
52. Job 39:14–16; Proverbs 17:6; Psalms 127:3–5; Jeremiah 32:35; Leviticus 20:25; II Samuel 21:8–14; II Kings 4:18–20; I Kings 3:16–27.
53. Sommerville, 1982, 1990, p. 33; de Vaux, 1961, p. 49; Sommerville, 1982, 1990, p. 35.
54. Genesis 30:1, 16:2, 30:3, 9; Carmody, 1979, p. 95.
55. de Riencourt, 1974, p. 88.
56. Isaiah 49:15, 66:13.
57. For example, Breiner, 1990, p. 88; Otwell, 1977; Trible, 1978; Meyers, 1988.
58. Genesis 2:18, 24; Proverbs 31:10–31.
59. de Vaux, 1961, p. 40; Exodus 20:17; de Riencourt, 1974, p. 87.
60. For example, Lerner, 1986, pp. 167–79; Carmody, 1979, pp. 92–97.
61. For example, Phyllis Bird (in Ruether, 1974, pp. 41–88); Breiner, 1990, pp. 70–98.
62. Ruth 4:11; Johnson, P., 1987, p. 46.
63. Johnson, P., 1987, p. 15.
64. Deuteronomy 22:13–21; Johnson, P., 1987, p. 36.
65. de Riencourt, 1974, p. 88.

3. The Sublime and the Ridiculous: Classical Mom

1. Golden, 1981; French in Grant, et al., 1988, 1989, p. 1357; Breiner, 1990, p. 50.
2. Cantarella, 1987, p. 44; Garland, 1985, p. 81; Pomeroy, 1983, p. 135.
3. See Edward Gibbon writing, in the late eighteenth century, *The Decline and Fall of the Roman Empire,* and Lecky a century later.
4. There were, however, outbreaks of disease, and a serious outbreak in the 420s B.C.
5. deMause, 1974, p. 10.
6. M. I. Finley, Philippe Ariès, Ivy Pinchbeck, Margaret Hewitt, Edward Shorter, Lawrence Stone.
7. Pollock, 1983, p. 25.
8. Valerie French, Eva Keuls.
9. Engels, 1980.
10. Golden, 1981; Harris, 1982.
11. Most notably John Boswell's *The Kindness of Strangers* (1988), though this is about a later period.
12. Keuls, 1985, p. 146.
13. Golden, 1981; Pomeroy, 1983.
14. Lefkowitz, 1991, p. 23; Keuls, 1985, p. 1.
15. Keuls, 1985, pp. 82–86, 114–17, 147; Pomeroy, 1975, pp. 57, 79–82, 87; Henderson, 1988, p. 1249.
16. Lefkowitz and Fant, 1982, p. 18.
17. Henderson, 1988, p. 1252; Golden, 1990, p. 49.
18. There is abundant feminist scholarship that asserts that women flourished within their spheres of influence (the *oikos,* as *hetairai*) (Lefkowitz, 1986, pp. 37–39; Boulding, 1976, pp. 258–63). But the fact remains that they were never empowered in any direct political, economic, or social area.
19. Pomeroy, 1975, p. 87; Dover, 1978; Dover, 1988; Massey, 1988, p. 5.
20. Downing, 1990, pp. 56–57.
21. Hermann, 1989, p. 56.
22. Cantarella, 1987, p. 52; Keuls, 1985, p. 144.
23. Aeschylus, *Eumenides* (fifth century B.C.).
24. Keuls, 1985, p. 332.
25. Plato, *Republic,* 8.549c–555c.
26. This was the conclusion of both Mark Golden (*Children and Childhood in Classical Athens,* 1990) and Valerie French in "Birth control, childbirth and early childhood" in *Civilization of the Ancient Mediterranean* (1988).
27. Golden, 1990, p. 89; Garland, 1985, p. 84; Garland, 1990, p. 144.
28. Zahn, 1970, pp. 23–25; French in Hawes and Hiner, 1991, p. 16.
29. Garland, 1990, p. 153; Tobey, 1991, p. 64; Fildes, 1986, p. 22.
30. French in Grant, 1988, 1989, p. 1359; Sommerville, 1982, 1990, p. 28; Garland, 1990, p. 107.

31. Boswell, 1988, p. 37n.
32. French in Grant, 1988, 1989, p. 1361; Golden, 1990, p. 91; Still, 1931, pp. 6–31.
33. Golden, 1990, p. 92.
34. This is the view of Garland, 1990; Breiner, 1990; Sommerville, 1982, 1990; Pomeroy, 1975; deMause, 1974.
35. Golden, 1990, p. 83.
36. Maternal mortality may have been as high as 2.5 percent (French in Grant, 1988, p. 135), though Garland, 1990, p. 65, implies that it may have been much higher.
37. Massey, 1988, p. 6.
38. Thirty to forty percent died within one year (Golden, 1990, p. 83).
39. Keuls, 1985, p. 144.
40. Garland, 1990, p. 98.
41. Ibid., p. 100.
42. Dick, 1987, p. 23.
43. Fildes, 1986, p. 211.
44. Fildes, 1988, p. 192.
45. Coote, 1983; Kahr, 1991; Breiner, 1990, p. 49.
46. Sommerville, 1982, 1990, p. 32.
47. Breiner, 1990, p. 45.
48. The power of the father was absolute within the family. He could punish any member in any way he deemed reasonable.
49. Cantarella, 1987, p. 159; Pomeroy, 1975, p. 96.
50. Suzanne Dixon, 1988; Paul Veyne, 1987; Thomas Wiedemann, 1989; and John Evans, 1991.
51. Kahr, 1991.
52. Cantarella, 1987, p. 130.

4. Sacred and Profane Callings: Medieval Mom

1. Carroll, 1986, p. xii.
2. Warner, 1976, p. 192.
3. Most notably Philippe Ariès, Lawrence Stone, Edward Shorter, Jean-Louis Flandrin, and Lloyd deMause. Also Barbara Kellum, Emily Coleman, Zefira Rokeah, R. Trexler, and others.
4. Demos, 1986, p. 75.
5. Readers may note that contemporary historians of the classical period also used this argument, but they derived their thinking from Ariès.
6. Tuchman, 1978, p. 50.
7. Dally, 1983, p. 29.
8. Ariès, 1962, p. 33.
9. In virtually all parts of Europe in the Middle Ages, the father's illegitimate children were part of the household (Nicholas in Hawes and Hiner, 1991, p. 38).

10. Goode, 1963.
11. Most notably Edward Shorter, Lawrence Stone, Randolph Trumbach, and Alan MacFarlane.
12. Shorter, 1975, chapter 5; deMause, 1974, pp. 1, 51.
13. Rybczynski, 1986, p. 28.
14. Luepnitz, 1988, p. 120.
15. Stone, 1977, p. 6; Shorter, 1975, pp. 218–19.
16. Stone, 1977, p. 7; Flandrin, 1979.
17. Stone, 1977, p. 56.
18. Ibid., pp. 105–106; Ariès, 1982, pp. 82, 90.
19. Shorter, 1975, p. 168; Trumbach, 1978, p. 247; MacFarlane, 1986, p. 664.
20. Most notably Shulamith Shahar, David Herlihy, Barbara Hanawalt, Linda Pollock, Ralph A. Houlbrooke, Peter Laslett, Richard Smith, John Hajnal.
21. See Ilene Forsyth for examples from the Carolingian, Ottoman, and Romanesque periods.
22. Boswell, 1988, p. 38.
23. Mount, 1982, pp. 118–19.
24. As quoted in Shahar, 1990, p. 152.
25. David Herlihy (1985) and Richard Smith (1979).
26. Hareven, 1991, p. 98.
27. Tuchman, 1978, p. xvii; Rybczynski, 1986, p. 33; Huizenga, 1924, p. 18.
28. King, 1991, p. 11; Boswell, 1988; Ibid., p. 432.
29. Sommerville, 1982, 1990, p. 61.
30. Tucker, 1974, p. 231; Matthew 19:14.
31. Sommerville, 1982, 1990, p. 58.
32. Ibid., pp. 60–61.
33. Tuchman, 1978, p. 49.
34. Josephus's *Wars of the Jews* in Greek; a work by the fifth-century Roman Hegesippus; the *Josippon* in the tenth century; Boccaccio's *Lives of Famous Men and Women;* a nineteenth-century painting by Wiertz, *Hunger, Madness, and Crime* (taken from Shahar, 1990, p. 138).
35. Atkinson, 1991, p. 136.
36. Baron, 1979–1980.
37. Atkinson, 1991, p. 164.
38. Miles, R., 1989, p. 99.
39. Ibid., p. 61.
40. Atkinson, 1991, p. 37.
41. Lederer, 1968, pp. 163, 178.
42. Herlihy, 1985, p. 144; Reuther, 1977, p. 38; Atkinson, 1991, p. 17.
43. Rogers, 1966, p. 19; McLaren, 1990, pp. 80–81.
44. Atkinson, 1991, chap. 3.
45. Herlihy, 1985, p. 122; Ruether, 1977, p. 44; Bynum, 1982, pp. 111–12; Atkinson, 1991, pp. 23–64, 240.

46. *Time,* Dec. 30, 1991, p. 66.
47. Bynum, 1982, p. 145.
48. Atkinson, 1991, p. 144.
49. Matter in Olson, 1990, p. 92.
50. Ibid., p. 91.
51. Miles, R., 1989, p. 74.
52. Carroll, 1986, p. 59.
53. Miles, M., in Suleiman, 1985, 1986, p. 202; Ross in deMause, 1974, p. 199; Kraus, 1967, pp. 41–62.
54. Reuther, 1977, p. 72.
55. Clark, 1969, p. 65.
56. Kristeva in Suleiman, p. 106.
57. A short list of famous misogynist works of the medieval period:

    Satire — John of Salisbury's *Policratus*

    — Walter Map's *De nugis curialim* (especially the letter of Valerius to Rufinum)

    — Andreas Capellanus's *Art of Courtly Love* (Book III)

    — *Quinze joies de mariage*

    — *Lamentations de Matheolus*

    the subgenre of debate poems

    the *fabliaux*

    the animal fable

    the comic theater or farce

    the *chantefable Aucassin et Nicolette*

    Adam de Halle's *Jeu de la feuilée*

    (taken from Bloch, 1991, p. 7). Also see Gies and Gies, 1978, p. 37.
58. As quoted in de Riencourt, 1974, p. 220.
59. Ibid., p. 216; Miles, M., in Suleiman, 1985, 1986, p. 201; Clark, 1969, p. 58.
60. de Riencourt, 1974, p. 216; deMause, 1974, pp. 20–21.
61. Miles, M., in Suleiman, 1985, 1986, p. 202.
62. McLaughlin in deMause, 1974, p. 115; Warner, 1976, p. 196.
63. Warner, 1976, pp. 206–33.
64. Ibid., p. 233.
65. de Beauvoir, 1952, p. 171.
66. Klapisch-Zuber, 1985, p. 115.
67. Herlihy, 1985, p. 127.
68. Nicholas in Hawes and Hiner, 1991, p. 32; McLaren, 1990, pp. 17, 63–64, 156; Herlihy, 1985, pp. 49, 54.
69. Wemple, 1976.
70. Mount, 1982, p. 19; Herlihy, 1985, p. 78.
71. McLaren, 1990, p. 107.
72. Nicholas in Hawes and Hiner, 1991, p. 32; Boswell, 1988, p. 228; Nicholas in Hawes and Hiner, 1991, p. 32.
73. Boswell, 1988, p. 177; Ibid., p. 178; Ibid., p. 225; Ibid., p. 157; Ibid., p. 3.

74. Steiner, 1989.
75. Coleman, 1976; Herlihy, 1985, p. 64.
76. Nicholas in Hawes and Hiner, 1991, p. 38.
77. Clark, 1969, p. 23.
78. Atkinson, 1991, p. 63; McLaughlin in deMause, 1974, p. 117; Clark, 1969, p. 68.
79. Bloch, 1991, p. 81; Mount, 1982, p. 227.
80. Kraus, 1967, p. 95; Tuchman, 1978, p. 216; Kelly-Gadol in Bridenthal et al., 1976, 1987, p. 182; Mount, 1982, p. 232.
81. Gies and Gies, 1978, p. 147.
82. Hanawalt, 1986, p. 158.
83. Ibid., pp. 96, 100; McLaren, 1990, p. 113.
84. As quoted in Tuchman, 1978, p. 50; McLaughlin in deMause, 1974, p. 118.
85. Nicholas in Hawes and Hiner, 1991, p. 36; Sommerville, 1982, 1990, p. 71.
86. Sommerville, 1982, 1990, p. 79.
87. As quoted in Mount, 1982, p. 119.
88. Ladurie as quoted in Boswell, 1988, p. 404.
89. As quoted in Ross in deMause, 1974, p. 198.
90. Shahar, 1990, p. 35; Atkinson, 1991, pp. 187–89.
91. McLaren, 1990, pp. 118–20; King, 1991, p. 2.
92. Shahar, 1990, p. 70; Labarge, 1986, p. 24.
93. McLaren, 1990, p. 117.
94. Piers, 1978, p. 51; Leibert, 1983, p. 13.
95. Shahar, 1990, pp. 66, 68; Dick, 1987, p. 34; Nicholas in Hawes and Hiner, 1991, p. 261.
96. As quoted in Gies and Gies, 1978, pp. 200–201; King, 1991, p. 14.
97. King, 1991, p. 13.
98. Shahar, 1990, p. 81; Hanawalt, 1986, p. 179.
99. Peiper, 1956, pp. 178–79; discussed by Sigmund Freud in a slight 1909 essay, "The Family Romance."
100. Shahar, 1990, p. 122; Pentikainen, 1968, pp. 60–61.
101. McLaughlin in deMause, 1974, pp. 133–39; Shahar, 1983, pp. 230–32; Nicholas in Hawes and Hiner, 1991, p. 39.
102. Kellum, 1973, p. 367; Hanawalt, 1986, p. 102; Shahar, 1990, pp. 128–29.
103. Hanawalt, 1986, p. 180; as quoted in King, 1991, p. 8.
104. Hanawalt, 1986, p. 181.
105. Boswell, 1988, p. 216; McLaren, 1990, p. 128.
106. I use "Renaissance" to refer to the period called the "late Middle Ages" everywhere except Italy. The Renaissance occurred later up north.
107. Stuard in Bridenthal et al., 1987, p. 167.
108. Sachs, 1971, p. 28; Stuard in Bridenthal et al., 1987, p. 168.
109. King in Labalme, 1980, pp. 66–90; Boulding, 1976, p. 526.
110. Stone, 1977, p. 151.

111. Herlihy, 1985, p. 158.
112. Stuard in Bridenthal et al., 1987, p. 167.
113. Herlihy, 1985, p. 158; Sommerville, 1982, 1990, p. 88.
114. Atkinson, 1991, p. 167.
115. Kahn in Garner et al., 1985, p. 82; Leites, 1986, p. 2.
116. Freud as quoted in Kahn in Garner et al., 1985, p. 84.
117. Boswell, 1988, p. 418; Klapisch-Zuber, 1985, p. 105.
118. Boswell, 1988, p. 451; Luepnitz, 1988, p. 124.

5. Father Knows Best: Early Modern Mom

1. A torture that resembles bungee jumping.
2. King, 1991, p. 144; Coudert in Brink et al., 1989, p. 61; Demos, 1982, p. 11.
3. Pinchbeck and Hewitt, 1969, p. 12; Flandrin, 1979, pp. 180–84; Shahar, 1990, p. 131; Hoffer and Hull, 1981, p. xi and chap. 2.
4. Shammas in Gordon, 1983, p. 199; Pleck, 1987, p. 81; Rybczynski, 1986, p. 4.
5. Stone, L., 1977.
6. For example, Laslett, Pollock, Herlihy, Hanawalt.
7. O'Faolain and Martines, 1973, pp. 196–97.
8. Schama in Rotberg and Rabb, 1988, p. 157; Goldberg in Ferguson et al., 1986.
9. Pleck, 1987, p. 81; Stone, 1977, p. 158.
10. Boulding, 1976, p. 547.
11. Anderson and Zinsser, 1988, p. 265.
12. de Riencourt, 1974, p. 259.
13. Woodbridge, 1986, p. 5.
14. Jankowski, 1992, p. 39; Stallybrass, 1986, pp. 126–27.
15. Atkinson, 1991, p. 217; Wiesner in Bridenthal et al., 1987, p. 208.
16. Jankowski, 1992, p. 38; Atkinson, 1991, p. 23.
17. Wiesner in Bridenthal et al., 1987, p. 243; Mount, 1982, pp. 130–33; Atkinson, 1991, p. 216.
18. Pinchbeck and Hewitt, vol. I, 1969, p. 201; Amussen, 1988, pp. 111, 117.
19. Coudert in Brink et al., 1989, pp. 71–72.
20. Ibid.
21. Schotz in Davidson and Broner, 1980, p. 45; Kahn in Ferguson, 1986, p. 40.
22. Pattison, 1978, p. 48.
23. Warner, 1991; Tatar, 1987, p. 3.
24. Bernikow, 1980, p. 23.
25. Klapisch-Zuber, 1985, p. 125; Nicholas in Hawes and Hiner, 1991, p. 37; Anderson and Zinsser, 1988, p. 263.
26. Ariès, 1962, p. 350; Goldberg in Ferguson et al., 1986, p. 16.

27. Montrose in Ferguson et al., 1986, p. xx; Levin in Brink et al., 1989, p. 97.
28. The epicenter of witch hunting was Germany, and, fittingly, the largest collection of this holocaust was assembled by the perpetrators of another, the Nazi SS (Monter in Bridenthal et al., 1987, p. 213).
29. Larner, 1986, p. 84; Coudert in Brink et al., 1989, p. 78.
30. Coudert in Brink et al., 1989, p. 64; Demos, 1982, p. 170; Hoffer and Hull, 1981, p. 21.
31. Chesler, 1987, p. 274; Newman, 1991, p. 58.
32. Rich, 1976, 1986, pp. 134–35.
33. Most recently by Jessica Mitford, Robbie Davis-Floyd, Jeanne Achterberg, and Richard and Dorothy Wertz. The classics are by Ehrenreich and English, and Rich.
34. Schama, 1988, chap. 7; pp. 402, 480, 523, 540.
35. Sommerville, 1992, p. 21.
36. Beales, in Hawes and Hiner, 1985, p. 24.
37. Sommerville, 1992, p. 13; Stone, 1977, p. 13; Schnuckler in Fildes, 1990, p. 108; Ozment, 1983, p. 135.
38. Sommerville, 1982, 1990, p. 103.
39. As quoted in Sommerville, 1982, 1990, p. 137.
40. Ehrenreich and English, 1979, p. 192.
41. Stone, 1977, pp. 139, 263.
42. Demos, 1986, p. 86; Beekman, 1977, p. 50; as quoted in Dally, 1983, p. 44.
43. Houlbrooke, 1984, p. 194.
44. Dick, 1987, p. 122.
45. As quoted in Greven, 1990, p. 20.
46. As quoted in King, 1991, p. 210.
47. Stone, 1977, p. 57; Flandrin, 1979, p. 115; Dally, 1983, p. 27.
48. As quoted in Ariès, 1962, p. 39.
49. As quoted in Badinter, 1980, p. 63.
50. Marvick in deMause, 1974, p. 273; Hunt, 1972, pp. 161–75; Stone, 1977, pp. 508–509.
51. Stone in Rosenberg, 1975, p. 40.
52. Stone, 1977, p. 77.
53. Beales in Hawes and Hiner, 1985, p. 24.
54. Demos, 1986, p. 74; Schnuckler in Fildes, 1990, p. 117.
55. Sommerville, 1982, 1990, p. 129.
56. Macfarlane, 1970, p. 15; Ozment, 1983, p. 149; Marshall in Hawes and Hiner, 1991, p. 62.
57. Sommerville, 1978; Wooden, 1986, p. xii.
58. Sommerville, 1991, p. 100; Ozment, 1983, p. 132; Maloney and Maloney, 1985, pp. 6–10.
59. Berry, 1993, p. 45.
60. Ariès, 1962, p. 39; Stone, 1977, p. 105; Shorter, 1975, p. 55.

61. Marshall in Hawes and Hiner, 1991, p. 55; Hardyment, 1983, p. 9; Dally, 1983, p. 27.
62. Fraser, 1984, p. 73; Ozment, 1983, p. 163; Houlbrooke, 1984, p. 137; Fraser, 1984, p. 72.
63. Pollock, 1987, p. 95.
64. Fraser, 1984, p. 60; Crawford in Fildes, 1990, pp. 6, 17.
65. Travitsky in Davidson and Broner, 1980, pp. 33–43; Houlbrooke, 1984, pp. 134–35; as quoted in Travitsky in Davidson and Broner, 1980, p. 38; as quoted in Pollock, 1987, p. 168.
66. Farrell, 1991, p. 11.
67. McLaren, 1990, p. 154; as quoted in Crawford in Fildes, 1990, p. 20; McLaren, 1990, p. 158.
68. Crawford in Fildes, 1990, pp. 55–57.
69. Ibid., p. 22; Erasmus, 1979, p. 19.
70. Pollock, 1987, p. 20.
71. Fraser, 1984, p. 69.
72. Beekman, 1977, p. 27.
73. Wilson in Fildes, 1990, p. 88; Hardyment, 1983, p. 3.
74. Hardyment, 1983, p. 3; Dick, 1987, p. 64.
75. Houlbrooke, 1986, p. 155; Marshall in Hawes and Hiner, 1991, p. 65.
76. Fildes, 1986, p. 156; Shorter, 1975, p. 177; Stone, 1977, p. 432.
77. Fildes, 1986, p. 156.
78. Pollock, 1987, p. 54; Fildes, 1986, p. 213, 290.
79. As quoted in Durston, 1989, p. 124.
80. Dick, 1987, p. 30; Gathorne-Hardy, 1973, pp. 37–38.
81. Fildes, 1986, p. 109; Stone, 1977, p. 100.
82. Fildes, 1988, p. 12.
83. Dick, 1987, pp. 21, 27; Fraser, 1985, p. 78.
84. Fildes, 1988, p. 971; Ibid., p. 235.
85. Fildes in Fildes, 1990, p. 166; Fildes, 1988, p. 158.
86. Fildes, 1988, p. 212; Beekman, 1977, p. 5; Sommerville, 1982, 1990, p. 118.
87. Stone, 1977, p. 473.
88. As quoted from Fildes in Fildes, 1990, p. 154.
89. McLaren, 1990, p. 159; Ransel, 1988, p. 15; as quoted in Fildes in Fildes, 1990, p. 15.
90. Watts, 1984, p. 69.
91. Atkinson, 1991, p. 195.

6. The Exaltation of Mother: Eighteenth- and Nineteenth-Century Mom

1. Bernard, 1974, p. 12; Bloch, 1978; Welter, 1966; Thackeray, 1968, pp. 488–89. The last witch hanging in England was in 1727 (Boulding, 1976, p. 610). From a poem by Coventry Patmore.
2. Ehrenreich and English, 1979, p. 5.

3. Zelitzer, 1981, p. 3.
4. Bloch, 1978.
5. Ehrenreich and English, 1979, p. 190.
6. In a letter from Howard Taylor Ricketts to Myra Tubbs, 11 July 1896, quoted in Demos, 1986, p. 57; as quoted in Miles, R., 1989, p. 212.
7. Lederer, 1968, pp. 175–77.
8. Luepnitz, 1988, p. 129.
9. Smith-Rosenberg, 1986; Coontz, 1988, p. 210; as quoted in Bernard, 1974, p. 213.
10. Luepnitz, 1988, p. 129.
11. Miles, R., 1989, p. 155.
12. Matthews, 1987, p. 91.
13. Anderson and Zinsser, vol. II, 1988, p. 217.
14. Boulding, 1976, p. 603.
15. Rybczynski, 1986, p. 77.
16. Woolf, 1942, pp. 237–38.
17. As quoted in Paglia, 1990, p. 233.
18. As quoted in Bernard, 1974, p. 4.
19. Tobey, 1991, p. 66.
20. Duncan in Broude and Garrard, 1982, pp. 201–207.
21. Langer, C., 1992, p. 98.
22. Bloch, 1978.
23. Tatar, 1987, pp. 110–11.
24. E. Kaplan, 1992, p. 4.
25. Hunt, L., 1992, p. 106; Schama, 1990, p. 227.
26. Sommerville, 1982, 1990, p. 153.
27. As quoted in Clark, 1969, p. 279.
28. Rosenblum, 1988, pp. 54–55; Brobeck, 1977; Calvert, 1982.
29. Kunzle in Tufte and Meyerhoff, 1979, p. 121.
30. Jordan, 1987, p. 91.
31. Boulding, 1976, p. 619.
32. Lerner, 1993, p. 135.
33. Dye and Smith, 1986.
34. Greven, 1977, pp. 227–33; Dally, 1983, p. 54; Dick, 1987, p. 123.
35. Griswold, 1993, p. 11.
36. Stone, 1977, p. 432.
37. Robertson in de Mause, 1974, p. 410; McLaren, 1990, pp. 163, 165.
38. Wertz and Wertz, 1977, p. 25.
39. One out of twenty women died; one out of five babies died (Anderson and Zinsser, vol. 2, 1988, p. 241). Dally, 1983, pp. 32–37.
40. Schama, 1988, p. 183; Hufton, 1974, pp. 318–51; Fildes, 1988, p. 146.
41. Dick, 1987, pp. 77, 128; Sommerville, 1982, 1990, p. 121.
42. Sommerville, 1982, 1990, p. 118; Dick, 1987, p. 128.
43. Stone, 1977, p. 471. Swaddling continued in France well into the nineteenth century.
44. Walzer in de Mause, 1974, p. 352.

45. Ransel, 1988, p. 15; Anderson and Zinsser, vol. 2, 1988, p. 246; Piers, 1978, pp. 71–78.
46. Sommerville, 1982, 1990, p. 122; Fildes, 1988, p. 17; Barret-Ducrocq, 1989, p. 41.
47. Dick, 1987, p. 131.
48. Pattison, 1978, p. 76.
49. Sommerville, 1982, 1990; Clark, 1969, p. 237.
50. Rogers, 1966, p. 207.
51. Lesser, 1991, p. 29.
52. Zimmerman in Davidson and Broner, 1980, p. 82; Hirsch, 1989, p. 14.
53. As quoted in Auerbach, 1978, p. 3; Olsen, 1972, 1979, p. 19; LeGuin, 1989, pp. 36–37.
54. Hirsch, 1989, p. 47; Johnson, 1958, vol. 2, p. 475.
55. Hirsch, 1989, p. 10; Rich, 1979, p. 91.
56. Gilbert and Gubar, 1979; Herman, 1989; Bernikow, 1980; Davidson and Broner, 1980; Daly and Reddy, 1991.
57. Cixous in Marks and de Courtivron, 1981, p. 251.
58. As quoted in Matthews, 1987, p. 50; Kaplan, E., 1992, pp. 127, 129; Tompkins, 1981, p. 81.
59. Kaplan, E., 1992, p. 128; as quoted in Gilbert and Gubar, 1979, p. 483.
60. Van Buren, 1989, p. 127; Tobey, 1991, p. 73.
61. As quoted in Porter in Boucé, 1982, p. 21.
62. Sternglanz and Nash in Birns and Hay, 1988, p. 18.
63. Ibid., p. 43; Bernard, 1974, p. 21.
64. Miles, R., 1989, p. 190; Homans, 1986, p. 155; Huet, 1993, p. 6.
65. Gordon, 1976, p. 21; Holbrook, 1873, pp. 14–15; Miles, R., 1989, p. 209.
66. Acton, 1857, p. 133; Degler, 1980, p. 467; Wertz and Wertz, 1989, p. 79.
67. Hays, 1964, p. 279; Shorter, 1975, p. 83; as quoted in Cott, 1978.
68. Degler, 1980, pp. 249–79; Comfort, 1967.
69. Paglia, 1990, p. 26; Freud, 1925.
70. As quoted in Dally, 1983, p. 133; Lerner, 1993, p. 137; Ruddick, 1989, pp. 13–28.
71. Hewlett, 1986, p. 180.
72. McLaren, 1990, p. 197.
73. As quoted in Lewis, 1986, p. 1; Anderson and Zinsser, vol. 2, 1988, p. 162; as quoted in Pearson and Pope, 1981, p. 47; as quoted in Hewlett, 1986, p. 182; Strasser, 1981, p. 227.
74. McLaren, 1990, pp. 178, 180; Brookes in Lewis, ed., 1986, p. 156.
75. Anderson and Zinsser, vol. 2, 1988, p. 242.
76. Dick, 1987, p. 34.
77. Robertson in deMause, 1974, p. 424; Gathorne-Hardy, 1973, p. 33.
78. Mintz and Kellogg, 1988, p. 58; Pleck, 1987, pp. 46–47; Robertson in deMause, 1974, p. 421.
79. Piers, 1978, p. 85; Robertson in deMause, 1974, p. 420.

80. As quoted in Pearsall, 1969, pp. 289, 290; Jordan, 1987, pp. 270–71.
81. Masson, 1984; Freud, 1917, p. 3701.
82. Kahr, 1991, p. 204.
83. Pearsall, 1969, p. 211; Sommerville, 1982, 1990, p. 189; Ehrenreich and English, 1979, p. 189.
84. Rose, 1986, p. 29.
85. Anderson and Zinsser, vol. 2, 1988, p. 245; Jordan, 1987, p. 92.
86. Jordan, 1987, p. 83.
87. Anderson and Zinsser, vol. 2, 1988, p. 247.
88. Langer, 1974; Fuchs, 1992, p. 5.
89. Klaus, 1993, p. 5; as quoted in Bernard, 1974, p. 13.

7. Fall from Grace: Twentieth-Century Mom

1. Koonz, 1987, p. 185; as quoted in Matthews, 1987, p. 184.
2. Apple, 1987, p. 97.
3. Skolnick, 1991, pp. 42–43.
4. From 1890 — when just one college-age woman in fifty continued her education — until 1910, female college enrollment tripled, doubling again during the teens (Mintz and Kellogg, 1988, p. 111). Participation in the labor force by college-trained women rose six times faster between 1900 and 1930 than did participation by single women (Berry, 1993, p. 87).
5. Skolnick, 1991, p. 46.
6. Mintz and Kellogg, 1988, p. 115.
7. Skolnick, 1991, p. 40.
8. Mintz and Kellogg, 1988, p. 114; Demos, 1986, p. 61; Ehrenreich and English, 1978, 1979, p. 210.
9. Bienstock in Tufte and Meyerhoff, 1979, p. 176; Berrol in Hawes and Hiner, 1985, p. 356.
10. Bienstock in Tufte and Meyerhoff, 1979, p. 174.
11. Ehrenreich and English, 1978, 1979, p. 188.
12. Sommerville, 1982, 1990, p. 186.
13. Hardyment, 1983, p. 122.
14. Margolis, 1984, p. 47.
15. Mintz and Kellogg, 1988, p. 120.
16. McCartney and Phillips in Birns and Hay, 1988, p. 160.
17. Anderson and Zinsser, vol. 2, 1988, pp. 209–211.
18. Harriss (ed.), 1991, p. 117.
19. Ibid.
20. Apple, 1987, p. 116; as quoted in Ehrenreich and English, 1978, 1979, p. 195.
21. Ehrenreich and English, 1978, 1979, p. 195.
22. Strasser, 1982, p. 135.
23. As quoted in Ehrenreich and English, 1978, 1979, p. 216.
24. Ibid., p. 198.

25. Hardyment, 1983, p. 100.
26. Strasser, 1982, pp. 232–33.
27. Apple, 1987, p. 181; Hardyment, 1983, p. 123.
28. As quoted in Beekman, 1977, p. 146.
29. Hardyment, 1983, p. 71.
30. Bernard, 1974, p. 96.
31. As quoted in Hardyment, 1983, p. 176.
32. Ehrenreich and English, 1978, 1979, p. 205.
33. Recall Marx and Engels in Chap. I.
34. Ransel in Hawes and Hiner, 1991, p. 485.
35. Mount, 1982, pp. 36–37; Harriss, 1991, p. 66.
36. Miles, R., 1989, p. 239.
37. Troen and Ackerman in Hawes and Hiner (eds.), 1991, p. 346; Kitzinger, 1978, p. 219.
38. Hardyment, 1983, p. 109.
39. Gay, 1988, p. 507; Schneiderman, 1990, p. 12.
40. Sayers, 1991, p. 13.
41. Gay, 1988, p. 505; Sprengnether, 1990, pp. 39–86.
42. Sprengnether, 1990, p. 64; Mahony, 1986, p. 35; Blacker and Abraham, 1982–1983.
43. Roazen, 1984, p. 445.
44. Rycroft, 1985, p. 102.
45. Freud, 1896, p. 63.
46. Freud, 1905, 1915, 1940, 1926, p. 170; 1915, pp. 122–23.
47. Freud, 1911, 1914, 1923, 1917.
48. Freud, 1931, 1933.
49. Gay, 1988, p. 506; Abraham, 1982–1983; Sprengnether, 1990, p. 19.
50. Freud, 1933, p. 133.
51. Abraham, 1982–1983.
52. As quoted in Ehrenreich and English, 1978, 1979, ch. 7, p. 214.
53. Ibid., 1978, 1979, ch. 7.
54. Hardyment, 1983, pp. 224–25; Margolis, 1984, p. 63; Sommerville, 1982, 1990, p. 256.
55. Sommerville, 1982, 1990, p. 266.
56. Mintz and Kellogg, 1988, p. 178.
57. Skolnick, 1991, p. 53.
58. Ibid., p. 51; Matthews, 1987, p. 210; Miller and Nowak, 1977, pp. 156–57.
59. Matthews, 1987, pp. 187, 192, 193, 195.
60. Ibid., pp. 215–16.
61. Snitow, 1992.
62. Skolnick, 1991, p. 78.
63. Reed, 1978.
64. Skolnick, 1991, pp. 102, 103.
65. Landers, 1976.
66. Hewlett, 1986, p. 270; Hardyment, 1983, p. 166; Buxbaum, 1951, p. 151.

67. Ehrenreich and English, 1978, p. 269.
68. Ibid., p. 216.
69. Weiss, 1978.
70. Hardyment, 1983, p. 225.
71. Wolfenstein, 1955; Marshall in Phoenix, Woollett, and Lloyd, 1991, p. 82.
72. Walters, 1992, pp. 47–54, 84–90.
73. Swigart, 1986, pp. 102–105; Swigart, 1991, p. 227.
74. deMause, 1974, p. 52.
75. Zuckerman in Rosenberg, 1975, p. 190; as quoted in Mintz and Kellogg, 1988, p. 187.
76. Hardyment, 1983, p. 245.
77. Zuckerman in Rosenberg, 1975, p. 183.
78. Ehrenreich and English, 1978, 1979, pp. 226–29.
79. Rich, 1976, p. 217.
80. Swigart, 1986, pp. 57, 62; Swigart, 1991, p. 211.
81. Smith, 1990; Marshall in Phoenix, Woollett, and Lloyd, 1991, pp. 73–74.
82. Chira, Susan, "The New Realities Fight Old Images of Mother," *New York Times,* Sunday, Oct. 4, 1992, pp. 1, 30.
83. Traub, 1986.
84. Hewlett, 1986, p. 268.
85. Snitow, 1992.
86. Walters, 1992, p. 145; *Wall Street Journal,* September 7, 1983, as quoted in Hewlett, 1986, 1987, p. 15; Woollett and Phoenix in Phoenix, Woollett, and Lloyd, 1991, p. 219.
87. Griswold, 1993, p. 245; Rogers, 1966, p. 263.
88. Rogers, 1966, p. 237; Walters, 1992, p. 75.
89. Caine, 1985, p. 14; Matthews, 1987, p. 207.
90. Ibid., p. 202.
91. Duncan in Davidson and Broner, 1980, p. 231.
92. Fishburn in Davidson and Broner, 1980, p. 215.
93. Koch, Jim, "Saint to Sinner," *New York Times,* Sunday, May 10, 1992, pp. 14, 17.
94. Chodorow and Contratto in Chodorow, 1989, pp. 79–97.
95. Ibid., p. 80.
96. Fine, 1979, p. 158.
97. Margolis, 1984, p. 72.
98. As quoted in Ehrenreich and English, 1978, 1979, p. 234.
99. Margolis, 1984, p. 260; Ehrenreich and English, 1978, 1979, p. 236.
100. Hardyment, 1983, p. 233; Bernard, 1974, p. 71.
101. Fine, 1979, p. 156; Eyer, 1992, p. 52.
102. Karen, 1990; Ehrenreich and English, 1978, 1979, p. 227.
103. Roazen, 1984, p. 486; Tizard in Phoenix, Woollett, and Lloyd, 1991, p. 178; Karen, 1990.
104. Eyer, 1992, p. 50.

105. Bowlby, 1951.
106. Birns, 1985, p. 6.
107. Tizard in Phoenix, Woollett, and Lloyd, 1991, p. 182.
108. Eyer, 1992; Marshall Klaus and John Kennell, 1976; Eyer, 1992, p. 67.
109. Rutter, 1972.
110. Eyer, 1992, p. 67; Clarke and Clarke, 1976; Schaffer and Emerson, 1964; Lamb, 1976.
111. Chess and Thomas, 1977; Birns, 1985, p. 5.
112. Caplan and Hall-McCorquodale, 1985.
113. Sayers, 1991, p. 10.
114. Barth, 1989.
115. Deutsch, 1945.
116. Sayers, 1991, p. 67.
117. Kestenberg, 1956; Parens, 1971.
118. Benedek, 1959; for example, Chasseguet-Smirgel, 1974; Kestenberg, 1976; and Stoller, 1976.
119. Barth, 1993.
120. Roazen, 1984, pp. 398–400, 428.
121. Greenberg and Mitchell, 1983, p. 80.
122. Sullivan, 1953, 1962; Fromm-Reichmann, 1950.
123. Freud, A., 1936; Hartmann, 1939.
124. Freud, A., 1965, p. 50.
125. Greenberg and Mitchell, 1983, p. 181.
126. Mahler, et al., 1975, p. 45.
127. Winnicott, 1975, Winnicott, 1945, Winnicott, 1958, 1971, Winnicott, 1953, Winnicott, 1969, Winnicott, 1957, p. vii; Winnicott, 1948.
128. Kohut, 1977, pp. 146–47.
129. Kohut, 1980.
130. Bergmann, 1987, p. 250.
131. Snitow, 1992.
132. Cowan, 1983, p. 199; Chira, 1992, pp. 1, 30.
133. Walsh, 1993; Brownmiller, 1984, pp. 221, 222, 230.
134. Walters, 1992, p. 186; Skolnick, 1991, pp. 122, 187; Berry, 1993, p. 148.
135. Haskell, 1988, p. 84.
136. Mintz and Kellogg, 1988, p. 240.
137. Snitow, 1992; Walsh, 1993.
138. Friedan, 1981.
139. Snitow, 1992.
140. Cobb, 1990.
141. Silverstein, 1991.
142. Margolis, 1984, p. 105.
143. Silverstein, 1991; Tizard in Phoenix, Woollett, and Lloyd, 1991, p. 185; Silverstein, 1991.
144. Belsky, 1988.
145. Faludi, 1991, pp. 42, 44–45.
146. West, 1984.

147. Gordon, 1991, p. 68.
148. Walters, 1992, p. 190.
149. E. Kaplan, 1992, pp. 202–209.
150. *New York Times,* July 21, 1993, p. A1.
151. Gordon, 1974, 1990, p. 458; Taitz, 1992, p. 12; Seinfels, 1992.
152. Gibbs, 1990, p. 42.
153. Whithead, 1993, p. 55.
154. Goodman, 1993.
155. Snitow, 1992.
156. Skolnick, 1991, p. 223.
157. Stern, 1977.
158. Sander, 1977; Brazelton, et al., 1975; Stone, et al., 1973.

BIBLIOGRAPHY

Abraham, Ruth. "Freud's Mother Conflict and the Formulation of the Oedipal Father." *The Psychoanalytic Review* 69 (1982–1983): 441–453.

Achterberg, Jeanne. *Woman As Healer.* Boston: Shambhala, 1990.

Acton, William. *The Functions and Disorders of the Reproductive Organs in Youth and Adult Age and in Advanced Life, Considered in Their Physiological Sound and Moral Relations.* London: J and A Churchill, 1857.

Adams, Paul. "The Mother Not the Father." *Journal of the American Academy of Psychoanalysis.* 15, no. 4 (October 1987): 465–480.

Adelman, Janet. *Suffocating Mothers: Fantasies of Maternal Origin in Shakespeare Plays, "Hamlet" to "Tempest."* New York: Routledge, 1992.

Ainsworth, Mary. "Attachment: Retrospect and Prospect." In *The Place of Attachment in Human Behavior,* edited by Colin Murray Parkes and Joan Stevenson. New York: Basic Books, 1982.

Albright, William F. *Yahweh and the Gods of Canaan.* New York: Doubleday, 1968.

Alexander, Franz. "Need for Punishment and the Death Instinct." *International Journal of Psychoanalysis* 10 (1929).

———. *Our Age of Unreason: A Study of the Irrational Face in Society.* New York: J. B. Lippincott, 1951.

al-Hibri, Azizah. "Reproduction, Mothering, and the Origin of Patriarchy: In *Mothering: Essays in Feminist Theory.* Lanham, Md.: Rowman and Littlefield, 1983.

Allcott, William. *The Physiology of Marriage.* Boston: Jewett, 1856.

Amussen, Susan Dwyer. *An Ordered Society: Gender and Class in Early Modern England.* Oxford: Basil Blackwell, 1988.

Anderson, Bonnie, and Judith Zinsser. *A History of Their Own: Women in Europe from Prehistory to the Present,* vols. 1 and 2. New York: Harper and Row, 1988.

Anderson, Michael. *Family Structure in Nineteenth-Century Lancaster.* Cambridge: Cambridge University Press, 1971.

Anthony, James, and Therese Benedek, eds. *Parenthood: Its Psychology and Psychopathology.* Boston: Little, Brown, 1970.

Apple, Rima. *Mothers and Medicine: A Social History of Infant Feeding, 1890–1950.* Madison: University of Wisconsin Press, 1987.

Applegarth, Adrienne. "Origins of Femininity and the Wish for a Child." *Psychoanalytic Inquiry* 8, no.1 (1988): 160–176.

Appleton, W. S. "The Mistreatment of Patients' Families by Psychiatrists." *American Journal of Psychiatry* 131 (1974): 655–657.

Ariès, Philippe. *Centuries of Childhood: A Social History of Family Life,* translated by Robert Baldick. New York: Knopf, 1962.

———. *The Hour of Our Death.* New York: Vintage, 1982.

Atkinson, Clarissa. *The Oldest Vocation: Christian Motherhood in the Middle Ages.* Ithaca: Cornell University Press, 1991.

Auerbach, Nina. "Artists and Mothers: A False Alliance." *Women and Literature* 6, no.1 (Spring 1978).

Bachofen, J. J. *Myth, Religion and Mother Right,* translated by Ralph Montheim. Princeton: Princeton University Press, 1967.

Badinter, Elizabeth. *Mother Love: Myth and Reality: Motherhood in Modern History,* translated by Roger de Gravis. New York: Macmillan, 1980.

Bainton, Roland. *Women of the Reformation in France and England.* Minneapolis: Augsburg Publishing, 1973.

Balint, Alice. "Love for the Mother and Mother-Love." In *Primary Love and Psychoanalytic Technique,* edited by Michael Balint, 91–108. New York: Liveright Publishing, 1965.

———. "Love for the Mother and Mother-Love." *International Journal of Psychoanalysis,* 30 (1949): 251–259.

Baring-Gould, William, and Ceil Baring-Gould. *The Annotated Mother Goose.* New York: Bramhall House, 1962.

Baron, F. Xavier. "Children and Violence in Chaucer's *Canterbury Tales.*" *Journal of Psychology* 7 (1979/80): 17–103.

Barret-Ducrocq, Françoise. *Love in the Time of Victorian Sexuality and Desire Among Working-Class Men and Women in Nineteenth-Century London,* translated by John Howe. New York: Penguin, 1989.

Barron, James, and Mary Tabor. "17 Killed and Life Is Searched for Clue." *New York Times* (Sunday, 4 August 1991): 1, 30.

Barstow, Anne. "The Prehistoric Goddess." In *The Book of the Goddess: Past and Present,* edited by Carl Olson. New York: Crossroads Publishing, 1983.

Barth, F. Diane. "Blaming the Parent: Psychoanalytic Myth and Language." *The Annual of Psychoanalysis,* 17 (1989): 185–201.

———. "Conflicts Over Selfishness: One Aspect of Some Women's Wish for a Baby." *Psychoanalytic Psychology* 10, no. 2 (1993): 169–185.

Barzilai, Shuli. "Reading 'Snow White': The Mother's Story." *Signs,* 15, no. 3 (Spring 1990).

Beales, Ross. "The Child in Seventeenth-Century America." In *American Childhood: A Research Guide and Historical Handbook,* edited by Joseph Hawes and N. Ray Hiner. Westport, Conn.: Greenwood Press, 1985.

Beekman, Daniel. *The Mechanical Baby: A Popular History of the Theory and Practice of Child Raising*. Westport, Conn.: Lawrence Hill and Co., 1977.

Beilin, Elaine. *Redeeming Eve: Women Writers of the English Renaissance*. Princeton: Princeton University Press, 1987.

Belsky, Jay. "Infant Daycare and Socioemotional Development." *Journal of Child Psychology and Psychiatry* 29 (1988): 397–406.

Benedek, Therese. "Parenthood as a Developmental Phase." *Journal of the American Psychoanalytic Association* 7 (1959): 379–417.

Benjamin, Jessica. *The Bonds of Love: Psychoanalysis, Feminism, and the Problems of Domination*. New York: Pantheon, 1988.

Bergmann, Martin. *The Anatomy of Loving*. New York: Columbia University Press, 1987.

Bernard, Jessie. *The Future of Marriage*. New York: Bantam Books, 1972.

———. *The Future of Motherhood*. New York: Dial Press, 1974.

———. *The Return of Motherhood*. New York: Penguin, 1979.

Bernikow, Louise. *Among Women*. New York: Harmony, 1980.

Berrol, Selma. "Ethnicity and American Children." In *American Childhood: A Research Guide and Historical Handbook,* edited by Hawes and Hiner, 343–375. Westport, Conn.: Greenwood Press, 1985.

Berry, Mary Frances. *The Politics of Parenthood, Child Care, Women's Rights and the Myth of the Good Mother*. New York: Viking, 1993.

Bettelheim, Bruno. *Children of the Dream*. New York: Avon, 1969.

———. *The Uses of Enchantment: The Meaning and Importance of Fairy Tales*. New York: Random House, 1972, Vintage Books, 1977.

Bienstock, Beverly. "The Changing Image of the American Jewish Mother." In *Changing Images of the Family,* edited by Virginia Tufte and Barbara Myerhoff, 173–193. New Haven: Yale University Press, 1979.

Bird, Phyllis. "Images of Women in the Old Testament." In *Religion and Sexism,* edited by Rosemary Ruether, 9–81. New York: Simon and Schuster, 1974.

Birns, Beverly. "The Mother-Infant Tie: Fifty Years of Theory, Science and Science Fiction." *Work in Progress* 21, Stone Center, Wellesley College, 1985.

Birns, Beverly, and Dale Hay, eds. *The Different Faces of Motherhood*. New York: Plenum, 1988.

Blacker, K. H., and R. Abraham. "The Rat Man Revisited: Comment on Maternal Influences." *International Journal of Psychoanalytic Psychotherapy* 9 (1982–1983): 704–731.

Blank, M. "Mother's Role in Infant Development." *Journal of the American Academy of Child Psychology* 30 (1964): 89–105.

Bleeker, C. J. "Isis and Hathor, Two Ancient Egyptian Goddesses." In *The Book of the Goddess: Past and Present,* edited by Carl Olson. New York: Crossroads Publishing, 1990.

Bloch, R. Howard. *Medieval Misogyny and the Inventor of Western Romantic Love*. Chicago: University of Chicago Press, 1991.

Bloch, Ruth. "American Feminine Ideals in Transition: The Rise of the Moral Mother, 1785–1815." *Feminist Studies* 4, no. 2 (1978).

Boswell, John. *The Kindness of Strangers: The Abandonment of Children in Western Europe from Late Antiquity to the Renaissance*. New York: Pantheon, 1988.

Boucé, Paul-Gabriel. *Sexuality in Eighteenth-Century Britain*. Manchester, England: Manchester University Press, 1982.

Boulding, Elise. *The Underside of History*. Boulder, Colo.: Westview Press, 1976.

Bowlby, John. *Attachment and Loss 1*. London: Hogarth Press, 1969.

———. *Attachment and Loss 2: Separation, Anxiety, and Anger*. London: Hogarth Press, 1973.

———. *Attachment and Loss 3: Loss, Sadness, and Depression*. London: Hogarth Press, 1980.

———. *Maternal Care and Mental Health*. Geneva: World Health Organization, 1951.

Bradley, Keith. *Discovering the Roman Family*. New York: Oxford, 1991.

Brazelton, T. Berry. "Working Parents." *Newsweek* 8, no. 7 (February 13, 1989): 66–72.

Brazelton, T. Berry, E. Tronick, L. Adamson, A. Als, and S. Wise. "Early Mother-Infant Reciprocity." In *Parent-Infant Interaction*, CIBA Foundation, Symposium 33 (1975), Amsterdam: Elsevier, 137–154.

Breiner, Sander. *Slaughter of the Innocents: Child Abuse Through the Ages and Today*. New York: Plenum, 1990.

Bridenthal, Renate, Claudia Koonz, and Susan Stuard. *Becoming Visible: Women in European History*. Boston: Houghton Mifflin, 1977, 2nd edition, 1987.

Briffault, Robert. *The Mothers*. New York: Johnson Reprint, 1969.

Brink, Jean, Allison Coudert, and Maryanne C. Horovitz, eds. *The Poetics of Gender in Early Modern Europe*. Tempe: Northeast Missouri State, 1989.

Brobeck, Stephen. "Images of the Family: Portrait Paintings as Indices of American Family Culture, Structure, and Behavior, 1730–1860." *Journal of Psychohistory* 5 (1977): 81–100.

Brody, Sylvia, and Sidney Axelrod. *Mothers, Fathers and Children*. New York: International Universities Press, 1978.

———, eds. *Anxiety and Ego Formation in Infancy*. New York: International Universities Press, 1971.

Bromberg, Pamela Starr. "Holding On: Letting Go." *Simmons Review* 69, no. 1 (Winter 1987).

Brookes, Barbara. "Women and Reproduction, 1860–1939." In *Labour and Love: Women's Experience of Home and Family, 1850–1940*, edited by Jane Lewis. Oxford: Basil Blackwell, 1986.

Broude, Norma, and Mary Garrard. *Feminism and Art History*. New York: Harper and Row, 1982.

Brown, Georgia. "Mother Inferior." *Lears* (July 1990): 88–89.

Brownmiller, Susan. *Femininity*. New York: Linden Press, 1984.

Buxbaum, Edith. *Your Child Makes Sense, A Guide for Parents*. London: Allen and Unwin, 1951.

Bynum, Caroline Walker. *Jesus as Mother*. Berkeley: University of California Press, 1982.

Caine, Lynn. *What Did I Do Wrong?: Mothers, Children, Guilt*. New York: Arbor House, 1985.

Calvert, Karen Lee. "Children in American Family Portraits, 1670–1810." *William and Mary Quarterly*, 3rd. series, 39 (1982): 87–113.

Campbell, Joseph. *Myths to Live By*. New York: Viking, 1972.

———. *The Hero with a Thousand Faces*. Cleveland and New York: World Publishing Co., 1968.

———. *The Masks of God: Primitive Mythology*. New York: Viking, 1972.

Cantarella, Eva. *Pandora's Daughters: The Role and Status of Women in Greek and Roman Antiquity*. Baltimore: Johns Hopkins University Press, 1987.

Caplan, Paula J. "Take the Blame Off Mother." *Psychology Today* 20 (October 1986): 70–71.

Caplan, Paula J., and Ian Hall-McCorquodale. "Mother-Blaming in Major Clinical Journals." *American Journal of Orthopsychiatry* 55 (1985): 348–353.

Carmody, Denise Lardner. *Women and World Religions*. Nashville: Abingdon, 1979.

Carroll, Michael. *The Cult of the Virgin Mary*. Princeton: Princeton University Press, 1986.

Chopin, Kate. *The Awakening*. New York: Capricorn, 1964.

Chasseguet-Smirgel, Janine. "Feminine Guilt and the Oedipus Complex." In *Feminine Sexuality*, edited by Janine Chasseguet-Smirgel, 94–103. Ann Arbor: University of Michigan Press, 1970.

———. *Feminine Sexuality*. Ann Arbor: University of Michigan Press, 1970.

Chesler, Phyllis. *Mothers on Trial*. New York: Harvest/HBJ Book, 1987.

Chess, Stella, and Alexander Thomas. "Infant Bonding: Mystiques and Reality." *American Journal of Orthopsychiatry* 52, no. 2 (April 1982): 213–222.

———. *Origins and Evolution of Behavior Disorders*. New York: Brunner/Mazel, 1989.

Chira, Susan. "New Realities Fight Old Images of Mother." *New York Times* (Sunday, 4 October 1992): 1, 30.

Chodorow, Nancy. *Feminism and Psychoanalytic Theory*. New Haven: Yale University Press, 1989.

———. *The Reproduction of Mothering: Psychoanalysis and the Sociology of Gender*. Berkeley: University of California Press, 1978.

Chodorow, Nancy, and Susan Contratto. "The Fantasy of the Perfect Mother." In *Rethinking the Family: Some Feminist Questions*, edited by B. Thorne and M. Yalom, 59–75. New York: Longman, 1982.

Christ, Carol. *Laughter of Aphrodite: Reflections on a Journey to the Goddess*. San Francisco: Harper and Row, 1987.

Cixous, Hélène. "The Laugh of the Medusa." In *New French Feminisms,* edited by Elaine Marks and Isabelle de Courtivron. Brighton: Harvester, 1975.

Clark, Kenneth. *Civilization.* New York: Harper Collins, 1969.

Clarke, Ann, and A.D.B. Clark, eds. *Early Experience: Myth and Evidence.* New York: Free Press, 1976.

Cobb, Nathan. "The Baby Grows." *Boston Globe Magazine* (June 7, 1990): 14–35.

Coleman, Emily. "Infanticide in the Early Middle Ages." In *Women in Medieval Society,* edited by S. M. Stuard, 47–79. Philadelphia: University of Pennsylvania Press, 1976.

Collins, A. Y. *Feminist Perspectives in Biblical Scholarship.* Chicago: Scholars Press, 1985.

Comfort, Alex. *The Anxiety Makers: Some Curious Preoccupations of the Medical Profession.* London: Thomas Nelson, 1967.

Condit, Polly. "The Analyst as Parent." *Current Issues in Psychoanalytic Practice* 4 (Spring-Summer 1987):1–2.

Coontz, Stephanie. *The Social Origins of Private Life.* New York: Verso, 1988.

———. *The Way We Never Were: American Families and the Nostalgia Trap.* New York: Basic Books, 1992.

Coote, Stephen, ed. *The Penguin Book of Homosexual Verse.* London: Allen Lane, 1983.

Cott, Nancy. *The Bonds of Womanhood: Women's Sphere in New England, 1780–1835.* New Haven: Yale University Press, 1977.

———. "Passionless: An Interpretation of Victorian Sexual Ideology, 1790–1850." *Signs* 4, no. 2 (Winter 1978).

Coudert, Allison. "The Myth of the Improved Status of Protestant Women: The Case of the Witchcraze." In *The Poetics of Gender in Early Modern Europe,* edited by Jean Brink, Allison Coudert, and Maryanne C. Horovitz, 61–93. Tempe: Northeast Missouri State, 1989.

Coveney, Peter. *Poor Monkey.* Bungay, Great Britain: Richard Clay and Co. Ltd., 1952.

Cowan, Ruth Schwartz. *More Work for Mother: The Ironies of Household Technology from the Open Hearth to the Microwave.* New York: Basic Books, 1983.

Crawford, Patricia. "The Construction and Experience of Maternity in 17th-Century England." In *Women as Mothers in Pre-Industrial England,* edited by Valerie Fildes, 3–39. London: Routledge, 1990.

Curtis, Homer. "Clinical Perspectives in Self Psychology." *Psychoanalytic Quarterly* 54 (1985): 339–377.

Dally, Ann. *Inventing Motherhood: The Consequences of an Ideal.* New York: Schocken, 1983.

Daly, Brenda O., and Maureen Reddy, eds. *Narrating Mothers: Theorizing Maternal Subjectivities.* Knoxville: University of Tennessee Press, 1991.

Daly, Mary. *Gyn/Ecology: The Metaethics of Radical Feminism.* Boston: Beacon, 1978.

Davidson, Cathy, and E. M. Broner, eds. *The Lost Tradition: Mothers and Daughters in Literature*. New York: Frederick Ungar, 1980.

Davies, Steve. "The Canaanite-Hebrew Goddess." In *The Book of the Goddess: Past and Present,* edited by Carl Olson. New York: Crossroads Publishing, 1981, 1990.

Davis, Elizabeth Gould. *The First Sex*. Baltimore: Penguin, 1971.

Davis, Floyd. *Birth as an American Rite of Passage*. Berkeley: University of California Press, 1992.

Davis, Glenn. *Childhood and History in America*. New York: Psychohistory Press, 1976.

Davis, Kingsley. "Wives and Work: A Theory of the Sex-role Revolution and Its Consequences." In *Feminism, Children and the New Families,* edited by Sanford M. Dornbusch and Myra H. Strober. New York: Guilford Press, 1988.

de Beauvoir, Simone. *The Second Sex*. New York: Vintage, 1952, 1987.

de Kanter, Ruth. "The Children's Home: An Alternative in Childrearing Practices in the Netherlands." In *The Different Faces of Motherhood,* edited by Beverly Birns and Dale Hay. New York: Plenum, 1988.

deMause, Lloyd. "The Evolution of Childhood." In *The History of Childhood,* edited by Lloyd deMause. New York: Peter Bedrick, 1974, 1988.

———, ed. *The History of Childhood*. New York: Peter Bedrick, 1974.

de Riencourt, Amaury. *Sex and Power in History*. New York: Delta, 1974.

Degler, Carl N. *At Odds: Women and the Family in America from the Revolution to the Present*. New York: Oxford, 1980.

———. "What Ought To Be and What Was: Women's Sexuality in the Nineteenth Century." *American History Review* 79 (December 1974): 1467–1490.

Demos, John P. *Entertaining Satan: Witchcraft and the Culture of Early New England*. New York: Oxford University Press, 1982.

———. "Images of the Family Then and Now." In *Past, Present, and Personal: The Family and the Life Course in American History*. New York: Oxford, 1986.

———. *Little Commonwealth: Family Life in Plymouth Colony*. New York: Oxford University Press, 1970.

de Vaux, Roland. *Ancient Israel: Its Life and Institutions*. New York: McGraw-Hill, 1961.

Dick, Diana. *Yesterday's Babies: A History of Baby Care*. London: Bodley Head, 1987.

Diner, Helen. *Mothers and Amazons: The First Feminine History of Culture*. New York: Julian, 1965.

Dinnerstein, Dorothy. *The Mermaid and the Minotaur*. New York: Harper, 1976.

Dixon, Suzanne. *The Roman Mother*. Norman: Oklahoma University Press, 1988.

Donington, Robert. *Opera and Its Symbols: The Unity of Words, Music, and Staging*. New Haven: Yale University Press, 1991.

Dover, Kenneth. *Greek Homosexuality*. Cambridge: Harvard University Press, 1978.

———. "Greek Homosexuality and Initiation." In *The Greeks and Their Legacy: Collected Papers*, vol. 2, 115–134. Oxford: Basil Blackwell, 1988.

———. *The Greeks and Their Legacy, Collected Papers*. Oxford: Basil Blackwell, 1988.

Downing, Christine. *The Goddess: Mythological Images of the Feminine*. New York: Crossroads Publishing, 1989.

———. "The Mother Goddess Among the Greeks." In *The Book of the Goddess*, edited by Carl Olson. New York: Crossroads Publishing, 1990.

Duncan, Carol. "Happy Mothers and Other New Ideas in Eighteenth-Century French Art." In *Feminism and Art History: Questioning the Litany*, edited by Norma Broude and Mary Garrard, 198–219. New York: Harper and Row, 1982.

Duncan, Erica. "The Hungry Jewish Mother." In *The Lost Tradition: Mothers and Daughters in Literature*, 231–242, edited by Cathy Davidson and E. M. Broner. New York: Frederick Ungar, 1980.

Durston, Christopher. *The Family in the English Revolution*. Oxford: Basil Blackwell, 1989.

Dye, Nancy Schrom, and David Blake Smith. "Mother Love and Infant Death, 1750–1920." *The Journal of American History* 73, no. 2 (1986): 329–353.

Eagleton, Terry. *Literary Theory: An Introduction*. Minneapolis: University of Minnesota Press, 1983.

Earle, Alice Morse. *Child Life in Colonial Days*. New York: Macmillan, 1899.

Eckstein-Diener, Berta. *Mothers and Amazons; The First Feminine History of Culture (by) Helen Diner*. Edited and translated by John Philip Lundin. New York: Julian Press, 1965.

Ehrenberg, Margaret. *Women in Prehistory*. Norman: University of Oklahoma Press, 1989.

Ehrenreich, Barbara, and Deirdre English. *For Her Own Good: 150 Years of the Experts' Advice to Women*. New York: Doubleday Anchor, 1978, 1979.

———. *Witches, Midwives and Nurses: A History of Women Healers*. Old Westbury, Conn.: The Feminist Press, 1973.

Eisler, Riane. *The Chalice and the Blade: Our History, Our Future*. San Francisco: Harper and Row, 1987.

Eissler, K. R. *Leonardo da Vinci: Psychoanalytic Notes on Enigma*. New York: International Universities Press, 1961.

Ellenberger, Henri. *The Discovery of the Unconscious*. New York: Basic Books, 1970.

Engels, Donald. "The Problem of Female Infanticide in the Greco-Roman World." *Classical Philology* 75 (1980): 112–120.

Engels, Friedrich. *The Origins of the Family, Private Property, and the State*. Chicago: Charles Kerr, 1884.

Erasmus, Desiderius. *The Praise of Folly*, translated by Clarence Miller. New Haven: Yale University Press, 1979.

Erikson, Erik. "Womanhood and the Inner Space." In *Identity, Youth and Crisis*. New York: W. W. Norton, 1968.

Evans, John K. *War, Women and Children in Ancient Rome*. London: Routledge, 1991.

Evans, W. N. "The Mother: Images and Reality." *Psychoanalytic Review* 59 (Summer 1972): 183–199.

Eyer, Diane. *Mother-Infant Bonding: A Scientific Fiction*. New Haven: Yale University Press, 1993.

Fairbairn, Ronald D. "Synopsis of an Object-Relations Theory of the Personality." *International Journal of Psychoanalysis* 44 (1963): 224–225.

Faludi, Susan. *Backlash: The Undeclared War Against American Women*. New York: Doubleday, 1991. Reprint, New Crown, 1991.

Farr, Cecilia Konchar. "Her Mother's Language." In *Narrating Mothers: Theorizing Maternal Subjectivities*, edited by Brenda O. Daly and Maureen Reddy, 94–108. Knoxville: University of Tennessee Press, 1991.

Farrell, Michèle Longino. *Performing Motherhood: The Sévigné Correspondence*. Hanover, N.H.: University Press of New England, 1991.

Felber, A. *Unzucht und Kindsmord in der Rechtsprechung der freien Reichstadt Nordlingen* von 15 bis 19 Jahrundert Bonn: 1961.

Ferguson, Margaret, Maureen Quilligan, and Nancy Vickers, eds. *Rewriting the Renaissance: The Discourses of Sexual Differences in Early Modern Europe*. Chicago: University of Chicago Press, 1986.

Figes, Eva. *Patriarchal Attitudes*. New York: London: Faber, 1970.

Fildes, Valerie. *Breasts, Bottles, and Babies: A History of Infant Feeding*. Edinburgh: Edinburgh University Press, 1986.

———. *Wet Nursing: A History from Antiquity to the Present*. London: Basil Blackwell, 1988.

———, ed. *Women as Mothers in Pre-Industrial England*. London: Routledge, 1990.

Fine, Reuben. *A History of Psychoanalysis*. New York: Columbia University Press, 1979.

———. *The Psychoanalytic Vision*. New York: The Free Press, 1981.

Finley, Moses I. "The Elderly in Classical Antiquity." *Greece and Rome* 28: 156–171. Cambridge: Cambridge University Press, 1988.

Fishburn, Katherine. "The Nightmare Repetition: The Mother-Daughter Conflict in Doris Lessing's *Children of Violence*." In *The Lost Tradition: Mothers and Daughters in Literature*, edited by Cathy Davidson and E. M. Broner. New York: Frederick Ungar, 1980.

Fisher, Elizabeth. *Woman's Creation: Sexual Evolution and the Shaping of Society*. Garden City, N.Y.: Doubleday, 1979.

Fishman, Robert. *Bourgeois Utopias: The Rise and Fall of Suburbia*. New York: Basic Books, 1987.

Flandrin, Jean-Lewis. *Families in Former Times: Kinship, Household, and Sexuality*. Translated by Richard Southern. Cambridge: Cambridge University Press, 1979.

Fluegel, J. C. *Man, Morals and Society*. London: Duckworth, 1945.

Foley, Helene. "Women in Greece." In *Civilization of the Ancient Mediterra-*

nean, vol. 1, edited by Michael Grant and Rachel Kitzinger, 1301–1317. New York: Scribner's, 1988.

Forsyth, Ilene. "Children in Early Medieval Art: Ninth through Twelfth Centuries." *Journal of Psychology* 4, no. 1 (Summer 1976): 31–71.

Fraiberg, Selma. *Every Child's Birthright: In Defense of Mothering.* New York: Basic Books, 1977.

———. *The Magic Years: Understanding and Handling the Problems of Early Childhood.* New York: Scribner's, 1959.

Fraser, Antonia. *The Weaker Vessel.* New York: Vintage, 1984.

French, Valerie. "Birth Control, Childbirth, and Early Childhood." In *Civilization of the Ancient Mediterranean,* vol. 1, edited by Michael Grant and Rachel Kitzinger, 1355–1362. New York: Scribner's, 1988, 1989.

———. "Children in Antiquity." In *Children in Historical and Comparative Perspective,* edited by Joseph Hawes and N. Ray Hiner. Westport, Conn.: Greenwood, 1991.

Freud, Anna. *Normality and Pathology in Childhood.* New York: International Universities Press, 1936.

———. *The Concept of the Rejecting Mother,* vol. 3 of the *Collected Papers,* 586–602. New York: International Universities Press, 1969.

———. *The Ego and the Mechanisms of Defense.* New York: International Universities Press, 1936.

Freud, Sigmund. *The Standard Edition of the Complete Psychological Works of Sigmund Freud,* edited and translated by James Strachey, Anna Freud, Alex Strachey, and Alan Tyson. London: Hogarth, 1953.

———. 1896. "Further Remarks on the Neuro-Psychoses of Defense." S.E. 3.

———. 1901–1905. "Three Essays on the Theory of Sexuality." S.E. 7.

———. 1905. "Three Essays on the Theory of Sexuality." S.E. 7.

———. 1910. "Leonardo da Vinci and a Memory of His Childhood." S.E. 11.

———. 1911. "Formulations on the Two Principles of Mental Functioning." S.E. 12.

———. 1914. "On Narcissism." S.E. 14.

———. 1915. "Instincts and their Vicissitudes." S.E. 14.

———. 1916–1917. "Introductory Lectures on Psycho-Analysis (part III): General Theory of Neuroses." S.E. 16.

———. 1917. "Mourning and Melancholia." S.E. 14.

———. 1920. "Beyond the Pleasure Principle." S.E. 18.

———. 1923. "The Ego and the Id." S.E. 19.

———. 1925. "Some Psychical Consequences of the Anatomical Distinction Between the Sexes." S.E. 19.

———. 1926. "Inhibition, Symptoms, and Anxiety." S.E. 20.

———. 1930. "Civilization and Its Discontents." S.E. 21.

———. 1933. "Femininity." S.E. 22.

———. 1937–1939. "An Outline of Psychoanalysis." S.E. 23.

Friedman, N., and S. Grant, eds. *Communicative Structures and Psychic Structures.* New York: Plenum Press, 1977.

Fromm, Erich. *The Anatomy of Human Destructiveness.* New York: Holt, Rinehart, and Winston, 1973.

Fromm-Reichmann, Frieda. *Principles of Intensive Psychotherapy.* Chicago: University of Chicago Press, 1950.

Fuchs, Rachel. *Poor and Pregnant in Paris: Strategies for Survival in the Nineteenth Century.* New Brunswick, N.J.: Rutgers, 1992.

Gadon, Elinor. *The Once and Future Goddess.* New York: Harper and Row, 1989.

Garland, Robert. *The Greek Way of Death.* London: Duckworth, 1985.

———. *The Greek Way of Life: From Conception to Old Age.* London: Duckworth, 1990.

Garner, Sherry Nelson, Claire Kahane, and Madelon Sprengnether, eds. *The (M)other Tongue: Essays in Feminist Psychoanalytic Interpretation.* Ithaca: Cornell University Press, 1985.

Gathorne-Hardy, Jonathan. *The Rise and Fall of the British Nanny.* London: Hodder and Stoughton, 1973.

Gay, Peter. *Freud: A Life for Our Time.* New York: Norton, 1988.

Gesell, Arnold, M.D. "A Half Century of Science and the American Child." *Child Study* (November 1938): 36.

Gibbs, Nancy. "Shameful Bequests to the Next Generation." *Time* (October 8, 1990): 42–46.

Gies, Frances, and Joseph Gies. *Women in the Middle Ages.* New York: Harper and Row, 1978.

Gilbert, Sandra, and Susan Gubar. *The Madwoman in the Attic.* New Haven: Yale University Press, 1979, 1984.

Gimbutas, Marija. *The Goddesses and Gods of Old Europe: 6500–3500 BC Myths and Cult Images.* Berkeley: University of California Press, 1982.

———. *The Language of the Goddess.* New York: Harper and Row, 1989.

———. "Women and Culture in Goddess-Oriented Europe." In *The Politics of Women's Spirituality,* edited by Charlene Spretnak. New York: Doubleday, 1982.

Givelber, Frances. "The Parent-Child Relationship and the Development of Self-Esteem in Childhood." In *The Development and Sustenance of Self-Esteem in Childhood,* edited by John Mack and Steven Ablan. New York: International Universities Press, 1983.

Gledhill, Christine, ed. *Home Is Where the Heart Is: Studies in Melodrama and the Women's Film.* London: BFI, 1987.

Goldberg, Arnold. *Advances in Self-Psychology.* New York: International Universities Press, 1980.

Goldberg, Jonathan. "Fatherly Authority: The Politics of Stuart Family Images." In *Rewriting the Renaissance: The Discourses of Sexual Differences in Early Modern Europe,* edited by Margaret Ferguson, Maureen Quilligan, and Nancy Vickers, 3–33. Chicago: University of Chicago Press, 1986.

Golden, Mark. *Children and Childhood in Classical Athens.* Baltimore: Johns Hopkins University Press, 1990.

———. "Demography and the Exposure of Girls at Athens." *Phoenix* 35, no. 4 (1981): 316–331.

Goode, W. J. *World Revolution and Family Patterns.* New York: Free Press, 1963.

Goodman, Ellen. "The Changing Form — and Often Conflicting Views — of the Family." *Boston Globe* (August 19, 1993): 19.

Goodrich, Norma. *Priestesses.* New York: Harper Perennial, 1989.

Gordon, Linda. *Woman's Body, Woman's Right: A Social History of Birth Control in America.* New York: Penguin, 1974, 1990.

Gordon, Michael, ed. *The American Family in Social and Historical Perspective.* New York: St. Martin's Press, 1983.

Gordon, Suzanne. "Parent-Bashing Is Back with a Vengeance." *Boston Sunday Globe,* 13 Feb. 1991, 65–68.

Gornick, Vivian. "The World and Our Mothers." *New York Times Book Review* (November 22, 1987): 1–54.

Grahn, Judy. "From Sacred Blood to the Curse and Beyond." In *The Politics of Women's Spirituality: Essays on the Rise of Spiritual Power Within the Feminist Movement,* edited by Charlene Spretnak. Garden City, N.Y.: Doubleday Anchor, 1982.

Grant, Michael. *The History of Ancient Israel.* London: Weidenfeld and Nicolson, 1989.

Grant, Michael, and Rachel Kitzinger, eds. *Civilization of the Ancient Mediterranean,* vols. 1 and 3. New York: Scribner's, 1988, 1989.

Graves, Robert. *The White Goddess.* New York: Knopf, 1948.

Green, Alberto Ravinoll. *The Role of Human Sacrifice in the Ancient Near East.* Missoula, Mont.: Scholars Press, 1975.

Greenberg, Jay, and Mitchell Stephen. *Object Relations in Psychoanalytic Theory.* Cambridge: Harvard University Press, 1983.

Greven, Philip. *Protestant Temperament: Patterns of Child-Rearing, Religious Experience, and the Self in Early America.* New York: New American Library, 1977.

———. *Spare the Child: The Religious Roots of Punishment and the Psychological Impact of Physical Abuse.* New York: Knopf, 1991.

Griswold, Robert. *Fatherhood in America.* New York: Basic Books, 1993.

Grossberg, Michael. *Governing the Hearth: Law and Family in Nineteenth-Century America.* Chapel Hill: University of North Carolina Press, 1985.

Grosskurth, Phyllis. "The New Psychology of Women." *The New York Review of Books* (October 24, 1991): 25–32.

Guntrip, Harry. "My Experience of Analysis With Fairbairn and Winnicott." *International Review of Psycho-Analysis* 2 (1975): 145–156.

Hajnal, John. "Two Kinds of Pre-Industrial Household Formation Systems." In *Family Forms in Historic Europe,* edited by Richard Wall, Jean Robin, and Peter Laslett, 65–104. Cambridge: Cambridge University Press, 1983.

Hamilton, Robert, and Michele Barrett, eds. *The Poetics of Diversity.* New York: New Left Books, 1986.

Hanawalt, Barbara. *The Ties That Bound: Peasant Families in Medieval England.* New York: Oxford University Press, 1986.

Harding, Esther. *Women's Mysteries.* New York: Bantam Books, 1973.

Hardyment, Christina. *Dream Babies: Three Centuries of Good Advice on Child Care.* New York: Harper and Row, 1983.

Hareven, Tamara. "Family Time and Individual Time: Family and Work in a Planned Corporation Town, 1900–1924." *Journal of Urban History* 1 (1975): 365–389.

———. "The History of the Family and the Complexity of Social Change." *American Historical Review* 8, no. 1 (1991).

Harris, William. "The Theoretical Possibility of Extensive Infanticide in the Graeco-Roman World." *Classical Quarterly* 32 (1982): 114–116.

Harrison, Roland Kenneth. *Old Testament Times.* Grand Rapids: William B. Eerdmans Publishing Co., 1970.

Harriss, John, ed. *The Family: A Social History of the Twentieth Century.* New York: Oxford, 1991.

Hartmann, Heinz. *Ego Psychology and the Problem of Adaptation.* New York: International Universities Press, 1958.

Haskell, Molly. "Hollywood Madonnas." *MS* (May 1988): 84–86.

———. "Meryl Streep: Hidden in the Spotlight." *MS* (December 1988): 68–72.

Havelock, Christine. "Mourners on Greek Vases: Remarks on the Social History of Women." In *Feminism and Art History,* edited by Norma Broude and Mary Garrard, 45–63. New York: Harper and Row, 1982.

Hawes, Joseph, and N. Ray Hiner. *American Childhood: A Research Guide and Historical Handbook.* Westport, Conn.: Greenwood, 1985.

———. *Children in Historical and Comparative Perspective.* New York: Greenwood Press, 1991.

Hawkes, Jacquetta. *Dawn of the Gods: Minoan and Mycenaean Origins of Greece.* New York: Random House, 1968.

Hays, Hoffman Reynolds. *The Dangerous Sex: The Myth of Feminine Evil.* New York: Pocket Books, 1964.

Heilbrun, Carolyn. *Hamlet's Mother and Other Women.* New York: Columbia University Press, 1990.

Helterline, Marilyn. "The Emergence of Modern Motherhood: Motherhood in England 1899–1959." *International Journal of Women's Studies* 3, no. 6: 590–614.

Henderson, Jeffrey. "Greek Attitudes Toward Sex." In *Civilization of the Ancient Mediterranean,* vol. 1, edited by Michael Grant and Rachel Kitzinger, 1249–1263. New York: Scribner's, 1988.

Herlihy, David. "Medieval Children." In *Walter Pressott Webb Memorial Lectures: Essays on Medieval Civilization,* 109–141. Austin: University of Texas, 1976.

———. *Medieval Households.* Cambridge: Harvard University Press, 1985.

Herman, Nini. *Too Long a Child: The Mother-Daughter Dyad.* London: Free Association, 1989.

Herodotus. *The Histories, Book 1,* translated by George Rawlensen. Tudor, 1949.

Hewlett, Sylvia Ann. *Lesser Life: The Myth of Women's Liberation in America.* New York: Warner, 1986.

———. *When the Bough Breaks: The Cost of Neglecting Our Children.* New York: Basic Books, 1991.

Hirsch, Marianne. *The Mother/Daughter Plot: Narrative, Psychoanalysis, Feminism.* Bloomington: Indiana University Press, 1989.

Hoffer, Peter, and Neil Hull. *Murdering Mothers: Infanticide in England and New England 1558–1803.* New York: New York University Press, 1981.

Holbrook, M. L. *Parturition Without Pain: A Code of Directions for Escaping From the Primal Curse.* New York: Wood and Holbrook, 1873.

Holt, Luther, Jr. *The Care and Feeding of Children: A Catechism for the Use of Mothers and Children's Nurses,* 183–184. New York: D. Appleton and Co., 1929.

Holzman, Philip. *Psychoanalysis and Psychopathology.* New York: McGraw-Hill, 1970.

Homans, Margaret. *Bearing the Word: Language and Female Experience in Nineteenth-Century Women's Writing.* Chicago: University of Chicago Press, 1986.

Honey, Maureen. *Creating Rosie the Riveter.* Amherst: University of Massachusetts Press, 1984.

Hopkins, Keith. *Death and Renewal.* Cambridge: Cambridge University Press, 1983.

Hochschild, Arlie, with Anne Machung. *The Second Shift: Working Parents and the Revolution at Home.* New York: Viking, 1989.

Horney, Karen. "The Flight from Womanhood." *International Journal of Psycho-Analysis* 12 (1926): 360–364.

———. "The Flight from Womanhood: The Masculinity Complex in Women as Viewed by Men and by Women." In *Women and Analysis,* edited by Jean Strouse, 171–186. New York: Grossman, 1974.

Houghton, Walter. *The Victorian Frame of Mind.* New Haven: Yale University Press, 1957.

Houlbrooke, Ralph A. *The English Family: 1450–1700.* London: Longman, 1984, 1986.

Huet, Marie-Helene. *Monstrous Imagination.* Cambridge: Harvard University Press, 1993.

Hufton, O. H. *The Poor of Eighteenth-Century France 1750–1789.* Oxford: Oxford University Press, 1974.

Huizinga, J. H. *The Waning of the Middle Ages: A Study of the Forms of Life, Thought and Art in France and the Netherlands in the 14th and 15th Centuries.* London: Edward Arnold, 1924.

Hunt, David. *Parents and Children in History: The Psychology of Family Life in Early Modern France.* New York: Basic Books, 1970.

Hunt, Lynn. *The Family Romance of the French Revolution.* Berkeley: University of California Press, 1992.

Irigaray, Luce. *Speculum of the Other Woman,* translated by Gillian G. Gill. Ithaca: Cornell University Press, 1985, a.

———. *This Sex Which Is Not One,* translated by C. Porter with C. Burke. Ithaca: Cornell University Press, 1985.

Jankowski, Theodora. *Women in Power in the Early Modern Drama.* Urbana: University of Illinois Press, 1992.

Jensen, Adolf. *Myth and Cult Among Primitive Peoples.* Chicago: University of Chicago Press, 1963.

Johansson, S. Ryan. "Centuries of Childhood/Centuries of Parenting: Philippe Ariès and the Modernization of Privileged Infancy." *Journal of Family History* 12, no. 4 (1987).

Johnson, Paul. *A History of the Jews.* New York: Harper and Row, 1987.

Johnson, Thomas, ed. *The Letters of Emily Dickinson.* Cambridge: Harvard University Press, 1958.

Jordan, Thomas. *Victorian Childhood: Themes and Variations.* Albany: State University of New York Press, 1987.

Kagan, Jerome. *The Nature of the Child.* New York: Basic Books, 1984.

Kagan, Jerome, and H. Moss. *Birth to Maturity: A Study of Psychological Development.* New York: John Wesley, 1962.

Kahn, Coppélia. "The Absent Mother in *King Lear.*" In *Rewriting the Renaissance: The Discourses of Sexual Differences in Early Modern Europe,* edited by Margaret Ferguson, Maureen Quilligan, and Nancy Vickers, 33–56. Chicago: University of Chicago Press, 1986.

———. "The Hand That Rocks the Cradle: Recent Gender Theories, and Their Implications." In *The (M)other Tongue: Essays in Feminist Psychoanalytic Interpretation,* edited by Shirley Garner, Claire Kahane, and Madelon Sprengnether, 72–89. Ithaca: Cornell University Press, 1985.

Kahr, Brett. "The Sexual Molestation of Children: Historical Perspectives." *Journal of Psychohistory,* vol. 19, no. 2 (Fall 1991).

Kaplan, E. Ann. *Motherhood and Representation: The Mother in Popular Culture and Melodrama.* New York: Rutledge, 1992.

———. "Mothering, Feminism and Representation: The Maternal in Melodrama and the Women's Film 1910–40." In *Home Is Where the Heart Is: Studies in Melodrama and the Woman's Film,* edited by Christine Gledhill, 113–138. London: BFI, 1987.

Kaplan, Meryle M. *Mother's Images of Motherhood.* London: Routledge, 1992.

Karen, Robert. "Becoming Attached." *The Atlantic Monthly* (Feb. 1990): 35–70.

Kastor, Elizabeth. "Magazine Boom: Mass Appeal to Yuppie Kids." *Boston Globe* (16 August 1990).

Kellum, Barbara. "Infanticide in England in the Late Middle Ages." *History of Childhood Quarterly* 1 (1973): 367–388.

Kelly-Gadol, Joan. "Did Women Have a Renaissance?" In *Becoming Visible: Women in European History,* 2nd ed., edited by Renate Bridenthal, Claudia Koonz, and Susan Stuard, 175–203. Boston: Houghton Mifflin, 1976, 1987.

Kerber, Linda. *Women of the Republic: Intellect and Ideology in Revolutionary America.* Chapel Hill: University of North Carolina Press, 1980, 1988.

Kestenberg, Judith. "On the Development of Maternal Feeling in Early Childhood." *Psychoanalytic Study of the Child* 11 (1956): 257–291.

———. "Regression and Reintegration in Pregnancy." *Journal of the American Psychoanalytic Association* 24 (suppl. 1976): 213–250.

Keuls, Eva. *The Reign of the Phallus: Sexual Politics in Ancient Athens.* New York: Harper and Row, 1985.

King, Margaret. "Book-Lined Cells: Women and Humanists in the Early Renaissance." In *Beyond Their Sex: Learned Women of the European Past,* edited by Patricia H. Labalme, 66–90. New York: New York University Press, 1980.

———. *Women of the Renaissance.* Chicago: University of Chicago Press, 1991.

———. "Women's Roles in Early Modern Venice." In *Beyond Their Sex: Learned Women of the European Past,* edited by Patricia H. Labalme, 129–152. New York: New York University Press, 1980.

Kinsley, David. *The Goddesses' Mirror.* Albany: State University of New York Press, 1989.

Kittay, Eva Feder. "Womb Envy: An Explanatory Concept." In *Mothering: Essays in Feminist Theory,* edited by Joyce Treblicot, 94–129. Lanham, Md.: Rowman and Littlefield, 1983.

Kitzinger, Sheila. *Women As Mothers: How They See Themselves in Different Cultures.* New York: Vintage, 1978.

Klapisch-Zuber, Christiane. "Childhood in Tuscany at the Beginning of the Fifteenth Century." In *Women, Family and Ritual in Renaissance Italy,* 94–117. Chicago: University of Chicago Press, 1985.

———. "The 'Cruel Mother': Maternity, Widowhood and Dowry in Florence in the Fourteenth and Fifteenth Century." In *Women, Family and Ritual in Renaissance Italy,* 117–131. Chicago: University of Chicago Press, 1985.

Klaus, Alisa. *Every Child a Lion: The Origins of Maternal and Infant Health Policy in the United States and France, 1890–1920.* Ithaca: Cornell, 1993.

Klaus, Marshall, and John Kennell. *Maternal-Infant Bonding: The Impact of Early Separation or Loss in Family Development.* St. Louis: Mosby, 1976.

Klein, Melanie. *Psychoanalysis of Children.* New York: Grove, 1932, 1960.

Koch, Jim. "Saint to Sinner: Movie Moms Are a Tough Act." *New York Times* (Sunday, 10 May 1992): 17.

Kohon, Gregorio. *The British School of Psychoanalysis: The Independent Tradition.* London: Free Association, 1986.

Kohut, Heinz. "Summarizing Reflections." In *Advances in Self Psychology,* edited by A. Goldberg. New York: International Universities Press, 1980.

———. *The Analysis of the Self.* New York: International Universities Press, 1971.

———. *The Restoration of the Self.* New York: International Universities Press, 1977.

Kolata, Gina Bari. "Kung Hunter-Gatherers: Feminism, Diet, and Birth Control." *Science,* 185: 932–934.

Koonz, Claudia. *Mothers in the Fatherland: Women, the Family, and Nazi Politics.* New York: St. Martin's, 1987.

Kramer, Heinrich, and Jacobus Sprenger. *Malleus Maleficarum,* translated by Montague Summers. London: Arrow Books, 1928.

Kramer, Samuel Noah. *History Begins at Sumer.* Garden City, N.Y.: Doubleday Anchor, 1959.

Kraus, Henry. "Eve and Mary: Conflicting Images of Medieval Women." In *Living Theatre of Medieval Art,* 41–62. Bloomington: Indiana University Press, 1967.

Kristeva, Julia. *Desire in Language.* New York: Columbia University Press, 1977, 1980.

———. "Stabat Mater," translated by Leon S. Roudiez. In *The Female Body in Western Culture,* edited by Susan Suleiman, 99–118. Cambridge: Harvard University Press, 1985.

Krull, Marianne. *Freud and His Father.* New York: W. W. Norton and Co., 1986.

Kunzle, David. "William Hogarth: The Ravaged Child in the Corrupt City." In *Changing Images of the Family,* edited by Virginia Tufte and Barbara Myerhoff, 99–140. New Haven: Yale University Press, 1979.

Kurtz, Donna. *Greek Burial Customs.* London: Thames and Hudson, 1971.

Labalme, Patricia. *Beyond Their Sex: Learned Women of the European Past.* New York: New York University Press, 1980.

Labarge, Margaret. *The Small Sound of the Trumpet: Women in Medieval Life.* Boston: Beacon Press, 1986.

Lacan, Jacques. *Écrits: A Selection,* translated by Alan Sheridan. Ithaca: Cornell University Press, 1977.

Ladurie, Emmanuel. *Montaillou: The Promised Land of Error,* translated by Barbara Bray. London, 1978.

Lamb, Michael E., ed. *The Role of the Father in Child Development.* New York: Wiley, 1976.

Landers, Ann. "Parenthood: Is It All Pain, Little Joy?" *Wisconsin State Journal* (June 16, 1976).

Langer, Cassandra. *Mother and Child in Art.* New York: Crescent, 1992.

Leites, Nathan. *Art and Life: Aspects of Michelangelo.* New York: New York University Press, 1986.

Lenz, Elinor. "The Generation Gap: From Persephone to Portnoy." *New York Times Book Review* (August 30, 1987).

Lerman, Hannah. *A Mole in Freud's Eye: From Psychoanalysis to the Psychology of Women.* New York: Springer Publishing, 1986.

Lerner, Gerda. *The Creation of Feminist Consciousness: From the Middle Ages to 1870.* New York: Oxford, 1993.

———. *The Creation of Patriarchy.* New York: Oxford University Press, 1986.

Lesser, Wendy. *His Other Half: Men Looking at Women Through Art.* Cambridge: Harvard University Press, 1991.

Lévi-Strauss, Claude. *The Elementary Structures of Kinship.* Boston, 1969.

Levin, Carole. "Power, Politics, and Sexuality: Images of Elizabeth I." In

The Politics of Gender in Early Modern Europe, edited by Jean Brink, Allison Coudert, and Maryanne C. Horovitz, 95–111. Tempe: Northeast Missouri State, 1987.

Levy, David. *Maternal Overprotection.* New York: Columbia University Press, 1943.

Lewis, Jane, ed. *Labour and Love: Women's Experience of Home and Family, 1850–1940.* Oxford: Basil Blackwell, 1986.

Lewis, Judith Schneid. *In the Family Way: Childbearing in the British Aristocracy, 1760–1860.* New Brunswick: Rutgers University Press, 1986.

Lichtenberg, Joseph. *Psychoanalysis and Infant Research.* Hillsdale, N.J.: Analytic Press, 1983.

Langer, William. "Infanticide: A Historical Survey." *History of Childhood Quarterly* (1974): 353–374.

Larner, Christina. *Enemies of God: The Witch-Hunt in Scotland.* London: Chatto and Windus, 1986.

———. "Witchcraft Past and Present." In *Witchcraft and Religion: The Politics of Popular Belief,* edited by Alan MacFarlane, 79–91. Oxford: Basil Blackwell, 1984.

Laslett, Peter. *The World We Have Lost,* 2nd rev. ed. London: Methuen, 1972.

Laslett, Peter, and Richard Walls, eds. *Household and Family in Past Time.* Cambridge: Cambridge University Press, 1972.

Lazarre, Jane. *The Mother Knot.* New York: McGraw-Hill, 1976.

Leacock, Eleanor. "Women in Egalitarian Societies." In *Becoming Visible: Women in European History,* edited by Renate Bridenthal, Claudia Koonz, and Susan Stuard. Boston: Houghton Mifflin, 1977.

Le Guin, Ursula. "The Hand That Rocks the Cradle Writes the Book." *New York Times Book Review* (22 January 1989).

Lederer, Wolfgang. *The Fear of Women.* New York: Harcourt, Brace, 1968.

Lee, Richard B., and Irven De Vore, eds. *Man the Hunter.* Chicago: Aldine, 1968.

Lefkowitz, Mary. "Liberty for Whom?" *New York Times Book Review* (November 17, 1991): 23.

———. *Women in Greek Myth.* Baltimore: Johns Hopkins University Press, 1986.

Lefkowitz, Mary, and Maureen Fant. *Women's Life in Greece and Rome.* Baltimore: Johns Hopkins University Press, 1982.

Leibert, Robert. *Michelangelo: A Psychological Study of His Life and Images.* New Haven: Yale University Press, 1983.

Lidoff, Joan. "Virginia Woolf's Feminine Sentence: The Mother-Daughter World of *To The Lighthouse.*" *Literature and Psychology* 32, no. 3 (1986): 43–59.

Luepnitz, Deborah Anna. *The Family Interpreted: Psychoanalysis, Feminism and Family Therapy.* New York: Basic Books, 1988.

Lundberg, Ferdinand, and Marynia Farnham. *Modern Woman: The Lost Sex.* New York: Harper Brothers, 1947.

MacDonald, Susan Peck. "Jane Austen and the Tradition of the Absent Mother." In *The Lost Tradition: Mothers and Daughters in Literature,* edited by Cathy Davidson and E. M. Broner, 58–70. New York: Frederick Ungar, 1980.

MacFarlane, Alan. *Marriage and Love in England 1300–1890.* New York: Basil Blackwell, 1986.

———. "Illegitimacy and Illegitimate in English History." In *Bastardy and Its Comparative History,* edited by Peter Laslett, Karla Osterveen, and Richard M. Smith. London: Edward Arnold, 1980.

———. *The Family Life of Ralph Josselyn: A Seventeenth-Century Clergyman.* Cambridge: Cambridge University Press, 1970.

———, ed. *Witchcraft and Religion: The Politics of Popular Belief.* Oxford: Basil Blackwell, 1984.

Mahler, Margaret. "On Human Symbiosis." In *Anxiety and Ego Formation,* edited by Sylvia Brody and Sidney Axelrod. New York: International Universities Press, 1971.

———. "Notes on the Development of Basic Moods: The Depressive Effect." In *Psychoanalysis: A General Psychology,* edited by R. M. Lowenstein, L. M. Newman, M. Schur, and A. J. Solnit, 152–168. New York: International Universities Press, 1966.

———. "On the First Three Subphases of the Separation-Individuation Process." *International Journal of Psychoanalysis* 53 (1972): 333–338.

———. "Thoughts About Development and Individuation." *Psychoanalytic Study of the Child* 18 (1963): 307–324.

Mahler, Margaret, F. Pine, and A. Bergman. *The Psychological Birth of the Human Infant.* New York: Basic Books, 1975.

Mack, John, and Steven Ablon. *The Development and Sustenance of Self-Esteem in Childhood.* New York: International Universities Press, 1983.

Mahony, Patrick. *Freud and the Rat Man.* New Haven: Yale University Press, 1986.

Maloney, Mercedes Lynch, and Anne Maloney. *The Hand That Rocks the Cradle: Mothers, Sons and Leadership.* New York: Prentice-Hall, 1985.

Marcus, Steven. *Freud and the Culture of Psychoanalysis.* Boston: George Allen and Unwin, 1984.

Margolis, Maxine. *Mothers and Such: Views of American Women and Why They Changed.* Berkeley: University of California Press, 1984.

Marks, Elaine, and Isabelle de Courtivron, eds. *New French Feminisms.* Brighton: Harvester, 1975.

Maroney, Heather J. "Embracing Motherhood: New Feminist Theory." In *The Politics of Diversity,* edited by Roberta Hamilton and Michele Barrett. London: Verso, 1986.

Marshall, Harriette. "The Social Construction of Motherhood: An Analysis of Children and Parenting Manuals." In *Motherhood: Meanings, Practices and Ideologies,* edited by Ann Phoenix, Anne Woollett, and Eva Lloyd, 66–86. London: Sage, 1991.

Marshall, Sherrin. "Childhood in Early Modern Europe." In *Children in His-*

torical and Comparative Perspective, edited by Joseph Hawes and N. Ray Hiner, 53–71. New York: Greenwood Press, 1991.

Marvick, Elizabeth. "Nature vs. Nurture: Patterns and Trends in Seventeenth-Century French Child-Rearing." In *The History of Childhood,* edited by Lloyd deMause, 259–303. New York: Peter Bedrick, 1974.

Massa, Aldo. *The Phoenicians.* Geneva, 1977.

Massey, Michael. *Women in Ancient Greece and Rome.* Cambridge: Cambridge University Press, 1988.

Masson, Jeffrey Moussaieff. *The Assault on Truth: Freud's Suppression of the Seduction Theory.* New York: Farrar, Straus and Giroux, 1984.

Matter, E. Ann. "The Virgin Mary: A Goddess." In *The Book of the Goddess: Past and Present,* edited by Carl Olson, 80–92. New York: Crossroads Publishing, 1990.

Matthews, Glenn. *Just a Housewife: The Rise and Fall of Domesticity in America.* New York: Oxford, 1987.

May, Elaine Tyler. *Homeward Bound: American Families in the Cold War Era.* New York: Basic Books, 1988.

McBride, Angela Barron. *The Growth and Development of Mothers.* New York: Harper and Row, 1973.

McCartney, Kathleen, and Deborah Phillips. "Motherhood and Child Care." In *The Different Faces of Motherhood,* edited by Beverly Birns and Dale F. Hay. New York: Plenum Press, 1988.

McLaren, Angus. *A History of Contraception: From Antiquity to the Present Day.* Oxford: Basil Blackwell Ltd., 1990.

McLaughlin, Mary M. "Survivors and Surrogates: Children and Parents from the Ninth to the Thirteenth Centuries." In *The History of Childhood,* edited by Lloyd deMause, 101–183. New York: Peter Bedrick, 1974.

Mead, Margaret. *Male and Female.* New York: Morrow, 1949.

Mead, Margaret, and Martha Wolfenstein, eds. *Childhood in Contemporary Cultures.* Chicago: University of Chicago Press, 1955.

Mellaart, James. *Catal Hüyük: A Neolithic Town in Anatolia.* London: Thames and Hudson, 1967.

Meyers, Carol. *Discovering Eve: Ancient Israelite Women in Context.* New York: Oxford University Press, 1988.

Miles, Margaret. *Images and Insight: Visual Understanding in Western Christianity and Secular Culture.* Boston: Beacon, 1985.

———. "The Virgin's One Bare Breast: Female Nudity and Meaning in Tuscan Renaissance Culture." In *The Female Body in Western Culture,* edited by Susan R. Suleiman, 193–209. Cambridge: Harvard University Press, 1985, 1986.

Miles, Rosalind. *The Women's History of the World.* New York: Harper and Row, 1989.

Miller, Daniel, and Guy Swanson. *The Changing American Parent.* New York: John Wiley and Sons, 1958.

Miller, Douglas T., and Marion Nowak. *The Fifties: The Way We Really Were.* Garden City: Doubleday, 1977.

Miller, Jean Baker. *Toward a New Psychology of Women*. Boston: Beacon Press, 1976.

Mintz, Steven, and Susan Kellogg. *Domestic Revolutions: A Social History of American Family Life*. New York: Free Press, 1988.

Mitchell, Juliet. *Psychoanalysis and Feminism*. New York: Pantheon, 1974.

Mitford, Jessica. *The American Way of Birth*. New York: Dutton, 1992.

Moi, Toril. *Sexual/Textual Politics: Feminist Literary Theory*. London: Methuen, 1985.

Montague, Ashley. *The Natural Superiority of Women*. New York: Macmillan, 1953.

Monter, E. William. "Protestant Wives, Catholic Saints and the Devil's Handmaid: Women in the Age of Reformation." In *Becoming Visible: Women in European History,* edited by Renate Bridenthal, Claudia Koonz, and Susan Stuard. Boston: Houghton Mifflin, 1977, 2nd. edition 1987.

———. "The Pedestal and the Stake: Courtly Love and Witchcraft." In *Becoming Visible: Women in European History,* edited by Renate Bridenthal and Claudia Koonz. Boston: Houghton Mifflin, 1977.

Montrose, Lewis. "*A Midsummer Night's Dream* and the Shaping Fantasies of Elizabethan Culture: Gender, Power, Form." In *Rewriting the Renaissance: The Discourses of Sexual Differences in Early Modern Europe*, edited by Margaret Ferguson, Maureen Quilligan, and Nancy Vickers, 65–88. Chicago: University of Chicago Press, 1986.

Mosca, Paul. "Child Sacrifice in Canaanite and Israelite Religion: A Study in *Mulk* and *Mlk*." Ph.D. diss., Harvard University, 1975.

Mount, Ferdinand. *The Subversive Family: An Alternative History of Love and Marriage*. London: Counterpoint, 1982.

Neumann, Erich. *The Great Mother: An Analysis of the Archetype,* translated by Ralph Manheim. Princeton: Princeton University Press, 1955.

Newman, Karen. *Fashioning Femininity and English Renaissance Drama*. Chicago: University of Chicago Press, 1991.

Nicholas, David. "Childhood in Medieval Europe." In *Children in Historical and Comparative Perspective,* edited by Joseph Hawes and N. Roy Hiner, 13–53. New York: Greenwood, 1991.

———. *The Domestic Life of a Medieval City: Women, Children and the Family in Fourteenth Century Ghent*. Lincoln: University of Nebraska Press, 1985.

Notman, Malkah, and Eva Lester. "Pregnancy: Theoretical Considerations." *Psychoanalytic Inquiry* 8, no. 1 (1988): 139–159.

O'Faolain, Julia, and Laura Martines, eds. *Not In God's Image*. New York: Harper Torchbooks, 1973.

Ochshorn, Judith. "Ishtar and Her Cult." In *The Book of the Goddess: Past and Present,* edited by Carl Olson. New York: Crossroads Publishing, 1990.

Olivier, Christiane. *Jocasta's Children,* translated by George Craig. London: Routledge, 1989.

Olsen, Tillie. *Silences*. New York: Doubleday, 1972, 1979.

Olson, Carl. *The Book of the Goddess: Past and Present*. New York: Crossroads Publishing, 1990.

Ortner, Sherry. "Is Female to Male as Nature Is to Culture?" In *Women, Culture and Society,* edited by M. Z. Rosaldo and Louise Lamphere, 67–88. San Francisco: Stanford University Press, 1974.

Osofsky, J.R. "Attachment Theory and Research and the Psychoanalytic Process." *Psychoanalytic Psychology* 5, no. 2 (Spring 1988).

Ostling, Richard. "Handmaid or Feminist?" *Time* 138, no. 26 (December 30, 1991): 62–69.

Otwell, John. *And Sarah Laughed: The Status of Women in the Old Testament*. Philadelphia: Westminster Press, 1977.

Ozment, Steven. *When Father Ruled: Family Life in Reformation Europe*. Cambridge: Harvard University Press, 1983.

Paglia, Camille. *Sexual Personae: Art and Decadence from Nefertiti to Emily Dickinson*. New York: Vintage, 1990.

Parens, H., L. Pollock, L. Stern, and S. Kramer. "On Girls' Entry Into the Oedipus Complex." *Journal of American Psychoanalytic Association* 24 (suppl. 1976): 79–108.

Parkes, Colin Murray, and Joan Stevenson-Hinde. *The Place of Attachment in Human Behavior.* New York: Basic Books, 1982.

Patai, Raphael. *The Hebrew Goddess*. New York: Avon, 1967.

Patterson, Cynthia. "Not Worth Being: The Causes of Infant Exposure in Ancient Greece." *Transactions of the American Philological Association. 135.*

Pattison, Robert. *The Child Figure in English Literature*. Athens: University of Georgia Press, 1978.

Pearsall, Ronald. *The Worm in the Bud: The World of Victorian Sexuality*. London: Weidenfeld and Nicolson, 1969.

Pearson, Carol, and Katherine Pope. *The Female Hero in American and British Literature*. New York: R. R. Bowker Co., 1981.

Peck, Ellen, and Judith Senderowitz, eds. *Pronatalism: The Myth of Mom and Apple Pie*. New York: Thomas Y. Crowell Co., 1974.

Peiper, Albrecht. *Geschichte der Kinderheil Kunde*. Leipzig, 1956.

Pentikain, Joha. *The Nordic Dead Child Tradition*. Helsinki: FF Communications, 22, 1968.

Phoenix, Ann, Anne Woollett, and Eva Lloyd, eds. *Motherhood: Meanings, Practices and Ideologies*. London: Sage, 1991.

Piers, Maria. *Infanticide*. New York: Norton, 1978.

Pinchbeck, Ivy, and Margaret Hewitt. *Children in English Society*. 2 vols. London: Routledge and Kegan Paul, 1969, 1973.

Pine, Fred. *Developmental Theory and Clinical Process*. New Haven: Yale University Press, 1985.

Pines, Malcolm. "Reflections in Memory." *International Review of Psychology* 11, no. 1 (1989): 27–92.

Plaza, Monique. "The Mother/The Same: Hatred of Mother in Psychoanalysis." *Feminist Issues* (Spring 1982): 75–99.

Pleck, Elizabeth. *Domestic Tyranny: The Making of American Social Policy Against Family Violence from Colonial Times to the Present.* New York: Oxford University Press, 1987.

Polatnick, M. Rivkal. "Why Men Don't Rear Children: A Power Analysis." In *Mothering: Essays in Feminist Theory,* edited by Joyce Treblicot. Lanham, Md.: Rowman and Littlefield, 1983.

Pollitt, Katha. "Are Women Morally Superior To Men?: Debunking 'Difference Feminism.'" *Utne Reader* (Sept./Oct. 1993): 101–109.

Pollock, Linda. *A Lasting Relationship: Parents and Children Over 3 Centuries.* Hanover: University Press of New England, 1987.

———. *Forgotten Children: Parent-Child Relations from 1500 to 1900.* Cambridge: Cambridge University Press, 1983.

Pomeroy, Sarah. *Goddesses, Whores, Wives, and Slaves: Women in Classical Antiquity.* New York: Schocken, 1975.

———. "Infanticide in Hellenistic Greece." In *Images of Women in Antiquity,* edited by Averil Cameron and Amalie Kuhrt. London: 1983.

Porter, Ray. "Mixed Feelings: The Enlightenment and Sexuality." In *Sexuality in Eighteenth-Century Britain,* edited by Paul-Gabriel Boucé. Manchester, England: Manchester University Press, 1982.

Rabuzzi, Kathryn. *Motherself: A Mythic Analysis of Motherhood.* Bloomington: Indiana University Press, 1988.

Radbill, Samuel. "Children in a World of Violence: A History of Child Abuse." In *The Battered Child,* fourth edition, edited by Ray Helfer and Ruth Kempe. Chicago: University of Chicago Press, 1987.

Ransel, David. *Mothers of Misery: Child Abandonment in Russia.* Princeton: Princeton University Press, 1988.

———. "Russia and the USSR." In *Children in Historical and Comparative Perspective,* edited by Joseph Hawes and N. Ray Hiner, 471–491. Westport, Conn.: Greenwood, 1985.

Reed, James. *From Private Vice to Public Virtue: The Birth Control Movement and American Society Since 1830.* New York: Basic Books: 1978.

Reik, Theodor. *The Creation of Women.* New York: Braziller, 1960.

Ribble, Margaret. *The Rights of Infants: Early Psychological Needs and Their Satisfactions.* New York: Columbia University Press, 1943.

Rich, Adrienne. *Of Women Born: Motherhood as Experience and Institution.* New York: W. W. Norton, 1976, 1986.

———. *On Lies, Secrets, and Silence: Selected Prose, 1966–1978.* New York: W. W. Norton, 1979.

Riley, Denise. *War in the Nursery: Theories of the Child and Mother.* London: Virago, 1983.

Roazen, Paul. *Freud and His Followers.* New York: New York University Press, 1984.

Robertson, Priscilla. "Home as a Nest: Middle-Class Childhood in Nineteenth-Century Europe." In *The History of Childhood,* edited by Lloyd deMause, 407–432. New York: Peter Bedrick, 1974, 1988.

Rogers, Katherine. *The Troublesome Helpmate: A History of Misogyny in Literature.* Seattle: University of Washington Press, 1966.

Rohrlich-Leavitt, Ruby. "Women in Transition: Crete and Sumer." In *Becoming Visible: Women in European History,* edited by Renate Bridenthal, Claudia Koonz, and Susan Stuard. Boston: Houghton Mifflin, 1977.

Rokeah, Zefira E. "Unnatural Child Death Among Christians and Jews in Medieval England." *Journal of Psychoanalysis* 18, no. 2 (Fall 1990): 181–226.

Rollin, Betty. "Motherhood: Fad or Myth." In *Pronatalism: The Myth of Mom and Apple Pie,* edited by Ellen Peck and Judith Senderowitz. New York: Thomas Y. Crowell Co., 1974.

Rosaldo, M. Z., and Louise Lamphere, eds. *Women, Culture and Society.* San Francisco: Stanford University Press, 1974.

Rose, Lionel. *The Massacre of the Innocents: Infanticide in Britain 1800–1939.* London: Routledge Kegan Paul, 1986.

Rosenberg, Charles, ed. *The Family in History.* Philadelphia: University of Pennsylvania Press, 1975.

Rosenblum, Robert. *The Romantic Child.* New York: Thames and Hudson, 1988.

Ross, James Bruce. "The Middle-Class Child in Urban Italy: Fourteenth to Early Sixteenth Century." In *The History of Childhood,* edited by Lloyd de Mause, 183–229. New York: Psychohistory Press, 1974.

Rotberg, Robert, and Theodore Rabb, eds. *Art and History: Images and Their Meaning.* Cambridge: Cambridge University Press, 1988.

Rothgeb, Carrie Lee, ed. *Abstracts of the Standard Edition of the Complete Psychological Works of Sigmund Freud.* Northvale: Jason Anderson, Inc., 1973.

Ruddick, Sara. *Maternal Thinking: Toward a Politics of Peace.* Boston: Beacon Press, 1989.

Ruether, Rosemary R. *Mary — The Feminine Face of the Church.* Philadelphia: Westminster Press, 1977.

———, ed. *Religion and Sexism.* New York: Simon and Schuster, 1974.

Ruskin, John. "Of Queens' Gardens." *Works,* 8, sect. 68 (1865): 122.

Rutter, Michael. *Maternal Deprivation Reassessed.* New York: Penguin, 1972.

Rybczynski, Witold. *Home: A Short History of an Idea.* New York: Penguin, 1986.

Rycroft, Charles. *Psychoanalysis and Beyond.* Chicago: University of Chicago Press, 1985.

Sachs, Hannelore. *The Renaissance Woman.* New York: McGraw Hill, 1971.

Sander, L. W. "Regulation of Exchange in the Infant-Caretaker System: A Viewpoint on the Ontogeny of 'Structures.'" In *Communicative Structures and Psychic Structures,* 13–34, edited by N. Friedman and S. Grant. New York: Plenum Press, 1977.

Sayers, Janet. *Mothers of Psychoanalysis: Helen Deutsch, Karen Horney, Anna Freud, Melanie Klein.* New York: W. W. Norton, 1991.

Scacheri, Robert. "The Early Birth Control Movement: Role of the Nineteenth-Century American Physician." *The Pharos* (Spring 1993): 15–20.

Schaffer, H. R., and P. E. Emerson. "The Development of Social Attachments in Infancy." *Monograph of the Society for Research in Child Development* 29 (1964).

Schaffer, Rudolph. *Mothering*. Cambridge: Harvard University Press, 1977.

Schama, Simon. *Citizens: A Chronicle of the French Revolution*. New York: Vintage, 1990.

———. "Domestic Environment in Early Modern England and America." In *The American Family in Social-Historical Perspective,* edited by Michael Gordon, 113–136. New York: St. Martin's Press, 1983.

———. "The Domestication of Majesty: Royal Family Portraiture, 1500–1850." In *Art and History: Images and Their Meaning,* edited by Robert Rotberg and Theodore Rabb, 155–185. Cambridge: Cambridge University Press, 1988.

———. *The Embarrassment of Riches: An Interpretation of Dutch Culture in the Golden Age*. Berkeley: University of California Press, 1988.

Schatzman, Morton. *Soul Murder: Persecution in the Family*. Hammondsworth: Penguin Books, 1976.

Schneiderman, Stuart. "Everybody's Mother Is a Woman." *New York Times Book Review* (Jan. 21, 1990): 12.

Schnucker, Robert. "Puritan Attitude Toward Childhood Discipline." In *Women as Mothers in Pre-Industrial England,* edited by Valerie Fildes. London: Routledge, 1990.

Schotz, Myra G. "The Great Unwritten Story: Mothers and Daughters in Shakespeare." In *The Lost Tradition: Mothers and Daughters in Literature,* edited by Cathy Davidson and E. M. Broner, 44–56. New York: Frederick Ungar, 1980.

Schur, M. *Freud: Living and Dying*. New York: International Universities Press, 1972.

Segal, Hanna. *Introduction to the Work of Melanie Klein*. New York: Basic Books, 1974.

Shackley, Myra. *Human Sacrifice: In History and Today*. New York: William Morrow and Co., 1980, 1981.

Shahar, Shulamith. *Childhood in the Middle Ages*. London: Routledge, 1990.

———. *The Fourth Estate: A History of Women in the Middle Ages*. New York: Methuen, 1983.

Shammas, Carol. "The Domestic Environment in Early Modern England and America." In *The American Family in Social-Historical Perspective,* 113–136, edited by Michael Gordon. New York: St. Martin's Press, 1983.

Shorter, Edward. *The Making of the Modern Family*. New York: Basic Books, 1975.

Silverstein, Louise. "Transforming the Debate About Child Care and Maternal Employment." *American Psychologist* 46, no. 10 (1991): 1025–1032.

Simonds, Wendy. *Women and Self-Help Culture: Reading Between the Lines*. New Brunswick: Rutgers University Press, 1992.

Sjoo, Monica, and Barbara Mor. *The Great Cosmic Mother.* San Francisco: Harper and Row, 1987.

Skolnick, Arlene. *Embattled Paradise.* New York: Basic Books, 1991.

Skolnick, Arlene, and Jerome Skolnick, eds. *Family in Transition,* 5th ed. Boston: Little, Brown, 1986.

Slater, Philip. *The Glory of Hera.* Boston: Beacon Press, 1968.

Smith, Janna M. "Mothers: Tired of Taking the Rap." *New York Times Magazine* (June 10, 1990): 32–38.

Smith, Richard. "Kin and Neighbors in a Thirteenth-Century Suffolk Community." *Journal of Family History* 4 (1979): 219–256.

———. "The Female World of Love and Ritual: Relations Between Women in Nineteenth-Century America." *Signs* 1 (Autumn 1975).

Snitow, Ann. "Feminism and Motherhood: An American Reading." In *Feminist Review,* 40 (Spring 1992): 32–51.

Sommerville, C. John. *The Rise and Fall of Childhood.* New York: Vintage, 1982, 1990.

———. *The Discovery of Childhood in Puritan England.* Athens: University of Georgia Press, 1992.

———. "English Puritans and Children: A Socio-Cultural Explanation." *Journal of Psychology* 5, no. 4 (1978): 113–139.

Soren, David, Aicha Ben Abed Ben Khaden, and Hedi Slim. *Carthage.* New York: Simon and Schuster, 1990.

Spitz, René. *The First Year of Life.* New York: International Universities Press, 1965.

Spock, Benjamin. *The Pocket Book of Baby and Child Care.* New York: Pocket Book Editions, 1954. Reprint, New York: Pocket Books, 1976. *The Common Sense Book of Baby and Child Care,* original edition. New York: Duell, Sloan and Pearce, 1946.

Sprengnether, Madelon. *The Spectral Mother: Freud, Feminism and Psychoanalysis.* Ithaca: Cornell University Press, 1990.

Spretnak, Charlene, ed. *The Politics of Women's Spirituality.* New York: Doubleday, 1982.

Stager, Lawrence, and Samuel Wolff. "Child Sacrifice at Carthage: Religious Rite or Population Control?" *Biblical Archaeology Review,* 10, no. 1 (January/February 1984): 30–51.

Stallybrass, Peter. "Patriarchal Territories: The Body Inclosed." In *Rewriting the Renaissance: The Discourses of Sexual Differences in Early Modern Europe,* edited by Margaret Ferguson, Maureen Quilligan, and Nancy Vickers, 123–142. Chicago: University of Chicago Press, 1986.

Steiner, George. "Poor Little Lambs." *The New Yorker* (February 6, 1989): 103–106.

Steinfels, Peter. "Seen, Heard, Even Warned About." *New York Times* (Sunday, 27 December 1992), "The Week in Review."

Stern, Daniel. *The First Relationship: Infant and Mother.* Cambridge: Harvard University Press, 1977.

Sternglanz, Sarah Hall, and Alison Nash. "Ethnological Contributions to the Study of Human Motherhood." In *The Different Faces of Motherhood,* edited by Beverly Birns and Dale Hay, 15–43. New York: Plenum Press, 1988.

Still, George. *The History of Paediatrics*. London: Oxford University Press, 1931.

Stiller, Nikki. *Eve's Orphans: Mothers and Daughters in Medieval English Literature*. Westport, Conn.: Greenwood, 1980.

Stoller, Robert. "Primary Femininity." *Journal of American Psychoanalysis* (suppl. 1976): 59–78.

Stone, Lawrence. *The Family, Sex and Marriage in England, 1500–1800*. New York: Harper and Row, 1977.

———. "The Rise of the Nuclear Family in Early Modern England." In *The Family in History,* edited by Charles E. Rosenberg, 13–15. Philadelphia: University of Pennsylvania Press, 1975.

Stone, L. Joseph, M. T. Smith, and L. B. Murphy. *The Complete Infant: Research and Commentary*. New York: Basic Books, 1973.

Stone, Merlin. *When God Was a Woman*. New York: Harcourt Brace, 1976.

Storr, Anthony. *Solitude*. New York: Free Press, 1988.

Strasser, Susan. *Never Done: A History of American Housework*. New York: Pantheon, 1982.

Strecker, Edward A. *Their Mothers' Sons*. Philadelphia: J. B. Lippincott, 1946.

Strouse, Jean, ed. *Women and Analysis*. New York: Grossman, 1974.

Stuard, Susan. "The Dominion of Gender: Women's Fortunes in the High Middle Ages." In *Becoming Visible: Women in European History,* 2nd ed., edited by Renate Bridenthal, Claudia Koonz, and Susan Stuard, 153–175. Boston: Houghton Mifflin, 1976, 1987.

———, ed. *Women in Medieval Society*. Philadelphia: University of Pennsylvania Press, 1976.

Suleiman, Susan R. "Writing and Motherhood." In *The (M)other's Tongue: Essays in Feminist Psychoanalytic Interpretation*. Ithaca: Cornell University Press, 1985.

———. "On Maternal Splitting: Apropos of Mary Gordon's *Men and Angels*." *Signs,* 14, no. 1 (Autumn 1988): 25–47.

Sullivan, Harry S. *Schizophrenia as a Human Process*. New York: W. W. Norton, 1962.

———. *The Interpersonal Theory of Psychiatry*. New York: W. W. Norton, 1953.

Sunley, Robert. "Early Nineteenth-Century American Literature on Child-Rearing." In *Childhood in Contemporary Cultures,* edited by Margaret Mead and Martha Wolfenstein, 150–167. Chicago: University of Chicago Press, 1955.

Sussman, George. *Selling Mother's Milk: The Wet-Nursing Business in France 1715–1914*. Urbana: University of Illinois Press, 1982.

Swigart, Jane. *The Mother in Modern Literature*. Dissertation for the State University of New York at Buffalo, University Microfilms, International, Ann Arbor, 1986.

———. *The Myth of the Bad Mother.* New York: Doubleday, 1991.

Taitz, Sonia. *Mothering Heights: Reclaiming Motherhood from the Experts.* New York: William Morrow, 1992.

Tanner, Nancy, and Adrienne Zihlman. "Women in Evolution, Part 1; Innovation and Selection in Human Origins." *Signs,* vol. 1, no. 3 (1981).

Tatar, Maria. *The Hard Facts of the Grimms' Fairy Tales.* Princeton: Princeton University Press, 1987.

Thackeray, William M. *Vanity Fair,* ed. J. I. M. Stewart. Middlesex: Hammondsworth, 1968.

Thomas, Alexander, and Stella Chess. *Temperament and Development.* New York: Brunner/Mazel, 1977.

Thorne, B., and M. Yalom. *Rethinking the Family: Some Feminist Questions.* New York: Longman, 1982.

Tizard, Barbara. "Employed Mothers and the Care of Young Children." In *Motherhood: Meanings, Practices and Ideologies,* edited by Ann Phoenix, Anne Woollett, and Eva Lloyd, 178–195. London: Sage, 1991.

Tobey, Susan B. *Art of Motherhood.* New York: Abbeville Press, 1991.

Tompkins, Jane. "Sentimental Power: Uncle Tom's Cabin and the Politics of Literary History." *Glyph* 8 (1981): 79–102.

Traub, James. "Goodby, Dr. Spock." *Harper's* (March 1986): 57–64.

Travitsky, Betty. "The New Mother of the English Renaissance: Her Writings on Motherhood." In *The Lost Tradition: Mothers and Daughters in Literature,* edited by Cathy Davidson and E. M. Broner, 33–44. New York: Frederick Ungar, 1980.

Treblicot, Joyce, ed. *Mothering: Essays in Feminist Theory.* Lanham, Md.: Rowman and Littlefield, 1983.

Trexler, Richard C. "Infanticide in Florence: New Sciences and First Results." *History of Childhood Quarterly* 2 (1975): 98–116.

———. "Infanticide in Florence: New Sources and First Results." *History of Childhood Quarterly* 1 (Summer 1973): 98–116.

———. "The Foundlings of Florence, 1395–1450." *History of Childhood Quarterly* 1 (1973): 259–328.

Trible, Phyllis. *God and the Rhetoric of Sexuality.* Philadelphia: Fortress Press, 1978.

———. "Women in the Old Testament." In *Interpreters Dictionary of the Bible, Supplementary Volume,* edited by K. R. Crim. Nashville: Abingdon, 1976.

Troen, Selwyn, and Walter Ackerman. "Israel." In *Children in Historical and Comparative Perspective,* 333–360, edited by Joseph M. Hawes and N. Ray Hiner. New York: Greenwood, 1991.

Trumbach, Randolph. *The Rise of Egalitarian Family: Aristocratic Kinship and Domestic Relations in 18th Century England.* New York: Academic Press, 1978.

Tuchman, Barbara. *A Distant Mirror: The Calamitous 14th Century.* New York: Ballantine, 1978.

Tucker, M. J. "The Child as Beginning and End: Fifteenth- and Sixteenth-

Century English Childhood." In *The History of Childhood,* edited by Lloyd deMause, 229–258. New York: Peter Bedrick, 1974.

Tufte, Virginia, and Barbara Myerhoff, eds. *Changing Images of the Family.* New Haven: Yale University Press, 1979.

Turnbull, Colin. *The Forest People.* New York: Simon and Schuster, 1968.

Van Buren, Jane. *The Modernist Madonna: Semiotics of the Maternal Metaphor.* Bloomington: Indiana University Press, 1989.

Veyne, Paul, ed. *A History of Private Life: From Pagan Rome to Byzantium.* Cambridge: Harvard University Press, 1987.

Walcott, Peter. "Images of the Individual." In *Civilizations of the Ancient Mediterranean,* vol. 3, edited by Michael Grant and Rachel Kitzinger. New York: Scribner's, 1988.

Walsh, Joan. "Up Front: The Mother Mystique." *Vogue* (August 1993): 96–102.

Walters, Suzanna Danuta. *Lives Together: Worlds Apart: Mothers and Daughters in Popular Culture.* Berkeley: University of California Press, 1992.

Walzer, John. "A Period of Ambivalence: Eighteenth-Century American Childhood." In *The History of Childhood,* edited by Lloyd deMause, 351–383. New York: Peter Bedrick, 1974, 1988.

Warner, Marina. *Alone of All Her Sex: The Myth and the Cult of the Virgin Mary.* New York: Knopf, 1976.

———. Op Ed, *New York Times* (Sunday, 12 May 1991).

Washington, Valora. "The Black Mother in the United States: History, Theory, Research, and Issues." In *The Different Faces of Motherhood,* edited by Beverly Birns and Dale F. Hay, 185–215. New York: Plenum Press, 1988.

Watson, John B. *Psychological Care of Infant and Child,* 9–10. New York: W. W. Norton and Co., 1928.

Watts, Sheldon. *A Social History of Western Europe: 1450–1720.* London: Hutchinson, 1984.

Weiss, Nancy Pottishman. "Mother, the Invention of Necessity: Dr. Benjamin Spock's *Baby and Child Care.*" *American Quarterly* 29 (1977).

———. "The Mother-Child Dyad Revisited: Perceptions of Mothers and Children in Twentieth-Century Child-Rearing Manuals." *Journal of Social Issues,* 34, no. 2 (1978): 29–45.

Welter, Barbara. "The Cult of True Womanhood: 1820–1860." *American Quarterly* 18 (1966): 151–174.

Wemple, Suzanne. "Sanctity and Power: The Dual Pursuit of Early Medieval Woman." In *Becoming Visible: Women in European History,* 2nd ed., edited by Renate Bridenthal, Claudia Koonz, and Susan Stuard, 131–153. Boston: Houghton Mifflin, 1976, 1986.

Wertz, Richard, and Dorothy Wertz. *Lying In: A History of Childbirth in America.* New Haven: Yale University Press, 1977.

West, Anthony. "Mother to Son." *New York Review of Books,* 31, no. 1 (March 1989): 9–11.

Whitehead, Barbara. "Dan Quayle Was Right." *The Atlantic* 10, no. 3 (Summer 1993): 47–84.

Wiedemann, Thomas. *Adults and Children in the Roman Empire*. London: Routledge, 1989.

Wiesner, Merry. "Spinning Out Capital: Women's Work in Early Modern Economy." In *Becoming Visible: Women in European History,* edited by Renate Bridenthal, Claudia Koonz, and Susan Stuard, 221–249. Boston: Houghton Mifflin, 1987.

Williams, Juanita. *Psychology of Women*. New York: W. W. Norton, 1987.

Wilson, Adrian. "The Ceremony of Childbirth and Its Interpretation." In *Wet Nursing: A History from Antiquity to the Present,* edited by Valerie Fildes, 68–108. Urbana: University of Illinois, 1990.

Wilson, Stephen. "The Myth of Motherhood and Myth: The Historical View of European Child-Rearing." *Social History* 9, no. 2: 181–198.

Winnicott, Donald Woods. *Babies and Their Mothers*. Reading: Addison-Wesley, 1987.

———. *Mother and Child: A Primer of First Relationships,* vii. New York: Basic Books, 1957.

———. *Playing and Reality*. Middlesex, England: Penguin, 1971.

———. 1945. "Primitive Emotional Development." In *Through Pediatrics to Psychoanalysis*. New York: Basic Books, 1975.

———. 1948. "Reparation in Respect of Mother's Organized Defense Against Depression." In *Through Pediatrics to Psychoanalysis*. New York: Basic Books, 1975.

———. "The Capacity to Be Alone." In *The Maturational Process and the Facilitating Environment*. New York: International Universities Press, 1965.

———. *The Maturation Process and the Facilitative Environment*. New York: International Universities Press, 1965.

———. "The Theory of the Parent-Infant Relationship." *International Journal of Psychoanalysis,* 41 (1960): 585–595.

———. "Transitional Objects and Transitional Phenomena." *International Journal of Psychoanalysis,* 34: 89–97.

Wolf, E. "On the Developmental Line of Self Object Relations." In *Advances in Self Psychology,* edited by A. Goldberg. New York: International Universities Press, 1980.

Wolfenstein, Martha. "Fun Morality: An Analysis of Recent American Child Training Literature." In *Childhood in Contemporary Cultures,* edited by Margaret Mead and Martha Wolfenstein, 168–178. Chicago: University of Chicago Press, 1955.

———. "The Emergence of Fun Morality." *The Journal of Social Issues* 7, no. 4 (1951): 15–25.

Wollheim, Richard. "So What Did They Want?" *New York Times Book Review,* Jan. 24, 1993, 21.

Woodbridge, Linda. *Women and the English Renaissance: Literature and the Nature of Womankind 1540–1620*. Urbana: University of Illinois Press, 1986.

Wooden, Warren. *Children's Literature of the English Renaissance*. Lexington: University of Kentucky Press, 1986.

Woollett, Anne, and Ann Phoenix. "Afterword: Issues Related to Motherhood." In *Motherhood: Meanings, Practices and Ideologies,* edited by Ann Phoenix, Anne Woollett, and Eva Lloyd, 216–233. London: Sage, 1991.

Woolf, Virginia. "Professions of Women." In *Death of the Moth and Other Essays*. New York: Harcourt Brace, 1942.

Wren-Lewis, J. "Love's Coming of Age." In *Psychoanalysis Observed,* edited by C. Rycroft. New York: Coward McCann, 1966.

Wylie, Philip. *Generation of Vipers*. New York: Holt, Rinehart and Winston, 1942.

Xenophon. *The Anabasis,* translated by A. D. O. Wedderburn and W. Collingwood. London: 1867.

Young-Bruehl, Elizabeth. "On Feminism and Psychoanalysis: In the Case of Anorexia Nervosa." *Psychoanalytic Psychology* 10, no. 3 (1993): 317–330.

Zahn, R. "Das kind in der Antiken Kunst." *Forschungen und Berichte* 12 (1970): 21–31.

Zelitzer, Vivian. *Pricing the Priceless Child: The Changing Social Value of Children*. New York: Basic Books, 1985.

Zimmerman, Bonnie. " 'The Mother's History' in George Eliot's Life, Literature, and Political Ideology." In *The Lost Tradition: Mothers and Daughters in Literature,* edited by Cathy Davidson and E. M. Broner. New York: Frederick Ungar, 1980.

Zuckerman, Michael. "Dr. Spock: The Confidence Man." In *The Family as History,* edited by Charles Rosenberg, 179–209. Philadelphia: University of Pennsylvania Press, 1975.

INDEX